SING A NEW SONG

The Psalms in the Sunday Lectionary

Irene Nowell, O.S.B.

A Liturgical Press Book

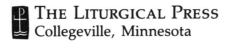

THE LITURGICAL PRESS
Collegeville, Minnesota

1   2   3   4   5   6   7   8   9

Library of Congress Cataloging-in-Publication Data

Nowell, Irene, 1940–
    Sing a new song : the Psalms in the Sunday lectionary / Irene Nowell.
        p.   cm.
    Includes bibliographical references.
    ISBN 0-8146-2043-4
    1. Bible. O.T. Psalms—Liturgical use. 2. Bible. O.T. Psalms—Criticism, interpretation, etc. 3. Catholic Church. Lectionary for Mass (U.S.). Sundays and feasts. 4. Catholic Church—Liturgy. I. Title.
BS1435.N686 1993
264'.02034—dc20   93-15752
                                                                        CIP

Contents*

*The bracketed numbers refer to the respective Psalm number in the Lectionary.

I. Introduction

After Israel has crossed the sea through the mighty power of God, Miriam leads them in song. After great victories over powerful foes, Deborah and Judith sing God's praises. Hezekiah sings his thanksgiving after he is delivered from illness. It seems natural for God's people, whenever they experience God's action in their lives, to burst into song. Where is that song in the life of today's Christian community and what is its effect?

A. The Responsorial Psalm in the Sunday Lectionary

One answer to that question is found in the responsorial psalm of the Sunday liturgy. According to *The General Instruction on the Roman Missal*, the psalm is "an integral part of the Liturgy of the Word."[1] The psalm, however, has been largely neglected in studies of the Lectionary readings and in aids for homilists. That is a loss, because attention to the psalm text can be greatly rewarding. Ralph Kiefer states regarding the Sunday liturgy: "The Responsorial Psalm constitutes a summation of the word for that day. . . . If there *is* a theme it is in the antiphon of the Responsorial Psalm."[2] Thus the psalm may provide a key to understanding the juxtaposition of the other readings.

The psalm has a second function. The sung chants are "the modes of liturgical expression whereby the laity express their role in the celebration of the word."[3] They contribute to the "conscious, active, and full participation of mind and body."[4] The psalms as poetry move the worshippers

[1] General Instruction on the Roman Missal, #36.
[2] Ralph Kiefer, *To Hear and To Proclaim: Introduction, Lectionary for Mass with Commentary for Musicians and Priests* (Washington: NPM, 1983) 81.
[3] *Ibid.*, 81.
[4] GIRM, #3.

from the discursive text which they hear, to an emotion-laden text in which they may participate. Because the psalms are sung, the power of the poetry is enhanced. Song penetrates the worshipper and remains long after the liturgy has ended. How often do we find ourselves humming little snatches of melody that we heard earlier in the day?

Therefore the psalm functions to lead the worshippers both to understand and to appropriate the readings. The readings tell the story of God's actions with the people. The psalm allows today's people to say: "Yes, we too are part of that story."

The responsorial psalms were chosen specifically to accompany the first reading (Old Testament except during the Easter Season) and the gospel. The three-year Sunday Lectionary is constructed around the gospel reading. In each of the three years one of the synoptic gospels (Matthew in Year A, Mark in Year B, Luke in Year C) is read from beginning to end with some passages omitted. The first reading complements the gospel, especially during Ordinary Time. The first reading enhances a theme, provides a contrast, demonstrates an Old Testament background, or presents a prophetic foreshadowing of the gospel. During Lent and Easter the first reading takes on a life of its own and presents the progress of salvation history in Israel and the early church. There is still some resonance with the gospel, however. The second reading (usually from the New Testament Letters) is independent of the other readings. The letter is also read from beginning to end, with some passages omitted. Even here, however, there may be some resonance with the gospel. Thus the psalm, which is chosen with the first reading and the gospel in mind, may be a key to all the readings.[5]

B. Purpose and Function of the Book

Because the focus of this book is on the psalm and not on the Sunday, the psalms which are used in the Sunday Lectionary are here divided by genre.[6] After a short analysis of the genre, each psalm will be analyzed briefly

---

[5]For a more thorough discussion of the structure of the lectionary, see the excellent article by Eileen Schuller, "The Bible in the Lectionary," *Catholic Study Bible,* ed. Donald Senior (New York: Oxford, 1990) 440–451.

[6]For genre classification I have consulted the following authors: Bernhard Anderson, *Out of the Depths: The Psalms Speak for Us Today* (rev. ed.; Philadelphia: Westminster, 1983); Richard J. Clifford, "Psalms," *The Collegeville Bible Commentary*, ed. Dianne Bergant and Robert J. Karris (Collegeville: The Liturgical Press, 1989) 754–786; John Kselman and Michael Barré, "Psalms," *The New Jerome Biblical Commentary* (Englewood Cliffs, N.J.: Prentice Hall, 1990) 523–552; Leopold Sabourin, *The Psalms: Their Origin and Meaning* (rev ed.; New York: Alba House, 1970); Carroll Stuhlmueller, *Psalms 1 and*

in its own right. Then each psalm will be considered in its relationship to each set of readings which it accompanies. Because there are many studies of the readings of the three-year Sunday Lectionary, this work will touch the other readings lightly, focusing primarily on the effect of juxtaposing this particular psalm with this set of readings.

The approach to psalms and readings is post-critical. The insights of critical scholarship are assumed and utilized. This book, however, is not a critical analysis. It is intended rather as a ministry to the imagination. It follows what Benedictines call the *lectio* approach. Images are pursued and linked. Connections are drawn because of the juxtaposition that would not be part of the analysis of any one of the readings.[7] The liturgical sense of feast and season is also used to open further meanings. It is hoped, however, that no violence has been done to either psalm or readings. The complex interweaving of liturgical readings forms, in the end, its own identity. It is this identity which this book explores.

C. How to Use this Book

This book is intended to be of service to those who preach the word, to those who plan liturgy and provide music, and most of all to everyone who prays and is nourished by the Sunday readings. It is intended to be used along with the Bible and the Lectionary or Missal. The following method is suggested: 1. Read and ponder the entire psalm in your Bible. 2. From this book read the introduction to the psalm and the introduction to the psalm's genre. 3. Read and ponder the Sunday or feast day readings from your Bible or a missal. 4. Read from this book the discussion of the psalm in the Sunday liturgy.

---

2 (Old Testament Message 21 and 22; Wilmington: Michael Glazier, 1983). For commentary I have also consulted Walter Brueggemann, *The Message of the Psalms* (Minneapolis: Augsburg, 1984); Mitchell Dahood, *Psalms I, II, and III* (Anchor Bible 16, 17, and 17A; Garden City, N.J.: Doubleday, 1966, 1968, and 1970); Hans-Joachim Kraus, *Psalmen* (5th ed.; BKAT 15.1 and 2; Neukirchen-Vluyn, Neukirchener Verlag, 1978); Patrick D. Miller, *Interpreting the Psalms* (Philadelphia: Fortress, 1986); and Claus Westermann, *Praise and Lament in the Psalms* (Atlanta: John Knox, 1981).

7 Gail Ramshaw ("The First Testament in Christian Lectionaries," *Worship* 64 [1990] 495) pleads "that all the readings, the psalm, the hymns, the other proper prayers, the choir pieces, the liturgical color, and the attendant art and design selections provide coherence to the [Sunday] event. . . ." This book is written in the spirit of that plea. Ramshaw's article is a fine study of the various techniques by which the Old (First) Testament can be used to complement the gospel.

II. The Psalms in The Lectionary

A. Historical Psalms

There are a few psalms in which the subject is primarily a recitation of the history of God's people. The content centers on the major events of exodus, desert wandering, and entrance into the land (cf. Deut 26:5-9). Other elements are sometimes added such as the stories of the ancestors (cf. Gen 12–50) or the story of David (1 Sam 16–1 Kgs 1). Psalms which may be included in this category are: 78, 105, 106, 135, 136. These psalms are united by content rather than form. Thus there are hymns such as Pss 105, 135 and 136, laments such as Ps 106, and a wisdom psalm, 78.

Why do we pray our history?[1] The answer is at the foundation of all liturgy. We pray in order to remember. The power of the community memory brings God's saving action of the past into the present. Christians have used the Greek word *anamnesis*, "memorial," to refer to the celebration of the Eucharist in which we remember that "Christ has died, Christ is risen, Christ will come again." Our remembering together brings the saving action of Christ—past and future—into our present. The historical psalms have a similar function. We pray our history in order to remember. We remember in order to bring God's salvation into our own time.

1. Psalm 78 (Davidic Covenant)

Psalm 78 is a long historical psalm (72 verses!) in which the importance of remembering is repeated over and over (78:7, 11, 35, 42). The psalm begins with the words of a wisdom teacher (see Wisdom Psalms below): "Attend, my people, to my teaching; listen to the words of my mouth. I will open my mouth in story, drawing lessons from of old" (78:1-2).[2] The sage teaches that the people must remember.

[1]See Irene Nowell, "The Prayer of History," *Sisters Today* 51 (1979) 205–214.
[2]The psalm translation used throughout is *The Revised Psalms of the New American Bible* (Washington: Confraternity of Christian Doctrine, 1991).

The psalm has a complex structure.[3] It opens with the wisdom introduction (1-11), which is followed by two long sections describing the desert wanderings (12-39) and the events on either side of the desert: the exodus from Egypt and entrance into the land (40-72). The two long sections form a kind of sandwich. The events of the latter section surround the experience of the former. In each long section there is a four-part movement similar to the stereotyped pattern of the stories in the Book of Judges: God's mighty work, the people's rebellion, God's anger and punishment, God's return to mercy.

Although the structure of the psalm is complex, the message is simple. When the people forget all God has done, they sin. Again and again they forget; again and again God, in spite of well-deserved punishment, cares for them. God is "mindful that they [are] flesh" (39), even though they forget God's great deeds. Finally God rejects the northern kingdom, Israel, and chooses Judah and the house of David (67-72). In all this God's fidelity does not fail.

18th Sun Year B (3-4.23-24.25.54) [114]

The Lord gave them bread from heaven (24).

The first reading for the Eighteenth Sunday of Year B (Exod 16:2-4, 12-15) is part of the desert tradition of murmuring. It recounts the story of murmuring about food. The people ask both for bread and for meat (cf. the parallel story in Num 11:1-6, 31-35; cf. also Deut 8:3; Pss 105:40; 106:14-15; Wis 16:20-29; 1 Cor 10:1-10). There are two patterns for the murmuring stories, one which emphasizes the providence of God and the other which emphasizes the weakness of the people. This story, in which there is a genuine need for food, follows the first pattern emphasizing God's providence. The portion of the chapter which is left out of this Sunday's reading (vv. 5-11) describes the grumbling of the people. The word "grumbling" occurs five times in those verses. In spite of their grumbling, however, God still cares for them.

The gospel passage for this Sunday (John 6:24-35) compares the manna given in the desert to the bread of life which Jesus is. In the second reading (Eph 4:17, 20-24) believers are exhorted not to be empty-headed but to "be renewed in the spirit of [their] minds" (17, 23) just as the Israelites were exhorted not to forget like their ancestors (Ps 78:8-11).

The verses chosen from Psalm 78 are 3-4, 23-24, 25, 54. These verses indicate the importance of remembering God's goodness and tell the story of the gift of manna and the gift of land. The antiphon, "The Lord gave them bread from heaven" (24), echoes the story of the manna in the Exo-

---

[3]I follow the structure from *The Revised Psalms of the New American Bible*.

dus reading. What is missing in these verses, however, is the consequence of forgetting which is a major part of this psalm. All indications of punishment are omitted. Since the first reading follows the pattern of murmuring stories in which there is no punishment, there is some consistency here. However, some mention of the fatal results of forgetting might strengthen the gospel reading in which Jesus warns his listeners that they should not seek signs but the food which gives eternal life. Remembering God's care is food for eternal life. To remember is to avoid the empty-headedness of the second reading and to be renewed in spirit.

Triumph of Cross (1-2.34-35.36-37.38) [638]

Do not forget the works of the Lord! (7).

The Feast of the Triumph of the Cross, when it falls on a Sunday, supercedes the regular Sunday readings. The first reading for the feast is a murmuring story from the desert tradition (Num 21:4-9). The people complain against God and Moses: "Why have you brought us up from Egypt to die in this desert, where there is no food or water? We are disgusted with this wretched food!" (21:5). This story follows the second pattern of murmuring stories in which the people's weakness is emphasized. There is no genuine need. Therefore God punishes the people for their complaining. Fiery serpents (*saraph* means "fiery") bite the people and many die. Moses is instructed to make a bronze serpent and mount it on a pole. Anyone who looks on it will live.

The Gospel of John (John 3:13-17) alludes to the desert event, drawing a parallel between the lifting up of the serpent and the lifting up of the Son of Man. The gospel reminds us that we have rebelled in the desert experience of our lives. We suffer the consequences of our sins, but God does not leave us there. God sent the Son to be lifted up "so that everyone who believes in him may have eternal life" (15). He is our example, the one among us who "did not regard equality with God something to be grasped" (Phil 2:6; second reading, Phil 2:6-11). His humble obedience heals our rebellious murmuring.

The selection of psalm verses for the Feast of the Triumph of the Cross begins with the wisdom instruction of the introduction. The remaining verses are from the long section about the desert wanderings (12-39). The reading from Numbers tells of a punishment for complaining without need. The psalm verses also include the mention of punishment. Like the reading, the psalm also concludes with the story of God's mercy. The antiphon, "Do not forget the works of God" (7), respects the main theme of Psalm 78. Forgetting results in sin and punishment; remembering results in mercy and care.

We too need to heed the wisdom of the psalmist who draws lessons from of old (2). We too suffer from amnesia. God's mercy surrounds us every day. How can we forget?

2. *Psalm 105 (Hymn)*

Psalm 105 is a hymn by form (see Hymns) and a historical psalm by content. It is a companion piece to Psalm 106, a communal lament, in which the emphasis is on the ingratitude of God's people. They may have been used together in liturgical worship also. Verses from both psalms are quoted together (along with Ps 96) in the story of David's bringing the ark to Jerusalem (1 Chr 16:8-36). Although both psalms concentrate on the period from the Exodus to the entrance into the land, the troubles of Psalm 106 are conspicuously absent in Psalm 105. The emphasis of Psalm 105 is on God's blessings. The psalm may be considered in six stanzas (1-6, 7-11, 12-15, 16-22, 23-38, 39-45).

The first stanza (1-6) establishes the psalm firmly as a hymn. The whole stanza is an extended call to praise. The descendants of Abraham and Jacob are called to remember God's mighty deeds and to give praise. The remaining 39 verses recite Israel's history as a motive for praise.

The second stanza (7-11) sets the history in the context of God's covenant with the ancestors, especially the covenant promise of land. Psalm 105 is the only psalm which tells the story of the ancestors, Abraham, Isaac, and Jacob. The third stanza (12-15) begins the story with the sojourning of the ancestors who are called both "anointed" (i.e., messianic) and "prophets" (i.e., messengers of God).

The sojourning continues with Joseph who preceded his family to Egypt in order to save them from famine (16-22). He is sent to Egypt by God's providence and the word of the Lord proves him true. Through Joseph, the whole family of Israel/Jacob enters Egypt (23-38). The psalm moves rapidly to the story of persecution. Then God's providence is seen in the people's history again through the "signs and wonders" of the plagues. The plagues are worked through Moses and Aaron, but are obviously the work of God. The interweaving of verbs throughout the stanza makes God's design clear. God "turned," "sent," "worked," "sent," "turned" (25-29). God "spoke," "struck," "spoke," "struck" (31-36). God is the subject of almost every verb in the stanza. This is God's work. The people have only to see and give praise (cf. 1-6).

The sixth stanza (39-45) gives an abbreviated version of the desert wanderings and the entrance into the land. There is no mention of the murmuring, only of God's providential gifts of food, water, and protection. The whole journey is portrayed as a joyful procession into the land promised to Abraham in the covenant (cf. 7-11). What is God's purpose in all this tender care? That the people might keep the law. Thus they will have long life in the land (cf. Deut 6:23-24; 30:15-20).[4] The psalm ends with the joyful shout of "Hallelujah," praise the Lord!

We may find Psalm 105 difficult to pray, both because of its length and because we are not accustomed to praying our history. Precisely there is the lesson of the psalm for us. This psalm teaches us that God is active through all the events of our history. God is not removed from our world, in a separate divine realm. God has chosen to enter our history. We Christians proclaim that truth on an even more profound level: God has chosen to take on our very flesh and become one of us. Psalm 105 encourages us to bring the daily paper and the nightly news to our prayer. Where is God to be found today?

Holy Family B [opt] (1b-2.3-4.5-6.8-9)

The Lord remembers the covenant forever (8a).

Only the opening verses of Psalm 105, the call to prayer and the announcement of the covenant, are selected for the Feast of the Holy Family B. Perhaps this is a suggestion that we must follow the introduction with examples of God's fidelity from our own history. The refrain supports this notion: The Lord remembers the covenant forever. God remembered not only in the time of Abraham and during the Exodus. God remembers forever. God remembers now.

In his summary of Psalm 105, H.-J. Kraus says, "The essential message of Ps 105 lies in the conclusion that Yahweh's covenant fidelity should arouse and make possible a new obedience to the commands of God."[5] Kraus' words also describe the essential message of the readings for this feast.

The first reading (Gen 15:1-6; 21:1-3) tells the story of God's covenant making with Abraham. God promises land, descendants, and blessing. Abraham, already an old man, cannot understand how God can do this. God renews the promise and Abraham, with no more evidence than God's word, believes. His faith is "credited . . . to him as an act of righteousness," an act of right relationship. The tangible sign of God's fidelity is found in the birth of Isaac, the son given to Abraham and Sarah in their old age. God may wait beyond the last possible minute, but God remembers the

---

[4]See Stuhlmueller 2.115 for a table of correspondences between Psalm 105 and Deuteronomy.

[5]"Die wesentliche Aussage des Ps 105 liegt in der Konsequenz beschlossen, dass Jahwes Bundestreue einen neuen Gehorsam gegen die Gebote Gottes erwecken und bewirken soll." Kraus 2.895; translation mine.

covenant forever (Ps 105:8). God's time is not our time; God's fidelity is beyond our imaginations!

The author of the Letter to the Hebrews delights in Abraham's faith (11:8, 11-12, 17-19). Abraham believed enough to leave his land and go, "not knowing where." Abraham's faith gave him "power to generate," even though he was "as good as dead." He believed "that the one who had made the promise was trustworthy." Then incredibly Abraham believed enough to offer back to God this one tangible sign of God's fidelity, his son Isaac. Because of his amazing faith "he received Isaac back as a symbol" that God can raise even from the dead. The covenant truly begins with this man whose faith is indeed righteousness. God is faithful and Abraham believes. This is the foundation of the everlasting covenant (Ps 105:10).

Psalm 105, the only psalm to discuss the story of the ancestors, is a fitting responsorial psalm with these two readings. We see Abraham's faith and God's fidelity and we give thanks. But even as we glory in God's wonderful deeds, we hear the call to see God's signs and words in our own lives. We recognize the demand to imitate Abraham's faith.

The gospel story (Luke 2:22-40) gives us the holy family as an example of covenant living. They follow the prescriptions of the law. They bring their firstborn son to the temple to redeem him according to the command in Exod 13. They see their actions as a continuation of the great song of praise to God who redeemed Israel, the firstborn, from Egyptian slavery (Exod 4:22; Ps 105:23-38). They are met by two old people who live by faith in God's promises. Simeon believed that God would grant him a vision of the Messiah before his death; Anna believed in the redemption of Jerusalem. Like Abraham, their lives give flesh to their faith. They have waited a long time; their faith has been rewarded. The Lord remembers the covenant forever (Ps 105:8).

How does this great covenant story relate to family life? Israel's best images of the covenant bond are drawn from the family: the bond between husband and wife and between parent and child. Today's readings infer that connection without drawing it directly. Abraham and Sarah, Joseph and Mary, Simeon and Anna, are all going about their lives fulfilling daily demands. Precisely in their ordinary lives are the signs of God's wonderful fidelity: the birth of a child, the customary worship, the joyful sight of young parents with a baby. The God who rules the whole earth chooses to be present in the ordinary events of human history, even the events of our ordinary lives. How grateful we must be for the wonder of happy families. How tireless must we be in bringing healing to those whose families are wounded. Our courage comes from Abraham who, even when there was no hope, believed that the Lord remembers the covenant forever.

3. *Psalm 136 (Hymn)*

Psalm 136 is formally a hymn (see Hymns below). Like the hymns it begins with a call to prayer (1-3) and continues with the reasons for praise (4-25 and the refrain). The psalm has the structure of a litany, which makes it unique in the psalter. Verses 3-25 are one long sentence, interrupted by the repeated refrain. Apparently a leader sang the first line of each verse and the congregation responded with the refrain.

The refrain is the real prayer of this psalm and the essence of its content: "God's love endures forever." The Hebrew word for this love is *hesed* which is the faithful love of the covenant bond. One of the best human images for *hesed* is the all-encompassing love one sees in a couple who have been married for many years. This is the love that has seeped into their very bones, that shapes every word and action.

Psalm 136 begins with a call to praise (1-3). The Lord, Israel's God, is good and does good things for the people. This God is the greatest god and mightiest lord. The repetition of a term, such as "God of gods, Lord of lords," is the Hebrew superlative. The good things God does, the acts of God's faithful love, include both creation (4-9) and historical events (10-22). God created the world; God delivers the people, leads them through the desert, and gives them a land. The final verses (23-25) summarize God's love. God continues to sustain and preserve all creation. God saves the people from misery, oppression, and hunger. God saves and sustains us now. We are still called to praise the God whose love endures forever (26).

The content of the psalm is the reason for including it with the historical psalms. Creation and history are one event in this psalm, however. All things are an expression of God's faithful covenant love.

Psalm 136 is probably post-exilic. The litany structure suggests that it belongs to liturgical worship. The refrain occurs also in other psalms (106:1; 107:1; 118:1, 29). It is also cited as an introduction to worship in 2 Chron 5:13; 7:3, 6; 20:21. The psalm is called the Great Hallel or Great Praise, and is sung in Jewish worship on Sabbath mornings and for Passover.

Easter Vigil Common (1-3.4-6.7-9.24-26) [*175*]
Easter Vigil Common (1.3.16.21-23.24-26) [*175*]

God's love endures forever (Refrain).

Psalm 136 is suggested as a common responsorial psalm for the Easter vigil. It is given in two forms, each using the refrain as the response. The first form (1-3, 4-6, 7-9, 24-26) omits all the verses which have to do with historical events: the plagues, the exodus, the desert, the conquest and gift of the land. Only the call to praise, creation, and the summary are included. The second form (1, 3, 16, 21-23, 24- 26) includes a mention of the desert and the gift of the land, but omits the creation and the exodus event. The omissions are strange since the readings of the Easter vigil celebrate precisely the same events that Psalm 136 celebrates, God's saving love from creation through history to the present.

The whole of Psalm 136 could be divided for use in the Easter vigil as follows:[6] Verses 1-9 after the first reading, Gen 1:1–2:2, the story of creation. Verses 1, 10-15 after the third reading, Exod 14:15–15:1, the exodus event. Verses 1, 16-22 after the fourth reading, Isa 54:5-14, promise of return from Exile. Verses 1, 23-26 after the fifth reading, Isa 55:1-11, promise of God's continued care.

B. Laments

There are more laments in the psalter than any other category. Perhaps this is a comment on the ever-present suffering in human life or on the human tendency to complain more often than to thank. Whatever the reason, the psalter gives us a rich variety of ways to express our suffering and complaints. There are both individual and communal laments as well.

The form of the lament is not as predictable as that of the hymns. Our suffering cannot be as neatly expressed as our joys. There are some standard elements, however, which appear in most laments:

a. The lament commonly opens with a *cry to God* which often includes the mention of God's name. Laments are almost always addressed directly to God.

b. Following the cry is a *main section* in which several things may happen. The suffering is described: the attack of enemies, sickness, the awareness of sin, imminent death. There is an attempt to move God to help the sufferer by reminding God of the covenant obligations or the relationship of the sufferer to God. The psalmist either claims to be innocent and thus unjustly punished or acknowledges personal sinfulness and lays claim to God's forgiveness. Sometimes the motivation is that God's own reputation will be ruined if others see one of God's servants in distress. The prayer for help may be a complaint against God who is seen as the origin of the distress or it may be a curse against the psalmist's enemies. In many laments the psalmist vows to offer sacrifice to God when the distress is relieved.

---

[6] I am not suggesting that the substitution of a common psalm for the specific psalms assigned to the Easter vigil is a good idea. However, if it is necessary, this is a possible arrangement.

c. The *final section* of the lament is often a dramatic shift from complaint to praise. There is a strong expression of trust in God and praise for God's deliverance. This dramatic shift has been explained as the response to an oracle of salvation, in which a cultic official assures the sufferer that God has heard and will answer the prayer. A few psalms include such an oracle, e.g., Ps 12: "Because they rob the weak, and the needy groan, I will now arise," says the LORD; "I will grant safety to whoever longs for it" (Ps 12:6; cf. also Pss 60:8-10; 91:14-16). Another explanation for the shift in tone may be that the psalm is recited from the perspective of deliverance already experienced. A better explanation, however, is faith. The psalms teach us that even in the midst of terrible distress it is possible to cling to faith in God. God has the power to save us; God's love can overcome all our suffering.

The variety of elements in the laments can be confusing. One way to simplify the approach is to consider the three relationships expressed in the lament: the relationship between the sufferer and God, between the sufferer and the enemies, between the sufferer and self.[1] We may be most comfortable with the last of the three relationships. We have learned to acknowledge our own sinfulness. We know that sometimes we are our own worst enemies. Even in this confession of sin, however, the psalms are a real challenge to us to confront the heart of our weakness.

The other two relationships expressed in the laments are more difficult.[2] We cringe at the violent curses hurled toward the enemies. We are even more uncomfortable flinging accusations in the face of God. Here too the laments have something to teach us. Rather than attacking enemies ourselves, we leave the exercise of vengeance to God. The outward expression in prayer of the violence that nests in every human heart at times is a way of robbing the violence of its power. Through the psalm we both acknowledge and let go of the anger and hatred.

The accusations against God are also an expression of faith. We challenge God because we believe that God has the power to relieve our distress. Therefore we cry, "Hurry up!" We challenge God because our only hope is to cling to that relationship even when God seems to be absent and so we cry, "Wake up!" We take refuge in the example of Job who complains against God through all his suffering and is declared by God to be the only one who spoke rightly (Job 42:8). Jeremiah too shows us how to complain against God and yet remain faithful (Jer 11:18–12:6; 15:10-21; 20:7-18).

---

[1]Claus Westermann, *Praise and Lament in the Psalms*, 267.

[2]See Walter Brueggemann, "A Shape for Old Testament Theology 2: Embrace of Pain," *CBQ* 47 (1985) 28–46, 395–415.

Another way to deal with the laments is to relate them to the other biblical stories.[3] The titles are an example of this method of interpretation. Many of the laments are connected through the titles with incidents in the life of David. Reading the Davidic story with the lament helps bring the lament to life. The juxtaposition of the laments with the biblical stories in the Lectionary, which is the task of this book, is another example of this method.

The laments are given to us that we might learn how to live in a world of suffering and injustice neither being conquered by evil nor abandoning hope in God. Perhaps that is why there are so many laments in the psalter.

1. Psalm 17

Psalm 17 is a declaration of innocence and a plea for God's justice. In the opening section (1-5) the psalmist cries out to God and submits to God's judgment, claiming that God, who tests in the night, has found no sin. Then the plea is renewed with greater intensity (6-12). The psalmist calls upon God's *hesed*, God's faithful covenant love, which is continually evident in wonderful deeds for the faithful. It is God who will answer, God who has power to deliver from the ravenous enemies. The final section (13-15) begins again with a plea to God to act. God is asked to exercise justice by punishing the enemies and rewarding the faithful (including, of course, the psalmist). The greatest reward is the enjoyment of God's presence (15).

Verse 14 is very difficult to translate, but the general sense of the verse is a call for God's retribution: punishment for the wicked who devour God's people as lions devour prey. The *Revised New American Bible* translates verse 14 as follows:

> Slay them with your sword;
>> with your hand, LORD, slay them;
>> snatch them from the world in their prime.
> Their bellies are being filled with your friends;
>> their children are satisfied too,
>> for they share what is left with their young.

Two things in this psalm may make us uncomfortable: the declaration of innocence and the plea for vengeance against the enemy. The declaration of innocence was a way of answering an accusation if no witnesses could be found for a trial (cf. 1 Kings 8:31-32). The accused took an oath, proclaiming the absence of guilt, and left the judgment to God. If guilt was indeed present, God would punish. If the accused was innocent, no

---

[3]See P. D. Miller, *Interpreting the Psalms*, 51–63.

one was guilty of false judgment. Job makes such a protestation of innocence when his friends try to convince him that his suffering comes because
of his sins (Job 31).

The righteousness (*sedeq*) claimed by the psalmist must be understood
in the biblical sense of relationship. The norm for righteousness is not an
abstract law but the demands of the relationship. It is the right of the relationship that Job claims. He has not let go of God; he is the only one in
the story who speaks to God! Therefore he calls upon God to honor the
relationship. In the same way the psalmist is claiming that the relationship
with God still stands. In contrast to the enemies the psalmist trusts God,
calls upon God, clings to God. God too maintains the relationship, the covenant love, and can be counted on to shelter the psalmist as tenderly as a
mother bird in the shadow of her wings (cf. Exod 19:4; Deut 32:11).

Vengeance against the enemies is difficult for us to face in prayer. The
heart of the cry is a plea for God to root evil out of the world and to establish goodness. Since throughout most of the Old Testament period there
was no firm belief in life after death, this victory of good over evil was longed
for during one's lifetime. The longing for God's victory over evil is certainly part of our longing too. It is part of the prayer, "Your kingdom
come." We must not be too squeamish to bring the longing directly to
God, nor too cowardly to trust God for the outcome.

32nd Sun Year C (1.5-6.8.15) [157]

Lord, when your glory appears, my joy will be full (15).

The first reading for the Thirty-Second Sunday of Year C (2 Macc 7:1-
2, 9-14) tells the story of the valiant mother who encourages seven sons
to be faithful even in the face of death and who is then martyred herself.
Her story is set at the time of the Maccabean revolt (165–142 BCE) when
the Syrian rulers were forcing Jews to abandon their religious customs: cir-
cumcision, dietary laws, Sabbath, and Torah. This woman is admirable not
only for her heroic fidelity but also for her theological wisdom. She encourages her sons by declaring her own faith in the resurrection of the dead
(7:23, 29). She has taught them well. At the point of death they too proclaim faith in God's power to raise the dead.

In the gospel (Luke 20:27-38) Jesus is challenged by the Sadducees concerning resurrection. They present what they consider an impossible
dilemma. Jesus tells them that they do not begin to understand the transformation that will take place at the resurrection.

In the passage from 2 Thessalonians (2:16–3:5) Paul asks for prayers that
he might be delivered from evil. He declares his faith in God whose love
will fill the lives of believers with everything that is good.

In the context of these readings, Psalm 17 takes on a richer meaning. Like Paul, the psalmist prays to be delivered from evil and hopes to receive good from God's love. But the psalmist has, if anything, only a glimmer that God's reward might last after death. The prayer, "when I awake, let me be filled with your presence," is a prayer for this life. But in the mouths of the Maccabean mother and her sons it becomes a prayer for eternal life. Jesus declares: God "is not God of the dead, but of the living." The psalmist knew only a shadow of that truth, only a shadow of the power of God's *hesed*.

Several verses of the psalm are omitted: most of the declaration of innocence (vv. 2-4); the description of the enemies (vv. 9-12); and the plea for vengeance (vv. 13-14). The understanding of righteousness as relationship would allow us to restore the declaration of innocence. The understanding of the prayer for vengeance as a plea to eradicate evil from the world would allow the use of verses 13-14. Perhaps the enemies have been sufficiently described in the reading from 2 Maccabees. The most inexplicable omission, however, is verse 7, the description of God's wonderful love:

> Show your wonderful love,
>> you who deliver with your right arm
>> those who seek refuge from their foes.

It would seem that this verse declares the reason for the faith which is proclaimed in all the other readings.

2. Psalm 22

Psalm 22 is the quintessential lament. It has all the elements of lament: cry to God, complaint, description of illness and of the enemies, expression of trust, and song of thanksgiving. It can be divided into four stanzas, two each for lament and thanksgiving: 2-12, cry to God for help; 13-22, complaint about enemies and illness; 23-27, promise of public thanksgiving; 28-32, extension of the thanksgiving through space and time.

The first two stanzas are rounded off by literary devices. The first stanza (2-12) begins and ends with the same key word, "far" (the device of inclusion). The psalmist complains that God is far away and pleads with God not to stay far away. The second stanza (13-22) describes the enemies in terms of animals. The animals are repeated in reverse order: bulls (13), lions (14), dogs (17), dogs (21), lions (22a), wild bulls (22b). This repetition in reverse order is called chiasm.

The literary devices are a key to the meaning. The psalmist is convinced in the first stanza that pain and distress are due completely to the absence of God. The plea alternates between complaint to God and expressions of confidence. The psalmist remembers that God helped people in times past and calls for the same help. The psalmist's own life has belonged to God from the very beginning, from the moment that God the midwife drew the baby from the womb. But even this trust in God becomes an opportunity for the enemies to taunt the psalmist: "You relied on the LORD—let [the LORD] deliver you!"

The second stanza (13-22) is a vivid description of suffering. The enemies are wild animals. The sufferer is sick and weak with dry throat and melting strength. The enemies are so sure of the advance of death that they already divide the victim's possessions. At this point the psalmist makes another appeal to God: "Do not stay far off!"

The poignant description of suffering intensifies the dramatic shift to thanksgiving. Throughout the two final stanzas (23-27, 28-32) the thanksgiving widens from the psalmist's community to all God's people, especially the poor who will share in the thanksgiving feast, and finally to all the ends of the earth and all people from the already dead to unborn generations. The psalmist proclaims that, no matter how deep the suffering, God does deliver the one who cries out. This is the message of the psalm. Against all evidence the psalmist places total trust in God and that trust is rewarded beyond belief.

Psalm 22 underlies the passion narrative in the gospels. From the Cross Jesus cries out, "My God, my God, why have you abandoned me" (cf. Matt 27:46; Mark 15:34). The mockery of bystanders echoes Ps 22:8-9 (Matt 27:39, 43; Mark 15:29). Jesus is thirsty (Ps 22:16; John 19:28). His executioners, according to custom, cast lots for his clothing (Ps 22:19; Matt 27:35; John 19:23-24).[4] The early Christian community recognized that Psalm 22, a description of terrible suffering and of rescue by God, gave them a way to understand the suffering and the victory of Jesus. Jesus took all of human suffering upon himself and, by total trust and obedience to his father, transformed suffering and death into life. All people, those already dead and unborn generations, rejoice in his victory.

Passion Sunday ABC (8-9.17-18.19-20.23-24) [38]

My God, my God, why have you abandoned me? (2).

Psalm 22 is an excellent choice for Passion Sunday, the beginning of Holy Week. Like the early Christians, we too find Psalm 22 a way of internalizing the truth of Jesus' passion, death, and resurrection. Most of the verses

---

[4]Verses 17c–18a, which have been textually damaged, have sometimes been translated: "They pierced my hands and feet . . .," and interpreted in light of the crucifixion. In *The Revised Psalter of the New American Bible*, it reads: "So wasted are my hands and feet that I can count all my bones."

chosen are those used by the evangelists in the passion narrative (8-9, 17-18, 19-20). The final verses are the beginning of the thanksgiving. Even as we enter this week of darkness and pain, we cannot forget the blazing light of Easter to come.

The first reading is the third Servant song from the Book of Isaiah (50:4-7). The sixth-century prophet who wrote the second section of Isaiah (chs. 40–55) was encouraging the people, saying that the Babylonian Exile would not last forever, that God could and would deliver them. The prophet describes a mysterious figure, a Servant called by God, whose suffering will win life for others (cf. also Isa 42:1-4; 49:1-7; 52:13–53:12). The Servant can be seen as Israel, as a prophet, as Moses, as a figure yet to come. The Servant, obedient to God, accomplishes God's will and brings light and life to God's people. The Servant could well have prayed Psalm 22.

The second reading is the hymn to Jesus as Lord from the Letter to the Philippians (2:6-11). Because Christ in total obedience emptied himself even to death, he has been exalted by God above all creation. The gospel reading for all three cycles is the passion narrative from one of the synoptic gospels (Matt 26:14–27:66; Mark 14:1–15:47; Luke 22:14–23:56). Psalm 22 gathers all these readings with the cry of terrible suffering: "My God, my God!" Psalm 22 also testifies to constant trust in the midst of that suffering. The Servant knows that he will not be put to shame (cf. Isa 50:7).

Holy Week Common (8-9.17-18.19-20.23-24) [175]

My God, my God, why have you abandoned me? (2).

Psalm 22 is the common psalm for Holy Week. The verses selected are the same as those for Passion Sunday (see above). They echo the passion narrative and anticipate the thanksgiving of Easter. The first reading for Passion Sunday was the third Servant song from the Book of Isaiah. On Monday, Tuesday, and Wednesday that reading and two of the other Servant songs are read (Isa 42:1-7; 49:1-6; 50:4-9). The gospel stories lead inevitably to the passion. Jesus is anointed by a woman, commissioned as Messiah (=anointed, John 12:1-11). Jesus predicts Judas' betrayal and Peter's denial (John 13:21-33, 36-38). Judas concludes the bargain to betray Jesus (Matt 26:14-25). Psalm 22 links the suffering of the Servant to the passion narrative of Jesus. The psalm emphasizes suffering, trust, and rescue. It keeps the images of the passion and the hope of Easter victory before us.

5th Sun Easter B (26-27.28.30.31-32) [54]

I will praise you, Lord, in the assembly of your people (26).

The Easter season shows us the thanksgiving side of Psalm 22. The verses used for the Fifth Sunday of Easter B are all from the thanksgiving song

(26-27, 28, 30, 31-32). They illustrate dramatically the ever-widening circle of praise begun by the psalmist's testimony. The expression of praise from all who have died, "all who sleep in the earth," is especially fitting in this season celebrating resurrection.

The readings for the Sundays of the Easter season are mostly from the Acts of the Apostles and the Johannine literature (the Letters of John, the Gospel of John, and the Book of Revelation). The opening reading for this Sunday is the story of Paul's entry into the Jerusalem community (Acts 9:26-31). It is a story both of suffering and peace. Paul is initially rejected by the disciples, who are afraid of him because of his past. But he is accepted into the community through the efforts of Barnabas who relates the story of his conversion and his preaching. After he is accepted by the Christian community, however, the Jews try to kill him because of his preaching. The reading ends on a note of peace. Paul escapes his enemies; the church is growing and at peace. Victory can be seen even through the suffering.

The gospel (John 15:1-8) tells the story of the vine and the branches. It is also a story of suffering and glory. The vine is pruned and cleansed. But when the pruning is over the yield of the vine increases. The one who lives in Christ the vine bears much fruit. The First Letter of John (1 John 3:18-24) goes to the heart of the matter. Christians are at peace because they keep God's commandments. The commandments are two: to believe in Christ and to love one another. By keeping these commandments Christians remain in the vine and bear much fruit. By keeping these commandments Christians can endure suffering because they believe in the victory which Christ has already won. As we know by the end of Psalm 22, God has indeed not abandoned us.

3. Psalm 25 (Acrostic)

Psalm 25 is an acrostic psalm. Each verse begins with a successive letter of the Hebrew alphabet. The form is carried through well. Only the letter *qoph*, which should begin verse 18, is missing. There is a final verse added to the psalm after the last letter of the alphabet. This final verse (22) begins with the letter *pe*. Thus the verses at the beginning, middle, and end of the psalm begin with the letters *'aleph, lamed,* and *pe*. These three letters spell the first letter of the Hebrew alphabet, *'aleph*.

Carefully calculated forms such as the acrostic are characteristic of Israel's wisdom literature. The message conveyed by the form is that every word, every letter, every tiny element of creation, leads to God. God is present "from A to Z." There are other wisdom elements in Psalm 25 as well, such as proverbial sayings (8, 12) and emphasis on God's "way" and on teaching.

Adherence to the acrostic form often makes it difficult for the poet to sustain a logical sequence of thought. Each verse tends to be self-contained. In Psalm 25, however, there is some flow of ideas. This flow suggests the individual lament. In verses 1-7, addressed directly to God, the psalmist pleads with God for forgiveness and instruction and promises to wait for God. Verses 8-15 are a declaration of trust and faith in God's goodness. In verses 16-22 the psalmist again pleads with God to relieve distress and save from enemies. The last verse extends the plea for the sake of all Israel.

The repetition of key words is an important indication of the message of this psalm. God is characterized by *goodness* (7, 8)[5], *truth* (5, 10) and *faithful love* (*hesed*, 6, 7, 10). The psalmist pleads with God to *remember* only the goodness, truth, and love which are part of the divine nature, and to forget the psalmist's own sins (6-7). Because God is good, true, and loving, the psalmist *waits* for God alone (3, 5, 21). God can be counted on to *teach* the right *way* to live (4, 5, 8, 9, 10, 12, 14).

1st Sun Advent C (4-5.8-9.10.14) [3]

To you, O Lord, I lift my soul (1).

Psalm 25 is particularly apt for Advent with its emphasis on waiting. The verb occurs three times (3, 5, 21) and it is sometimes inserted also into verse 1: "I wait for you, O Lord; I lift up my soul to my God" (1991 NAB). However, the verses chosen for the First Sunday of Advent C include only one of these "waiting" verses (5). The emphasis in the selected verses is on God's teaching and God's way. A verse concerning God's faithful love is also included (10). Love and fidelity (*hesed* and *'emeth*) are the primary virtues of the covenant. Both God and Israel are bound to faithful love as they nourish this bond which is described as the bond between husband and wife or between parent and child. Thus "the covenant instructs" God's faithful (14).

The first reading (Jer 33:14-16) is from a section of the Book of Jeremiah that is sometimes called the Book of Consolation (chs. 30–33). It is an echo of an earlier oracle (23:5-6) in which the hope for a continuation of the Davidic dynasty in a specific king is expressed. This king will be called, "The Lord, our justice" or Zedekiah. In chapter 33 there is a renewal of God's promise to sustain the Davidic dynasty (cf. 2 Sam 7), but now it is Jerusalem which will be called "The Lord, our justice." The fulfillment seems set in the distant future.

The First Letter to the Thessalonians is characterized by extensive thanksgiving. Paul is very grateful for the way in which the Thessalonians have

---

[5]The line, "because of your goodness, Lord," has been transposed in the *Revised Psalter of the New American Bible* to the end of v. 5.

accepted the faith and are living it. The reading for this Sunday's liturgy (1 Thess 3:12–4:2) concludes Paul's thanksgiving and begins his continuing instruction to the Thessalonians concerning Christian life. The gospel (Luke 21:25-28, 34-36) is part of a discourse concerning the end of the world and the last judgment. The style of this discourse is called apocalyptic, or "revealing," because it is a revealing of the end times. The description of cosmic catastrophe is characteristic of Jewish writing on this subject around the last centuries before Christ.

Thus the three readings address the three facets of Christian waiting: past, present, and future. Christians see the fulfillment of the promise to David in Jesus, the true Son of David, the true anointed king (=messiah/christ). Paul's exhortation applies to Christian living today as well as it did in the first century. Finally, we are all waiting for the end of time and the arrival of God's kingdom. Psalm 25 weaves these readings together from at least two angles. The emphasis on God's faithful love gives us confidence that God will continue to fulfill the promises and to care for faithful people. The emphasis on God's way reminds us that, like the Thessalonians, we must make still greater progress in what we have learned, and, in order to be ready for the end of time, we must continue to be on guard. In all this we are confident because the Lord who is good and upright shows sinners the way.

Advent Common (4-5.8-9.10.14) [175]

To you, O Lord, I lift my soul (1).

Psalm 25 is one of two psalms suggested as a common psalm for Advent. (For the other, see Psalm 85.) The verses suggested are the same as those for the First Sunday of Advent C (see above). The psalm is particularly suited to the First Sunday of Advent A and B as well (see Pss 122 and 80 respectively for a fuller discussion). The gospel for each of those Sundays concerns the end of time (Matt 24:37-44; Mark 13:33-37) and the need to be faithful to God's way. In both years the second reading (Rom 13:11-14; 1 Cor 1:3-9) also exhorts Christians to live faithful lives now in order to be ready for the end time. The first reading for Cycle A (Isa 2:1-5) is an appeal to come to God's house in order to be instructed in God's ways. The first reading for Cycle B (Isa 63:16-17,19; 64:2-7) is an appeal to God to forgive and to remember love and compassion. There is a wish to be mindful of God in our ways.

Psalm 25 might also be used for the Fourth Sunday of Advent in all three cycles (see Pss 24, 89, and 80). The first reading for all three years has to do with the promise to David and the hope for a king like David (Isa 7:10-14; 2 Sam 7:1-5, 8-11, 16; Mic 5:1-4). The psalm assures us of God's fidelity. The gospel (Matt 1:18-24; Luke 1:26-38; 1:39-45) tells us how the faithful God has indeed fulfilled the promises and the second reading (Rom 1:1-7; 16:25-27; Heb 10:5-10) interprets the fulfillment for us. "All the paths of the LORD are faithful love."

1st Sun Lent B (4-5.6-7.8-9) [23]

Your ways, O Lord, are love and truth, to those who keep your covenant (10).

The verses of Psalm 25 chosen for the First Sunday of Lent are primarily from the first stanza, pleading for forgiveness and instruction. This is the heart of the psalm, describing God as good (7, cf. 8), true (5, cf. 10), and loving (6, 7, cf. 10). The psalmist begs God to remember the love that is part of God's own nature, not to remember the psalmist's sins (6-7). The psalmist trusts God to teach the way to life (4, 5, 8, 9, 10).

The first reading (Gen 9:8-15) is a part of the primeval history, Gen 1–11. The primeval history tells a story of the increasing alienation caused by sin: humans from God, the earth, animals, and each other. But the story is permeated by God's mercy and blessing. God continues to strive toward reconciliation with wayward human beings. At the end of the flood story (Genesis 6-9), God blesses Noah and his family and makes covenant with them. The covenant extends to all creation. This covenant will be the beginning of new creation. God remembers faithful love and forgets human sin (cf. Ps 25:6-7). God makes covenant to show humans the way (cf. Ps 25:10). God even sets the rainbow as an everlasting reminder.

The gospel tells the beginning of God's ultimate victory over sin and death: the temptation of Jesus (Mark 1:12-15). The selection from the First Letter of Peter (3:18-22) spells out this mystery of God's love: "Christ . . . suffered for sins once, the righteous for the unrighteous, that he might lead you to God" (18). Our way of participating in Christ's victory is through baptism, a bath of water which saves us just as the ark saved Noah and his family from the waters of the flood. This is the mystery of God's goodness and love. This is the hope of the catechumens and of all of us beginning Lent. This is the hope expressed in Psalm 25 when we pray that God will remember love and show us the way.

3rd Sun Year B (4-5.6-7.8-9) [69]

Teach me your ways, O Lord (4).

The verses of Psalm 25 chosen for the Third Sunday of Year B are the same as those for the First Sunday of Lent B (see above). The refrain, however, is different: "Teach me your ways, O Lord." Many people are on the way in this Sunday's readings. Jonah, a very reluctant prophet, is finally persuaded by a storm and a fish and the repeated voice of God to fulfill his mission to Nineveh. He preaches destruction, and immediately the people of Nineveh turn from their evil ways. God too (to the dismay of the prophet) turns from threatened evil, forgets sin, and remembers compassion. Later in the book the prophet complains to God that this is precisely why he did not want to go to Nineveh: "I knew that you are a gracious and merciful God, slow to anger, rich in clemency, loathe to punish." Jonah knows what the psalmist knows. God is good, true, and loving.

In the gospel (Mark 1:14-20) Jesus begins preaching God's kingdom. He calls four disciples and immediately they follow him. The incarnation of God's love has begun teaching the way of the Lord. Paul reminds his readers that the time of Christ's return may be sooner than we think (1 Cor 7:29-31). The attention of Christians should remain on God's way, rather than on the passing events of daily life.

There is an enlightening tension between the readings and Psalm 25 as we look down the long stretch of Ordinary Time. The readings all express a certain urgency. The Ninevites repent immediately. Jesus announces the imminent arrival of the kingdom of God. Paul says the time is running out. Yet Psalm 25 begins, "I wait for you, O LORD." The psalmist can afford to go through all the letters of the alphabet in prayer because no one who waits for God will be disgraced. Whether the time is long or short, it is God who knows the way. It is God who is good and true and loving. We can enter the year with courage. The God in whom we trust will not abandon us.

26th Sun Year A (4-5.6-7.8-9) [137]

Remember your mercies, O Lord (6).

The compassionate love of God is the focus for the Twenty-Sixth Sunday of Year A. The heart of Psalm 25, which calls upon God's *hesed*, is sung today. *Hesed* is the faithful enduring love demanded and nourished by the covenant. The evidence of God's *hesed* is the never-ending forgiveness extended to human beings. With God it is never too late. As soon as the sinner turns to God, God forgives.

Ezekiel (18:25-28) reminds the people in Exile that they cannot hide behind the excuse that they suffer for the sins of previous generations. God promises life to anyone who repents. The righteous, however, should not coast complacently, relying on past good deeds. They must strive daily to follow God's way.

The two sons of the gospel parable (Matt 21:28-32) illustrate the two ways open to us: lip service or true obedience. The one who chooses to do the father's will, no matter what preceded, is the one who truly learns

God's ways. God, hearing the plea of the psalmist, forgets the sins of youth and remembers *hesed*.

Hesed is a covenant obligation imposed on both God and God's people. The demand of *hesed* is total. Paul reminds Christians that our attitude must be the same as Christ's (Phil 2:1-11). God's *hesed* led Christ to empty himself of everything, even life, in order to do God's will. Because of this loving obedience, God exalted him over everything else that exists. He is perfectly united with the Father. He is the incarnation of God's faithful love. He is the witness that God remembers *hesed*. His self-emptying is the model for faithful love demanded of Christians. His example is the way that God has made known to us, the *hesed* that we must remember.

All Souls (6-7.17-18.20-21) [791]

To you, O Lord, I lift my soul (1).

The readings for All Souls Day are from the Common of the Dead. Psalm 25 is one of the suggested psalms. Most of the verses chosen are from the final stanza of the psalm (16-22) in which the psalmist pleads for God's protection and rescue. Verses 6-7 are also included which contain many of the significant key words of the psalm: goodness, faithful love, remembering. Interestingly, the line of verse 7 asking God to forget youthful sins is omitted. The plea for forgiveness appears, however, in verse 18. The selection ends with the request for honesty and virtue as protective escorts while the psalmist waits for God.

Old Testament readings which Psalm 25 might appropriately accompany include the following: Job 19:1, 23-27, which expresses undying trust and waiting for God; Wis 3:1-9, which ends with a testimony concerning truth, mercy and faithful love; Isa 25:6-9, the victory song of those who waited for God; Lam 3:17-26, which declares that God is good to those who wait. Some of the New Testament readings also echo themes of Psalm 25: Rom 5:5-11, which describes the proof of God's love for us; Rom 8:14-23 in which the whole created world awaits God's revelation; Rom 8:31-35, 37-39, the great hymn to God's love; Phil 3:20-21 which declares our eager expectation of Christ; and 1 John 3:1-2, another description of God's great love.

A few of the suggested gospel readings can be linked to Psalm 25: Matt 25:1-13, in which the wise bridesmaids are prepared to wait for the groom; Luke 12:35-40, in which the faithful servants wait for the master; Luke 23:33, 39-43, in which the crucified criminal is forgiven despite the sins of his youth. If verses are included which ask God to teach the way (4, 5, 8, 9, 10, 12, 14), Psalm 25 would reinforce the message of John 14:1-6 in which Thomas asks how we can know the way.

4. *Psalm 31*

Psalm 31 is an expression of undying trust in God. The psalmist calls God rock (3 ,4 [two different terms]), refuge (3, 5, cf. 2, 20), fortress (4), and fortified city (22). In the first stanza alone the psalmist expects God to deliver (2), listen (3, cf. 23), hurry and rescue (3), save (3, cf. 17), lead (4), guide (4), free (5), redeem (6). As the psalm progresses God is trusted to punish the enemies and save the faithful psalmist from distress (15-19). God's face will shine upon the sufferer (17) and will become a shelter from enemies (21).

The prayer comes out of a situation of terrible distress. Enemies lie in wait (5, 9). Sickness and sorrow wear out the body (10-11). Friend and enemy alike avoid the afflicted one (12-14). Trust in God is the only support for this miserable person. Expressions of trust penetrate even the descriptions of suffering. "Into your hands I commend my spirit; you will redeem me, LORD, faithful God" (6). "I trust in you, LORD; I say, 'You are my God.' My times are in your hands" (15-16). "How great is your goodness, LORD, stored up for those who fear you" (20).

The psalmist who has suffered so terribly can exhort all believers to have courage, to trust and love God (24-25). God has heard the plea of this person who was forgotten like the dead, shattered like a dish (13). All who hope in the Lord can hope to be heard.

In expressing this overwhelming suffering and unquenchable trust, Psalm 31 uses the standard phrases of all Israel's lament. It is as if the powerful emotions can only be contained in the formulas familiar to all worshippers. The psalm is similar to Jeremiah's confessions (see the Twenty-Second Sunday of Year A) and to many of the laments. There is also a strong element of thanksgiving. The psalm can be considered in three stanzas: 2-9, call for help and declaration of trust; 10-19, description of misery; 20-25, thanksgiving.

Good Friday ABC (2.6.12-13.15-16.17.25) [41]

Father, I put my life in your hands (Luke 23:46).

Just as Matthew and Mark put Psalm 22:2 in the mouth of Jesus at the moment of his death, so Luke uses verse 6 of Psalm 31: "Into your hands I commend my spirit" (Luke 23:46). The psalm, an expression of trust in mortal suffering, is fitting for the passion narrative and for Good Friday.

The reading which precedes the psalm on Good Friday is the fourth Servant song from the Book of Isaiah (52:13–53:12). The Servant's suffering makes him repulsive to those who see him. Yet his suffering is our suffering; he endures the consequences of our sins. His silent suffering wins justification for many. His suffering becomes his victory. This understanding of vicarious suffering is virtually unique in the Old Testament. The mysterious figure of the Servant is sometimes understood to be Israel itself, whose endurance through suffering preserved the covenant for future generations. Sometimes the figure is thought to be a prophet, caught between God and the people, who faithfully delivers God's message in spite of suffering. From the time of the gospels Christians have used the wisdom of the Servant songs to interpret the passion and death of Jesus.

The gospel for Good Friday is the passion narrative from the Gospel of John (18:1–19:42). Jesus, in this narrative, is completely in control of events. Thus his submission from the moment of his arrest until his death is a dramatic expression of obedience to his father. The reading from the Letter to the Hebrews (4:14-16; 5:7-9) interprets the event: "Son though he was, he learned obedience from what he suffered." This obedience has become the source of our salvation.

Psalm 31 is well chosen to highlight these readings. The verses selected emphasize the element of trust (2, 6, 15-17, 25) and the hopelessness of suffering (12-13). Like the Servant, at the very moment that he is a horror to all who see him, Christ wins their salvation if they will accept it. His total trust is in his Father and his trust is not in vain. God does indeed rescue him in faithful love. We have every reason to be strong and take heart as we make Christ's words our own: "Father, into your hands I commend my spirit."

9th Sun Year A (2-3.3-4.17.25) [86]

Lord, be my rock of safety (3).

Psalm 31 draws from the other readings for the Ninth Sunday of Year A the importance of trust. The reading from Deuteronomy (11:18, 26-28) is a call to trust the word of God. Moses declares flatly that obedience to God's word is blessing and life, disobedience is curse and death (cf. Deut 30:15-20). The choice is clear; there is no middle ground. At the end of the sermon on the mount (Matt 7:21-27) Jesus makes a similar statement. Everyone who listens to his words and acts on them will be like the wise person who builds a house on rock. The foolish person, on the other hand, who disregards his words, builds a house on sand.

The psalmist knew that only God could be counted on as rock and refuge. Only God could be counted on for salvation and life. The psalmist makes no claim to perfect obedience, only to unwavering trust (v. 23 notwithstanding). It is God's righteousness that is the hope for deliverance, God's name that is the hope for safety. The reason for courage is hope in God.

This is Paul's message in the Letter to the Romans (3:21-25, 28). No one has a right to salvation; all have sinned. But we have been freely justified by God's grace through redemption in Christ Jesus. It is not the works of the Law which provide our claim to salvation. It is our trust in God's free gift which comes from God's own righteousness. God is our only rock.

5. *Psalm 42–43*

Psalm 42–43 is actually only one psalm. There is a refrain (42:6, 12; 43:5) which binds the whole work together. In addition the psalm is united by echoed lines such as, "Where is your God?" (42:4, 11), and "Why must I go about mourning . . ." (42:10; 43:2). The refrain marks out the divisions of the psalm: 2-6, longing for God based on memories of the past; 7-12, description of present distress; 43:1-5, plea for protection in the future and promise of thanksgiving.

There is a masterful interweaving of themes in this psalm. The psalm opens with the image of longing for God as the deer longs for water. Water is seen both in a positive and negative light. God is like living water (cf. v. 3). The water of tears has become the psalmist's food (4). The headwaters of the Jordan remind the psalmist of God's power and the power of the waters of chaos (7-8). The deep, *tehom*, often refers to primeval chaos. Water in this psalm stands for both life and death.

In verse 2 the psalmist's *nephesh* longs for God. The word *nephesh*, which is sometimes translated "soul," refers to the essence of one's life. Originally the word meant "throat," and sometimes it is still used in that sense. Because the health of the throat is so essential to life, the word came to mean life. It can also imply desire. The word is particularly strong in verse 2. The psalmist's throat/desire/life longs for God. The word occurs throughout the psalm. In verse 3 the *nephesh* thirsts for God; in verse 5 the psalmist pours out the *nephesh* as if it were water. In verses 6-7 the *nephesh* is downcast or crushed and groans in distress (cf. also 12 and 43:5).

The psalmist longs for God, but particularly longs to be able to worship God with the community in the temple, the special place of God's presence. For some reason, the psalmist is not in Jerusalem, but to the north, somewhere in the Hermon range. The enemies are taunting and grief shatters the bones. The terrible question is: "Where is your God?" Yet the psalmist clings to the assurance that God is faithful, that patient waiting for God will again lead to the opportunity for praise. Light and Fidelity, personified as messengers of God, will lead the psalmist back to Mount Zion and God's altar. That is the delight the *nephesh* longs for.

Easter Vigil 7 (3.5; 43:3.4) [42]

Like a deer that longs for running streams, my soul longs for you, my God (2).

Psalm 42-43 is an excellent choice for the Easter Vigil. The images of water and of longing for God with one's whole being underscore the waiting of this sacred night. The *Exsultet* tells us that "this is the night when God led the Israelites dry-shod through the sea. This is the night when Christians everywhere, washed clean of sin . . . are restored to grace and grow together in holiness." On this night catechumens wait to plunge into the deadly waters of baptism so that they might emerge with Christ into new life (42:8-9). As the deer longs for streams of water, they long for the living water of God's life (Ps 42:2). Reflecting this psalm, ancient baptistries were often decorated with the motif of the deer. On this night all Christians wait to renew their baptismal vows and to celebrate Christ's victory over death. On this night the whole community assembles at the altar of God (42:5; 43:4).

The reading from Ezekiel (36:16-28) is the promise that the covenant will be renewed and God's people restored to their own land. For the sake of the divine name, God will sprinkle clean water upon the people to cleanse them from all their impurities. God will give them a new heart and a new spirit, God's own spirit. The unity pledged by the covenant, which is the desire of God and of the people, will be restored: "You shall be my people, and I will be your God." The longing for God will be satisfied; the whole people will give thanks in God's house.

All Souls (2.3.5; 43:3.4.5) [791]

My soul is thirsting for the living God; when shall I see God face to face? (42:3).

Psalm 42-43 expresses ardent longing for God. The use of this psalm in the Common of the Dead reveals the Christian faith that after death one is united with the living God. The refrain captures the heart of faith in the face of death. "When can I go and see the face of God?" The selected verses are the same as those chosen for the Easter Vigil (see above) with the addition of the psalm's refrain (43:5), a cry of hope that sorrow will come to an end. This echo of the Easter celebration reminds us also of our hope for resurrection and of baptism, the reason for our hope.

Some of the Old Testament readings suggested in the Common of the Dead have a particular resonance with Psalm 42-43. Job (19:1, 23-27) longs to see God and believes courageously that he will. The prophet Isaiah (25:6, 7-9) presents a vision in which God will wipe away all tears and all people will find salvation on God's holy mountain. The poet of Lamentations (3:17-26) is downcast, but hopes in Yahweh who is good to all who seek, who renews mercy every morning.

New Testament readings also echo images from the psalm. In Rom 5:5-11 the love of God is described pouring out like water for the thirsty. The longing for God is expressed in Rom 8:14-23. The great vision of the New Jerusalem in Rev 21:1-5, 6-7 reminds us that God wipes away every tear and gives life-giving water to all who thirst.

Four gospel selections would be supported by Psalm 42- 43: Matt 5:1-12, blessings for the sorrowing, thirsty, single-hearted; Matt 11:25-30, the revelation of God in Jesus and rest for the weary; Luke 24:13-35, unbelievable hope for the downcast disciples; and John 6:51-58, Jesus' gift of himself to satisfy the thirsty.

6. *Psalm 51 (Penitential)*

Psalm 51 is the best known of the penitential psalms (Pss 6, 32, 38, 51, 102, 130, 143). Tradition has designated these psalms as particularly appropriate prayers of repentance for sin. Masterfully, the psalmist begs for forgiveness and rejoices in renewal. The psalm falls into two major stanzas (3-10, 11-19) with an appendix (20-21).

The first major section (3-10) is preoccupied with the reality of sin. Verses 3-4 introduce the subject with three terms for sin balanced by three terms of hope. The former terms describe sin as rebellion (*pesha'*), perversion (*'awon*), and missing the mark (*hatta'*). The latter terms state the reason for hope. The psalmist cries out for mercy (*hanan*) because of God's love (*hesed*, cf. Ps 25), and compassion (*rahamim*). God's compassion is like that of a mother for the child of her womb (*rehem*).

The psalmist makes no excuses, but knows the reality of sin and the one whom sin offends (5-6). The psalmist recognizes that the inclination to sin is imbedded within us from the beginning (7-8). Therefore it is God, the very one whom sin offends, who must scrub it away (9, cf. 4). Only God can restore the whole person, flesh and bones, to the joy of life (10).

The second stanza (11-19) begins with another plea that God blot out sin and guilt (11, cf. 3). The psalmist then begins to describe God's restoration. Because sinful tendencies are rooted in us from the beginning (cf. 7-8), God must re-create us from the inside out (12-14). The verb *bara'* (create) is predicated only of God. Only God can make new the spirit (*ruah*). The psalmist begs God not to withdraw the holy spirit/breath that gives life (cf. Gen 2:7), but through that spirit, to recreate a strong and free spirit and a clean heart within the psalmist. Then the psalmist will teach God's ways and praise God's salvation (15-17). Then the psalmist's heart and spirit will be completely broken open to God (18-19, cf. 8, 12-14).

The appendix (20-21) is a late response to the statement about sacrifice in verses 18-19. The point of the earlier verses is that sacrifice is worthless without the love and devotion of the worshiper. Lest they be misinterpreted as denying the value of sacrifice altogether, a prayer for Jerusalem has been added expressing the worth of genuine sacrifice.

This psalm is carefully woven together. The plea for cleansing in verse 4 reappears in verse 9 with the verbs reversed (A:B:B:A, a literary device called chiasm). This interlocks with the expression of desire that sin and guilt be blotted out (3, 11). The need for inner renewal weaves throughout the psalm (7-8, 12-14, 18-19). A vivid expression of the psalmist's need is found in the verb of verse 9, *hatta'*, a form of the common word for sin which in one form or another appears in verses 4, 5, 6, 7, 11, and 15. Verse 9 begins literally, "Unsin me!"

The title (1-2) relates the psalm to David's repentance after his sin with Bathsheba (2 Sam 12:13-25). David becomes an example to us of genuine repentance and complete trust in God. (See Psalm 54 for a further discussion of psalm titles.)

Two theological problems must be noted regarding verse 7. The verse has sometimes been understood as a statement about original sin. The doctrine of original sin was not fully developed until New Testament times. Paul in Romans 5 draws the contrast between Jesus and Adam and states that through Adam's sin condemnation came to all (Rom 5:18). In the Old Testament there is certainly an understanding of the human inclination to sin. Genesis 3 is part of an attempt to explain our weakness. Psalm 51:7 is the psalmist's acknowledgment of the deep roots of sin within us. The idea, however, of inheriting the inclination and/or the sin from Adam is not an Old Testament idea.

A further problem may surface in interpreting verse 7. Because of the mention of the mother's conceiving, the verse was sometimes understood to mean that the act of intercourse was itself sinful, especially for the woman. This is totally foreign to biblical thought which asserts that sexuality is a creation of God and is therefore good (cf. Gen 2:21-25; Song of Songs). Only the perversion of sexuality (as of any of God's good gifts) is sinful.

1st Sun Lent A (3-4.5-6.12-13.14.17) [22]

Be merciful, O Lord, for we have sinned (3).

Psalm 51 is well-chosen for the beginning of Lent. As we begin our retreat with the catechumens awaiting baptism, we acknowledge our need for re-creation from the inside out. The verses chosen for this First Sunday of Lent A include the confession of guilt and the plea for God's mercy (3-6), the prayer for inner renewal (12-14), and a promise of praise (17). The troublesome verse 7 is omitted, perhaps a wise decision. A less happy decision is the omission of verses 18-19 which describe the true sacrifice of an open heart. This concept certainly relates to Lent and to the obedience of Jesus.

The first two readings (Gen 2:7-9; 3:1-7; Rom 5:12-19) immediately present the challenge of the teaching concerning original sin. This challenge, if confronted head-on, may be a wonderful opportunity to explain the development of the doctrine and to emphasize that we all share in the sinful condition of humanity. We cannot blame Adam any more than the man could blame the woman or the woman the serpent (Gen 3:12-13). It is not Adam's fault that we are sinners. We can each sing: "My sin is always before me."

The first reading is a severely abbreviated version of the Yahwist story of human creation and sin. It would be well to read the whole story (2:4a–3:24) in order to find God's command about the trees, the creation of the animals, the creation of the sexes, the goodness of sexuality, and the consequences of sin.

Within the Genesis reading we find God creating and giving life through divine breath (although neither *bara'* nor *ruah* are used). The psalm pleads for new creation, a new infusion of God's spirit (12). The serpent in Genesis implies that God has evil intentions toward humankind; the psalm reverses that by confessing that only God can recreate and renew life. The Genesis story explains the incursion of sin and evil into human life. The psalm allows us to appropriate that story by acknowledging that we too have sinned (3-6).

The reading from Romans and the gospel (Matt 4:1-11) together proclaim the wonder of God's love and compassion (*hesed* and *rahamim*). To renew our spirit, to cleanse and create us again (Ps 51:12-14), God sent the Son to share our weak human condition and to reverse our misery by turning us back to God through his obedience. Jesus was led by the Spirit to be tempted. His temptation, like the one in Genesis, was to snatch at being like God. His response, unlike the one in Genesis, was complete trusting obedience to God. God's merciful love has worked a marvelous transformation. "For our sakes [God] made him to be sin who did not know sin, so that we might become the righteousness of God in him" (2 Cor 5:21, cf. Ash Wednesday). This is God's new creation.

5th Sun Lent B (3-4.12-13.14-15) [35]

Create a clean heart in me, O God (12).

The refrain and verses selected from Psalm 51 for the Fifth Sunday of Lent B center on the plea for new creation (12-14). The last verse is a promise to teach sinners God's way. The direct acknowledgment of guilt is omitted (5-6); the only allusion to sinfulness is in the opening verses (3-4).

The reading from Jeremiah (31:31-34) is God's promise of new creation, a new covenant with the people. The covenant bond is the creation of the people, their unity and their identity. They are God's people; Yahweh is their God. The new covenant will be rooted within them; God's instruction (*torah*) will be written on their hearts. The psalm pleads for God to fulfill the promise, to create within the people a clean heart, a new spirit (12-14). Because the new covenant is written on hearts, there will be no need to teach it any more. Yet in the psalm the people pledge to teach God's way in order to hasten the new creation, to build the new covenant community (15). In the new covenant God will not only forgive but will forget their sins. When God ceases to remember something, it no longer exists. God's forgetting permanently blots out sin. In the new covenant all will know the Lord, all will be enlivened by God's holy spirit.

The New Testament readings (Heb 5:7-9; John 12:20-33) seem paradoxical. They point out the price of new creation. "Unless a grain of wheat falls to the ground and dies, it remains just a grain of wheat" (John 12:24). Unless one is willing to surrender the old life, the new cannot come. The clean heart, the steadfast willing spirit, spring from the sacrifice of a broken spirit, a crushed heart (Ps 51:19).

Still only God can create the new heart; only God can establish the new covenant. God chooses to do this through Jesus, the Son who learned obedience from what he suffered (Heb 5:8). Jesus, who conquers sin and death by his obedience, draws everyone to himself (John 12:32) and becomes the source of eternal salvation for all who obey him (Heb 5:9). He is the new covenant, the bond between God and the people. He is the beginning and the source of the new creation.

Ash Wednesday (3-4.5-6.12-13.14.17) [220]

Be merciful, O Lord, for we have sinned (3).

The refrain and psalm verses chosen for Ash Wednesday are the same as those for the First Sunday of Lent A (see above).

The reading from the prophet Joel (2:12-18) is the proclamation of a fast. The reasons for fasting surround the call. "Perhaps [God] will again relent . . . the LORD . . . took pity on [the] people" (2:14, 18). The psalm (including verses not selected for this day) acts out the call from the reading. God cries out in the words of the prophet: "Return to me with your whole heart, . . . rend your hearts, not your garments" (Joel 2:12-13). In the psalm we promise the sacrifice of a broken heart (Ps 51:19) and we beg God, who alone has power, to renew and make whole our hearts (Ps 51:12). We count on the creedal statement that God is gracious (*hanún*), merciful (*rahúm*), and rich in love (*hesed*), as we plead, "Have mercy on me (*honneni*), God, in your goodness (*hesed*); in your abundant compassion (*rahamim*) blot out my offense." The priests in the reading seem to pray the psalm for us, "Spare . . . your people." Even the appendix to Psalm 51 (20-21) echoes the prophetic hope that God will leave behind a blessing, the grain and wine and oil which will make sacrifice possible. The confidence in the psalm is not in vain. "The LORD . . . took pity on [the] people" (Joel 2:18).

The New Testament readings (2 Cor 5:20–6:2; Matt 6:1-6, 16-18) give us two warnings as we undertake our fast. The first warning has to do with time. The call is urgent. Now is the acceptable time to be reconciled to God. Now is the acceptable time to take the prayer of Psalm 51 into the center of our being. God's grace is given to us; God's holy spirit is present to us. The time to acknowledge guilt honestly and to be open to new creation is now.

The second warning has to do with attitude. The good works of almsgiving, prayer, and fasting must come from a willing, generous spirit (Ps 51:14). The term *nadîb*, "willing," connotes freedom and nobility, voluntary and generous giving. Good works which spring from such a noble spirit are free, without regard for reward. There is no ulterior motive of self-glorification. The psalm keeps us aware that we are sinners, in desperate need ourselves of God's loving mercy. Only through God's new creation are we able to do good works at all.

Lent Common (3-4.5-6.12-13.14.17) [175]

Be merciful, O Lord, for we have sinned (3).

The fact that Psalm 51 is used for Ash Wednesday and for two Lenten Sundays already indicates its appropriateness for the Common of Lent. The verses and the refrain are the same as those for the First Sunday of Lent A (see above). During the Lenten season, however, the psalms assigned to the Sundays are so well chosen that if at all possible it would be advisable to use the proper psalm.

Although Psalm 51 resonates with the whole Lenten season, there are a few Sundays which echo parts of the psalm more specifically. On the Third Sunday of Lent A (see Ps 95 for a fuller discussion) the reading from Exodus (17:3-7) tells of the murmuring of the people. A plea for mercy might well follow. The plea is answered in Rom 5:1-2, 5-8: God's love is proved to us because, while we were still sinners, Christ died for us. The woman at the well then becomes an example of new creation (John 4:5-42).

God's merciful response to Israel's cry of distress is described in the call of Moses, the first reading of the Third Sunday of Lent C (Exod 3:1-8, 13-15; see Ps 103). Paul reminds us, however, that their example of murmuring is not to be followed (1 Cor 10:1-6,10-12), but that we continually stand in need of God's mercy. The gospel (Luke 13:1-9) is a parable of God's mercy, the story of the fig tree.

The reading from 2 Chronicles (36:14-17, 19-23) on the Fourth Sunday of Lent B describes the Exile as a result of the people's sin (see Ps 137). Recognizing our own sin we might identify with them in crying out for mercy. The reading from Eph 2:4-10 begins: "God is rich in mercy." Our salvation is God's gift; we are a new creation in Christ Jesus (cf. Ps 51:12-14).

The New Testament readings of the Fourth Sunday of Lent C tell of reconciliation and new creation (see Ps 34). Each is used (whole or in part) with Psalm 51 on another Sunday: 2 Cor 5:17-21 (see Ash Wednesday), Luke 15:1-3, 11-32 (see Twenty-Fourth Sunday of Year C). The concept of new creation and the lifegiving force of God's Spirit is central to the Fifth Sunday of Lent A (Ezek 37:12-14; Rom 8:8-11; John 11:1-45; see Ps 130). Psalm 51, especially verses 12-14, would be appropriate for this Sunday (cf. the refrain and verses for the Fifth Sunday of Lent B).

Easter Vigil Alt 7 (12-13.14-15.18-19) [42]

Create a clean heart in me, O God (12).

Psalm 51 is suggested as an alternate response to Ezekiel 36:16-28 in the Easter Vigil (see also Ps 42-43). The refrain, "Create a clean heart in me, O God," focuses the response on new creation. The selected verses include not only the prayer for a new heart and spirit (12-14) but also the promise to sacrifice a broken spirit and crushed heart (18-19). The reading from Ezekiel is a promise of new covenant. (See Fifth Sunday of Lent B where a parallel new covenant passage, Jer 31:31-34, is discussed.) God reminds the people that the Exile was a just punishment for their sins (cf. Ps 51:6). Now, however, God will renew the covenant, will cleanse them and give them a new heart and spirit; God's spirit will give them life (cf. Ps 51:12-14). Their restoration will prove God's own holiness to the nations. They will become an example of God's merciful way (cf. Ps 51:15).

24th Sun Year C (3-4.12-13.17.19) [133]

I will rise and go to my father (Luke 15:18).

The psalm refrain for the Twenty-Fourth Sunday of Year C is taken from the gospel. The verses of Psalm 51 include the plea for forgiveness (3-4) and new creation (12-13), and the promise of praise (17) and true sacrifice (19).

All the readings portray generous and undeserved forgiveness. In Exod 32:7-11, 13-14, God threatens to destroy the people for making the image of a golden calf. Moses' prayer turns God's heart. Moses reminds God of the promise to the patriarchs and God relents. Moses knows God. In the Hebrew Scriptures God repents (*niham*) far more often than people do. We

too trust in God's willingness to forgive as we sing Psalm 51. With the Israelites we need to plead for God's mercy. With Moses we need to beg for
God's compassion on our sinful world.

The author of 1 Timothy, writing in Paul's name, also proclaims the
wonder of God's forgiveness (1 Tim 1:12-17). He acknowledges his sinfulness and claims that, precisely because he is the foremost of sinners, God
dealt with him mercifully. Thus he becomes an example of the abundance
of God's compassion (Ps 51:3). The gospel is the familiar collection of the
"lost" parables (Luke 15:1-32). Jesus tells these parables in defense of his
practice of eating with sinners. The parables assert that God eats with sinners and not only eats with them but throws a party to celebrate their return (6, 9, 23-24). As we sing Psalm 51 we know that God is not only
forgiving us but is rejoicing at our sacrifice of a broken heart and spirit. With
Paul and the younger son, we may go with confidence to our father. May
the bitter elder son find the spirit of Moses and plead for his younger brother.
God, have mercy on us all.

7. Psalm 54

Psalm 54 is an expression of trust in the name of God. God's name,
Yahweh, is a great gift to Israel. Exod 3:13-15 tells the story of the revelation of the name to Israel. The name, Yahweh, is derived from the verb
"to be." It signifies not only that God's essence is Being, but also that God
is present and active. God is the one who will be there for the people. It
is this presence and care that is the hope of the psalmist who cries, "By
your name save me" (3). When the distress is over the psalmist promises
to praise the name, Yahweh (LORD), because the name has rescued the
sufferer (8-9).

The psalm can be considered in two parts: verses 3-5 are the psalmist's
cry for help; verses 6-9 are an expression of trust and promise of praise.
"God" is mentioned four times in verses 3-6 and "Lord" ('*adonai*) once,
but only in verse 8 does the psalmist call out God's personal name, Yahweh. The promised praise of God's name begins at the end of v. 8 with
the phrase *kî tôb*, "how good!" (translated "gracious" in NAB). Just as God
praised creation in Gen 1 by proclaiming "how good" it is (Gen 1:4, 10,
12, 18, 21, 25, 31), so the psalmist returns the praise to God.

The reason for the lament is the persecution of enemies who are not
aware of God's presence (5). God, faithful to the trusting believer, destroys
the enemies and saves the psalmist.

Most of the psalms in this section of the psalter (Pss 51–65, 68–70) are
attached to David (cf. Ps 72:20). Many of them have a lengthy title connecting the psalm to some event in David's life. These titles are later addi-

tions to the psalm, but they often give us a valuable clue for interpretation. Psalm 54 is related to an incident when David, fleeing from Saul, was betrayed by a foreign tribe (1 Sam 23:14-28). The connection may have been drawn because Saul was "seeking David's life" (1 Sam 23:15; Ps 54:5).

25th Sun Year B (3-4.5.6-8) [135]

The Lord upholds my life (6).

On the Twenty-Fifth Sunday of Year B all of Psalm 54 is used except the last verse. Verse 9 is probably omitted because of the reference to gloating over enemies. The omission, however, also takes out the reference to rescue through the power of God's name. The psalm refrain is part of the psalmist's expression of confidence.

The readings for this Sunday give us a picture of trust in God in the face of persecution. The Book of Wisdom is the latest book in the Old Testament, written about 50 BCE. It is one of the few books of the Old Testament which declare a firm hope in life after death. The hope in life after death turns upside down problems of early death, childlessness, suffering of the innocent, prosperity of the wicked. The wicked have not believed in life after death, and so they seize pleasure and trample the powerless. The very presence of a just person is a judgment against them, and so they taunt and persecute the righteous, mocking them with their very trust in God. Psalm 54 allows the congregation to identify with the just and to express again unshakeable trust in God in spite of persecution.

The gospel passage is Jesus' second prediction of his passion (Mark 9:30-37). Each of the predictions is followed by an example of the disciples' misunderstanding and a teaching by Jesus. Here the disciples have failed to understand that real power comes from trust in God, not from greedy grasping. It is God who sustains our lives (Ps 54:6). The reading from the Letter of James (3:16–4:3) also contrasts contentious greed with the wisdom of trusting in God. No deprivation, not even death, can defeat that trust.

Psalm 54 emphasizes the power of God's name. There are several other names in the readings for this Sunday. In the Book of Wisdom the just one is challenged by the title "son of God" (Wis 2:18). The title here does not imply divinity, but childlike trust in God's power (cf. Mark 9:36-37). The mockery of the wicked suggests that God will not save the trusting child. The psalm asserts that God will indeed save. Jesus in the gospel is identified as "Son of Man," a title connoting his share in our human nature as well as his future role as judge at the end of time. Because of his humanness, Jesus can and will suffer. Because of his trust in God, he will also rise. His resurrection is our hope for the end of time. God indeed sustains our life!

8. Psalm 63

Psalm 63 is only tentatively included among the laments. Because of the longing and distress of verses 2 and 10-12, it is usually classified as a lament.[6] The center section, however, expresses thanksgiving and confidence which leads some scholars to include the psalm either with Songs of Thanksgiving or Psalms of Confidence.[7] Dahood regards the psalm as a prayer of the king (cf. v. 12) which suggests royal elements as well.[8]

The mood of lament is conveyed by the holding together of seeming opposites. The opening verses (1-2) portray a desert; the middle verses are set in God's sanctuary (3-9). The psalmist yearns (2) and anticipates being satisfied (6). All who trust in God will be rewarded; the wicked are destined for ruin (10-12).

The longing of the psalmist involves the whole person, not only flesh (*basar*) but that which makes one live (*nephesh*). *Nephesh*, often translated "soul" or "life," originally meant "throat" (see Psalm 42-43 for a longer discussion on *nephesh*). The term unites this psalm, occurring at beginning, middle, and end. The throat/life thirsts for God (2), but will be satisfied by the richness of a banquet offered in praise of God (6). On the other hand, the enemies who seek to destroy the psalmist's throat/life will themselves be destroyed (10).

Other important images portray the psalmist's longing and the hope which inspires it. The first verb for longing in verse 2 is derived from the word for dawn, *shahar*.[9] The longing is similar to that of Psalm 130:6, like the longing of sentinels for dawn. The psalmist may be making a night vigil at the sanctuary (cf. v. 7) and eagerly awaiting God's revelation at dawn. The psalmist rejoices under God's wings (8), perhaps the wings of the cherubim over the ark. The ark is also suggested in verse 3 by the word "power" (*'oz*) which is sometimes a name for the ark (cf. Pss 78:61; 132:8). The psalmist regards God's love (*hesed*) as better than life (4, see discussion with Pss 25 and 136). The prayer is made to God's name (see Ps 54).

This is another psalm attached to David's life by the title (see Ps 54). The opening desert imagery is linked to David's sojourn in the Judean wilderness when he was fleeing from Saul (1 Sam 23-26). The psalm, with its

[6]So Sabourin (250). Stuhlmueller (1.54) classifies it as a Prayer of Supplication. Kraus (2.600-601) calls it a *Gebetslied*, i.e., song of supplication. He notes that it also contains elements of thanksgiving and trust.

[7]Clifford (768) says the psalm contains elements of lament, thanksgiving, and trust. Anderson (240) and Kselman-Barré (536) include Psalm 63 with songs of trust.

[8]Dahood, 2.95-102.

[9]See Stuhlmueller 1.288.

references to the ark in the temple is certainly later than David and Solomon, but the title gives us a focus for sharing in the mood of the psalm.

12th Sun Year C (2.3-4.5-6.8-9) [97]

My soul is thirsting for you, O Lord my God (2).

On the Twelfth Sunday of Year C, Psalm 63 sets the theme of longing by the use of verse 2 as a refrain. All the verses of the psalm are used except verse 7, which refers to the night vigil, and the last three verses (10-12), which refer to the enemies and the king.

The first reading (Zech 12:10-11) is one of the most mysterious passages in the Old Testament. The second section of the Book of Zechariah (chs. 9–12), the work of unknown post-exilic prophets, contains a series of oracles which seem to refer to the final days of cosmic battle and God's victory in Jerusalem. The oracles are favorites of the evangelists who use them as a witness to Christ, especially to his passion (e.g., Zech 9:9 in Matt 21:5 and John 12:15; Zech 11:12-13 in Matt 26:15 and 27:9-10). Today's passage is part of a vision of the great battle around Jerusalem. Someone (the king?) has been killed and those responsible will mourn him. It is a vision both of suffering and of repentance at the final crisis. The Gospel of John connects the vision to the piercing of Jesus' side (John 19:37). The juxtaposition of a gospel passage in which Jesus predicts his passion (Luke 9:18-24) enhances the overtones of suffering in the Zechariah passage. The gospel, however, takes us a step beyond repentance: All who wish to come after Jesus must deny themselves, take up their Cross daily, and follow him. The passage from Galatians (3:26-29) tells us why this is necessary: Through baptism we "have clothed [ourselves] with Christ"; we "are all one in Christ Jesus" (3:27, 28). Therefore we must suffer with him in order to inherit the promise.

In the context of these readings Psalm 63 paradoxically expresses our longing for God, our trust in God. In Christ we are able to sing, "your love (*hesed*) is better than life" (4). In Christ we are able to assert, "your right hand upholds me; . . . in the shadow of your wings I shout for joy" (9,8). The psalm allows us to become both the mourners for him who was pierced and Christ surrendering to God's faithful love. Unity with God, whatever the cost, is the only banquet which will satisfy our longing.

22nd Sun Year A (2.3-4.5-6.8-9) [125]

My soul is thirsting for you, O Lord my God (2).

The refrain and verses of Psalm 63 used for the Twenty-Second Sunday of Year A are the same as those used for the Twelfth Sunday of Year C (see above). Again the mood of longing is connected to the passion of Christ and to the cost of discipleship. The interweaving of readings, however, is clearer than on the Twelfth Sunday C.

The passage from the prophet Jeremiah (20:7-9) begins the last of his "confessions" (12:1-5; 15:10-21; 17:12-18; 18:18-23; 20:7-18). These laments show Jeremiah's struggle with God over the terrible cost of his prophetic mission. In today's passage he accuses God of overpowering him. Yet the preaching of God's word is a compulsion, a fire within his bones.

Psalm 63 is an excellent response. We take on Jeremiah's struggle, both the yearning for God and the awareness of suffering for God's sake. It would be appropriate to include the final verses of the psalm (10-12), which are not in the Lectionary. Part of Jeremiah's suffering is caused by mortal enemies. In the passage immediately preceding today's selection he is punished in the stocks.

The gospel is Matthew's version of Jesus' first passion prediction (Matt 16:21-27). (For Luke's version of the same event see Sunday 12 C above.) Peter's response to Jesus' discussion of his impending suffering is denial. "God forbid, Lord!" After rebuking Peter, Jesus begins to instruct the disciples concerning the way to follow him. Disciples too must be ready to embrace the Cross and abandon even life itself. The reward is nothing less than life in God's kingdom. Paul (Rom 12:1-2) puts the matter directly: "Offer your bodies as a living sacrifice . . . do not conform yourself to this age."

With Psalm 63 we accept God's will for us and more. We long for whatever God's love will bring us. We enter Jeremiah's struggle; we speak for a converted Peter. With Christ we open ourselves to the Father.

32nd Sun Year A (2.3-4.5-6.7-8) [155]

My soul is thirsting for you, O Lord my God (2).

The psalm refrain for the Thirty-Second Sunday of Year A is the cry of longing from Psalm 63:2. The verse selection, however, is slightly different from the two Sundays discussed above. Verse 7 concerning the night vigil has been added. Verse 9, which implies trust in God no matter what the danger, is omitted. Verses 10-12, which never appear in the Lectionary, are also omitted. The effect of the omissions is a mood of longing and fulfillment with no sense of threat.

This quiet mood corresponds to the readings which center on wisdom. The opening reading (Wis 6:12-16) is taken from the Wisdom of Solomon, a deutero-canonical book recognized by Roman Catholics but not by Jews or Protestants. The book is the last of the Old Testament works to be written (ca. 50 BCE). Its author, who probably lived in Alexandria, wrote in Greek and used the fruits of Greek philosophy. Its words are set in the mouth of Solomon and today's reading is part of an exhortation to kings and rulers concerning the value of wisdom. Wisdom is presented as a wonderful woman; the readers are urged to court her and take her as a bride. As the chapters proceed, she herself is recognized as a manifestation of God.

The refrain of the psalm follows the exhortation perfectly. We are exhorted to seek Wisdom; we respond with a cry of longing for Wisdom-God. We are promised that those who watch for her at dawn will find her. In the psalm we declare that we long for her as the dawn (2) and that we will remember her help in the watches of the night (7).

The gospel (Matt 25:1-13) echoes the imagery of wedding and night watch, but the gender of seekers and sought is reversed. Ten virgins wait for the arrival of the bridegroom. Only five of them have made friends with Wisdom. Only five are prepared for the length of the wait. The exhortation is: Stay awake! Do not let your longing fade! The other New Testament reading (1 Thess 4:13-18) specifies the message of the gospel parable. Jesus the Bridegroom will return. Then we, both dead and alive, will meet him and be with him forever. This is the goal of our longing (Ps 63:2). This is the sanctuary toward which we gaze (3); this is the banquet we await (6). This is the love that is better than life (4).

All Souls (2-3.3-4.5-6.8-9) [791]

My soul is thirsting for you, O Lord my God (2).

The readings for All Souls Day are taken from the Common of the Dead. Psalm 63 is one of the possible selections for the responsorial psalm. The refrain and verses are the same as those for the Twelfth Sunday of Year C (see above). The refrain focuses the mood on longing for God. The omitted verses concern the night vigil (7), the enemies (10-11), and the king (12). Verse 7, watching for God through the night, might well be added in certain circumstances.

Psalm 63, like Psalm 42-43, makes a firm statement of faith in the face of death. As we sing, we declare that God's love is better than life (4). No matter what the danger, God is our help; God's right hand sustains us (9). Therefore, even in desert and darkness, we long for God, we cling to God (2, 7-8). We know the end of desert thirst is the rich banquet of God's praise (6). We see the darkness as the shadow of God's wings and we shout for joy (8).

Readings which Psalm 63 might appropriately accompany are: Job 19:1, 23-27, in which Job expresses his consuming longing and his faith that he will see God in his own flesh; Isa 25:6, 7-9, which describes God's final banquet (better if all of Isa 25:6 is included) and the watchfulness of the faithful; Lam 3:17-26, a valiant expression of faith in God's goodness to those who seek; Rom 8:14-23, the longing of all creation for God's kingdom; Rom 8:31-35, 37-39, the certainty that nothing, not even death, can separate us from God's love which is better than life. Two gospel passages pick up themes from Psalm 63: Matt 5:1-12, in which the hungry and thirsty are declared blessed; and John 6:51-58, the banquet in which Jesus himself is food and drink.

Year Common (2.3-4.5-6.8-9) [175]

My soul is thirsting for you, O Lord my God (2).

Psalm 63 is one of eight psalms suggested for common use during the Season of the Year. The refrain and verses are those of the Twelfth Sunday of Year C (see above). The use of Psalm 63 for specific Sundays indicates themes for which it is particularly appropriate: longing or waiting for God; suffering and passion; night vigils; and God's banquet.

A few suggestions: The Twentieth Sunday of Year A centers on the acceptance of the Gentiles. (See the fuller discussion with Psalm 67.) The Canaanite woman (Matt 15:21-28) longs for the crumbs from Jesus' table. The Gentiles described in Isa 56:1, 6-7 will be joyful in God's house. Paul hopes that the welcome of the Gentiles will awaken the longing of the Jews (Rom 11:13-15, 29-32).

The gospel for the Twenty-Fifth Sunday of Year B includes one of Jesus' passion predictions (Mark 9:30-37). (See Psalm 54; see also the discussion of passion predictions with the Twelfth Sunday of Year C and the Twenty-Second Sunday of Year A.) The first reading (Wis 2:12, 17-20) describes the mockery and vindication of one who trusts implicitly in God. The reading from James 3:16–4:3 lists examples of wise and unwise longing.

The gospel parable of the Thirty-Third Sunday of Year A (Matt 25:14-30) is a warning to be vigilant (see Psalm 128; see also the Thirty-Second Sunday of Year A for a similar parable). The reading from 1 Thess 5:1-6 is part of Paul's exhortation concerning preparation for the final day. The first reading (Prov 31:10-13, 19-20, 30-31) may well be a portrayal of the Wisdom Woman now as wife. This Sunday continues the themes of the previous Sunday in which Psalm 63 was the responsorial psalm.

Psalm 63 might also be substituted for Psalm 42-43 when the main emphasis is thirst and longing.

9. Psalm 69

Psalm 69 is a long and beautifully crafted lament of a person in mortal danger. The psalm can be divided into stanzas by noting three objects of attention: God, the psalmist, and others—both enemies and the faithful.

In the opening stanza (2-5) the psalmist cries out the desperate situation. The repeated word "I" directs the focus. The psalmist, threatened by the waters of chaos or death, complains, they "have reached my neck (*nephesh*)." The play of meanings of the word *nephesh* (see Psalm 42-43) indicates the threat to life itself. God seems absent; enemies making false accusations are too present.

The focus shifts to God in the second stanza (6-13) with the emphatic "you" in verse 6. God knows all the sins of the psalmist. God also knows that the psalmist suffers for God's sake, is somehow accused because of devotion to God's temple. God is thus the cause of suffering and the only hope for relief. The psalmist, the subject of enemies' mockery, prays not to be a scandal to believers.

The third stanza (14-22) begins with an emphatic "I" (14) and ends with an emphatic "you" (20). Attention is focused on the relationship between God and the psalmist. The vocabulary of the first stanza is repeated (15-16): mire, water, flood, depths, sink, overwhelm, enemies. But the distress is surrounded by trust in God's faithful love (*hesed*) and hope for God's answer (14, 17-18). The psalmist continues with a plea for ransom and redemption (19), key words from the exodus account, and ends with a renewed declaration of faith that God knows all the insult and injury (20-22).

The enemies are the subject of the fourth stanza (23-29). It is a prayer for God's vengeance against them. As the psalmist's eyes have failed (4), may their eyes fail (24). As the flood overwhelms the psalmist (3), may God's anger overtake them (25). As the psalmist is abandoned by friends and relatives (8-9), may their dwellings be left desolate (26). As they accused the psalmist (5), may God accuse them (28-29). May all this come because they added to the pain of one wounded by God.

The final stanza (30-37) weaves between the psalmist (note "I" in verse 30), God, and God's faithful people. The subject is the psalmist's vow to praise God. Thanksgiving to God must always take place in a communal setting. The one giving thanks must bear witness to everyone of God's great goodness. In this psalm the vow will be fulfilled with song rather than sacrifice. The psalm ends with the hope that God will rebuild Zion, the city of God's house for which the psalmist is so zealous (cf. v. 10).

Psalm 69 is a favorite of New Testament writers. It is cited most often in connection with Christ's passion (e.g., v. 5 in John 15:25; v. 22 in Matt 27:34 par; v. 26 in Acts 1:20) and the cleansing of the temple (v. 10 in John 2:17).[10] Christ is one who suffers for God's sake, who is wrongly believed to be a sinner because he suffers (5, 8-13). He is victorious in his

---

[10]See Stuhlmueller (1.312) for a wonderful table on v. 10 and John 2:17.

struggle with death because of God's great love and mercy (14, 16-17). In his victory he himself becomes both ransom and redeemer (19).

The verses most often cited in the New Testament come from the prayer for vengeance. Thus we Christians must face our discomfort with such prayers. It is undeniable that human sin causes suffering, often in innocent victims. The fullness of Christ's victory will be the rooting out of all evil and the healing of all suffering. We share in the struggle; we share in the pain. We must also share in praying for the eradication of evil in our world.[11]

12th Sun Year A (8-10.14.17.33-35) [95]

Lord, in your great love, answer me (14).

The selection of verses from Psalm 69 for the Twelfth Sunday of Year A is greatly abbreviated. The selection includes verses 8-10, part of the plea that God is the cause of the distress; verses 14 and 17, the prayer of confidence in God's love which, in the psalm, surrounds the recapitulation of the distress; and verses 33-35, the song of praise which will fulfill the vow. The refrain (14) teaches us how to bear suffering: by crying out to God with trust in God's great love. Missing is the description of the watery depths of chaos (2-3, 15-16), as well as most of the description of the enemies (5, 20-29). The prayer for vengeance has entirely disappeared.

The first reading (Jer 20:10-13) is one of the confessions of Jeremiah (see the Twenty-Second Sunday of Year A). Jeremiah suffers from mocking enemies (cf. Ps 69:12-13), yet trusts in God who hears the poor (cf. Ps 69:34). Jeremiah prays for God's vengeance on his enemies (cf. Ps 69:23-29) and even hopes to see it. Psalm 69 is well chosen to resonate with Jeremiah's distress. The psalm seems to be a summary of Jeremiah's suffering. Jeremiah was thrown in a cistern and sank in its muck (Jer 38; Ps 69:2-3). His family plotted against him (Jer 12:6; Ps 69:9). He suffered shame and disgrace for God's sake (Jer 15:10-17; 20:7-8; cf. Ps 69:8). He pleads for God's vengeance against his enemies (Jer 17:14-18; 18:18-23; cf. Ps 69:23-29). The whole psalm could certainly be prayed in Jeremiah's voice.

The gospel (Matt 10:26-33) returns us to the confidence of the psalm refrain. No distress, not even the mortal struggle described by the psalmist, should cause God's people to fear. Only God is to be feared, and it is God who in great love will answer us when we cry out. Another echo of the psalm is heard in the last sentence of the gospel: "Whoever denies me . . . I will deny" (10:33). The psalmist became an outcast to family and friends. Woe to those who unwittingly cast out the suffering Christ.

---

[11]For further discussion of the prayer of vengeance, see Stuhlmueller 1.312–315; Anderson, 87–90.

Paul (Rom 5:12-15) turns to the subject which is the central problem of the psalm, the power of sin and death in the world. The psalmist's plea to God for an answer (Ps 69:14, 17-18) is a plea to remove the evil that causes the psalmist's own suffering. Verses 23-29 make the plea specific. Paul acknowledges the power of evil and declares God's answer. In faithful love God has given the answer of life in Jesus Christ. He is the gift of God's abundant love. His victory over sin and death is the reason we need not fear. The Lord hears the poor; see and be glad! (cf. Ps 69:33-34).

15th Sun Year C (14.17.30-31.33-34.36.37) [106]

Turn to the Lord in your need and you will live (33).

The verses chosen from Psalm 69 for the responsorial psalm of the Fifteenth Sunday of Year C come from the psalmist's prayer of trust and vow of praise. All descriptions of the enemy are omitted and the suffering is only mentioned directly once (30). Thus the heart of the psalm has been omitted. The refrain, a paraphrase of the song which fulfills the psalmist's vow, mentions need but focuses on the help of God.

The juxtaposition of Psalm 69 and the reading from Deut 30:10-14 is initially jarring. The Deuteronomy passage is snipped from the middle of a chapter (mid-sentence actually) in which the exilic author, speaking with the voice of Moses, is exhorting the people to repentance. If they repent and obey, God will delight in their prosperity. Following today's reading the choice is set before the people: life or death, life if they love and obey God, death if they turn to other gods. Thus the command which is in their mouths and hearts is the command to return to God, to love God and to demonstrate their love through obedience. With the psalm refrain then, we repeat the advice to an exiled people: "Turn to the Lord in your need, and you will live."

The gospel (Luke 10:25-37) expands the command to love God by the command to love neighbor (also an Old Testament command, from Lev 19:18). Jesus illustrates the dual command with the parable of the Good Samaritan. The reading from Col 1:15-20 draws the whole together. Christ, the image of God, has been sent to reconcile everything in his person. The thread running through all the readings and the psalm is reconciliation.

There is a paradoxical irony in the use of Psalm 69 within a context of reconciliation. The psalmist has cried out to God in the midst of terrible suffering, brought in part by enemies. The psalmist thinks that the resolution of the problem is in the destruction of the enemies (23-29). God, however, has a different answer in mind (cf. 14, 17). God's answer to evil is reconciliation, the reconciliation won by Jesus through the blood of his Cross. Reconciliation is the answer of God's abundant love. But the struggle against evil continues. The reconciliation won by Christ must be given flesh in our lives. Thus the command is not only to love God but neighbor as well. This is the command in our hearts. Then the lowly and poor, the robbed and beaten, will know God's answer and be glad (cf. 33-34). Then we will all live and inherit the kingdom of God (cf. 33, 36-37).

10. Psalm 71

Psalm 71 is the prayer of an elderly person who has always trusted God. Now in time of distress that trust is used both to motivate God to help and to strengthen the petitioner to endure. The psalm has an air of confidence even in the midst of suffering (cf. 5-7, 19-20). It is carefully woven of repeated words and synonyms, especially terms for refuge and rescue.

The psalm can be divided into three almost equal stanzas (1-8, 9-16, 17-24) by the recurrent motif of promised praise (vv. 8, 14-16, 22-24). In each stanza the psalmist reminds God of faithful service from youth until the present (5-6, 9, 18). The psalmist begs not to be abandoned now in old age (9, 12, 18). Praise is promised which will extend God's glory even to every coming generation (18).

The psalm is filled with standard phrases and themes found in other psalms, perhaps indicating the psalmist's years of experience with the praying community. There is a striking affinity with Psalm 22 (see above).[12] The psalmist is supported by God from the womb, an image suggesting the immediate care of the midwife (Pss 71:5-6; 22:10-11). The psalmist begs God not to be distant (Pss 71:12; 22:2, 12, 20). The psalmist promises to proclaim God's praise to coming generations (Pss 71:18; 22:31-32).

4th Sun Year C (1-2.3-4.5-6.15-17) [73]

I will sing of your salvation (15).

The selected verses of Psalm 71 for the Fourth Sunday of Year C represent most of the first stanza, concluded by the promise of praise which ends the second stanza. These opening verses heap up terms for refuge and rescue along with sure expression of confidence: You are my rock, my fortress, my hope, my trust, my strength. The reliance on God from birth is brought out, but the fact that the psalmist is old is not mentioned. The selection ends with the psalmist's declaration of faithful service. The refrain is taken from the psalmist's vow of praise.

The psalm as a whole presents an interesting contrast to the readings. The psalm is the prayer of an old person at the end of a faithful life. The readings describe beginnings.

[12]See Stuhlmueller (1.317) for a list of correspondences between the two psalms.

The first reading (Jer 1:4-5, 17-19) is part of the call of Jeremiah. It tells of God's encounter with the prophet, the commissioning, and repeats God's reassurance to the reluctant youth. Jeremiah's objection, "I am too young," although it is not included, should not be far from our minds. Through the psalm we become Jeremiah, proclaiming, "From my mother's womb you are my strength" (Ps 71:6). The refrain, however, represents more of a struggle than is at first obvious. Jeremiah will indeed meet opposition and will need God as rescue and refuge (1-4). But through the struggle Jeremiah will continue to sing of God's salvation. Remembering the whole psalm calls to mind Jeremiah's long and faithful service as God's prophet.

The gospel is Luke's story of the beginning of Jesus' ministry (Luke 4:21-30). After reading a passage from Isaiah, Jesus proclaims its fulfillment. The people of his own town, however, reject him. After he reminds them that "no prophet is accepted in his own native place," they even attempt to kill him. But he walked through their midst and went away. Like Jeremiah, Jesus faces rejection and persecution from the beginning (cf. Ps 71:1-4). Like Jeremiah, he never ceases proclaiming God's justice, singing of God's salvation (Ps 71:15-17).

Paul's hymn to love (1 Cor 12:31–13:13) adds another layer to the themes of this Sunday. Love is not mentioned in Psalm 71, nor does it occur in either of the other two readings. But love is the foundation of all of them. It is love, the love that never fails, which supports the faithful service of the psalmist (and of Jesus and Jeremiah). It is love, the love that is patient and enduring, which allows each of them to endure suffering and persecution. It is knowledge of the love of God, even though seen as in a mirror, which inspires trust in God's rescue, praise of God's justice. Love remains. Even in old age we will sing of God's salvation.

11. Psalm 80 (Communal)

Psalm 80 is a national lament, a lament of the whole people. There is a great deal of debate over the specific calamity which inspired the psalm. The reference to Joseph, a name used to signify the northern kingdom, and Ephraim and Manasseh, northern tribes, leads to the proposal that the psalm belongs to the period around the collapse of the northern kingdom in 722 BCE. The prayer for the king (18-19) and the use of the titles "LORD of hosts" and "enthroned on the cherubim," which suggest the ark of the covenant, imply that Jerusalem may be the scene of the prayer. Perhaps the time is the reign of Josiah (640–609 BCE). Josiah attempted to expand the borders of Judah to include territory formerly belonging to the northern kingdom. It was a time of reform and resistance. Josiah instituted a reform, inspired by the newly discovered book of Deuteronomy. In the face of great resistance Jeremiah preached insistently the need for return to God (*shûb*, a word used in the refrain of Psalm 80). It was also a time of disaster. Josiah was killed in 609 battling Pharaoh Neco at Megiddo. The nation was defeated by Babylon in 597, again in 587 and taken into Exile.

The specific calamity, however, is not as important as the content of the psalm, which teaches us how to pray in any disaster. The plea of the psalm is contained in the refrain: "LORD of hosts, restore us. Let your face shine upon us, that we may be saved" (4, 8, 20; cf. 15). The refrain calls upon God to do two things, which in the end are the same thing: restore us, shine upon us. "Restore us" comes from the verb, *shûb*, which means "turn." The form in the refrain is causative, "make us turn." It means both "make us return to you and be faithful again," and "turn our lives around and restore our good fortune." How will this happen? Only if God is kind to us. "Let your face shine upon us, then we will be saved." The increasing insistence in the plea is signified by the variations in the naming of God: "God" (4), "God of hosts" (8), "LORD, God of hosts" (20). The title "LORD/God of hosts" appears also in verses 5 and 15, echoing the refrain and reminding us of its plea.[13]

The refrain divides the psalm into three stanzas (2-4, 5-8, 9-20). The first stanza is an appeal to God, stressing both God's responsibility to care for the people as shepherd and guide (see Psalm 23), and the great power of the one enthroned upon the cherubim. The two concepts are united in the simple plea: "Stir up your power, come to save us."

The second stanza (5-8) describes the people's distress. They are at the mercy of neighbor and enemy. They eat and drink the tears of their misery. There is no doubt in their minds that God is the cause: "you burn . . . you have fed . . . you have left." Yet only God can relieve their misery. "Your people pray . . . restore us."

The third stanza (9-20) begins with motivation for God: *You* brought this vine from Egypt in the exodus (see the Twenty-Seventh Sunday of Year A for further discussion on the image of Israel as vine). *You* made space for it and planted it. Because of *you* it prospered. Now it is in distress because *you* have broken down its vineyard walls. Responsibility is laid squarely at God's feet. Therefore at the turning point of this long stanza (15) responsibility for restoration is also given completely to God: Turn again. Attend to the vine. Punish its enemies. Only in the last verse before the refrain (19) do we make a promise: If you restore us, "then we will not withdraw from you." The petition of the refrain closes the psalm.

---

[13] *The Revised Psalter of the New American Bible* has altered the text to read "LORD of hosts" (*yhwh seba'ot*) in all five cases.

1st Sunday Advent B (2-3.15-16.18-19) [2]

Lord, make us turn to you, let us see your face and we shall be saved (4).

The refrain of Psalm 80 is used as the response for the First Sunday of Advent B. The verses represent almost exclusively the petitions of the psalm. The first stanza, calling upon the powerful shepherd, is used in its entirety. The selection then leaps to the midpoint of the third stanza, using the whole final petition with the exception of the prayer for vengeance against the enemy (17). Omitted also are the description of distress (5-7) and the motivation for God to act (9-14).

The opening reading from Isa 63:16-17, 19; 64:2-7 picks up some of the themes omitted from the psalm and introduces others which the response will echo. The oracle represents another time of national disaster, the Babylonian Exile (587- 539 BCE) and the time of return in which the effort of rebuilding seemed overwhelming. Like the psalm, the prophetic oracle reminds God of the Exodus (63:11-14), using that past saving action to motivate God to save them again. God is named father and redeemer. God is given responsibility for the people's weakness (63:17). Thus it is God who must return (*shûb*) and save them. They admit their guilt, their apathy: "There is none who calls upon your name" (64:6). Finally they return to the titles of care and responsibility: father, potter, creator. With the psalm we repeat their cry to God to return and save us. We promise that, once revived, we will call on God's name (19).

The second reading (1 Cor 1:3-9) proclaims that God has returned to save us. The divine face has shone upon us. We have been strengthened and made blameless through Christ, the gift of God's faithfulness. But there is yet another return, a complete restoration for which we wait. The gospel warns us that God will indeed answer our prayer: "Stir up your power, come to save us." But we must be ready. "Would that you might meet us doing right" (Isa 64:4). We must take care to be on guard at the same time as we recognize God's power. If your face shines upon us, Lord, then we will be saved.

4th Sun Adv C (2-3.15-16.18-19) [12]

Lord, make us turn to you, let us see your face and we shall be saved (4).

The refrain and verses of Psalm 80 chosen for the responsorial psalm of the Fourth Sunday of Advent C are the same as those for the First Sunday of Advent B (see above.) One of the selected verses (18) is a prayer for the king, the "man at [God's] right hand." Every prayer for the king is to some degree messianic. The king is the anointed one (=Messiah) who is "son of God," beloved by God. At the end of the Advent season the messianic tone comes to the fore. God's return will be in the person of the anointed one, the christ.

The reading from the prophet Micah (5:1-4) announces that Judah's restoration will come through an anointed king like David, born in David's birthplace of Bethlehem, practicing David's occupation of shepherding. The psalm repeats the shepherd image, calling upon God, the shepherd, to come and save us. We ask for the light of God's face; we ask to be given new life.

The two New Testament readings (Heb 10:5-10; Luke 1:39-45) show us the wonder of God's plan. God's return to save us is in the person of Jesus, the Messiah. Through his flesh, the body prepared for him (cf. Heb 10:5), the face of God shines on us. Through his flesh, offered in obedience, we are saved. The gospel tells the story of one of the first proclamations of God's arrival to save us: "Blessed is the fruit of your womb." The Son of God has taken flesh in Mary's womb. God has come to revive us; let us call on the holy name!

27th Sun Year A (9.12.13-14.15-16.19-20) [140]

The vineyard of the Lord is the house of Israel (Isa 5:7).

The predominant image for the Twenty-Seventh Sunday of Year A is the vineyard. The refrain for the responsorial psalm is the climax of the first reading: "The vineyard of the Lord is the house of Israel." The verses chosen from Psalm 80 come from the third stanza in which the vine image is used to motivate God to restore the people. The verses omitted from the stanza concern the growth of the vine (10-11), the enemies (17), and the king (18, although 18b is printed in brackets in the Lectionary). The absence of the first two stanzas diminishes the awareness of distress (5-7) and the strong plea to God (1-3).

The vine or vineyard is a frequent image for God's people. God cares for the vine and delights in it (Isa 27:2-3, 6; Hos 14:8-9), but will prune it and even destroy it if it fails to produce good fruit (Isa 27:4-5; Jer 2:21; Ezek 15:1-8; Hos 10:1-2). The message of the first reading for this Sunday (Isa 5:1-7) is that God is going to abandon the vine because it produces rotten fruit. The song functions like a parable. The audience is drawn in through the first stanza (1-2): The singer has a friend whose vineyard, in spite of prudent care, produces bad grapes. In the second stanza (3-4) it seems that the owner of the vineyard is the singer, who calls on the audience to judge the case against the vineyard. But the third stanza (5-7) reveals the true situation. "The vineyard of the LORD of hosts is the house of Israel." God expected them to produce the good fruit of justice and judgment. Instead they produced violence and bloodshed.

The juxtaposition of the psalm with the first reading causes a stunning shift in perspective. With the refrain we reiterate the crucial sentence. It is true that we are God's vineyard. But then, through the psalm verses, we boldly ask God: "Why have you broken down the walls?" Isaiah's song has told us why, because the fruit is rotten. But in the confidence of true biblical prayer we remind God that only through divine help can we even now produce good fruit. The vine still belongs to God; only God can restore it.

The gospel (Matt 21:33-43) turns the vineyard image in yet another direction. The crisis in Jesus' parable is not poor fruit but wicked tenants. The owner is still deprived of the produce. In their resistance the tenants even go so far as to kill the owner's son. As a result the owner will lease the vineyard to others who will deliver the produce. Again the audience is drawn into a judgment. "When the chief priests and the Pharisees heard his parables, they knew that he was speaking about them" (Matt 21:45). The message in Matthew's Gospel is that now the vineyard will be entrusted to a wider group, Jews and Gentiles alike. The message to us is a strong reminder to produce good fruit and to deliver it to the owner. The Letter to the Philippians (Phil 4:6-9) encourages us in two ways. We are given a description of the good fruit; we are reminded that God is in charge of the vineyard. God has restored the vine; we are called to the fidelity we promised (Ps 80:19).

12. Psalm 85 (Communal)

Like Psalm 80, Psalm 85 is a national lament. There is some debate concerning the occasion for the psalm. The mood is calm, so it does not seem that the people face imminent disaster. The language echoes the latter chapters of the Book of Isaiah (40-66). Possibly the psalm reflects the difficulties experienced by the first returnees from Babylon as they struggled to rebuild the land (cf. Haggai, Zech 1-8). The promise of a good harvest (10-14) may connect the psalm to Sukkoth, the autumn festival which celebrated the final harvest of olives and grapes and looked forward to the first rains which would introduce the growing season.

The psalm can be considered in three stanzas (2-4, 5-8, 9-14). The first stanza (2-4) reminds God of past favor and forgiveness. Does this reflect return from Exile? The land (*'eres*) is certainly important in this psalm. It appears in verses 2, 10, 12, and 13. Walter Brueggemann points out that land is always a covenant partner.[14] The concept of restoration and return

---

[14]Walter Brueggemann, *The Land* (Overtures to Biblical Theology; Philadelphia: Fortress, 1977). See especially 47–53.

(*shûb*) is also important (vv. 2, 4, 5, 7, 9; see Psalm 80 for a fuller discussion of *shûb*).

The second stanza (5-8) is a plea for renewed restoration and forgiveness. Its themes echo Psalm 80: new life and an end to anger. The third stanza (9-14) is a prophetic oracle with a formal introduction. Many laments seem to presuppose this kind of oracle, signified by the dramatic change from complaint to new hope (e.g., Pss 12:6; 20:7; 22:22-23; 27:4-5).[15] The oracle promises a restoration of the covenant relationship between God and the people. The covenant virtues of love (*hesed*) and truth (*'emeth*) arrive as personified bearers of good tidings (see Psalms 25 and 136 regarding *hesed*). They announce the presence of the Lord who comes surrounded by faithful servants, justice (*sedeq*) and peace (*shalom*). God's justice (*sedeq*) guarantees the right relationship between all parts of creation; thus it results in prosperity. God's peace (*shalom*) guarantees to everyone what is needed for a full life; thus it brings good fortune. All the covenant partners, including the land, enjoy God's salvation.

2nd Sun Adv B (9-10.11-12.13-14) [5]

Lord, let us see your kindness, and grant us your salvation (8).

The psalm refrain for the Second Sunday of Advent B is the final plea of the lament section of Psalm 85. The verses represent the whole prophetic oracle of salvation. Thus the situation of the lament is almost totally absent; only the answer remains. The oracle puts strong emphasis on the covenant and covenant virtues. God's faithful love will bring prosperity to the people.

The first reading (Isa 40:1-5, 9-11) begins the collection called Second or Deutero-Isaiah (chs. 40-55). This collection represents the preaching of an unknown prophet whose message encouraged Jews toward the end of the Babylonian Exile. They will return to Jerusalem, led by God across desert and wasteland. Psalm 85 is ideally suited to accompany readings from Second Isaiah since the vocabulary and concepts are so abundantly shared. The prophet tells the people that their guilt has been expiated (cf. Ps 85:2-4); the restoration of their land is imminent (cf. Ps 85:10-14). The glory of the Lord will fill the land (cf. Ps 85:10). Jerusalem will come out to herald the arrival of God (cf. Ps 85:14).

In Mark 1:1-8 this passage from Isaiah is used to introduce John the Baptist, the messenger announcing the arrival of God's Messiah. The preparation John announces also has to do with forgiveness. John proclaims a

---

[15]See Westermann (65–71) for further discussion of this change within the psalm; cf. also Anderson, 108–109.

baptism of repentance which leads to the forgiveness of sins. This preparation is necessary because One more powerful is coming, One who will baptize in the Holy Spirit. The passage from 2 Peter (3:8-14) also speaks of an arrival, the return of Christ on the day of judgment. Even though it seems that the Lord is slow in coming, the delay is granted that we might have time to repent. Not only must we stand ready, we must hasten the coming of the day of God by our holiness and devotion.

Psalm 85 expresses both our longing for God's arrival and abiding presence and our confidence that the Lord will indeed come, with justice and peace in attendance. God's faithful love assures us that the promise will be kept.

Advent Common (9-10.11-12.13-14) [*175*]

Lord, let us see your kindness (8).

Psalm 85 is one of two choices for the Advent Common (see Psalm 25 for the other). The verses selected are the same as those for the Second Sunday of Advent B (see above). The refrain, however, is abbreviated: "Show us, Lord, your love." God's faithful love (*hesed*) is the source of our confidence during the Advent Season. The psalm is assigned to the Second Sunday of Advent B. It might also be used on the Second Sundays of Cycles A and C (see the fuller discussion of these Sundays with Psalms 72 and 126). The gospels for each of these Sundays (Matt 3:1-12; Luke 3:1-6) introduce John the Baptist who prepares for Christ's arrival. Luke's Gospel also echoes Psalm 85:8: "All flesh shall see the salvation of God." In the first reading of the Second Sunday of Advent A (Isa 11:1-10) justice (*sedeq*) is an important characteristic of the Messiah, a key word also in Psalm 85. The peaceful creation is a result of God's justice and peace (Ps 85:10-14). Paul exhorts us to exhibit the same harmony with one another (Rom 15:4-9).

The first reading of the Second Sunday of Advent C (Bar 5:1-9) is similar to the Isaiah passage of the Second Sunday of Advent B. Jerusalem is called to rise from her misery, wrap herself in justice, and stand on the heights to see her people return. God leads them home "in joy, by the light of [divine] glory," with love and justice for company (Bar 5:9; cf. Ps 85:14). The correspondence of theme and vocabulary to Psalm 85 is striking. The prayer from Philippians (1:4-6, 8-11) is that Christians be filled with the fruit of justice that comes through Jesus Christ. It is this harvest for which the psalm prays.

The psalm also echoes themes of the Third Sunday of Advent in all three cycles (see Ps 146, Isa 12, and Luke 1:46-54). In the Third Sunday of Advent A, Isaiah's portrayal of the blossoming desert and the arrival of God (Isa 35:1-6, 10) seems to be a fuller description of the blessings described in the oracle of Ps 85:10-14. The reading from James (5:7-10) is an encouragement to trust in God's promises. The gospel (Matt 11:2-11) describes the prosperity and good fortune which accompany Jesus' arrival.

Justice and salvation are key words in the first reading of the Third Sunday of Advent B (Isa 61:1-2,10-11). The second reading (1 Thess 5:16-24) is again encouragement to trust God's promises (cf. Ps 85:9-10). On the Third Sunday of Advent C the opening reading (Zeph 3:14-18) announces joy to Jerusalem because God has forgiven her (cf. Ps 85:2-4) and has arrived to restore the people (cf. Ps 85:10-14). The second reading (Phil 4:4-7) echoes the joy that God is near. The gospels for both Sundays (John 1:6-8,19-28; Luke 3:10-18) present the Baptist's proclamation of the Messiah's arrival.

15th Sun Year B (9-10.11-12.13-14) [105]

Lord, let us see your kindness, and grant us your salvation (8).

The refrain and verses from Psalm 85 chosen for the Fifteenth Sunday of Year B are the same as those for the Second Sunday of Advent B (see above). The whole oracle of salvation is represented. The opening stanzas which contain the lament are omitted.

The readings all treat the mystery of God's choice. The juxtaposition of Psalm 85 with these readings draws our awareness to the arrival of God in those who are chosen. The prophet Amos (7:12-15) expresses his own amazement at his call: "I was no prophet." But he is equally certain that God did call him. He meets with rejection because of the message he carries. The psalm presents us with an interesting dilemma. We plead to see God's love and to enjoy God's salvation. We hear the cantor sing the promise that God's salvation is near. Amos teaches us, however, that God may arrive in a prophet we do not recognize. We must indeed listen for the word of God (Ps 85:9).

Jesus also warns his disciples as they start out on their mission that they may be rejected (Mark 6:7-13). He shares with them his authority (cf. Mark 1:27, 34); his presence goes with them. The consequences of their arrival at any place depend on the acceptance given them. People who reject the arrival of Christ in them receive only the dust from their feet. Those who accept them enjoy the benefits of God's peace and justice (cf. Ps 85:13-14).

The thanksgiving hymn from Ephesians (Eph 1:3-14) proclaims that we are all chosen. God has favored us and forgiven us in Christ (cf. Ps 85:2-4). In God's plan we have all been chosen to praise the divine glory filling our land (cf. Ps 85:10). When the fullness of time has arrived, we will see the richness of God's promise, which we sing in Psalm 85. Then we will know God's love and salvation, offered to us now in hidden ways, but then in the brightness of divine glory.

19th Sun Year A (9.10.11-12.13-14) [116]

Lord, let us see your kindness, and grant us your salvation (8).

For the Nineteenth Sunday of Year A the psalm verses represent the oracle of salvation from Psalm 85. The lament has been omitted (see also the Second Sunday of Advent B). The refrain is the closing verse of the lament. On this Sunday, like the one discussed previously, there is a focus on recognizing the God whose arrival is announced in Psalm 85.

In the first reading (1 Kgs 19:9, 11-13) Elijah has traveled to Mount Sinai to consult with God and to escape the wrath of Jezebel whose prophets he has slaughtered. God comes to renew his commission as prophet. But Elijah's experience is not like that of Moses on the same mountain (cf. Exod 19–20). God arrives, not in fire and storm and earthquake, but in a tiny whispering sound. When he hears, Elijah knows that this is the presence of God.

In the psalm we beg to see God's love, to know God's salvation. With the prophet we pledge to listen to God's word. We accept the oracle with its wonderful promise.

The gospel story (Matt 14:22-33) confronts the disciples with the truth of Jesus' identity. When the weary disciples see Jesus walking toward them on the lake, at first they do not recognize him at all. "It is a ghost," they say. After Jesus reassures them, Peter risks an identification, "Lord, if it is you. . . ." When Jesus gets into the boat they worship him, saying, "Truly, you are the Son of God." They have moved from non-recognition to a confession of faith. Peter is blessed with yet another recognition. He recognizes not only Jesus, but the power of God working within himself.

Paul (Rom 9:1-5) is grieved that his own people, the Israelites, do not recognize the presence of God in Christ. The oracle of salvation has been brought to them. God's love and salvation have been offered, but the offer has as yet not been accepted. Their unbelief is a warning to us. We beg God to show us love and grant us salvation (8). We must be open to the divine presence however it comes—in fire or breeze, over the water or in another person. Near indeed is salvation. We listen for the word of God.

13. Psalm 86

The lament of Psalm 86 is poured out by a person who, even in the midst of distress, has great confidence in God. This person is steeped in the tradition. Standard phrases found in other psalms flow out in this cry for help.[16]

---

[16]For a lengthy list of correspondences to other psalms, see Stuhlmueller 2.52.

The psalm has a distinctive structure. After the lament (1-7), praise (8-10), and thanksgiving vow (11-13), the lament begins anew (14-17). The distress is not over; the cry to God continues.

The first stanza (1-7) is the cry for help, characteristic of laments. It is demarcated by an inclusion (the same words or phrase at the beginning and end): "Hear me, Lord, and answer me" (1); "Lord, hear my prayer . . . you will answer me" (6, 7). The inclusion expresses the psalmist's confidence. God will indeed answer.

Two elements which weave the whole psalm together are introduced in the first stanza. The first is the interplay between "servant" and "lord," which is striking in this psalm. This vocabulary is even thought by some to signify the relationship between the king and God. The psalm is seen somewhat as a royal letter to God.[17] The English word "lord" is confusing in modern translations. When printed in small capital letters (Lord), it substitutes for the divine name Yahweh. Other occurrences of "Lord" translate the Hebrew term *'adonai*, which is used as a title for God and also as a term of respect for important persons, somewhat as we use "sir." It is *'adonai* which is frequently used in Psalm 86 (3, 4, 5, 8, 9, 12, 15). The corresponding term is "servant" (2, 14, 16). The psalmist is the servant of a great Lord.

The second element that links all three stanzas of the psalm is a statement about God's nature, addressed to God with an emphatic "you" (5, 10, 15; cf. also 3). In the midst of lament, at the end of the hymn, and again in the renewed lament the psalmist declares God's greatness and mercy. Verse 15, the final cry of praise, is a standard formula found in Pentateuch, psalms, and prophets (Exod 34:6; Neh 9:17; Pss 103:8; 145:8; Joel 2:13; Jonah 4:2). This "little creed" is Moses' comfort and Jonah's despair, the hope of the repentant in Joel's time and the strength of this suffering psalmist (see Psalm 51 for a discussion of *rahûm* and *hanûn*, Psalm 25 for *hesed*.)

The second stanza (8-10) is a hymn of praise. The psalmist's attention has turned completely to God (not with complete disinterest, however). If other gods exist (and the psalmist seems to presume so), the Lord is greater than they—so great that all nations will come to worship the Lord, so great that indeed Yahweh alone is God.

In the third stanza (11-17) the focus shifts again to the psalmist, first in a vow of praise (11-13), then in a renewed plea for help (14-17). The psalmist, knowing that God is true and loving (15), asks to be led in truth and made single-hearted in order to praise God's name. God's love (*hesed*) has already been made evident in the rescue from Sheol. Sheol is the place of the dead, a place without light or memory, with neither pain nor joy

[17]Dahood, 2.292.

(cf. Job 3:13-19). All human beings were thought to go to Sheol in the centuries before belief in resurrection. After the vow of praise, however, the misery breaks out again in the presence of godless enemies. The faithful servant begs again for rescue, trusting still in God's faithful love.

16th Sun Year A (5-6.9-10.15-16) [107]

Lord, you are good and forgiving (5).

The theme for the Sixteenth Sunday of Year A is the great mercy of God. The expression of faith in the great and loving God which weaves through Psalm 86 (cf. 5, 10, 15) is repeated again and again in the readings. The refrain of the responsorial psalm is the first of those faith statements: "Lord, you are kind and forgiving." Two verses are chosen from each of the three stanzas. All three variations of the "little creed" are included. In addition there is one verse each from the initial lament, the repeated lament, and the central hymn. Thus the mood of the whole psalm is well represented. Only the vow of praise (11-13) is missing (and also the single mention of enemies, 14).

The first reading (Wis 12:13, 16-19) is from the Wisdom of Solomon, a late Old Testament book (ca. 50 BCE) accepted by Roman Catholics but not by Jews or Protestants. The book was written in Greek and shows the careful precision of Greek thought. Today's selection is from a long meditation on God's mercy (11:17–12:22). The heart of the message is that, because God is all powerful, God is "lenient to all." Precisely in God's might is our hope, because that might is demonstrated in mercy. This also is a lesson for human beings that, like God, "those who are just must be kind."

Psalm 86 is an apt response. The statement of God's greatness (9-10) is surrounded by proclamations of God's mercy (5, 15). Thus we cry out in confidence (6, 16), assured that God will answer us (7).

Both New Testament readings (Rom 8:26-27; Matt 13:24-43) emphasize the mercy of God. The gospel is part of Matthew's collection of kingdom parables. The tone is set by the parable of the weeds in the wheat which begins the selection and is interpreted at the end. The owner allows the weeds to remain, so that the wheat might not be damaged in the uprooting. There is separation at the end, however. Just so, God allows the wicked to live, but at the judgment they will be cast out. God's mercy allows time for repentance, but human beings are free to choose. God's mercy is powerful, but it will not violate our freedom. A second lesson is that we must not be too harsh in uprooting evil, but must trust God's power to prevail in the end.

The second reading is part of Paul's great hymn to God's love (Rom 8). Even as we wait in hope for the fullness of God's kingdom, God's Spirit comes to help us. We do not even know how to pray, but the Spirit prays for us. God's loving mercy is so great that God's own Spirit intercedes for us. Truly God is "merciful and gracious, . . . slow to anger, most loving and true" (Ps 86:15).

14. Psalm 90 (Communal)

Psalm 90 is a community lament with a strong wisdom flavor. The first two stanzas (1-6, 7-12) are meditations on wisdom themes. Only in the final stanza (13-17) do we find the lament proper.

The concern of the first stanza (1-6) is the brevity of human life. God exists eternally. From before creation to the last human generation God is God. Humans, on the other hand, are fleeting like sleep at dawn or grass in the desert sun. In a moment at God's command, humans return to dust (3). The phrase is reminiscent of Gen 3:19, but there are two significant vocabulary distinctions. In the psalm the terms for human beings are *'enosh*, which comes from a root meaning "weak," and *bene 'adam*, children of earthlings. The term in Genesis 3, *'adam*, is related to *'adamah*, the earth from which the human creature was formed (cf. Gen 2:7). The word in the psalm for "dust" is not the common word *'apar* found in Genesis 3, but *dakka'*, which comes from a root meaning "crushed." At the beginning of this psalm, as we recognize God's everlasting power, we acknowledge the frailty of all human creatures.

The second stanza (7-12) moves the meditation to a further point. Our lives fade away because of God's wrath. We are sinful; God is angry. Even at best—seventy or eighty years was an unheard-of life span in those centuries—most of our days are sorrow and toil. The stanza ends with a prayer for wisdom that we might learn from the shortness of our lives. The psalmist has already provided us with a meditation on the significance of time, highlighted by the words "year" and "day." For God a thousand years are a day (4). Our days ebb away under God's wrath; our years pass away like a sigh (9). The "days of our years" are seventy or eighty years at most (10). We pray for wisdom to count our days (12) and for days to sing for joy (14). We hope for years of joy to match our days of sorrow (15).

The third stanza (13-17) begins with typical phrases of the lament: relent (*shûb*, cf. 3; see also Psalm 80), how long, have pity (*niham*, cf. Twenty-Fourth Sunday C). The plea is fittingly couched in terms of time. "Fill us at daybreak with your love" (*hesed*, cf. Psalm 25), we who disappear like morning sleep (5). The morning was the traditional time for God's deliverance. Often petitioners prayed and fasted through the night, hoping for God's saving action in the morning. We pray also that the time of affliction may be balanced by the time of joy. We ask to see God's saving deeds so that our own work may prosper.

The whole psalm is framed by a prayer of trust. We call on God as "lord" (*'adonai*, see Psalm 86) at beginning and end (1, 17). We proclaim the Lord our refuge; we ask for the continued favor of the Lord through all our days.

The title of the psalm attributes Psalm 90 to Moses, the only psalm under his name. Psalm titles were added late in the history of the psalter (see Ps 54). Their chief function is to give us a direction for interpretation. Moses is credited with poetic praise of God in Exod 15:1 and in Deut 31:30 and 33:1. In Psalm 90, as in Deut 33:1, Moses is named "man of God" (cf. Elijah, 1 Kgs 17:18; Elisha, 2 Kgs 4:7). At the beginning of Israel's history, Moses was God's man, bringing God's word to the people; yet Moses died before entering the land of promise. The image of Moses reminds us that human life is fleeting; God is our refuge through all generations.

23rd Sun Year C (3-4.5-6.12-13.14.17) [130]

In every age, O Lord, you have been our refuge (1).

The psalm refrain for the Twenty-Third Sunday of Year C is the opening verse of Psalm 90. It sets the theme of God's eternity and human frailty. The verses represent primarily the first and third stanzas of the psalm. The meditation on God's anger at our sinfulness is omitted. The verses chosen emphasize the wisdom of knowing how short human life is (cf. 12). They begin with the observation that God soon sends us back to dust and end with a prayer that God will prosper the works of our hands, however fleeting. Only God can give us wisdom; only God can give us joy.

The reading from the Wisdom of Solomon (9:13-18) approaches from a Greek standpoint the same mystery of God's greatness and human weakness. Humans are timid and insecure, barely able to understand what is right in front of them. The author, influenced by Greek philosophy, attributes this weakness to the body (an idea foreign to the Hebrew mind). God, on the other hand, is unhindered by flesh and thus unreachable for human beings. It is only because God has sent Wisdom as a guide that human beings can approach God at all. How could the author have known that God in unsearchable wisdom would take on the burden of human flesh to lead us securely in Wisdom's path!

The psalm echoes the thought that we are frail and fleeting. It also emphasizes the point that precisely because of our weakness the eternal God is our refuge. It is the Lord who will teach us wisdom, give joy to our days, prosper our works.

The gospel (Luke 14:25-33) confronts us again with the mystery of God's wisdom. The two parables are easy to understand. It is their conclusion which is difficult for us. Even weak human beings know the value of planning ahead, of making all the necessary preparations for an important venture. Even human beings whose years are limited know the need to count life's days (Ps 90:12). But Jesus says that the real preparation needed is to take up the Cross, to renounce all possessions. The true wisdom is to embrace the weakness. Our lives are fleeting; therefore we should let go of them. Christ took on the frailty of human flesh in order to show us how to let go of it. This is God's wisdom; this is the answer to our prayer: Have pity on us; teach us wisdom.

Paul's Letter to Philemon (Phlm 9-10, 12-17) gives a concrete example of God's paradoxical wisdom. To the human mind, keeping a slave and punishing a runaway may seem a wise course of action. Paul, however, asks Philemon to welcome his runaway slave, now baptized, as a brother in Christ. Who could imagine this? "Scarce do we guess the things on earth . . . but when things are in heaven, who can search them out?" (Wis 9:16). "Whoever does not carry [the] cross and come after me cannot be my disciple" (Luke 14:27). Teach us, Lord, that we may gain wisdom of heart.

28th Sun Year B (12-13.14-15.16-17) [144]

Fill us with your love, O Lord, and we will sing for joy (14).

The tone for the Twenty-Eighth Sunday of Year B is set by the psalm refrain: "Fill us with your love, O Lord, and we will sing for joy" (Ps 90:14). Even though the verses come primarily from the lament portion of the psalm (13-17), the overwhelming mood is one of joy because of God's faithful love.

The opening reading (Wis 7:7-11) is taken from the Wisdom of Solomon. A major focus of this book is praise of God's wonderful Wisdom. Lady Wisdom is to be preferred above all treasure because she is herself the source of all good things. The author, speaking in Solomon's name, uses all his skill to persuade us that Wisdom is the greatest of God's gifts, is in fact God's own self.

The psalm refrain momentarily seems to sidetrack us. Why do we not ask immediately for Wisdom? Instead we ask for God's love (*hesed*) which is both the source and the expression of God's wisdom. In God we learn that wisdom is faithful love. Then we ask for wisdom and pity, joy and prosperity. All gifts come from Wisdom; all gifts come from God's love.

Because God's love is the source of all good things, any good thing may be abandoned in response to that faithful love. That is the message of the gospel (Mark 10:17-30). The rich man cannot believe that following Jesus is worth more than all his possessions. He cannot believe that all good things come at the hands of Wisdom. He does not know that it is God's love which fills our lives with song.

Our days are short. It is God who is eternal (Ps 90:1-6). It is God who holds the wisdom of the ages. Therefore God's word is living and effective, penetrating to the center of our being. It is God who is our refuge. It is God whose love fills us with joy. Anything else we treasure is a little sand, a little dry grass.

15. Psalm 123 (Communal)

Psalm 123 is one of the Songs of Ascent. There are fifteen psalms (120-134) given this title. With the exception of Psalm 132 they are all brief. They are characterized by earthy, everyday imagery, and often use a form of staircase parallelism in which a phrase from one line is repeated as a building block in the next line. There are many explanations for the title: Songs of Ascent. The most convincing is the theory that these psalms were used by pilgrims on their journey to and from Jerusalem.[18]

The key word in Psalm 123 is "eyes." The first stanza of the psalm (1-2) builds on this image in four successive bicola (two-part lines). The image progresses from the psalmist's eyes through the eyes of servant and maid to the whole community's eyes. All eyes are focused on a generous superior upon whom the subject is dependent. The figures of master and mistress sharpen the picture of dependence upon God, who is not mentioned until the final line of the stanza. The repetition intensifies the mood of expectant waiting.

The second stanza (3-4) builds on the final word of the first. The first stanza closes with the declaration that our eyes will be on the Lord until we are shown favor. The second stanza opens with a direct plea for favor, repeated twice, surrounding the name of God which has just been introduced. The psalm closes with the description of distress. We are sated with contempt. Our *nephesh* (throat/soul/life, cf. Psalm 42-43) is sated with contempt and insult.

Psalm 123 is deceptively simple. There are only two statements: We raise our eyes to God for mercy; we are up to our necks in insult. These two statements, however, represent the heart of our prayer: We are in need; only God can help us. The psalm begins in the singular, but it is soon evident that this is a community lament. Repetition, along with the move from singular to plural, heightens the intensity of the psalm. It is not hard to imagine a group of pilgrims singing Psalm 123 on their way to God's house, God's throne upon earth.

---

[18]For further discussion of the Songs of Ascent, see Stuhlmueller, 2.156; Sabourin, 317.

Our eyes are fixed on the Lord, pleading for mercy (2).

The juxtaposition of Psalm 123 with the readings for the Fourteenth Sunday of Year B focuses attention on distress from insult and contempt. The whole psalm is used. The refrain presents our only solution to such distress: "Our eyes are on the LORD, . . . till we are shown favor."

The reading from Ezek 2:2-5 is part of the prophet's call. In the midst of his commission he is confronted by the trials of his prophetic ministry. God tells him that it is the habit of the Israelites to resist God's word. Nevertheless the prophet must preach God's word so that they have a chance to listen and reform.

We sing Psalm 123 with Ezekiel's voice. The prophet did indeed experience insult and scorn. Yet as a true prophet he stood for all the people, pleading for God's favor. The plea is not in the name of the prophet, who suffers the mockery of his own people, but in the name of the people themselves, who suffer the humiliation of exile. The prophet turns the eyes of all toward God until favor is finally granted.

The gospel (Mark 6:1-6) shows Jesus suffering rejection and contempt from the people of his own town. They took offense at him. Jesus also sings the psalm with us and for us. Jesus carries the plea a step farther. In Jesus the favor of the Lord arrives for us; in Jesus the humiliation of sin and death are finally conquered.

Paul's description of his own torment (2 Cor 12:7-10) adds another aspect. Weakness and humiliation are allowed us to protect us from pride. Without the insult and contempt we too easily forget God and consider ourselves master and mistress of our lives. Weakness reminds us to raise our eyes to the Lord, whose favor alone gives us life (Ps 123:2).

16. Psalm 126 (Communal)

Psalm 126 is another Song of Ascents (see Psalm 123). Like Psalm 123 it is characterized by repetition and brevity. The structure of the psalm is similar to that of Psalm 85 (see above). God's saving deeds of the past are recalled (126:1-3). There is a new plea for restoration (126:4). The psalm concludes with words of assurance, a prophetic oracle or a wisdom saying.

The first stanza (1-4), which contains both the recollection of the past and the renewed plea, is demarcated by an inclusion (see Psalm 86): "When the LORD restored the fortunes of Zion, . . . restore again our fortunes" (1, 4). Repetitions move inward in concentric circles. The next circle describes the people's joy (2a, 3b). At the center is the reason for past joy and present hope: "The LORD has done great things for them/us" (2b, 3a).

The hope for restoration rests on the power of God, who through the winter rains can make the desert of the Negeb bloom.

The second stanza (5-6) is a reassurance that the hope is not in vain. Verse 5 is like a proverb, reminding the petitioners that sorrowful beginnings often end in joy. Verse 6 expands the proverb, providing another occasion for repetition. Through repetition the second stanza picks up the recollection of past joy from the first stanza and transforms it into hope for future joy.

The occasion for the psalm may be the distress of those who have returned from the Babylonian Exile. They have witnessed God's mighty power in restoring them to their own land. Now they plead for help in rebuilding the devastated country. The psalm ends with hope that all will end in joy.

2nd Sun Adv C (1-2.2-3.4-5.6) [6]

The Lord has done great things for us; we are filled with joy (3).

The psalm refrain for the Second Sunday of Advent C is the central statement of the first stanza of Psalm 126. It is the reason for past joy and future hope. God exercised great power for us when we were helpless; God will continue to restore us.

The first reading is from Baruch (5:1-9). The book of the prophet Baruch is deutero-canonical (accepted by Roman Catholics but not by Jews or Protestants). The book, which is ascribed to Jeremiah's secretary (cf. Jer 36:5, 32), was written toward the beginning of the second century BCE. The author used the example of the exiles to inspire his contemporaries to repent and hope in God.

The passage chosen for this Sunday is part of a poem consoling Jerusalem with the news that her children are about to return. The dream of restoration is coming true. "God is leading Israel in joy" (Bar 5:9). With Psalm 126 we proclaim our delight at God's great deeds. The departure was in sorrow, but the return is in joy (Bar 5:6; Ps 126:5). God is showing Jerusalem's splendor to all the earth (Bar 5:3). The nations are saying, "The LORD has done great things for them" (Ps 126:3).

The gospel (Luke 3:1-6) describes hope for a different restoration. All flesh is enslaved to sin. John the Baptist arrives announcing the good news that "all flesh shall see the salvation of God" (Luke 3:6). In preparation he proclaims a baptism of repentance for forgiveness of sins. "Those who sow in tears will reap with cries of joy" (Ps 126:5).

The second reading (Phil 1:4-6, 8-11) reassures us that God will indeed complete this great work in us. We hope for a harvest "filled with the fruit of righteousness that comes through Jesus Christ for the glory and praise of God" (Phil 1:11). Carrying those sheaves we will shout for joy. "The LORD has done great things for us."

5th Sun Lent C (1-2.2-3.4-5.6) [36]

The Lord has done great things for us; we are filled with joy (3)

The psalm refrain and verses for the Fifth Sunday of Lent C are the same as those chosen for the Second Sunday of Advent C (see above).

The readings for this Sunday insert us into the whole experience of restoration proposed by Psalm 126, from the joy of initial restoration through the hope of the weeping sowers to the new restoration of God's people.

Second Isaiah exults over God's new thing (Isa 43:16-21). This prophet of the Babylonian Exile encouraged the people to believe that God could and would restore them to their homeland. The return from Exile is portrayed as a new exodus. God once opened a way through the sea and led the people to freedom. Now God will open a way through the desert to deliver them. This is God's new thing, modeled on the old. It catches us in the midst of Psalm 126. We know God once restored Zion; we pray for a new restoration. Although the first restoration in the psalm is probably the return from Exile, the juxtaposition of the Isaiah reading leads us to move back a step and consider the exodus as the restoration of verse 1. This movement reveals the fact that God is continually restoring the people and leads to the general hope that is expressed in the proverb of verse 5. Over and over again it is true that "those who sow in tears will reap with cries of joy," because God continues to do great things for them.

The woman in the gospel (John 8:1-11) is brought to Jesus for judgment, not for restoration. Her accusers are not seeking new life for themselves either. All they want is the condemnation of the woman and the possibility of trapping Jesus. But God's new thing will not be hindered by such people. Jesus challenges the accusers to judge themselves, thereby giving them a genuine opportunity to repent, to sow in tears. They apparently do not choose to sow, and thus do not reap. The woman is the only one who waits for Jesus' judgment. The woman is the only one who hears Jesus' words of forgiveness. God has done great things for her. How happy she must be!

Paul (Phil 3:8-14) reminds us, however, that we must continue to beg God to restore us. He has sown in tears, considering everything else as loss for the sake of Christ. But he knows well that righteousness cannot be claimed as his own possession, but is an ongoing gift from God. He has not yet won the prize; it is not yet harvest time. He strains ahead, persevering in hope.

The Lectionary for this Sunday nourishes our hope. God, who gave life to the people in the exodus and revived them after the Exile, will continue to restore our fortunes. But even though the Lord has done great things for us, we have not yet arrived. We must continue to work toward the harvest.

30th Sun Year B (1-2.2-3.4-5.6) [150]

The Lord has done great things for us; we are filled with joy (3).

The psalm refrain and verses chosen from Psalm 126 for the Thirtieth Sunday of Year B are the same as those for the Second Sunday of Advent C (see above).

The psalm refrain gives focus to this Sunday's readings: "The Lord has done great things for us." Jeremiah's oracle (31:7-9) is from a section of the book sometimes called the Book of Consolation (chs. 30-33). The oracles initially expressed hope that the northern kingdom, which had been taken into captivity by the Assyrians in 722 BCE, would be restored. When eventually the southern kingdom suffered defeat and Exile in 587 BCE, these oracles were also applied to them. Throughout they proclaim the conviction that God will restore the fortunes of the people. Today's reading describes a procession of people returning to their land. The prophet is exhorted to proclaim to the nations: "The LORD has done great things for them." They departed in tears, but God will lead them gently home. How happy they will be!

The miracle story of the gospel (Mark 10:46-52) describes a different kind of restoration. Bartimaeus, a blind man, begs Jesus for sight and immediately it is granted to him. He too can say, "The LORD has done great things" for me.

But there is a deeper layer to this miracle story. In the Gospel of Mark there are two stories of blind men being healed. In the story previous to today's gospel (Mark 8:22-26) the miracle takes a little time. The two stories surround a section in which Jesus' disciples are blind to his mission. They understand that he may be the Messiah. They cannot grasp the message that he must also suffer. They are certainly not ready to accept the news that those who follow him will also suffer. The stories of the two blind men comment on the situation of the disciples. They too are blind; it will take a little time, but they too will be granted vision. The disciples are like us. We do not understand when we must sow in tears. We must continue to plead, "Restore again our fortunes, LORD."

A third level can be discerned in the gospel story. Jesus' miracles are a sign that the power of Satan is broken. The power of sin and suffering and death has been defeated in Jesus through his death and resurrection. Jesus the high priest has offered the ultimate sacrifice for us, through tears and suffering (Heb 5:1-6, cf. 5:7-9). Through him, the kingdom of God has broken into the world. This is the restoration for which we all pray, the deliverance for which we all hope. This is the great thing the Lord has done for us (cf. Ps 126:3)

17. Psalm 130 (Penitential)

The opening phrase of Psalm 130, "out of the depths," is familiar to almost everyone. This cry from the depths speaks to a universal human experience. Psalm 130 belongs to the collection of Songs of Ascent (see Psalm 123). Like the previous two psalms, it too is characterized by brevity and repetition. Psalm 130 is also the sixth of the seven penitential psalms (cf. Psalm 51).

The psalm can be divided into two stanzas by the shift in the person addressed. Verses 1-4 are addressed to God, verses 5-8 to the community. The first stanza (1-4) is a longing cry for mercy. The psalmist calls from the watery depths (cf. Ps 69:3, 15), the symbol of chaos, the place of death. Sin has exiled the psalmist to this desperate place. But the situation is not without hope. The psalmist cries and cries to God for a hearing, because God is one who forgives. If it were not so, if God kept track of sin, no human being could survive.

The wonder of God's forgiveness leads to fear. Fear of the Lord, an attitude recommended by the wisdom teachers (e.g., Prov 1:7; Sir 1:9-18), is awe at the great mystery of God.[19] This awe is inspired not only by God's immense power and magnificence but also by God's tender care and undying love. Thus the psalmist wisely knows that the amazing gift of God's forgiveness inspires fear. God's love for us, even when we are in the depths, is utterly beyond us.

The second stanza (5-8) turns to hope. The repeated phrases convey the psalmist's longing. "I wait . . . my soul waits . . . . My soul looks for . . . let Israel look for . . . ." The longing is directed entirely toward God. The sentinels who wait for dawn are an apt analogy (also repeated). The psalmist waits for the word, the oracle that proclaims forgiveness (see Psalm 85). Israel and the psalmist wait for God, because with God there is kindness (*hesed*, cf. Psalm 25). It is God's faithful love from which forgiveness comes. It is God's faithful love which brings full redemption, full redemption for Israel from all their sins (note repetition).

---

[19]For perceptive discussions of fear of the Lord, see G. von Rad, *Wisdom in Israel* (Nashville: Abingdon, 1972) 66–73; Kraus, 2.1050–51; Brueggemann, *Message*, 105; and K. O'Connor, *The Wisdom Literature* (Message of Biblical Spirituality 5; Wilmington: Michael Glazier, 1988) 52–53, 140–141.

5th Sun Lent A (1-2.3-4.5-6.7-8) [34]

With the Lord there is mercy, and fullness of redemption (7).

On the Fifth Sunday of Lent A the refrain from Psalm 130 is the heart of the psalm's conclusion. With God is faithful love (*hesed*) and redemption in full measure. That conviction supports the whole psalm, from desperate cry to longing hope. God is loving. God forgives. God redeems. The whole psalm is used on this Sunday with the exception of one bicolon (two-part line): "My soul looks for the Lord, more than sentinels for daybreak" (6a). The omission removes two of the repetitions which intensify the mood of the psalm. One wonders if the sentence was omitted in order to even out the number of bicola at eight. The re-insertion of the missing material would improve the flow of the psalm.

The insistent statement in the readings for this Sunday at the end of Lent is that God gives us new life. The reading from Ezekiel 37:12-14 is from a section of the book in which the prophet is encouraging his fellow exiles. His message is that God will bring new life to the exiled and scattered people; God will restore them to their own land. The prophet's vision in chapter 37 is a field of dry bones. The Lord asks if these bones can return to life and the prophet wisely answers, "you alone know that." The answer leaves the door open for hope. Then the prophet is told to command the bones to hear God's word. The word of the Lord, which created all things in the beginning (Gen 1:1–2:4a), recreates flesh and sinew to join the bones into bodies. Then the prophet is told to summon the wind/spirit to breathe into the bodies (cf. Gen 2:7), and they come alive and stand upright. Finally the prophet is instructed to interpret the vision for the people: "I will open your graves, . . . put my spirit in you, . . . settle you upon your land." The nation which is now as dead as dry bones will be given new life by God.

The reading from Ezekiel casts new light on Psalm 130. The psalm is the lament of an individual. At the end the individual joins the community and uses the individual experience as an example for the whole community. The reading is a prophetic encouragement to the whole people. In the juxtaposition the intimate bond between individual and community is brought to light.

That same bond is important to an understanding of the gospel (John 11:1-45). The story of the return of Lazarus to this earthly, mortal life is a sign for the gift of eternal life which Jesus wins for us. Martha announces its meaning before the miracle happens: "I know he will rise, in the resurrection on the last day" (John 11:24). Jesus works the miracle as a sign that he is the resurrection and the life. Ironically the miracle leads to his death, his final act of obedience in winning life for us (cf. John 11:47-53).

As is so often the case, the second reading (Rom 8:8-11) interprets the other readings in terms of the Christian community. "If the Spirit of the one who raised Jesus from the dead dwells in you, the one who raised Christ from the dead will give life to your mortal bodies also" (Rom 8:11). The same Spirit who breathed new life into the disheartened community during the Exile, will raise us to eternal life. The same Jesus who returned Lazarus to life wins eternal life for us through his death and resurrection.

In this context Psalm 130 becomes a cry of hope even in the face of death. The depths of chaos, of Sheol, are not enough to prevent God from hearing our cry. The depths of sin are not enough to keep God from forgiving us. And so we wait and hope. "For with the LORD is kindness, . . . full redemption, and God will redeem [the people] from all their sins" (Ps 130:7-8).

Lent Common (1-2.3-4.4-6.7-8) [175]

With the Lord there is mercy, and fullness of redemption (7).

Psalm 130 is one of three psalms suggested for the Lenten Common (cf. Pss 51, 91). The Lenten psalms are so well chosen, it would be better to use the specific psalm of the day. However, Psalm 130 certainly has the specific Lenten theme of hope in God's mercy even in the face of sin and death. Only one half-verse of the psalm is missing (6c). One wonders if that is a printer's error.

Psalm 130 is already used for the Fifth Sunday of Lent A (see above). There are four other Lenten Sundays on which it would be particularly appropriate.

On the First Sunday of Lent A (see the fuller discussion with Psalm 51) the readings focus on temptation and sin, death and redemption. Psalm 130 gives voice to the cry from the depths and the unshakeable hope in God's salvation. The theme for the First Sunday of Lent C (see Psalm 91) is similar. The readings assure us that whoever calls on the Lord will be saved.

The Second Sunday of Lent B (see Psalm 116) emphasizes absolute trust in God and the overwhelming love God has for us. These are the grounds both for fear of the Lord and for hopeful waiting in Psalm 130. On the Fourth Sunday of Lent B (see Psalm 137) we proclaim that God is rich in mercy, that God loved the world enough to give the only Son. "For with the LORD is kindness (*hesed*), with [God] is full redemption" (Ps 130:7).

10th Sun Year B (1-2.3-4.5-6.7-8) [90]

With the Lord there is mercy, and fullness of redemption (7).

The psalm refrain and verses for the Tenth Sunday of Year B are the same as those for the Fifth Sunday of Lent A (see above).

The conflict between the power of evil which brings death and the power of God who gives life is the focus of this Sunday's readings. The first reading (Gen 3:9-15) describes the consequences of the sin in the garden. Sin inevitably leads to separation. The human beings hide from God. The man blames the woman and the woman blames the serpent. Then God declares that the serpent will be separated from all the other animals. The ultimate consequence of sin is the ultimate separation, death. This spreading separation is the power of evil in the world.

In the face of this overwhelming power of evil we sing: "With the LORD is kindness, with [God] is full redemption." Overcome by evil, we cry to the Lord from the depths. We know that if God marks our sins we are doomed. Yet we wait in hope because God is forgiving. The forgiveness of God is mightier than the power of evil. Because of this we stand in awe.

The gospel story (Mark 3:20-35) confronts us with the importance of interpreting Jesus' miracles correctly. The scribes accuse Jesus of casting out evil by the power of evil. He replies that his miracles are the sign that the power of evil is broken. Satan's kingdom has been defeated by the kingdom of God. Sin and death no longer have total sway over human beings. The sin that cannot be forgiven, the sin against the Holy Spirit, is the refusal to believe that God has conquered evil, that Jesus, acting in the power of the Holy Spirit, has defeated sin and death. It is the refusal to believe that with God is forgiveness, kindness, and full redemption.

Paul, in the Second Letter to the Corinthians (2 Cor 4:13–5:1), expresses his belief in God's power manifested in Jesus' resurrection. Everything is ordered to our benefit. Our trust in the power of God's faithful love glorifies God and gives us courage. We wait with the psalmist, waiting for God's word. We know God is forgiving, therefore we wait in awe. "With [God] is full redemption!" (Ps 130:7).

All Souls (1-2.3-4.4-6.7-8) [791]

Out of the depths I cry to you, Lord (1).

Psalm 130 is one of the selections in the Common of the Dead, used for All Souls Day. The whole psalm is used, in contrast to its use in the Sunday Lectionary. The intense hope for God's redemption, expressed even from the depths of Sheol, makes Psalm 130 an ideal choice as we face the mystery of death.

Several Old Testament readings from the common go well with Psalm 130: Job 19:1, 23-27, in which Job expresses his hope for vindication and his longing for God; Isa 25:6, 7-9, in which we say, "This is the LORD for whom we looked"; and Lam 3:17-26, which is a cry of hope out of the depths. Apt New Testament selections are: Rom 5:5-11, God proves love for us even while we are still sinners; Rom 8:14-23, with all creation we await God's revelation; and 2 Cor 5:1, 6-10 (see Tenth Sunday of Year B, above). From the gospel selections the following echo themes of Psalm 130: Matt 25:1-13, the wise virgins waiting like sentinels; Luke 12:35-40, the wise servants waiting like sentinels; and John 11:17-27 or John 11:32-45 (see Fifth Sunday of Lent A above).

18. Psalm 137 (Communal)

Psalm 137, a communal lament, reminds one of a folk song. It begins like a ballad about the heart-rending experience of the Babylonian Exile (587–539 BCE). By the end its tone has changed to a bitter curse against the enemies. The whole psalm is characterized by intense emotion.

The psalm falls into three stanzas: 1-4, a lament over the sorrows of Exile; 5-6, a self-curse if Jerusalem is forgotten; 7-9, a curse against Edom and Babylon. The first stanza (1-4) contrasts weeping and singing. The exiled people have been asked to sing "a song of Zion." Their refusal marks several layers of impossibility. How can they sing a song of joy in the midst of dreadful sorrow? How can they "sing a song of the LORD in a foreign land?" To subject sacred texts and rituals to the mockery of non-believers could be blasphemous. How can they sing the songs of Zion (cf. Pss 46, 48, 76, 84, 87, 122), which proclaim that God's city stands forever, when it seems that all is lost? How can they endure the taunting which points out the failure of their belief in the words of their own songs?[20] They are like the dead in Sheol who cannot sing God's praises.[21]

The second stanza (5-6), however, is a song of praise for Jerusalem. The singer would curse the precious possessions of hand and tongue, essential for a musician, rather than forget Jerusalem. A wordplay in verse 5 displays the singer's talent and heightens the intensity. The root *shakah* can mean "forget" (Hebrew), or "wither" (cf. Ugaritic).[22] With poetic justice the singer proclaims, "If I forget . . ., may my right hand wither."

The same poetic justice is demanded in the final stanza (7-9). The psalmist asks God to remember the treachery of the Edomites, and blesses those who pay back to the Babylonians what they have done to God's people. The word "pay back" comes from the same root as the word *shalom*, usually translated "peace." The understanding is not that peace is won at the price of vengeance, but rather that there is a right order in the world. Evil recoils on the heads of its perpetrators; blessing returns to those who do good.

[20]See Kraus 2.1084.
[21]Cf. Dahood 3.270.
[22]Dahood 3.271.

The goal of the prayer is that God will eradicate all evil and restore the holy city in peace.

The enemies who are the object of this terrible curse are the Edomites and Babylonians. Judah was subject to Babylonian rule from the end of the seventh century until 587 BCE, when Nebuchadnezzar destroyed the city, burned the temple, and took the leading citizens into Exile. The Edomites, Judah's southern neighbors, aided the Babylonians and, when the war was over, looted and pillaged Judah at will. The psalm portrays their action as rape with the cry, "Strip her, strip her!" (7, Heb.). Because they took advantage of the people at their weakest moment, the Edomites were bitterly hated. The whole Book of Obadiah is a cry for vengeance against Edom.

The blatant prayer for vengeance in Psalm 137 makes us very uncomfortable. We cringe at the thought of smashing infants against a rock. This very discomfort is the value of Psalm 137. Perhaps if we continue to pray it, we will begin to recognize the horror of war, which has now reached demonic proportions through the advances of modern technology. Perhaps the intensity of this psalm's emotion will break through our paralyzing complacency. Perhaps our revulsion at the thought of crushed babies will lead us finally to seek genuine peace, the *shalom* in which everyone has what is necessary for a full life.

4th Sun Lent B (1-2.3.4-5.6) [32]

Let my tongue be silenced, if I ever forget you (6).

God's answer to the terror of war and the horror of sin is complete vulnerability. That is the message in the readings for the Fourth Sunday of Lent B. Psalm 137 reminds us of the power of those who cry to God in utter helplessness. The curse of the enemies (7-9) is omitted. Only the cry of sorrow and the pledge to remember are included. The oath to remember, which is a valiant declaration of hope, is emphasized through the refrain. To continue to remember and to remind God never fails to persuade the compassionate Lord.

The first reading (2 Chr 36:14-17, 19-23) describes the destruction of Jerusalem, the Exile, and the decree of Cyrus which permitted return. The blame for the Exile is laid squarely on the sinful people. Their evildoing has brought evil upon them. Their complacency in the face of prophetic warning has led to their humiliation. Now, when they have no hope except in God, God restores them. The psalm follows perfectly: mourning for Jerusalem, pledging constant hope. Even now that the Exile is over, the people must not forget what they have learned, what God has done for them.

The New Testament readings (Eph 2:4-10; John 3:14-21) portray the effects of evil at a deeper level. We have all been exiled from God's city, from God's presence by sin. In our foolishness we have loved darkness because we have feared to let our vulnerability be seen. We have been enslaved by sin and unable to sing a song of the Lord. But God has redeemed us from exile through no merit of our own. This is the gift of God. God loved the world enough to send the only Son, "so that everyone who believes in him might not perish but might have eternal life" (John 3:16). God's answer to the prayer to remember our enemies and bless those who exact vengeance on them is the total vulnerability of love.

By making the words of the psalm our own we pledge undying hope and agree to leave vengeance to God. God, rich in mercy, brings us to life with Christ. Our surrender to God's love is the vulnerability demanded of us.

C. Songs of Thanksgiving

The songs of thanksgiving are related both to the laments and to the hymns. The laments often end with an expression of thanksgiving for anticipated deliverance. The songs of thanksgiving are an extension of that section of the lament. There is a critical difference, however. In the lament, the deliverance is anticipated; in the song of thanksgiving the deliverance has just been experienced. The song of thanksgiving tells the story of a specific deliverance. Reflection on God's many rescues of the people develops into the general praise of the hymn.

Because the suffering has ended just moments before, there is a certain fragility in the song of thanksgiving. There is a strong awareness of dependence on God for everything—life, breath, relief from pain, joy. The songs of thanksgiving reveal a thin-skinned emotion. Joy is heightened because of the memory of recent pain; praise is rich because of the knowledge of recent helplessness.

Songs of thanksgiving were probably used in the liturgical ceremony of the thanksgiving offering (cf. Lev 7:11-21). In the midst of distress the sufferer had promised to offer sacrifice to God and has now come to fulfill the vow. References in the psalm reveal the liturgical setting: the assembly, the sacrifice, the public witness to God's saving act.

The form of the song of thanksgiving is simple. In the *introduction* the psalmist proclaims the intent to thank God for the deliverance. Usually the thanksgiving is addressed directly to God although some songs of thanksgiving are addressed to the community. The *main body* of the song is a description of the psalmist's experience. The story of suffering or danger is told. The appeal to God is repeated. God's wonderful rescue is recounted with thanksgiving and praise. The *conclusion* often includes a promise to continue to bear witness to God's saving deeds and/or a prayer for God's continued help. There are both individual and communal songs of thanksgiving.

Songs of thanksgiving represent one of the smallest categories of psalms in the psalter. Fortunately we have a few to remind us of God's constant care and our own need to express our gratitude.

1. Psalm 18 (Royal)

Psalm 18, a royal song of thanksgiving, is parallel to 2 Sam 22:1-51. This section of 2 Samuel (chs. 21–24) is often characterized as an appendix. In these chapters there are four incidents from David's life and two poems. In contrast to the earlier descriptions of David, the king is here portrayed as weak and fallible, dependent upon God and other people.[1] The connection to 2 Samuel gives us two important clues for interpreting Psalm 18. First is the linking of this psalm to David himself. The language of the psalm indicates that it may indeed date as far back as the tenth century BCE. In the core of Psalm 18 we may have an original Davidic psalm. Secondly, the movement of the psalm is from depth to height, height to depth. The king is in deepest distress (5-7) and aligns himself with the lowly (28). The Most High God comes down to save him (7-20), stoops to exalt the king (36-49). Set in the context of David's weakness, this psalm teaches the paradox that God fills our weakness with divine strength. God stoops to raise us up.

Psalm 18 may be considered in six stanzas: 1-4, title and invocation; 5-20, description of distress and theophany; 21-31, God's rescue of the righteous; 32-35, hymnic praise; 36-46, victory; 47-51, praise and thanksgiving.

The title connects the psalm to David's life before the glories of his kingship. The rest of the first stanza is an exclamation of praise for God who is the secure refuge of the king. The opening phrase, "I love you," is a puzzle. The verb, *raham* (see Ps 51) is never used with God as object. It is God who is the source of this tender, womb-like love.[2] Is it possible to read the first stanza as a dialogue? "I love you," God says to David. In wonder, David exclaims, "LORD, my strength!"

---

[1] See W. Brueggemann, "2 Samuel 21–24: An Appendix of Deconstruction?" *CBQ* 50 (1988) 383–397.

[2] See Stuhlmueller 1.129; Kraus 1.287. Kraus emends to *ramam*, "I will exalt you."

The second stanza (5-20) is long and full of mythical allusions. The psalmist is caught in death's clutches. The floods of Belial terrify him (see Ps 41). Sheol draws him in (cf. Jonah 2; see above, Ps 69. For Sheol see Ps 86). In the midst of this distress the psalmist cries out, "Lord!" It is enough. At that moment the rescue begins. God comes in a dramatic theophany to save the loyal servant. Earthshaking imagery of storm and volcano describes the divine arrival (cf. Deut 33:2; Hab 3:3-15). God's anger against evil erupts in flame. Like the Canaanite god Ba'al, Yahweh hastens to the rescue on the wings of the wind, mounted on a cherub, one of the mythical creatures guarding the ark of the covenant and supporting the throne. God is at once hidden in darkness and revealed by the violence of the storm. The sudden appearance of God shakes creation to its foundations. The bed of the sea appears, reminiscent of the divine rescue from Egypt. All this power is unleashed for one purpose: to save the one who cries out, "Lord!"

The quiet of the third stanza (21-31) is in stark contrast to the frenzy of the second. The thankful psalmist now reflects on the meaning of God's rescue. The Lord honors the terms of the relationship. Those who cling to God, who do not abandon the relationship, who cry out, are considered righteous (21, 25). God acts in righteousness toward them. Those who honor the demands of covenant love (*hesed*, 26), who know their strength is in God, are saved (28). The king is overwhelmed by the power God gives him. The fourth stanza (32-35) expresses his amazement: Who is this God? Who but the Lord *is* God?

The fifth stanza (36-46) spells out the effects of this divine gift. The king is protected. The king's enemies are soundly defeated. The king is exalted over nations. God stoops to exalt the king.

Like the first stanza, the final stanza (47-51) is an exclamation of praise. With a great shout the king exalts God who has exalted him. The final verse proclaims the true glory of the Davidic dynasty: God gives victory to the king; God shows faithful love (*hesed*) to the anointed one, the Messiah, i.e., to David and his descendants forever. For Christians the final manifestation of God's *hesed* to the Messiah is in the lasting victory of Jesus over Sheol, the realm of death. "The LORD lives!"

30th Sun Year A (2-3.3-4.47.51) [*149*]

I love you, Lord, my strength (2).

The verses of Psalm 18 chosen for the Thirtieth Sunday of Year A are taken only from the first and last stanzas of the psalm, i.e., the two exclamations of praise. Thus the whole drama of distress and deliverance is missing. Missing also is the wisdom reflection that the mighty God lifts up the lowly who cry out. The inclusion of some verses from the second and third stanzas would certainly add to the effect of the psalm.

The opening reading (Exod 22:20-26) is part of covenant law concerning treatment of the poor and lowly. The Law is based on the underlying principle: Be like God. God cares for aliens, widows and orphans; God is compassionate. Therefore God's covenant people must care for the poor with compassion. This is the righteousness demanded of them (cf. Ps 18:21-25). In return Psalm 18 assures us that those who are compassionate can expect compassion from God (cf. Ps 18:26-27). Those who identify with the needy can expect God to hear their cry (cf. Ps 18:7-20). In singing this psalm of thanksgiving we praise God for rescuing us from distress, for saving us from death. Implicitly we pledge to treat others as God has treated us.

Care for less fortunate members of society was a special obligation of the king. Because of the king's power, he had responsibility to care for the powerless. Psalm 18 is the king's song of thanksgiving. There is a special note of praise at the end for God who gives power to the king and shows favor to the anointed. As we sing this psalm a claim is put on our own power. We cannot sing this psalm and refuse to use our own power to care for the powerless.

Jesus, God's anointed (=Messiah) and Son of David, put all the power at his disposal into the service of the poor and needy. Thus when he is asked about the greatest commandment he is able to link the two commandments concerning love: Love the Lord your God; love your neighbor (Matt 22:34-40). This is the whole Law; this is the fulfillment of the covenant demands. This is the example that Jesus, king and Messiah, left for his followers. For love of us he was delivered to the breakers of death, the cords of Sheol (Ps 18:5-7). God rescued him from death, drew him out of the deep waters (Ps 18:17-20). God gave him victory over his enemies and dominion over nations (Ps 18:36-46). He humbled himself and God saved him (Ps 18:28).

Paul (1 Thess 1:5-10) praises the Thessalonians who have become imitators of Christ, "receiving the word in great affliction" and "with joy from the holy Spirit" (1 Thess 1:6). Shortly after Paul had come to preach to them he was forced by enemies to flee (cf. Acts 17:1-15). The Thessalonians know that he came to them, not for personal gain, but out of love (1 Thess 2). It is this love which they are called to imitate (cf. 1 Thess 3:11-13).

Psalm 18 provides an interesting context for these three readings. It allows us to claim the responsibility of the anointed Christian for the weak and to acknowledge the covenant demand of love. It also allows us to claim our need and to sing our thanksgiving that God has rescued us. It allows us to hear God say, "I love you," and it gives us words for our own responding love.

31st Sun Year B (2-3.3-4.47-51) [153]

I love you, Lord, my strength (2).

The refrain and verses of Psalm 18 chosen for the Thirty-First Sunday of Year B are the same as those for the Thirtieth Sunday of Year A (see above).

The gospel for this Sunday (Mark 12:28-34) is the Markan parallel to the gospel for the Thirtieth Sunday of Year A (see above). Mark quotes a larger portion of Deut 6:2-6 which is the first reading of this Eucharist. The central message of both readings is the commandment to love God above all else. Deuteronomy introduces the command with a promise: long life and prosperity are the effect of obedience. Jesus links the command with a second from Leviticus 19: You shall love your neighbor as yourself. In Mark the scribe who asked the question praises Jesus' answer and Jesus in turn commends the scribe.

"Love" is obviously the key word in both readings and in the psalm refrain. The nuances of the word's uses are worth exploring. In Deuteronomy the love of God is equated with fear of the Lord and with obedience to God's commands. This fear is awe and wonder rather than paralyzing terror. The obedience demanded is not slavish but a willing surrender to God's wisdom and care.

The same understanding of love is found in Jesus' use of Deuteronomy. Two elements are added in the gospel. Jesus ranks this commandment as the first and the foundation of all others. The whole Law is a law of love. The scribe recognizes that fulfilling this command is the true sacrifice, the genuine whole burnt offering. Jesus then adds the second commandment: Love your neighbor as yourself. Two loves are commanded here: love of self and love of neighbor. Both hang from the command to love God and therefore to love those whom God loves. The command requires us to acknowledge God's love for us and to imitate God's love for others.

Psalm 18 encompasses all these nuances. The opening phrase, "I love you," may be understood as God's word to us. "LORD, my strength," is our response in awe and thanksgiving. The psalm continues with a description of the lengths to which God will go in expressing love for us (5-20). The third and fourth stanzas (21-35) are a reflection on our responsibilities in face of this overwhelming love. We accept the Law and the covenant demands. The final section is a shout of thanksgiving for the great and awesome love of God for us.

The second reading (Heb 7:23-28) presents Jesus as the eternal high priest who offers the perfect sacrifice. His offering, recognized by the scribe in the gospel, is the offering of love, better than any burnt offering. His offering is perfect love of God and perfect love of us. In him the first phrase of Psalm 18 is united: God proclaiming love for us; we in Christ proclaiming love for God. "I love you, LORD, my strength!" (2).

2. Psalm 30

Psalm 30 is the thanksgiving of someone who has been healed of a mortal illness. The psalmist fulfills the important responsibility of bearing witness to personal experience of God's great mercy. It is possible to lament alone, but one needs the whole community to join in thanks and praise.

The title indicates that in later years this psalm must have been used in the celebration of Hanukkah, the feast of re-dedication of the temple in 164 BCE under Judas Maccabeus (cf. 1 Macc 4:36-59; 2 Macc 10:1-8). The use is appropriate. The temple too had been threatened with death and was restored through the healing mercy of God. This re-use is a clue for us concerning the prayer of the psalms. Whatever our present situation, there is something in the psalms to fit the occasion.

There are four stanzas in Psalm 30: 2-4, initial declaration of thanksgiving with reasons; 5-6, call to praise with reasons; 7-11, report of distress and lament; 12-13, renewed thanksgiving.

In the first stanza the psalmist begins the repetition of the name, Yahweh (LORD) which characterizes this psalm. The name is repeated nine times; only four of the twelve verses do not have it (6, 7, 10, 12). The psalmist knows where healing came from.

God is praised for drawing up, healing, and delivering from the realms of death. God draws up from the pit as one raises a bucket from a well.[3] The pit is the equivalent of Sheol, the place of death (see Ps 86). The sickness is already a sign of death's encroachment. The enemies delight in their assumption that the psalmist's suffering indicates sinfulness. God delivers from all this. Therefore the psalmist gives thanks.

In the second stanza (5-6) the psalmist calls all the faithful to join in thanksgiving. The faithful are named *hasidim*, keepers of *hesed*, covenant love. Thanks are due to God because joy has conquered sorrow. God's anger, seen as the source of suffering, lasts only the blink of an eye. God's favor, the source of healing, lasts throughout life.

The third stanza (7-11) is the report to the community of the psalmist's experience. Good health and prosperity had led to complacency. Like the godless in Psalm 10:6, the psalmist said, "I shall never be shaken." Too late comes the recognition that God, not self, is the origin of good fortune. When God's presence seemed to vanish, everything fell apart. Precisely at this point the psalmist shows true faith by crying out to the God who seems

[3]Dahood 1.182; Kraus 1.387.

to be absent. The argument of the psalmist's lament is traditional. It is certainly to God's advantage to keep a faithful servant alive, since no one gives praise in Sheol. The reported lament ends with the cry, "Hear, O LORD, have mercy on me."

The final stanza (12-13) reports God's wonderful act. God has transformed mourning into dancing. God removes the clothing of repentance and dresses the psalmist in joy. The psalmist declares that it is impossible ever to stop giving praise. The psalm ends as it began, with the name of God and the cry of thanks.

Easter Vigil 4 (2.4.5-6.11-12.13) [42]

I will praise you, Lord, for you have rescued me (2).

Psalm 30, a song of thanksgiving for deliverance from death, is well chosen for the Easter Vigil. This psalm, which served an individual cured of a serious illness and a community celebrating the restoration of their temple, now becomes the song of the Christian community celebrating the final victory over death, the resurrection of the everlasting temple, Christ.

Most of the psalm is used. Only two verses of the opening stanza appear; verse 3 about healing is omitted. Almost all of the report of the psalmist's experience is missing (7-10). The verses may have been omitted because they describe terror at the absence of God and pleading for mercy. Just those concepts, however, describe the agony of Christ's final hours. There is also a connection to the reading for which Psalm 30 is assigned: "For a brief moment I abandoned you; . . . In an outburst of wrath, for a moment I hid my face from you" (Isa 54:7-8).

Isa 54:5-14 is the fourth reading of the Easter Vigil. It is an oracle of God's deliverance from the Babylonian Exile. God is portrayed as a husband who divorced his wife in a moment of anger (see Hos 2), but who now calls her back. His anger lasts a moment, but his *hesed* lasts forever (cf. Ps 30:6). God pledges everlasting love and restoration beyond any imagining.

In our singing of Psalm 30 we join the community of the past, Israel in Exile, in giving thanks for God's deliverance. We join the worldwide community of present and future in praising God for the ultimate deliverance of resurrection. We call our own community to join us in bearing witness to God's great mercy in saving us from sin and death through baptism. The song of praise must go on. "O LORD, my God, forever will I give you thanks!" (13).

3rd Sun Easter C (2.4.5-6.11-12.13) [49]

I will praise you, Lord, for you have rescued me (2).

The refrain and verses of Psalm 30 chosen for the Third Sunday of Easter B are the same as those for the Easter Vigil (see above).

The readings of this Sunday make clear that it is through Christ, through his death and resurrection, that all deliverance comes. We join the endless praise of the whole Church giving thanks for the Easter mystery.

In the first reading from the Acts of the Apostles (5:27-32, 40-41) Peter and the apostles give witness to God's salvation wrought through Jesus' death and resurrection. Giving this witness is more important than obedience to human authority. Thanksgiving must be proclaimed. The apostles pay the price of being jailed and interrogated for their witness (cf. Acts 5:17-33). Paradoxically they even rejoice in this ill-treatment. Through Christ they have learned that deliverance from death comes through death. Death lasts a moment; God's love lasts for life eternal. Weeping comes for death's dark night; at the dawn of resurrection there is rejoicing. God indeed raises up from Sheol. No suffering can dampen the thanksgiving for that mighty act. So we join the apostles in the paradox. Immediately after we hear of their rejoicing over ill-treatment we sing, "I will praise you, Lord, for you have rescued me."

The second reading (Rev 5:11-14) continues the shout of thankful praise. In John's vision the whole community of heaven joins the song. "Worthy is the Lamb that was slain," the one who went to Sheol that we might all be raised up with him. Worthy is the Lamb of all praise. In our endless praise we echo the "Amen" of the four living creatures and the worship of the elders.

The gospel (John 21:1-19) relates two personal experiences of the power of Christ's resurrection. The disciples have gone fishing, but the night was a total loss. Just at dawn Jesus appears, standing on the shore. He tells them where to find the fish and fixes their breakfast. Homey things. Deceptively simple. But in the dailiness the disciples recognize the Lord. In the transformation of deadly dailiness there is rejoicing.

The second incident is a more dramatic experience of deliverance from death. Peter, who thought he could never be shaken (John 13:37; cf. Ps 30:7), three times denied the Lord. Now he is given three opportunities to express his love, and three times he is given a commission to feed others as he has been fed. Finally, sealing the renewed relationship, Jesus says as at the beginning, "Follow me." Peter's mourning has been turned into dancing. He has been raised up from the depths of Sheol. With him we sing, "I will praise you, Lord, for you have rescued me."

10th Sun Year C (2.4.5-6.11.12.13) [91]

I will praise you, Lord, for you have rescued me (2).

The verses and the refrain from Psalm 30 for the Tenth Sunday of Year C are the same as those for the Easter Vigil (see above). The readings for this Sunday describe deliverance from death. With the words of Psalm 30 we join in thanksgiving to God for this mighty work.

The first reading (1 Kgs 17:17-24) tells part of the story of Elijah and the widow of Zarephath. When the widow's son dies, she presumes that it is because Elijah's presence has drawn God's special attention to her and to her sinfulness. She also recognizes Elijah's power as a "man of God." Elijah pleads with God for the life of the child and his prayer is granted. The psalm expresses the thanks of the widow, her son, and Elijah. In different ways each pleaded with God for mercy; each was raised up from the pit.

The gospel story (Luke 7:11-17) is parallel to the first reading. Jesus witnesses the funeral procession of a widow's only son. Moved with pity, he restores the young man to life. Not only the three participants give thanks, but fear seizes the whole crowd and moves them all to praise of God. The endless praise for deliverance from death spreads to the whole countryside.

Paul tells a different story (Gal 1:11-19). He describes the transformation worked in him by God's call. Paul has been changed from a misguided zealot persecuting God's Church to a dedicated preacher of the faith he once tried to destroy. He has been shaken from his complacency (cf. Ps 30:7), healed, and sent to proclaim the Good News of our deliverance from death by God. He calls out, "Sing praise to the LORD, you faithful" (Ps 30:5). And they glorify God because of him (Gal 1:24).

In Psalm 30, the psalm of many uses, we gather all who give thanks to God for the gift of new life. Our song continues the pledge of endless praise (Ps 30:13).

13th Sun Year B (2.4.5-6.11.12.13) [99]

I will praise you, Lord, for you have rescued me (2).

The refrain and verses from Psalm 30 for the Thirteenth Sunday of Year B are the same as those of the Easter Vigil (see above). The readings emphasize the theme of deliverance from death, which characterizes all the uses of this psalm in the Sunday Lectionary.

The Book of Wisdom, the last book of the Old Testament to be written (ca. 50 BCE), is one of the few Old Testament books to express a firm belief in life after death. The reading for this Sunday (Wis 1:13-15; 2:23-24) states that belief clearly. The basic principle underlying the belief is that righteousness is undying (Wis 1:15). Biblical righteousness is always the expression of a relationship, and so the conclusion is that the relationship of the faithful person with God cannot die. Therefore the faithful person cannot die! The question then arises, "Where did death come from?" The Book of Wisdom is equally clear in this answer: "By the envy of the devil, death entered the world." Those who maintain a relationship with the devil are subject to death.

Israel's sages and faithful people struggled for centuries with the problem of death. The gradual coming to birth of the revelation that God raises the faithful from death is cause for great rejoicing. Psalm 30 becomes the thanksgiving song for all people who cling to God even through death. What wonderful news! "LORD, you brought me up from Sheol; you kept me from going down to the pit" (Ps 30:4).

The revelation of God's gift of eternal life attains its fullness in Jesus. It is Jesus whose death and resurrection won life for all of us. Throughout his ministry Jesus worked miracles which demonstrated that the devil's death-dealing power had been broken. Today's gospel (Mark 5:21-43) tells of two such miracles. The stories of two women are woven together. One is cured while Jesus is on the way to heal the other. By the time Jesus arrives, the young girl is already dead, already facing Sheol, the pit. Jesus raises her up and restores her to her parents. The older woman is just as dead. For twelve years she has suffered the enforced separation from normal human interaction because of ritual uncleanness. Sheol has already claimed her. A single touch of Jesus' clothing cures her and restores her to normal life.

It is our responsibility to sing the thanksgiving song for both these women: "You changed my mourning into dancing; you took off my sackcloth and clothed me with gladness" (Ps 30:12). Paul reminds us that, like these women, we too are made rich through Christ's willing acceptance of poverty (2 Cor 8:7, 9, 13-15). We too have been given the very gift of life. Because of this gift, our responsibility extends to all others in need. This is our call to righteousness, the relationship with God that is undying (cf. Wis 1:15). We become ministers of God in keeping others from going down to the pit (cf. Ps 30:4), so that all together we might give endless praise to God (Ps 30:13).

3. Psalm 32 (Penitential, Wisdom Elements)

Psalm 32, a thanksgiving for God's forgiveness, is the second penitential psalm (see also Pss 51, 130). A strong wisdom flavor permeates the psalm. Anderson claims it is St. Augustine's favorite psalm.[4]

The psalm may be considered in four stanzas: 1-2, beatitude for the for-

---

[4]Anderson, 93.

given sinner; 3-7, psalmist's experience of forgiveness; 8-9, oracle from Yahweh; 10-11, wisdom reflection and call to prayer.

The two beatitudes of the opening stanza declare the theme of the whole psalm: How happy is the one whom God forgives. The first verse is compellingly compact in Hebrew: Happy the "fault-forgiven," the "sin-pardoned." The three classic terms for sin appear in these two verses: *pesha'*, rebellion; *hatta'*, missing the mark; and *'awon*, perversion (see Psalm 51). The forgiveness includes sin in all its aspects. This psalm is not about the sinless but about those who know the agony of sin and the delight of forgiveness.

In the second stanza the psalmist turns to personal experience. The message is clear. Keeping silence, hiding guilt, results in sickness and sorrow. Declaring sin openly to God results in forgiveness and security. The turning point is in verse 5: I said, "I confess my faults to the LORD." Even the literary form highlights verse 5 as the center. The three terms for sin appear in a chiasm (A:B:C:B:A): sin (*hatta'*), guilt (*'awon*), fault (*pesha'*), guilt (*'awon*), sin (*hatta'*).

The psalmist knows from experience what modern psychologists have also discovered: suppressing sin takes its toll on our bodies and makes us sick, naming our sin and acknowledging it to God frees us to live. The turning point is in the confession: "I declared my sin to you; . . . and you took away the guilt of my sin."

In the third stanza (8-9) we hear the voice of God. Just as thanksgiving psalms often report the lament that preceded deliverance, they sometimes report the divine oracle which comes in answer to the prayer. The meter of the psalm shifts to longer lines for the voice of God. God promises wisdom to those who obey. Following God's instruction will lead to life; further disobedience will bring distress again. The wise person can learn from instruction; the senseless, like horses or mules, learn only from pain.

The final stanza (10-11) is a wisdom saying and a call to prayer. Verse 10 is a proverbial contrast (cf. Prov 28:13). In proverbial style the contrast is drawn cleanly. But proverbs always leave room for thought. First of all, the two groups of people are not the wicked and the sinless but the wicked and those who trust in the Lord. The psalmist is an example of one who trusts. The confession of sin is a surrender to God in trust. Thus both groups of people are sinners. The difference is found in trust. Secondly, the other terms of contrast are not exact opposites either. The wicked experience sorrow; the trusting are surrounded by love (*hesed*). One would expect sorrow-joy, or, in the context of the rest of the psalm, sorrow-healing. But love surpasses either joy or healing. *Hesed*, the re-establishment of the covenant bond of faithful love between God and the one who surrenders in trust, is better than life itself (cf. Ps 63:4). Nothing more could be desired.

The psalm closes with a call to prayer. Thanksgiving is never sufficient without the help of the community. There can never be enough praise, and so the psalmist calls for others to join in. The people called are the just (*saddiqim*) and the upright of heart (*yishre-leb*), those who maintain the relationship with Yahweh, those who walk straight on the way God shows them. There is no talk of innocence or sinlessness, only of faithful clinging to God, faithful following of God's way.

6th Sun Year B (1-2.5.11) [78]

I turn to you, Lord, in time of trouble, and you fill me with the joy of salvation (cf. 7).

The verses chosen from Psalm 32 for the Sixth Sunday of Year B include the introductory beatitude (1-2), the turning point of the psalm (5), and the concluding call to prayer (11). The refrain is a paraphrase of verses 5 and 7. The omissions remove much of the impact of the psalm. There is no description of the psalmist's trouble before the decision to acknowledge sin. The full description of the security resulting from open confession to God is missing. The divine oracle and the proverb have also been left out.

The use of Psalm 32 with the readings of this Sunday places us squarely in the midst of a theological problem: the relationship between sin and sickness. The psalm is clearly about sin, real sin, and the sickness that results from concealing it. The readings are about sickness and the connection to sin is more remote. The problem is, of course, that this is not the simple equation: Sin results in sickness; therefore sickness is a sign of sin. The Old Testament sages knew well that this equation did not work (cf. Job, Qoheleth).

But there is a connection between sickness and sin. Our own sins can indeed make us sick. More to the point, our sins as a society can make others sick. Pollution, waste, greed, and war mean starvation, sickness, and death for thousands, perhaps millions, of people. In this Sunday's readings we must face the fact of being both sinful and sick.

The reading from Lev (13:1-2, 44-46) outlines the actions prescribed in Israelite society for one suffering from skin disease. The priests, as head of the community, have the responsibility to declare a person unclean, unfit to live within the community, or clean, fit to return to community life. The reasons for this legislation, which seems harsh to us, are twofold. First of all, there is a genuine concern to protect the community from contagious diseases. But also there is an awareness that sickness is a manifestation of evil and a disruption of the order of creation. Something is askew. Lest the whole community be infected by this outbreak of the power of evil, the affected person is separated.

The gospel (Mark 1:40-45) tells the story of one of Jesus' miracles, the cure of a man afflicted by skin disease. Jesus then instructs the man to follow the prescriptions laid down in Leviticus that he might be re-admitted to the community by the priestly declaration. Jesus' miracles, taken as a whole, are a sign that the power of evil, the power of Satan, is broken (cf. Mark 3:22-30). Jesus has power over sickness, sin, and death. Through him the power of God's kingdom overcomes the power of Satan.

The problem, of course, is that the suffering and the sin may not reside in the same person. Why excommunicate the sufferer instead of the sinner? Why must one suffer for the sins of another? We must recognize that the problem permeates our own society. Why are the poor, the homeless, addicts and the starving, the handicapped and the unemployed, hidden from those of us who are "well." Who are the "unclean" in our society? For whose sins do they suffer? Who can or will declare them clean?

It is a bold act for us to sing Psalm 32 on this Sunday. By proclaiming happy the sinner who acknowledges guilt and is forgiven, we commit ourselves to face and acknowledge the sins for which our society suffers. God promises instruction and warns us not to be like stubborn mules. The proverb promises sorrow for those who are silent, love for those who walk bravely on God's way.

We face an overwhelming challenge. Paul (1 Cor 10:31–11:1) defines it: "Do everything for the glory of God." Seek not your own advantage "but that of the many that they may be saved. Be imitators of me as I am of Christ." We must imitate Christ, that is, follow the way of love even to death. It is Christ who has broken the power of evil. We are to spend our lives spreading his victory over sin, suffering, and death. We act with courage, for all the way we will be called happy; all the way we will rejoice in being forgiven, in being surrounded by the love of God.

11th Sun Year C (1-2.5.7.11) [94]

Lord, forgive the wrong I have done (cf. 5).

The verses of Psalm 32 used for the Eleventh Sunday of Year C are the same as those for the Sixth Sunday of Year B (see above) with the addition of verse 7, the description of God's protection which surrounds the forgiven sinner. The refrain is a paraphrase of the central point of the psalm, the acknowledgment of sin.

The readings all concern sin, judgment, and forgiveness. David (2 Sam 12:7-10, 13) has committed the double sin of adultery and murder. Nathan has come to him with a parable about sheep (2 Sam 12:1-4), leading the king to pronounce judgment on himself: "The man who has done this merits death!'' (2 Sam 12:5). Today's reading continues Nathan's exhortation to the sinner who has now recognized his sin.

Nathan reminds David of all that God has done for him while David's response has been these terrible sins. David immediately acknowledges his sin and Nathan announces God's forgiveness. The evil set in motion by sin, however, does not magically disappear. Violence has taken root in his house. His children will suffer and commit rape, incest, and murder. We sing Psalm 32 in David's voice: Lord, forgive the wrong I have done. We declare him happy for being forgiven. But we also remember the paradox of the proverb in verse 10: "Many are the sorrows of the wicked, but love surrounds those who trust in the LORD." There is no claim that the forgiven have no sorrows. Rather the psalm reveals the strength to deal with life's sorrows, the enduring covenant love of God.

The gospel (Luke 7:36–8:3) is another story of forgiveness. An unnamed woman washes Jesus' feet with her tears, dries them with her hair, and anoints them with oil. It is also a story of judgment. The town and Simon judge her to be a sinner and, because of her, judge Jesus to be no prophet. Jesus looks instead at her love and judges Simon by her standard. Because of her love and the action it inspires, Jesus declares that she has been forgiven all her sins. Of all the people present, she is the happiest. "Happy the sinner whose fault is removed, whose sin is forgiven"; love surrounds her (Ps 32:1, cf. 10).

In the Letter to the Galatians (Gal 2:16, 19-21) Paul explains the source of our forgiveness. We are justified, not by our own works but by the death and resurrection of Christ. Our faith in Christ opens us to new life in him. With David and the unnamed woman we are the happy ones to whom the Lord imputes no guilt because he has borne our sins on the cross. We are now surrounded by safety and love (Ps 32:7, 10). "Be glad in the LORD and rejoice, you just; exult, all you upright of heart!" (Ps 32:11).

4. Psalm 34 (Acrostic, Wisdom Elements)

Psalm 34 is a thanksgiving psalm with a strong wisdom flavor. The psalm is an acrostic or alphabetical psalm. Each verse begins with a successive letter of the alphabet. One letter is missing between verses 6 and 7. The final verse returns to the letter "p" (cf. Ps 25). Thus the first letters of the first verse of the poem (2), the middle verse (12), and the final verse (23) spell the Hebrew word *'aleph*, the name of the first letter of the alphabet.

Acrostic poems often lack strict logical sequence and this is true of Psalm 34. There is, however, a flow of thought between stanzas. The first stanza (2-4) reports the vow of thanksgiving and calls others to praise. The second stanza (5-11) describes the psalmist's experience and calls others to learn from it. The third stanza (12-23) is a wisdom teaching based on the psalmist's experience.

The title refers the psalm to David's experience when he was fleeing from Saul. He fled to the court of Achish, king of Gath,[5] but when the servants of Achish recognized him he feigned madness, drumming on the doors and drooling onto his beard (1 Sam 21:11-16). Achish sent him away and he escaped to the cave of Adullam. The title, a later addition, gives us a clue for interpretation. David, through all his troubles, never ceased to expect good things from God, and God never failed him. We strive to pray Psalm 34 in the same spirit of unshakable confidence.

In the first stanza (2-4) the psalmist announces the intention of the psalm: "I will bless the Lord at all times." Sometimes we are too shy to consider blessing God. It is true that God is the source of all blessing. For us to bless God, however, means to return to God what we alone can give, to pour out the strength and goodness of our lives in praise and thanksgiving. This first stanza focuses especially on the poor, the *'anawim* (3). These are the people who know their only hope is in God. The psalmist identifies with them and calls them to join in the thankful praise of God.

The second stanza (5-11) begins with the psalmist's experience. There is scant description of the distress, however; all attention is fixed on God, the deliverer. The psalmist cannot let go of this wonderful God. The name of God, Yahweh (LORD), is repeated in sixteen of the twenty-two verses. The psalmist cannot let go of the poor either. "I am one of you," verse 7 cries. "In my misfortune I called, the LORD heard." The psalmist knows God saves and therefore turns again to instruction so others might know it too. Look to God! Fear the Lord! Learn to savor God's goodness! Why? From personal experience the psalmist knows that power brings poverty in the end, but those who seek the Lord lack no good thing (11).

The final stanza (12-23) is an extended wisdom teaching on the goodness that comes to the just and the destruction that comes to the wicked. The psalmist calls out like Lady Wisdom, "Come, children, listen to me" (cf. Prov 8:4; 9:4-5). Verse 13 declares the goal of wisdom, the good life. Verses 14-15 echo the teaching of Proverbs (Prov 3:7; 4:24; 13:3, 19; 16:6, 17; 21:23). Verse 16 returns to the motivation for maintaining the right relationship with God. As the psalmist knows, God cares for the just even though they suffer, but the evil to which the wicked cling kills them in the end.

This is a psalm of joy for the poor who cling to God. They are the just who maintain the covenant bond with God. They are the holy ones who

---

[5]The king's name is confused in the psalm.

fear God because of God's goodness, who seek God because of their own powerlessness.

4th Sun Lent C (2-3.4-5.6-7) [33]

Taste and see the goodness of the Lord (9).

The readings for the Fourth Sunday of Lent C certainly give reason for thanksgiving. The verses chosen for this Sunday from Psalm 34 represent the clearest thanksgiving elements of the psalm: the introductory vow and call to praise (2- 4), and the report of the psalmist's own experience of deliverance (5-7). The refrain turns to the didactic element of the psalm. The psalmist will share the benefits of experience by instructing and exhorting others.

The most obvious connection between the psalm and the first reading (Josh 5:9, 10-12) is in the suggestion of eating. The link is deeper, however. To taste the goodness of the Lord is far more than the physical taste of manna, Passover bread, or the produce of the promised land, although all these foods are symbolic of the deeper reality. To savor the goodness of the Lord is to know by experience that God nourishes the poor when there is no other source of help. To savor the goodness of the Lord is to know by experience that God delivers from the terror of oppression and slavery. To savor the goodness of the Lord is to know God's invitation to eat well in the land of promise, the kingdom. This knowledge is the call both to thankful praise and to teach others how good the Lord is.

Jesus tells the parable of the Prodigal Son (Luke 15:1-3, 11-32) in response to those who criticize him for eating with sinners. The parable points out that even God welcomes sinners and eats with them. The '*anawim*, like the son (Luke 15:14-18), know their only hope is in a merciful Father. Their hope is not disappointed. "The LORD heard and saved me from all distress" (Ps 34:7). Only the elder son, who thinks he has a right to something, fails to join in the rejoicing. Both the other son and the father give thanks for the gift they have received.

In the Second Letter to the Corinthians (2 Cor 5:17-21) we learn the extent of God's gift. In Christ God has made us a new creation. An answer beyond the imagination of those who repeat the question: "Who among you loves life?" (Ps 34:13). God in Christ has been reconciled to the whole world, thus giving new life to all the '*anawim*. The response must be twofold: thanksgiving to God, teaching for others. God has entrusted to us the message of reconciliation. God has commissioned us to teach the good news. "Come, children, listen to me. Learn to savor how good the LORD [really] is!" (Ps 34:12, 9).

Taste and see the goodness of the Lord (9).

For the next three Sundays as we read the discourse on the Bread of Life from John 6 we will sing our response with various verses of Psalm 34, all held together by the refrain: Taste and see the goodness of the Lord. The verses chosen for the Nineteenth Sunday of Year B are from the first and second stanzas: the announcement of praise (2-4) and the psalmist's own experience (5-8) which is transformed into instruction (9).

In the first reading (1 Kgs 19:4-8) the prophet Elijah is fleeing from the wrath of Queen Jezebel. Elijah has just executed 450 prophets of Ba'al for false worship (18:40). Jezebel, their patron, has sworn to execute Elijah as well. Elijah himself is on the verge of giving up and prays for death. But God has further plans for the prophet. He will be commissioned for new tasks at Mount Horeb (=Sinai). So God sends an angel to strengthen Elijah for the journey with food and drink. "The angel of the LORD who encamps with them delivers all who fear God" (Ps 34:8). Elijah has been delivered from Jezebel's terror. The angel of the Lord comes to teach God's servant to savor the goodness of the Lord. Elijah has been fed by God's presence.

Elijah on his way through the desert to Mount Sinai is a figure of Israel journeying through the desert to receive the revelation of God. Just as the Israelites murmured in the desert, so their descendants murmur at God's new revelation in Jesus (John 6:41-51). Jesus announces that he is the nourishment sent by God, the bread of life. Manna sustained the people in the desert; the Law received at Sinai gave them life. Now Jesus who has seen the Father has come as the new Law to reveal God. Jesus himself is the living bread. He has come to ask, "Who among you loves life?" (Ps 34:13). Those who eat this bread will live forever. With his own flesh he will teach us to savor how good the Lord is.

The Letter to the Ephesians (Eph 4:30–5:2) exhorts us to imitate Christ. Christ loved us and handed himself over for us. We must live in that same generous spirit. We, who have been delivered from all fears, saved from all distress (Ps 34:5-7), fed with the bread of life by Christ's sacrifice, must proclaim our thanks and call others to join us in praise (Ps 34:2-4). We must also give flesh to our thankful praise. As Christ himself is the revelation of God's love, we must become the revelation of God's compassion and forgiveness. As Christ became the food for the journey, we must spend our energy, our lives, in solving the problems of hunger in our world. We must find the ways to distribute food and eradicate famine. We must find the ways to bring the bread of life to the thousands of Christian communities deprived of Eucharist. These actions will proclaim our message better than words: "Learn to savor how good the LORD is!" (Ps 34:9).

20th Sun Year B (2-3.10-11.12-13.14-15) [120]

Taste and see the goodness of the Lord (9).

The verses of Psalm 34 chosen for the Twentieth Sunday of Year B are part of the explicit wisdom instruction of the psalm. With these verses the refrain leads us to consider the goodness of God who orders creation and cares for the poor.

The reading from Proverbs (Prov 9:1-6) presents Lady Wisdom who invites the poor and the naive to her banquet. Wisdom's food is nourishment for life (Prov 9:6). "She is a tree of life to those who grasp her" (3:18). She calls to those who love life (cf. Ps 34:13) and promises life's nourishment. She is the firstborn of God (Prov 8:22) and the designer of creation (8:30). To find her is to find God (cf. 8:35).

Jesus is the incarnation of God's Wisdom. In the name of Wisdom he invites us to the banquet (John 6:51-58). He repeats Wisdom's promise: Whoever eats this bread will live, and live forever! The food that he gives is his own flesh and blood. To eat his flesh and drink his blood is to live by his life. Just as he lives because he shares life with the Father, those who feed on him will live because they share his life.

How carefully then must we live, not as foolish persons but as wise (Eph 5:15-20). How thankful must we be, always and for everything. Psalm 34 gives us the words for our thanksgiving song: "I will bless the LORD at all times; praise shall be always in my mouth" (34:2). How great our responsibility to proclaim to others God's gifts, to teach them the grateful fear of the Lord. How urgent the call to proclaim the good news to all people, to lead all to savor how good the Lord is.

21st Sun Year B (2-3.16-17.18-19.20-21.22-23) [123]

Taste and see the goodness of the Lord (9).

The verses chosen from Psalm 34 for the Twenty-First Sunday of Year B are, after the introduction (2-3), the final portion of the psalm (16-23). In these final verses the distinction between the just and the wicked is clearly delineated. The just may suffer along with the wicked, but their cry is heard and they are saved by the Lord.

The readings for this Sunday present God's people with the necessity and challenge of choice. There are two possible ways to go. One way leads to life, the other to death. The first reading (Josh 24:1-2, 15-17, 18) describes a covenant renewal ceremony at Shechem. The generation of the exodus has died in the wilderness. The generation of the entrance into the land is getting old. The cultural situation has changed. It is necessary to face the new generation with the challenge: Serve the Lord or serve other gods, the gods of the ancestors or of the Amorites. The covenant must always be a choice. The people choose immediately, "We . . . will serve the LORD." But Joshua warns them, "You may not be able to serve the LORD." To choose the covenant relationship with the Lord is to forsake all other gods. To choose the covenant is to learn to savor the Lord in bad times as well as good, to trust the Lord in trouble and to wait in patience for deliverance.

Jesus' listeners are faced with a similar choice (John 6:60-69). The crowd is repulsed by the words about eating his flesh and drinking his blood. Even the disciples acknowledge, "This saying is hard." But just as the Sinai covenant was sealed in blood and a meal (Exod 24:1-11), so the new covenant is sealed in blood and a meal. Sharing blood, sharing food, signify the sharing of life. God and the people are bound in an intimate unity. It is a bond that cannot be broken without destroying life. The disciples are faced with the choice. Many abandon him, but Peter answers for us who choose to stay: "Master, to whom shall we go? You have the words of eternal life" (John 6:68).

The reading from Ephesians (5:21-32) describes the one life-sharing human relationship that is closest to the life-sharing covenant bond with God. The reading is only one part of a whole section on relationships: husband and wife, children and parents, slaves and master (5:21–6:9). The whole section hangs from a single sentence: "Be subordinate to one another out of reverence for Christ." Each group of people is called to appropriate deference toward the other out of respect for the great mystery of God's life which is in each one and which is shared by all.[6] The same covenant choice is seen in each relationship, the choice to serve the Lord living in the other person or to serve the strange gods of dominance, selfishness, and exploitation. Covenant-making requires a choice, a free choice to share life.

The sharing of life in marriage is an image of the covenant sharing of life with God. To share God's life is to know God through intimate experience, to learn to savor the goodness of the Lord (Ps 34:9). To share God's life is to be in that right relationship with God that is righteousness. To share God's life is to be the just whom God sees and hears and saves. The share in God's life heals the broken-hearted and saves the suffering (34:19-20). It is a choice to be just or wicked, to serve the Lord or strange gods. To whom shall we go? The Lord has the words of eternal life. "Learn to savor how good the LORD is; happy are those who take refuge in [God]" (Ps 34:9).

---

[6]The sentence following the topic sentence actually has no verb in Greek. It simply continues, "wives to their husbands. . . ."

30th Sun Year C (2-3.17-18.19.23) [151]

The Lord hears the cry of the poor (cf. 7).

Psalm 34 is a psalm of the poor, the '*anawim* who know their only help is God. The verses chosen from the psalm for the Thirtieth Sunday of Year C emphasize God's care for the poor. The refrain is a paraphrase of the psalmist's own testimony: "In my misfortune I called, the LORD heard" (Ps 34:7).

The Wisdom of Jesus ben Sira is a wisdom of the middle class, of those who have something.[7] Ben Sira gives careful advice about investments and loans, about social contacts and the value of a good education. He also knows, however, that wealth does not save and that power belongs to God (cf. Sir 5:1-10). Before God everyone is needy, everyone is powerless. The sage reminds us in today's reading (35:12-14, 16-18) that God, although just, has a special care for the poor and powerless. There is a double moral to Ben Sira's wisdom. If you want God to hear you, recognize your own lowly status. Secondly, be like God and hear the cry of the poor.

By Ben Sira's standard the tax collector in Jesus' parable (Luke 18:9-14) is wise and the Pharisee is foolish. The tax collector who acknowledges his sinfulness and appeals to God's mercy goes home justified because he has maintained the relationship with God. The Pharisee who uses prayer to exalt himself is not really speaking to God and is not heard by God. "When the just cry out, the LORD hears. The LORD is close to the brokenhearted" (Ps 34:18, 19). Like many parables this one turns things upside down. The parable is addressed to those who are convinced of their own righteousness and yet despise everyone else. The parable warns that the truly righteous may be "the rest of humanity, . . . even like this tax collector." The self-righteous may find themselves in the dangerous position of hating the just, and "those who hate the just are condemned" (Ps 34:22). O God, be merciful to us sinners!

The author of 2 Timothy presents Paul as a genuine just man who does know his own righteousness (2 Tim 4:6-8, 16-18). He knows both sides of the relationship. He knows that he has kept the faith. He also knows that it is the Lord who gave him strength. Like the author of Psalm 34, he gives the glory to God and trusts in God's care for him. He is confident because he is faithful and he is needy. "The LORD redeems loyal servants;" the LORD hears the cry of the poor (Ps 34:23, cf. 7).

---

[7]See Dianne Bergant, " 'Blest are the Not-So-Poor . . .': Admonitions for the Middle Class," *TBT* 101 (March 1979) 1962–1968.

Peter & Paul (2-3.4-5.6-7.8-9) [591]

The angel of the Lord will rescue those who fear God (8).

When it falls on a Sunday the Solemnity of Peter and Paul supersedes the Sunday of Ordinary Time. The verses of Psalm 34 chosen for this solemnity come from the first part of the psalm, the introductory vow of praise and the report of the psalmist's own experience of deliverance. The refrain is the psalmist's expression of total confidence. The angel of the Lord who protects God's people in battle (cf. Exod 23:20-23) and who is often the Lord in disguise (cf. Gen 16:7-13; Exod 3:2-6) will be sent to deliver the poor one who cries out.

The first two readings (Acts 12:1-11; 2 Tim 4:6-8, 17-18) relate experiences of Peter and Paul in which God rescued them from danger (see also Thirtieth Sunday of Year C for 2 Tim 4:6-8, 16-18). Peter was released from prison by an angel; Paul was defended in a trial. Both saints know their own weakness and trust in God's strength. Both saints know the happiness of taking refuge in God (Ps 34:9).

The gospel (Matt 16:13-19) tells the story of another gift to Peter, the revelation that Jesus is the Messiah, the Son of the living God. Jesus in turn names him Rock, foundation of the Church, and promises that the gates of death will not prevail against the Church. The Church too must know that it is the Lord who gives strength; it is the Lord who delivers those who fear God. These saints sought God in their misfortune and were answered. We the Church follow in their footsteps: "Magnify the LORD with me; let us exalt [the] name together" (Ps 34:4).

Year Common (2-3.4-5.6-7.8-9) [175]

I will bless the Lord at all times (2).

Psalm 34 is one of eight psalms suggested for the Season of the Year (see also Pss 19, 27, 63, 95, 100, 103, and 145). The refrain is the introductory pledge of thankful praise. The verses continue the call to praise and relate the psalmist's own experience of deliverance by God. The response would thus be fitting for any Sunday in which the theme is thanksgiving, especially for deliverance from danger. The psalm is already used for three Sundays in which feeding is the theme (Nineteenth to Twenty-First Sundays of Year B). The psalm also emphasizes God's care for the poor. Sundays on which those are particular emphases might also be good occasions for the use of Psalm 34.

Two Sundays which emphasize feeding would be appropriate liturgies for Psalm 34. The gospel for the Eighteenth Sunday of Year A is Matthew's version of the multiplication of the loaves (Matt 14:13-21; see the fuller discussion of this Sunday with Ps 145). The first reading (Isa 55:1-3) is the prophetic call to come to God and eat and drink. The second reading (Rom 8:35, 37-39), declares that no affliction can separate us from the love of God. The gospel for the Eighteenth Sunday of Year B introduces the Bread of Life discourse from the Gospel of John (John 6:24-35; see Ps 78). Psalm 34, which is used for the following three Sundays, might be introduced here. The first reading describes the miracle of manna (Exod 16:2-4,12-15).

Three Solemnities of the Lord also lend themselves to the use of Psalm 34. The gospel for Corpus Christi Year A is the conclusion of the Bread of Life discourse (John 6:51-58; see Ps 147). The first reading (Deut 8:2-3, 14-16) is Deuteronomy's meditation on the gift of manna; the second reading (1 Cor 10:16-17) is Paul's meditation on the gift of Eucharist. On Corpus Christi Year C the gospel is Luke's version of the multiplication of the loaves (Luke 9:11-17; see Ps 110). The first reading (Gen 14:18-20) describes Melchizedek's offering of bread and wine; the second reading (1 Cor 11:23-26) is Paul's account of the institution of the Eucharist. The gospel for the Solemnity of the Sacred Heart Year C tells the first two lost and found parables (Luke 15:3-7; see Ps 23). The first reading (Ezek 34:11-16) describes God's care for the sheep; the second reading (Rom 5:5-11) makes explicit God's care for us even when we were still sinners.

It would be wise throughout Year C to keep Psalm 34 in mind as a possible substitute psalm. The poor who are a focus of Psalm 34 are also a special interest in the Gospel of Luke.

5. Psalm 40

Psalm 40 has a puzzling structure. The first section (2-11) is a song of thanksgiving; after a transition (12-13), the second section (14-18) is a lament almost identical to Psalm 70. While laments do occur within songs of thanksgiving, ordinarily they are presented as a report of earlier distress and occur toward the beginning of the psalm. In Psalm 40 the lament has the urgency of present distress and occurs at the end. It has been proposed that this lament is a separate psalm. However, there are verbal connections between the two parts of the psalm: God does not want (*hps*) sacrifice (7), I want (*hps*) to do God's will (9), but enemies want (*hps*) my ruin (15); I have proclaimed God's salvation (11, *teshu'a*), may all who long for God's salvation (*teshu'a*) give praise (17).[8] The move from thanksgiving to lament teaches us that our hold on any position of security is tenuous. We may never forget our need for God.

---

[8] For other connections, see Brueggemann, *Message*, 130–131. Many of the connections are between the thanksgiving and the transition.

The thanksgiving song (2-11) falls into three stanzas. In the first (2-4) the psalmist declares the personal reason for thanksgiving. In response to desperate trust ("I waited, waited"), God drew the psalmist from the muddy grip of death and provided this new song of thanksgiving. Even the thanksgiving is God's gift. The second stanza (5-6) is a general reflection on God's wonderful deeds for us. How happy those who trust in the power of such a merciful Lord! The third stanza (7-11) contrasts the offering of sacrifice with obedience and praise. The psalmist echoes a thought found throughout the Old Testament: obedience is better than sacrifice (1 Sam 15:22; cf. Hos 6:6; also Isa 1:10-20; Amos 5:21-24; Mic 6:6- 8; Pss 50; 51). Perhaps this is part of the prophetic critique of ritual without devotion, or perhaps it reflects a situation such as exile in which the psalmist is unable to offer sacrifice. In either case the thanksgiving offering made here is glad public testimony of God's great goodness.

The second section consists of transition (12-13) and lament (14-18). The transition ties the lament to the thanksgiving. I have not restrained the praise of my lips (10); Lord, do not restrain your compassion (12). I cannot count your wonderful deeds (6), nor can I count the evils around me or the sins within me (13). I did not hide your deeds within my heart (11), but now my heart fails me (13).

The lament (14-18) is an intense plea for immediate help. The first verse is familiar to many as the opening invocation of the Liturgy of the Hours. The heart of the lament has two prongs: disgrace my enemies, give joy to all who seek you. Verbal expression is important. The psalmist has announced God's great deeds in the thanksgiving and now hopes that those who speak scornfully will be shamed and those who are faithful will join the song of praise. The psalm ends with a poignant appeal to God who cares for the poor: "Though I am afflicted (a pun in Hebrew, *'ani 'ani*) and poor, the Lord keeps me in mind. You are my help and deliverer; my God do not delay!" (Ps 40:18).

2nd Sun Year A (2.4.7-8.8-9.10) [65]

Here am I, Lord; I come to do your will (8, 9).

The verses of Psalm 40 chosen for the Second Sunday of Year A are all from the thanksgiving song. The selection emphasizes the importance of obedience to the call to bear witness. God's gift to the psalmist is not only rescue but a new song. As the earlobe of a willing slave was pierced as a sign of obedience, God has cut open the ears of the psalmist (Exod 21:6; Deut 15:17). The psalmist is delighted with God's call and proclaims God's greatness to a vast assembly.

The readings for this Sunday also emphasize call and witness. The Servant has been called from the womb to bear witness not only to Jacob/Israel, but even to the ends of the earth (Isa 49:3, 5-6). In the first Servant song (42:1-4) the sign of the Servant's call is the outpouring of God's Spirit upon him. In the third Servant song (50:4-11) the Servant proclaims that God has given him a well-trained tongue to bear witness and has opened his ear to obey. The ambiguous figure of the Servant is at once the prophet and all God's people, Moses and one who is to come. From suffering and deliverance (cf. Isa 52:13–53:12) the Servant learns the new song of God's salvation which reaches to the ends of the earth.

In the opening salutation of the First Letter to the Corinthians (1:1-3), Paul announces his own call to be a witness of Christ and reminds the Corinthians of their call. The idea of living by their call to be holy will be an important theme throughout the letter.

The gospel (John 1:29-34) presents the Baptist's witness to Jesus. He announces that he has been called to introduce the one upon whom the Spirit remains, the one who will baptize with the Holy Spirit. John proclaims Jesus as the Lamb who takes away the sin of the world. He is the one who is lowly and poor, but who also comes to bring God's salvation. He is the one who comes in obedience and the one who is himself the perfect sacrifice (Ps 40:7-9; cf. Heb 10:5-10).

We sing Psalm 40 in the person of each of these figures presented to us in the readings. John, Jesus, and the Servant, Paul and the Corinthians, all cry out with us: "Here I am, Lord; I come to do your will." Each knows the intense waiting for the Lord's deliverance and the awesome experience of the new song. Each announces God's greatness to the vast assembly as God is the witness. May our song join with theirs; may our witness continue the spread of God's good news.

2nd Sun Year B (2.4.7-8.8-9.10 [66]

Here am I, Lord; I come to do your will (8, 9).

The psalm verses and the refrain for the Second Sunday of Year B are the same as those for the Second Sunday of Year A (see above).

As on the Second Sunday of Year A, the emphasis in this Sunday's readings is on call and witness. The first reading (1 Sam 3:3-10, 19) is the story of Samuel's call. The young man's ready answer of obedience, "Here I am," even when he does not know who calls, is echoed in the psalm (40:8). Eli, older and wiser, advises Samuel on how to answer the Lord. Samuel follows his advice and announces his open ears, "Speak, LORD, for your servant is listening" (1 Sam 3:9; cf. Ps 40:7). Samuel is called to announce God's deeds to a great assembly (cf. Ps 40:10). In turn the Lord does not permit any word of Samuel's to be without effect (1 Sam 3:19).

The gospel (John 1:35-42) continues the story of the Baptist's witness to Jesus and its effect (see above, Second Sunday of Year A). On the strength of the Baptist's words, two of his disciples follow Jesus. The witness starts a chain reaction. One of the disciples who heard John now gives his own witness to his brother Simon. The number of those called expands because of the expanding witness. Andrew has already learned the new song and given it to his brother.

Paul's message (1 Cor 6:13-15, 17-20) moves the responsibility for witness to the use of one's own body. One's use of food (cf. 1 Cor 6:12-13a) and sexuality bears eloquent witness to one's faith in Christ. Even the body of a Christian belongs to God, purchased by Christ and filled with the Holy Spirit. The body itself will share in Christ's resurrection. Thus even the body announces God's wondrous deeds. The Greek version of Psalm 40 expresses more clearly the call to use the body in glorifying God: Sacrifice and offering you did not desire, but a body (*sóma*) you prepared for me (Ps 39[40]:7 LXX; cf. Heb 10:5). It is in the body that we are delivered by God's mercy (cf. Ps 40:2-3); it is through the body that we proclaim, "The LORD be glorified" (cf. Ps 40:17).

With John and Andrew we sing the new song of God's wonderful deed in Christ. With Samuel and Paul we say, "Here I am; I come to do your will." With the Corinthians we dedicate our energy and our skill, every movement of our bodies to announce our thankful praise. God's Law is in our hearts, in our very flesh. We may not keep God's enduring kindness a secret. May our witness bring many to look on in awe and to trust in God (cf. Ps 40:4).

20th Sun Year C (2.3.4.18) [121]

Lord, come to my aid! (14).

The lament theme of Psalm 40 is emphasized on the Twentieth Sunday of Year C. The refrain is taken from the opening verse of the lament. The verses, most of which are taken from the thanksgiving portion of the psalm, report the psalmist's distress and God's wonderful rescue. The selection ends with the final verse of the lament and of the psalm, expressing trust in God's care for me because I am afflicted, and pleading for immediate help.

Psalm 40 could be the thanksgiving song of Jeremiah himself (Jer 38:4-6, 8-10). For the sake of the message which God entrusted to him, Jeremiah was threatened with death many times. In today's reading his enemies conspire to have him thrown into a muddy pit where he will certainly die of starvation. He is saved through the intercession of Ebed-Melech, an

Ethiopian courtier of the king. Ebed-Melech, whose name means "Servant of the King," is certainly functioning as a servant of God, drawing Jeremiah "out of the pit of destruction, out of the mud of the swamp" (Ps 40:3). God heard the prophet's cry; God came quickly to help him.

The gospel too confronts us with the cost of fidelity to God (Luke 12:49-53). The passage occurs in the midst of Jesus' warnings to be prepared and to understand the signs of the times. There is a tension between the urgency of Jesus' message and the evangelist's awareness that the parousia has been delayed. The Christian is urged to maintain vigilance in spite of the delay, to respond to Jesus' urgent desire to set the whole world on fire. Jesus yearns to accomplish his mission, even though it leads through the "baptism" of death. The follower of Jesus must be prepared also to face opposition and suffering, and yet never to give up. Our own longing is expressed in the psalm, "I waited, waited for the LORD." The second line is the source of our courage: The Lord "bent down and heard my cry" (Ps 40:2).

Further encouragement is found in the Letter to the Hebrews (Heb 12:1-4). "For the sake of the joy that lay before him [Jesus] endured the cross" (12:2). He now reigns at the right of the throne of God. We draw strength from remembering him and the opposition he endured. Our hearts do not fail us (cf. Ps 40:13). Even as we long for God's help, we continue to say, "the LORD be glorified" (Ps 40:17).

Psalm 40 reminds us that God does not forget the afflicted and poor. God answers those who trust with awesome deeds. The readings for this Sunday warn us of the suffering we will surely face if we follow Christ faithfully. The psalm teaches us how to endure. "I waited, waited for the LORD." The psalm teaches us even to rejoice in our weakness, because we trust in the power of God. "You are my help and deliverer; my God, do not delay" (Ps 40:18).

6. Psalm 41

Psalm 41 is a thanksgiving psalm with the remembered lament inserted into it. The psalm has three sections: 2-4, a wisdom pronouncement; 5-11, the remembered lament; 12-13, thanksgiving. Verse 14, a doxology, marks the end of Book 1 of the psalter.

The Book of Psalms is divided into five books, possibly in imitation of the five books of the Torah. Each book ends with a doxology, a proclamation of praise (cf. Pss 72:18-20; 89:53; 106:48; 150). The doxology is not part of the psalm, but an addition somewhat as we add the "Glory be . . ." to the end of a psalm or "For the kingdom . . ." to the end of the Our Father.

The opening instruction of Psalm 41 (2-4) begins with a beatitude, a typical wisdom form (cf. Ps 1:1). The content, however, is unique. The beatitude begins by praising the person who deals wisely: We expect the beatitude to acclaim the person who is wise in regard to God. Instead the psalm proclaims happy the person who is wise in regard to the poor. God's concern for the poor is so strong, that God will reward anyone who cares for them.

The psalmist then remembers a time of distress (5-11). The common conception that sickness and suffering were caused by sin and therefore a sign of sinfulness is evident in these verses. The psalmist prays for healing and forgiveness. The enemies presume the psalmist is a sinner, and gossip about the certain fate of such a one. They presume that the deadly disease, "a thing from Belial" (9, Heb.), is a punishment from God. The word "Belial," which means "worthless" or "evil," suggests the possibility even of demonic involvement in the suffering. Even the close friend, "the one of peace," whose sharing of food signified sharing of life, has turned against the psalmist. The section ends with a prayer for healing and vengeance. The psalmist too presumes that God rewards virtue and punishes wickedness. Therefore the enemies should be punished.

In the final verses (12-13) the psalmist thanks God for healing and vindication. The enemy no longer jeers. The psalmist, assured of integrity, enjoys the presence of God in the temple.

We may be a little uncomfortable both with the psalmist's confidence and with the wish for vengeance. If, however, we remember that there was no strong belief in life after death, we can understand the psalmist's view that the wicked must be punished and the just rewarded in this life. The real instruction of the psalmist is that God cares for those who care for the poor. The psalmist knows this from experience. This is the wisdom of the psalm.

7th Sun Year B (2-3.4-5.13-14) [81]

Lord, heal my soul, for I have sinned against you (5).

Psalm 41 is used only once in the Sunday Lectionary, on the Seventh Sunday of Year B. The whole wisdom instruction is included, along with the opening of the lament and the conclusion of the thanksgiving. Even the doxology is added! All the verses concerning the enemy have been omitted. This omission was no doubt made to avoid confusion concerning the enemies' presumption that sin caused the sickness and to avoid scandal concerning the wish for vengeance.

The gospel reading (Mark 2:1-12), however, also suggests the connection between sickness and sin. When Jesus sees the paralyzed man, he says to him, "your sins are forgiven." This is the first and greatest miracle of the story. The scribes are scandalized that Jesus takes power which belongs only to God, and so Jesus works the second miracle as sign of the first: "Rise, pick up your mat and go home." Jesus has demonstrated his authority over both sin and death, both "things of Belial."

The reading from Second Isaiah (43:18-19, 21-22, 24-25) is part of a sixth-century prophet's comfort to the exiles in Babylon. The prophet assures them that God not only can restore them to their own land but will do so. Just as God led them out of Egypt across the desert, so God will lead them out of Babylon. It is true that their sinfulness led to the distress of Exile. But God, being God, wipes out their sinfulness as well as their suffering. "Your sins I remember no more" (43:25). The assurance of the prophet is picked up by Paul in 2 Cor 1:18-22. God is faithful; Christ is the expression and fulfillment of God's fidelity. The Spirit is our sign and pledge that God will indeed save us from sin and death.

We know that it is impossible to draw a one-to-one connection between sin and suffering. A person who suffers cannot be judged therefore to be a sinner, or to be a saint for that matter. But in our time we certainly know that there is a larger connection between sin and suffering. We see wars and poverty caused by greed, famine and sickness caused by unconcern and the quest for comfort. Children do suffer for the sins of their elders. Nations suffer for the sins of world powers. Psalm 41 assures us that God cares for those who care for the lowly and poor. Their reward is the presence of God.

7. Psalm 65 (Communal)

Psalm 65 is difficult to classify. It blends the elements of thanksgiving and hymn. Claus Westermann divides psalms of praise into two categories and names them declarative psalms of praise (thanksgiving) and descriptive psalms of praise (hymn).[9] The declarative psalm of praise is a thanksgiving to God for a specific act of deliverance. It usually contains a description of the distress, a reference to the vow of praise and thanksgiving, and vocabulary such as "cry," "hear," "answer." The descriptive psalm has moved from the specific occasion to praise of God's never-ending goodness. It often refers to creation and history. God's acts and attributes are listed in a series of participles.

---

[9]Westermann, *Praise and Lament*, 31–32.

Psalm 65 refers to the vow of praise (2), and God's act of hearing and answering prayer (3, 6). The psalm also lists God's awesome deeds in creation and history with a series of participles (7-8). The psalm seems to be a community thanksgiving for forgiveness which has overflowed into a hymn of praise to God who sustains all creation. It may possibly be connected to the fall feasts of Yom Kippur (Day of Atonement) and Sukkoth (Tabernacles) which was a celebration of the last harvest of the year. The emphasis on rain corresponds to the fall season when the first rains begin.[10]

Psalm 65 can be considered in two stanzas: 2-5, thanksgiving; 6-14, praise. The first stanza begins by directing our attention to God: "to you . . . to you . . . to you." The community has assembled at the temple of Mount Zion to thank God for forgiveness and a new beginning. The hymn of praise, the vow of thanks, are due to God who hears prayer. The burden of guilt is too much for creatures of flesh; only God can forgive. How happy the chosen ones who know that God *does* forgive. They enjoy the presence of God in the temple; they are filled with the good things of the thanksgiving banquet.

The second stanza (6-14) moves to general praise of God. God's awesome deeds fill the whole world. God created all things—mountains and seas—and keeps the world in order. There is a suggestion of the mythological battle in which God defeats and restrains the seas of chaos in order to bring forth the created world. God's creative might is the hope of all people and leads them to worship in joyful fear. God's creative work is justice, establishing everything in right relationship. God's creative power is never exhausted. Every year God sends the rains to make the earth fertile and to provide food. The earth itself shouts for joy.

The link between the two parts of this psalm is instructive for our present world. The destruction of the earth caused by the sinful selfishness of a whole society is becoming ever more obvious. Only when there is a way for all of us together to come before the Creator to beg for forgiveness and promise amendment will there be a renewal of the earth. God's care enriches the earth; our unrepented sins destroy it.[11]

15th Sun Year A (10.11.12-13.14) [104]

The seed that falls on good ground will yield a fruitful harvest (Luke 8:8).

The verses of Psalm 65 chosen for the Fifteenth Sunday of Year A come entirely from the hymn to the Creator in the last part of the psalm. God

---

[10]See Stuhlmueller 1.292. Dahood (2.108–117) considers the final section to be a prayer for rain.

[11]Brueggemann, 135–136.

is praised as the one who sustains all creation by sending life-giving rain. The refrain is taken from the gospel parable of the sower.[12]

The first reading (Isa 55:10-11) is a prophetic encouragement to the people in Exile that God can and will fulfill the promises made to them. The earlier verses (55:6-9) urge the people to seek the Lord and to beg forgiveness. Their sinfulness may have led them into Exile, but now God is planning a glorious return (55:12-13). The sign of God's power and willingness to do this is the rain. Just as the rain fulfills its purpose of giving life to the earth, so God's word gives life to the people. This is God's awesome deed of justice which fills the whole world with hope (Ps 65:6).

In the gospel parable (Matt 13:1-23) Jesus expands the comparison between God's word and the fertility of the earth. God sows good seed, the word of life. The productivity of the seed, however, depends on the preparedness of the soil which receives it. The Isaiah reading, which compared God's word to the rain, emphasized the unfailing power of that word. The gospel parable regards the same mystery from a different angle and points out the importance of human response. Only those who welcome the word with understanding will produce the full harvest. It is sin which prevents the hearer from receiving the seed of the word and bearing fruit. Greed, anxiety, cowardice, and rejection of God stifle and kill the promise of the seed. Psalm 65 leads us as a community to bring the burden of our guilt to God who forgives (Ps 65:3-4). The land suffers because of our sin; our repentance will save the earth. Then we may expect the answer of abundant growth and joyous harvest.

We have already received the firstfruits of the Spirit (Rom 8:18-23). But along with the rest of creation we groan in labor awaiting the full harvest. What we suffer now is nothing compared to the glory to be revealed for us. We await God's awesome deeds. With all creation we wait in hope and fear (Ps 65:6, 9). We give thanks for our deliverance from the corruption of sin through Christ (Rom 8:21; Ps 65:2-5). We sing our hymn of praise to the God whose word roots within us.

8. Psalm 67 (Communal)

Like Psalm 65, Psalm 67 is a thanksgiving for God's gift of the harvest. The psalm is divided by the refrain (4, 6). The first stanza (2-4) begins with the priestly blessing of God's people (Num 6:24-25). But the psalm calls

---

[12]The Lectionary cites the Lukan parallel to this Sunday's gospel. Since almost the same phrase occurs in Matthew, one wonders why!

for the extension of God's blessing over the whole earth. Then all nations will know, i.e., experience, God's way of salvation. The second stanza (5-6) awaits the joyful praise of the nations who experience God's tender care and just guidance. The third stanza (7-8) describes the physical evidence of God's blessing, the harvest. The psalm concludes with a prayer that God's blessing will continue to extend through time and space.

Blessing in biblical terms is an enhancement of life and is always expressed in tangible ways.[13] Signs of God's blessing are long life, many children, good health, and abundant harvests (cf. Job 1:10; 42:12; Pss 49:19; 65:10; 107:38; 128:5; 132:15; Prov 10:22; 24:25). All of these gifts signify a share in the life of the Creator God. To extend a blessing is to give life. The prayer of this psalm is both the thanksgiving for God's gift of life-sustaining food and a prayer that God's renewing blessing might be shared with all peoples.

The tragedy of poverty and famine in our own century demonstrates the blockage of God's blessing through sin. We who make this psalm our prayer are called by it to give flesh to our request. The psalm calls us to use our own power and energy to bring the fruits of the harvest to all who are in need. Effective sharing of the world's resources is a compelling witness to the just rule of God. If our hope really is that the ends of the earth may revere God, then our attention must be given to the spread of God's blessing.

Mother of God ABC (2-3.5.6.8) [18]

May God be gracious to us and bless us (2).

All of Psalm 67 is used for the Solemnity of Mary, Mother of God, except verse 7 concerning God's gift of the harvest. It is unfortunate that verse 7 is omitted, because it gives the physical evidence of God's blessing and the immediate reason for the thanksgiving prayer of the psalm. Even in our urban age, when the immediacy of God's gift of nourishment is hidden from many people, the linkage of blessing to tangible reality would be healthy. It is good to realize on this New Year's Day that the material things which sustain our lives are gifts of God. Otherwise it becomes too easy to think of blessing only in spiritual terms. Without the physical evidence our awareness is too often hazy and our thanksgiving too often limp. It also becomes too easy to wish other people well and never move to assist their lives.

The first reading for this solemnity is the instruction for priestly blessing from the Book of Numbers (6:22-27). This section of Numbers contains a set of ritual laws which in the context of the book become the prepara-

[13]See Irene Nowell, "The Narrative Context of Blessing in the Old Testament," *Concilium: Blessing and Power*, ed. M. Collins and D. Power (Edinburgh: T & T Clark, 1985) 3–12.

tion for the march from Sinai to the promised land. The priestly blessing strengthens the people for the journey. The sign of God's blessing is peace, *shalom*, the situation in which each person has what is necessary for a full life.

Psalm 67 flows immediately from the instruction and puts it into action. We call for God's blessing and pray that all nations may enjoy it. The result of experiencing God's blessing will be worship of God by all peoples.

The two New Testament readings describe the ultimate physical sign of God's life-giving blessing, the incarnation. God became human in order to share life with us. In the Letter to the Galatians (Gal 4:4-7) Paul describes this sharing in divine life as the gift of God's Spirit. We receive this gift through the Son, who was sent to ransom us from slavery and to win for us the status of children of God.

The gospel (Luke 2:16-21), which continues the infancy narrative, reminds us that this day is the Octave of Christmas. The story presents the shepherds, the first outside witnesses to the incarnation in Luke's Gospel. The shepherds witness the sign of God's great blessing and return glorifying God. They bear witness to the truth of the psalm: Experience of God's blessing leads to knowledge of God's saving ways; knowledge of God's saving ways leads to praise. God still blesses us. In this New Year may we find tangible ways to share the blessing so that all the ends of the earth may revere our God.

6th Sun Easter C (2-3.5.6.8) [58]

O God, let all the nations praise you! (4).

Psalm 67, thanksgiving for God's blessing and a prayer for its universal extent, is used in the liturgy as thanksgiving for God's greatest blessing, the Incarnation. Its placement toward the beginning of the Christmas season (New Year's Day) and toward the end of the Easter season brackets our liturgical celebration of this great mystery.

The verses chosen are the same as those for the Solemnity of the Mother of God (see above). The refrain of the psalm is used on this Sunday as the people's response. The refrain highlights the psalm's universal character. All nations are called to praise God.

The first reading (Acts 15:1-2, 22-29) is Luke's description of a controversy in the early church concerning law. How much of Jewish Law are Gentile Christians expected to observe? The Jerusalem community, assembled together and relying on the presence of the Spirit in their midst, decides that the only necessary laws are those which enable genuine sharing of life. Gentile Christians are asked to observe dietary laws which make possible the sharing of meals, and sexual purity which preserves the sharing in marriage. The living community which such laws sustain is a sign of God's continued blessing, of the sharing of life with God. The witness of such a living community will spread the good news of God's blessing to the ends of the earth.

The gospel (John 14:23-29) teaches the paradoxical nature of shared life with God. Those who keep Jesus' word will enjoy the presence of the Trinity. Jesus and the Father will come to stay; the Spirit will come to teach. Yet Jesus announces a separation: he is going to the Father. The disciples will learn that the tangible evidence of God's blessing is a sign of deeper reality. Even without physical presence, Jesus will remain with them. Their sign that God still shares life with them is peace, *shalom*. Peace reigns when everyone has a full share of God's blessing.

The vision of Revelation (Rev 21:10-14, 22-23) is a vision of the final accomplishment of God's blessing. All God's people, symbolized by the number twelve, will be citizens in God's city and live by the light of God's presence. This is the final answer to the prayer: "May God be gracious to us and bless us; may God's face shine upon us" (Ps 67:2).

This Sunday's readings take the idea of God's blessing all the way from the first disciples to the fulfillment in the heavenly Jerusalem. The fulfillment comes through the active efforts of God's people to find ways to share the good news in all cultures and languages. The early church recognized that the sharing of life was the essential purpose of the Law. The cultural shaping of the Law is not essential. It is the sharing of life which is blessing, which is peace. "May all the nations praise you, God!"

20th Sun Year A (2-3.5.6.8) [119]

O God, let all the nations praise you! (4).

The verses of Psalm 67 for the Twentieth Sunday of Year A are the same as those for the Solemnity of the Mother of God (see above). The refrain, which emphasizes the spread of God's blessing to all nations, is the same as that of the Sixth Sunday of Easter C (see above).

This Sunday's readings force us to look at the outcasts from our communities. Whom do we wish to exclude from God's blessing? The first reading (Isa 56:1, 6-7) begins the final section of the Book of Isaiah. This series of prophetic oracles was addressed to people rebuilding the community after the Exile. Two streams of thought concerning non-Jews can be discerned in this post-exilic community. Some believed that the way to ensure pure devotion to God was to exclude all foreigners who might lead God's people astray (cf. Neh 13:1-3, 23- 31). Others were aware that the very experience of Exile and return demonstrated that their God was the God of the whole world (cf. Jonah). The latter opinion is expressed in this final section of Isaiah (chs. 56-66).

The opening oracle distinguishes between what is necessary for membership in the community and what is not. Those who love God's name, observe the Sabbath, refrain from evildoing, and keep the covenant are welcome as members of God's people. They may no longer be excluded because they are foreigners or eunuchs (cf. Deut 23:2). God will even choose ministers of prayer from these former outcasts (Isa 56:6; cf. 66:21). "Their holocausts and sacrifices will be acceptable on [God's] altar" (56:7). God will gather even more people than may be anticipated (56:8). "May all peoples praise you, God!"

The gospel story (Matt 15:21-28) illustrates the influence of exclusion even on the ministry of Jesus. When a Canaanite woman begs for a miracle, Jesus does not answer her and the disciples want to send her away. Jesus finally tells her, "I was sent only to the lost sheep of the house of Israel" (15:24). When she continues to beg, he insinuates that she is a dog (a pejorative term for a Gentile). But refusing to be insulted she turns his words to her advantage. Jesus, who delights in wit, is conquered by her faith. The miracle is a sign of the opening of God's kingdom even to the Gentiles.

The second reading (Rom 11:13-15, 29-32) reverses the parties but the temptation to exclusion is the same. Paul exhorts Gentile Christians to long as he does for the unity of Jews and Gentiles in the same community. The gifts received by the Jews have become blessing for the Gentiles. How great it will be when the gifts received by the Gentiles will become blessing for the Jews.

We pray in Psalm 67 for the opening of God's kingdom to all peoples. Who are the outcasts within our own communities? Where do we prevent God's blessing from reaching its intended goal, all peoples? Our singing of this psalm is a pledge to open our doors and share our blessings with all who love the Lord's name and keep the covenant. God, "may all the peoples praise you!"

9. Psalm 92

The title of Psalm 92 designates it a Sabbath song. During the Second Temple period (515 BCE–70 CE) a specially designated psalm was sung every day after the morning sacrifice. Psalm 92 is the only psalm with a such a designation in the Hebrew psalter. In the Greek translation Psalms 24, 48, 93, and 94 also are set apart for specific days of the week.[14] The musical indications within the psalm also suggest that it belongs in a liturgical setting.

[14]Sabourin 289–291.

The psalm praises God for vindication over enemies. There are three stanzas (2-5, 6-10, 11-16). The first stanza proclaims the intent to praise. Time is no object. God's praise must continue day and night. God keeps the covenant through love (*hesed*) and fidelity. God's acts bring joy to the faithful.

The second and third stanzas are more specific about God's acts. The second stanza (6-10) declares that even though the wicked may prosper now, they are already doomed. God's enemies (presumed to be the same as the psalmist's) will certainly perish. Only the wise who wait for God can understand this. The third stanza (11-16) focuses on the just. God's works fill the just with delight. Their lives are rich. They are vigorous as a wild animal, productive as a flourishing tree. Even into old age they continue praising God.

The psalmist claims to be anointed by God (11). The anointing may be a symbol of joy (cf. Ps 45:8) or strength (parallel to "horn" in 11a; cf. Ps 89:21-22), or the psalmist may be the anointed king or priest. If the psalmist is a priest, that strengthens the liturgical orientation of the psalm. If the psalmist is the king, the psalm should be read in light of other royal psalms (e.g., Ps 18).

8th Sun Year C (2-3.13-14.15-16) [85]

Lord, it is good to give thanks to you (2).

The verses chosen from Psalm 92 for the Eighth Sunday of Year C are taken from the first and third stanzas of the psalm. The verses declare the intent to praise God continually and describe the vigor of the just.

The readings for this Sunday emphasize testing and enhance the wisdom contrast in the psalm between good and bad. The sage Ben Sira (Sir 27:4-7) proposes a way to judge a person's character. The test is a person's speech. Just as the kiln proves the pot and the fruit proves the tree, so conversation proves the true worth of a person.

In the gospel (Luke 6:39-45) Jesus warns against judging others and excusing ourselves. He also uses the image of a tree's fruit to describe the true test of a person's virtue. A good person produces goodness; an evil person produces evil. Each one speaks from the heart's abundance.

Psalm 92 describes the good tree even more closely. The wicked, even though they seem to flourish, will die. The just, however, bear fruit even in old age. They praise God day and night, declaring, "The LORD is just" (Ps 92:13, 16). They know the true source of their goodness and praise God for the harvest of good fruit.

Paul (1 Cor 15:54-58) writes of the test of the final harvest. For those who are steadfast and persevering, the final harvest is everlasting life. The just know that their toil is not in vain when it is done in the Lord. The Lord gives them the strength of a wild bull (Ps 92:11) and plants them in the holy place. They shall bear fruit forever and give thanks to God without end.

The wisdom theme of testing the just and the wicked through speech is worth our consideration this Sunday. We speak from our heart's abundance; our conversation is the test. Our words reveal where we are planted.

11th Sun Year B (2-3.13-14.15-16) [93]

Lord, it is good to give thanks to you (2).

The refrain and verses of Psalm 92 chosen for the Eleventh Sunday of Year B are the same as those for the Eighth Sunday of Year C (see above). The reason for the choice of Psalm 92 for this Sunday is obvious (as it was for the Sunday described above). The image of trees and plants predominates in the readings.

In chapter 17 the prophet Ezekiel compares God's people to a great tree. An eagle cropped off the top of the tree, i.e., Babylon took the powerful of the land into Exile in 597 BCE. The tree then became a lowly vine but turned its roots toward another eagle, Egypt. Therefore God will bring the Babylonians back to destroy the land and take more of the people into Exile (587 BCE). Today's reading (17:22-24) ends the chapter. God will save a remnant of the exiled people (the tender shoot) and will restore them in the land (planting the shoot on the mountains of Israel). It is God who has the power; those who trust in God will flourish even though now they seem to wither.

The psalm addresses the same issue. Even though the wicked flourish now, they are doomed (Ps 92:8). The just, on the other hand, will bear fruit even in old age (92:13-15). They trust in the Lord, the rock in whom there is no wrong.

The two parables of Jesus (Mark 4:26-34) illustrate the hidden and mysterious growth of God's kingdom. The seed scattered by the farmer grows through the power of God. Even the smallest seed can grow into a large plant. The underlying message is again trust in God. It is God who gives growth to the plant; it is God who gives growth to the kingdom.

Paul expresses his own trust in God (2 Cor 5:6-10). It is God who decides whether we are in the body or not. But Paul adds an important insight. Knowing that God has the power, we exercise every human effort to please God. Psalm 92 describes the different fate of just and wicked. The wicked perish; the just flourish. Paul describes the same judgment. Each receives recompense according to life in the body. The wicked will wither like grass (cf. Ps 92:8); the just shall flourish like the palm tree (Ps 92:13). "The LORD is just, our rock in whom there is no wrong" (Ps 92:16).

10. Psalm 107 (Communal)

Psalm 107 is an all-purpose song of thanksgiving. The beginning and ending put all thanksgiving in the context of God's covenant love (*hesed* = merciful deeds, v. 43). The four stanzas following the introduction (4-9, 10-16, 17-22, 23-32) each state a specific kind of danger and call for thanksgiving to God who saves. Kraus proposes that the original situation may have been a communal celebration of thanksgiving similar to a mass celebration of marriage or general absolution performed in time of need. Each person comes prepared to offer the individual thanksgiving sacrifice. The psalm is the general introduction to this communal liturgy.[15]

The introduction (1-3) presents the key concepts: give thanks, Yahweh's *hesed*, the redeemed, the gathered. The whole psalm is a call to give thanks in all life's situations. God's covenant love endures forever (cf. Psalm 136). In faithfulness God has redeemed the people, has acted as the next-of-kin (*go'el*) who is responsible for their lives. In faithfulness God has gathered them from every corner of the world.

The four stanzas single out four specific groups: desert wanderers, the imprisoned, the sick, and seafarers. The first three stanzas could be related to the journey from Egypt to the promised land or to the return from Exile as well as to individual experiences. God saves the nation; God saves its individual members. The second and third stanzas relate the cause of danger to sin. Even though the relationship between the two is ambiguous— the sufferer is not always the sinner—it is a wise insight that sin causes suffering somewhere. The one giving thanks may not forget that fact.

The structure of the four central stanzas is an instruction on how to give thanks. Each stanza opens with a description of the problem (4-5, 10-12, 17-18, 23-27). A refrain follows: "In their distress they cried to the LORD" (6, 13, 19, 28). There is a lesson here on what to do in danger. In Egypt when the people cry out God begins the process of Exodus (Exod 2:23). Throughout the Book of Judges, when the people cry out God sends a judge to save them from their enemies (Judg 3:9, 15; 4:3; 6:6-7). In Psalm 107, when they cry out God rescues, saves, brings out. A second refrain follows the description of deliverance: "Let them thank the LORD for such kindness (*hesed*), such wondrous deeds for mere mortals" (8, 15, 21, 31). In the first two stanzas the thanksgiving refrain is followed by a statement of God's deliverance (9, 16). In the third and fourth stanzas it is followed by

[15]Kraus 2.910–911; cf. Sabourin 291.

a further specification of the thanksgiving: offer sacrifice (22), give praise in the assembly (32). The four stanzas combined teach us how to give thanks.[16]

The final stanza (33-43) is a hymn to God's power. God can and will give all good things to the people who trust, but the wicked will lose even what they seem to have. The psalm closes with a wisdom saying: "Whoever is wise will take note of these things, will ponder the merciful deeds (*hesed*, pl.) of the LORD."

12th Sun Year B (23-24.25-26.28-29.30-31) [96]

Give thanks to the Lord whose love is everlasting (1).

The verses chosen from Psalm 107 for the Twelfth Sunday of Year B are taken from the fourth description of danger, that of seafarers. The specific attention to the sea relates to the gospel story of Jesus calming the storm at sea. The refrain is the introductory call to thanksgiving.

The readings all set before us the overwhelming power of God. The first reading is taken from the Yahweh speeches in the Book of Job. Throughout the book Job has demanded an answer from God concerning his sufferings. His friends have made the too-simple equation, sufferer equals sinner. Job knows that is not right, and demands God's explanation. And so the mighty God, cloaked in the whirlwind, comes to speak to Job. The speeches of Yahweh do not explain Job's experience. Instead they introduce Job into God's experience, the experience of a creator who cares for all things in wisdom and love. Job begins to see from another perspective and surrenders to the care of God (42:1-6).

This Sunday's reading (Job 38:1, 8-11) describes God's power in terms of the mythological defeat of the sea, symbol of chaos. In contrast to the Canaanite god Ba'al, who has to do battle with the sea, Yahweh speaks and the destructive power of the sea is limited.

The psalm also celebrates Yahweh's power over all the destructive expressions of chaos including sin and suffering. "Let [us] thank the LORD for such kindness, such wondrous deeds for mere mortals" (Ps 107:31).

The gospel (Mark 4:35-41) tells the story of Jesus calming a storm at sea. The disciples, who are slow to understand in the Gospel of Mark, wake Jesus with the words, "Do you not care that we are perishing?" After Jesus calms the storm they ask the right question, "Who then is this whom even wind and sea obey?" Who indeed is this, who participates in the very creative power of God?

---

[16]See Stuhlmueller 2.123 for an outline of the structure.

The second reading (2 Cor 5:14-17) tells us the extent of God's creative power in Christ. In Christ all have died and have been created anew. The sea is a symbol of chaotic power; Jesus' stilling the storm symbolizes his victory over chaos. In Christ God has defeated the ultimate manifestations of chaos, sin and death, and has established for all time the new creation.

We have seen the great power of God's *hesed*. Our experience gives us a two-fold challenge. We who have experienced God's creative love are called to limit and defeat the power of chaos in our world today, homelessness, imprisonment, sickness, starvation, and death. We are also called to gather all people to join us in thanksgiving for God's merciful deeds. "Give thanks to the LORD, . . . whose love endures forever!"

11. Psalm 116

Often thanksgiving psalms shift back and forth between praise of God and description of past danger. This alternating mood adds to the intensity of Psalm 116. The shift is found in each of the three stanzas (1-4, 5-9, 10-19).

The first stanza (1-4) opens not with thanksgiving but at the deeper level of love. The only worthy response to the God who listens and delivers is love. In this stanza is the first description of distress. Death itself draws the psalmist down to Sheol. Deliverance comes because the psalmist calls upon the name of the Lord. The call in the first stanza is a call out of agony and dread. The phrase, "call on the name of the LORD," occurs twice more, both times in thanksgiving (13, 17). The act of calling is the turning point.

The second stanza (5-9) begins with general statements about God, deduced from the specific experience of deliverance. The covenant God is indeed gracious, just, and merciful. The psalmist is now certain that God saves the vulnerable. The psalmist can rest in confidence because of the Lord's goodness. The meditation on God leads to a renewed thanksgiving for deliverance. The psalmist again turns to God. Every part of the person has been saved—soul, eyes, feet. No longer threatened with death, the psalmist vows to walk before the Lord in the land of the living.

The final stanza (10-19) returns again to the terrible experience of suffering. Even in the face of human treachery, the psalmist continued to trust God. The remainder of the psalm is an ecstatic outburst of thanksgiving to God who did not abandon the sufferer. The psalmist exclaims that no thanksgiving can ever match God's goodness. Nonetheless vows must be paid; the thanksgiving sacrifice must be offered (13, 17). The psalmist, who has escaped the bitter cup of suffering, will raise the cup of salvation. The cup of salvation is either a libation, poured out as part of the thanksgiving sacrifice (cf. Exod 29:40; Num 28:7) or a cup shared as part of the thanksgiving banquet (cf. Ps 23:5; 1 Cor 10:16).[17] In either case the psalmist calls on the name of the Lord, bearing witness that the Lord saves. The psalmist, comparing himself to a houseborn slave with no possibility of release (cf. Exod 21:4), praises God for caring too much to let a faithful one die: "Too costly in the eyes of the LORD is the death of [the] faithful" (Ps 116:15). The psalm ends with a renewed promise of a thanksgiving sacrifice in the Jerusalem temple.

2nd Sun Lent B (10.15.16-17.18-19) [26]

I will walk in the presence of the Lord, in the land of the living (9).

The refrain for the Second Sunday of Lent B is the psalmist's joyful vow, having escaped death, to be faithful to God in life. The verses are all taken from the final stanza. Verse 10 is the psalmist's declaration of constancy even in the midst of terrible suffering. Verse 15 is praise of God who would not let the faithful servant suffer death. The rest of the verses are the pledge from this lifelong servant to offer a sacrifice of thanksgiving.

The Genesis reading (22:1-2, 9, 10-13, 15-18) tells the story of God's test of Abraham: "Take your son Isaac, your only one whom you love, and . . . offer him up as a holocaust." It is a story of agony and dread, of trust in the face of terrible suffering. Abraham obeys without question, but "too costly in the eyes of the LORD is the death of [the] faithful" (Ps 116:15). God substitutes a ram for Isaac. Both Abraham and Isaac have been saved from the snares of Sheol. Both can walk before the Lord in the land of the living.

We sing the psalm in the voices of both Abraham and Isaac. Abraham kept faith, even when he said, "I am greatly afflicted" (Ps 116:10). Isaac's death was too costly for God. Together we can sing the thanksgiving of both men.

The reading from Rom 8:31-34 presents us with a paradox. God did not spare his own Son but handed him over for us all. God, who finds the death of the faithful too costly, delivers his own Son to death. His death is even more costly to God. Therefore God releases him from death and us along with him. Death has been conquered through the obedience of Christ. Now all of us can walk before the Lord in the land of the living, even into eternal life (Ps 116:9). How can we repay the Lord for all the good done for us (12)? We will offer a sacrifice of thanksgiving and call on the name of the Lord (17).

The gospel (Mark 9:2-10) gives us a glimpse of God's glorious life shining through Jesus. The obedient Son, who places no obstacle before the

---

[17]For more on "cup," cf. Kraus 2.972; Dahood 3.149.

will of the Father, becomes completely transparent to the Father's glory. Death has been conquered; we rejoice in the land of the living.

Holy Thursday: Mass of the Lord's Supper ABC (12-13.15-16.17-18) [40]

Our blessing cup is a communion with the blood of Christ (1 Cor 10:16).

The refrain for Holy Thursday is taken from 1 Corinthians 10. It refers to the blessing cup of the Eucharist. In Judaism the blessing cup is the third cup of the Passover celebration. Psalm 116 also refers to a cup, the cup of salvation, which may have been a libation cup offered in sacrifice or a cup shared at the sacrificial banquet. The richness of the image is fitting for the Mass of the Lord's Supper. The psalm verses are all from the thanksgiving section of the final stanza. The psalmist proclaims the impossibility of ever thanking God enough and vows to offer the customary thanksgiving sacrifice.

The first reading (Exod 12:1-8, 11-14) is the priestly legislation for the celebration of Passover. The Passover is the memorial of God's deliverance of the chosen people from Egyptian slavery. The exodus is the experience which defines God and the people. God is the one who delivers them when they are helpless. Every thanksgiving song of God's people is a reminder of the constant thanksgiving due to God for that primary experience of salvation. "How can I repay the LORD for all the good done for me" (Ps 116:12).

In 1 Cor 11:23-26, Paul recites the traditional narrative of the primary Christian memorial of God's deliverance in Christ. This memorial, like Passover, refers to a festival meal and to blood, signs of shared life. The blessing cup of each celebration unites those who share it with each other and with God. Each blessing cup is a cup of salvation, marking God's rescue of the costly lives of the faithful. Each memorial is a celebration of thanksgiving to God for so great a love.

The gospel (John 13:1-15) describes the other Christian memorial of our salvation in Christ. Just as he will lay down his life for the sake of others and take it up again, Jesus lays down his outer garments in service and takes them up again. This is the model for his disciples to follow. As he has done, we also must do. This is another sign of shared life. This is another memorial. This is another sacrifice of thanksgiving.

24th Sun Year B (1-2.3-4.5-6.8-9) [132]

I will walk in the presence of the Lord, in the land of the living (9).

The first two stanzas of Psalm 116, with the exception of verse 7, are used on the Twenty-Fourth Sunday of Year B. The psalmist sings his love for God who has saved him from death. The refrain is the psalmist's pledge to follow God's ways throughout life.

Trust in God even in the face of suffering is the theme of this Sunday's readings. The refrain is a brave statement of faith as well as thanksgiving. The reading from Isaiah (50:4-9) is the third Servant song. The element of suffering increases throughout these four songs. In this third song the Servant stands before God in obedience (an open ear) and trust. God is a secure help, therefore the Servant is able to submit to persecutors. The Servant knows that no opposition is stronger than God's support. The Servant trusts God as the ultimate defense.

Psalm 116 looks at the reality of suffering from the other side. The psalmist has already experienced God's deliverance. The psalmist knows in fact what the Servant asserts in hope.

In the gospel (Mark 8:27-35) we find the paradox of Jesus, the Messiah, announcing his impending suffering and death. No one escapes suffering, not even God's Servant, not even God's Messiah. Jesus' followers cannot expect to escape either. Whoever of you wish to come after me must deny yourselves, take up your cross, and follow me.

Our faith in Christ takes us even farther. We believe that he is risen, that God indeed saved his life. We believe that his death and resurrection have won life for us, that through him God has freed our souls from death, our eyes from tears, our feet from stumbling. We sing Psalm 116 in a spirit of both thanksgiving and trust, thanksgiving for Christ's victory over death, trust that we shall walk in his presence in eternal life.

The Letter of James tells us, however, that faith is useless without works (Jas 2:14-18). Our faith in eternal life has value only insofar as we walk in God's presence in this present life. To walk in God's presence is to follow God's Law day after day (cf. Gen 17:1). Jesus equates following him with taking up the Cross. James is quite specific in telling us how to do this. If we do not feed the hungry or clothe the naked, how can we claim to walk in God's presence? Who can believe either our trust in God or our thanksgiving for God's gift of life if we spend all our energy insulating ourselves from the demands of others? We must be prepared to recognize the genuine commitment in singing this Sunday's refrain: "I will walk in the presence of the LORD in the land of the living."

Corpus Christi B (12-13.15-16.17-18) [169]

I will take the cup of salvation and call on the name of the Lord (13).

The verses of Psalm 116 chosen for Corpus Christi B are the same as those for Holy Thursday (see above). The refrain is the psalm's reference to the cup of salvation. (See Holy Thursday for a discussion of the "cup.")

In the three-year cycle the Corpus Christi readings focus on different elements of the mystery of the Body of Christ. In Cycle B the focus is on the "blood of the covenant." The first reading (Exod 24:3-8) describes the sealing of the Sinai covenant. There are in fact two rituals of sealing, a blood rite (24:3-8) and a shared meal (24:1-2, 9-10). Both rituals signify shared life. Only the blood rite is proclaimed on this feast.

Throughout the ancient world blood is a sign of life. God's people are forbidden to eat meat with the blood still in it because in the blood is the life and the life belongs to God (cf. Gen 9:4-6; Lev 17:10-11, 14; Deut 12:23-25). In this ritual at Sinai the blood of sacrificed animals is sprinkled on the altar, which signifies God, and on the people. The people thus become blood relatives of God. God is their next-of-kin, who is responsible for their lives. That is the significance of the covenant.

In Psalm 116 we see that God is indeed just (116:5). God honors the responsibility of the covenant and protects the lives of the covenant people. "Too costly in the eyes of the LORD is the death of [the] faithful" (15). The next-of-kin is also responsible to ransom a relative from slavery. We sing, "you have loosed my bonds," now "I am your servant" (cf. 16). The psalm is the joyful thanksgiving of one of God's covenant people.

The New Testament readings teach the real depth of the covenant bond between God and the people. The gospel (Mark 14:12-16, 22-26) describes the sealing of the new covenant, again with the life-sharing rituals of meal and blood. The Letter to the Hebrews (Heb 9:11-15) reminds us that in this ritual the blood is not that of sacrificed animals but of Christ himself. The sharing of life has moved from sign to reality. This sharing of life not only makes us blood relatives of God but incorporates us into the life of God's Son. We become, through the sharing of this blood, the Body of Christ.

Confronted by this mystery, we are grateful for the psalmist's words: "How can I repay the LORD for all the good done for me?" (12). We will raise the cup of salvation, the cup of our Passover celebration, the banquet cup of shared life, the cup which contains the new covenant in Christ's blood. We will raise the cup which is our thanksgiving sacrifice and call on the name of the Lord.

Through this mystery we are bound also to one another, more intimately than we are bound even to our own bodies. We take on the responsibility of shared life, of the next-of-kin. We are responsible to release those enslaved by ignorance, drugs, the structures of our society and Church. We are responsible for the lives of those threatened by war, violence, poverty. "Too costly in the eyes of the LORD is the death of [the] faithful" (15). Too costly in our eyes also.

All Souls (5.6.10-11.15-16?) [791]

I will walk in the presence of the Lord, in the land of the living (9).

Psalm 116 is one of ten possible choices for All Souls Day (Common of the Dead). The refrain shows an enlightening ambiguity. In the mind of the psalmist "the land of the living" meant this present life. The psalmist thanks God for deliverance from death and promises to follow God's Law in life. In the context of Christian revelation God's deliverance from death is believed to be even beyond physical death, a notion which appears only in very late Old Testament books. Through Christ's death and resurrection, the lasting power of death has been conquered forever (cf. Ps 116:15). God found the death of the faithful too costly and has loosed our bonds forever. The psalm verses praise God for mercifully saving the helpless (5-6). The psalmist clings to faith in God even in great danger (10-11), and gives thanks for God's wonderful deliverance (15-16). Both thanksgiving and faith inspire the refrain "I shall walk before the LORD in the land of the living."

Any readings which express a belief in God's rescue from death would go well with Psalm 116. Some possibilities from the Old Testament readings are: Wis 3:1-9, "their hope [is] full of immortality"; Dan 12:1-3, "many of those who sleep in the dust . . . shall awake"; 2 Macc 12:43-46, "the resurrection of the dead in view."

Four New Testament letters are particularly apt: Rom 8:14-23, "the sufferings of this present time are as nothing compared with the glory to be revealed for us"; Rom 8:31-35, 37-39, "neither death, nor life . . . will be able to separate us from the love of God"; Rom 14:7-9, 10-12, "whether we live or die, we are the Lord's"; 1 Cor 15:51-57, "where, O death, is your victory?"

Four gospel passages emphasize that the death of the faithful is too costly in the eyes of the Lord: Mark 15:33-39; 16:1-6, "He has been raised; he is not here"; Luke 23:44- 49; 24:1-6, "Why do you seek the living one among the dead?"; John 11:17-27, "I am the resurrection and the life"; John 11:32-45, "If you believe you will see the glory of God." The emphasis on God's revelation to the lowly in Matt 11:25-30 is also echoed in Ps 116:6: "The LORD protects the simple; I was helpless but God saved me."

12. Psalm 118

Psalm 118 is an individual thanksgiving that has been shaped into a liturgy. The resulting psalm is an excellent illustration of the interweaving of individual and communal prayer. The individual relationship with God always flows from the communal experience of covenant, the communal prayer is always nourished by the individual experience of God.

The effectiveness of Psalm 118 consists in its frequent intensifying repetition and its free-flowing structure. The introduction (1-4) is a liturgical call to prayer, unique in the psalms of thanksgiving. The large middle section (5-18) consists of one or many individual songs of thanksgiving. The psalm concludes (19-29) with a ritual dialogue of praise, blessing, and acclamation.

The liturgical introduction (1-4) consists of a litany in which three groups are called to give thanks to Yahweh whose love (*hesed*) endures forever (cf. Ps 136). *Hesed* is the bond of covenant love which obligates both God and the people. God's faithfulness to that love is the source of every good thing for the people. All thanksgiving ultimately focuses on God's *hesed*. (See Psalms 25, 136 for further discussion of *hesed*.) The house of Israel, God's people, is called to give thanks. The house of Aaron, the priestly clan, is called along with all those who fear the Lord, who are awed at God's great goodness.

The middle section (5-18) has been variously interpreted. There are signs of royal thanksgiving, a victory song in triumph over all the nations. It is also possible that various people are assembled to give thanks, beginning in turn at verses 5, 10, 17, for example. In either case, whether of the king or several individuals, the deliverance becomes a cause for the entire community to give thanks. Throughout this section it is the Lord who is the center of attention. The name Yahweh occurs in every verse from 5-20 (in vv. 5, 14, 17, 18, 19, the ancient form of God's name, Yah, appears).

The first part of the thanksgiving (5-9) sounds like the response to a salvation oracle: "Fear not; I am with you." The enemy is identified simply as humanity, '*adam* (6). Two wisdom sayings (8-9) advise that it is better to trust God than any human being, no matter how powerful. The thanksgiving continues with a description of battle against the enemies (10-14). As in the Exodus paradigm, it is God who has the power. The Lord's name is the weapon which wins the victory. The Lord is strength and might (cf. Exod 15:2; Isa 12:2). The victory is proclaimed (15-18) in the "tents of the just" (*saddiqim*, 15). Justice or righteousness is always based on relationship. Those who have clung to God experience the victory. Their trust in the relationship brings God's answering fidelity. God's power is used for them. In the same light even their suffering is seen as an expression of God's care for them. Their restoration to life is a call to bear witness to God's goodness.

The liturgical orientation of the psalm returns in the call to open the gates of victory/justice (*sedeq*, 19) for the thanksgiving procession of the victors/just (*saddiqim*, 20). The petitioner gives thanks (21); the congregation responds with a proverb proclaiming the paradox of rescue and exaltation (22). Their song continues, attributing the wonderful deed, the wonderful day, to God (23-24). In their joy they link petition and praise: "LORD, grant salvation," in Hebrew *hoshi'a-na'*, from which we derive "hosanna!"[18]

The petitioner, the one who comes in the Lord's name, is blessed by the priests, the house of Aaron (3), with the priestly blessing (26-27, cf. Num 6:25). The psalm concludes with the repeated thanksgiving of the individual (28) and the acclamation of the people (29), which repeats the first verse of the psalm and binds the thanksgiving into a circle: "Give thanks to the LORD, who is good, whose love endures forever!"[19]

Easter Vigil 8 (1-2.16.17.22-23) [42]

Alleluia, Alleluia, Alleluia!

Psalm 118 is the Church's Easter psalm *par excellence*. The great alleluia, which has been silent since Ash Wednesday, returns in the Easter vigil accompanied by Psalm 118. Throughout the Easter octave the alleluia verse is taken from Ps 118:24: "This is the day the LORD has made!" The verses of Psalm 118 which accompany the alleluia of the Easter vigil are taken from all three sections of the psalm: the liturgical introduction (1-2); the individual thanksgiving for deliverance from death (16-17); and the community's thankful response (22-23). Thus as we sing the alleluia we are able to lead the call to give thanks, to declare with Christ God's victory, and to respond in joy as God's people.

The alleluia comes at the end of a long recital of God's bringing life from death, beginning with the defeat of chaos in Gen 1 and ending with Paul's proclamation (Rom 6:3-11) that God in Christ has given us all eternal life. We who have been baptized into Christ have gone with him into death. But through his resurrection we have been delivered from death once and for all. With him we can shout: "I shall not die but live and declare the deeds of the LORD" (17).

The gospel tells the story of the empty tomb, the first human inkling of the tremendous mystery of resurrection (Matt 28:1-10, Year A; Mark 16:1-8, Year B; Luke 24:1-12, Year C). This is God's greatest deliverance; it calls for our most profound thanksgiving. God's *hesed* does indeed endure forever.

[18]For further discussion in hosanna, cf. Stuhlmueller 2.150.
[19]Psalm 118 is widely used in the NT; cf. Stuhlmueller 2.150–151; Sabourin 170.

Easter Sunday ABC (1-2.16-17.22-23) [43]

This is the day the Lord has made; let us rejoice and be glad (24).

The verses of Psalm 118 selected for Easter Sunday ABC are the same as those for the Easter Vigil (see above). The refrain is the joyful shout of the assembled community as the thanksgiving procession enters: "This is the day the Lord has made; let us rejoice and be glad."

The first reading (Acts 10:34, 37-43) is Peter's speech on the occasion of the baptism of Cornelius. Through the story Luke describes the opening of Christianity to Gentiles as well as Jews. During Peter's speech the Holy Spirit falls upon all present. The circumcised believers are astounded that God's gifts are given to Gentiles too. The good news which Peter preaches is that in Christ God has rescued Gentiles too from death. Not only the house of Israel, not only the house of Aaron, but all who fear the Lord are called to give thanks (118:4). Not only Israelites may enter the gates of victory, but all the just whose relationship with God has been won in Christ (118:19-20). Those who have been rejected are discovered to be the cornerstone. This is God's doing; it is wonderful in our eyes (118:22-23).

God's wonderful deed has transformed all of human life, has abolished all the old categories (cf. Col 3:1-4; 1 Cor 5:6-8). The sacrifice of thanksgiving consists in letting go of the old life, the old yeast. Even the old pain which centers on self must be transformed into praise of God. The Lord's right hand won the victory; in the Lord's name I triumphed (118:15-16, 10-12). "The LORD is with me; I am not afraid" (118:6). There is no longer the need for defensive separation between people. "What can mortals do against me?" (118:6). What can mortality do against me! "I shall not die but live and declare the deeds of the LORD"(118:17).

The gospel (John 20:1-9) is the fourth empty tomb story (the other three are used in the Easter Vigil). The relationship of the characters in the story again suggests a blurring of distinctions left over from the old yeast, the old life. Magdalene discovers the empty tomb first and runs to tell Peter, the apparent leader of the disciples. Peter and the Beloved Disciple run to confirm the news. The Beloved Disciple, leader of the Johannine community,[20] arrives first but defers to Peter. Peter enters first but the Beloved Disciple is the first of whom faith is reported: "He saw and believed" (20:8). The story is followed by the first appearance of the risen Christ, not to either of the men, but to Magdalene. Thus her story surrounds and supports theirs.

The expected distinctions are blurred. God shows no partiality (Acts 10:34). God's *hesed* extends to all who fear the Lord (cf. 118:1-4). All have

[20]See R. E. Brown, *The Community of the Beloved Disciple* (New York: Paulist, 1979) for a full description of the Johannine community.

been rescued from death; all are called to give thanks—Peter, Cornelius, Magdalene, the Beloved Disciple, and all of us. The joyful shout of deliverance is heard in the tents of the victors: "The LORD's right hand strikes with power!" (118:15). "Open the gates of victory; [we] will enter and thank the LORD" (118:19). No one may be excluded; all join in procession (118:27). "This is the day the LORD has made; let us rejoice in it and be glad" (118:24).

2nd Sun Easter ABC (2-4.13-15.22-24) [44] [45] [46]

Give thanks to the Lord who is good, whose love is everlasting (1).

Although there are separate selections in each of the three cycles for the first two readings of the Second Sunday of Easter, the gospel and the responsorial psalm are the same. Therefore the three Sundays will be treated together.

The refrain is the introductory call to praise. God is faithful to the bond of covenant love. This fidelity is evident in God's goodness toward the people. Therefore all are called to give thanks. The selected verses of Psalm 118 continue with a liturgical litany, calling various groups to answer in thanksgiving. The reason for thanksgiving is taken from the middle part of the psalm: God rescued me from death (13-15). The verses conclude with the community celebration of thanksgiving from the final section of the psalm.

The gospel for the Second Sunday of Easter ABC reports John's account of Jesus' appearance to the disciples after the appearance to Magdalene (John 20:19-31). There are two appearances, one week apart. There are obvious consequences of both appearances. On the first occasion Jesus offers the resurrection gift of peace. The experience of his presence and of seeing his wounds results in joy and faith. Jesus breathes the new life of the Spirit into the disciples and gives them the power to spread that new life through reconciliation. He commissions them to do as he has done. Between the two appearances Thomas, who was absent on the first occasion, declares that without experience of the risen Christ he will not believe. Jesus returns to minister to Thomas, whose declaration of faith surpasses that of the other ten. The passage ends with two sayings. Jesus declares those blessed who have not seen and have believed. The evangelist announces that his intention in writing is that we may come to believe and thus have life.

The story of Thomas shows that experience of the risen Christ is necessary for faith. But how is that experience possible for those who "have not seen." The evangelist tells us one way, through the written good news. The first reading of the three cycles for this Sunday tells us another, which is suggested by the commissioning in the gospel. People come to believe through experience of the risen Christ within the community. The community which lives in peace through mutual forgiveness and love mediates the presence of Christ to others.

Luke's three summaries of the ideal Christian life (Acts 2:42-47; 4:32-35; 5:12-16) show us the result of faith in Christ: a community of one heart and one mind. Spiritual needs are cared for in common through the teaching of the apostles, the breaking of bread, the prayers, and the communal life itself. Material needs are cared for through the sharing of possessions. The witness of this communal life fulfills Jesus' commission, "as the Father has sent me, so I send you," and draws others to join them. Their common life gives others the experience of the risen Christ necessary for faith.

In Year A the second reading (1 Pet 1:3-9) is an exhortation to Gentile Christians to praise God for their new birth into faith. Suffering cannot diminish such faith which is characterized by joy and love. These Christians, although they have never seen Christ, believe because of the ministry of other believers who preached the good news to them through the Holy Spirit (cf. 1 Pet 1:12). Through them they have touched the risen Christ.

In Year B the First Letter of John (1 John 5:1-6) tells us that those who believe that Jesus is the Christ are begotten by God. The love which binds the Christian community together is the love of God's children for one another. This love is demonstrated in the commandments which can be summarized in two: love God and love one another. This life of love is the gift of the risen Christ. It is the sign of the Spirit within the community. It conquers the world because it draws all people to faith that Jesus is indeed the Son of God.

The reading from Revelation for Year C (Rev 1:9-11, 12-13, 17-19) describes the author's experience of the risen and glorified Christ, the first and the last and the one who lives. Like the disciples in the gospel, the visionary is commanded to bear witness. He is called to write the vision that others may share his experience of the risen Christ and come to believe.

How fitting that the responsorial psalm should be an individual song of thanksgiving that has become a community liturgy. The opening litany calls all people to praise in an ever widening circle. The experience of death's threat is always individual. God's rescue teaches us one by one to proclaim that the Lord, "my strength and might, came to me as savior" (14). But thanksgiving must overflow in praise. None of us has sufficient strength to give thanks alone. The community, which grows in faith because of the experience of each believer, shouts in joyful praise of God who delivers. One by one each rejected stone supports the building. "By the LORD has this been done; it is wonderful in our eyes. This is the day the LORD has made; let us rejoice in it and be glad" (118:23-24). May our common life bring all people to experience the risen Christ that all may join in the cry: "Give thanks to the LORD, who is good, whose love endures forever" (1).

4th Sun Easter B (1.8-9.21-23.26.21.29) [51]

The stone rejected by the builders has become the cornerstone (22).

The psalm refrain for the Fourth Sunday of Easter B is the verse of Psalm 118 which is quoted in the first reading. In the psalm the community identifies the former sufferer as one who was rejected but has now been exalted. In the New Testament this phrase is applied to Jesus (Acts 4:11; 1 Pet 2:7; cf. Matt 21:42; Luke 20:17). The verses are chosen from throughout the psalm. They include the introductory call to give thanks (1), two wisdom sayings concerning trust in God (8-9), several verses from the dialogue at the temple gates (21-23, 26), and the repeated call to praise (29). The individual thanksgiving of verse 21 is repeated. Why? There is also a verse in sequence which is an individual thanksgiving (28) which seems to serve just as well. Perhaps verse 21 is repeated for the sake of the word "savior" (cf. Acts 4:12).

The first reading (Acts 4:8-12) continues Luke's story of the early church. Peter and John are interrogated by the Sanhedrin for a miracle they have worked. They declare that the healing power resides in the name of Jesus, the only name by which we are to be saved. Peter identifies Jesus as the sufferer of Psalm 118 whom God rescued from death. He addresses the Sanhedrin as enemies who rejected the sufferer whom God has now made the cornerstone. Through his suffering and exaltation all other sufferers are now healed. All other sufferers may now join in the thanksgiving hymn of Psalm 118. Through him God has answered us all.

Jesus, the Good Shepherd (John 10:11-18), has freely laid down his life for his sheep. He has become both the sufferer and the savior. His resurrection, his rescue from death, is at once his own experience of God's enduring love and the gift of God's love to us. God's enduring love has made us with him children of God (1 John 3:1-2). Our rejection by the world corresponds to the rejection of God's Son, the cornerstone. He has been exalted by God and it is wonderful in our eyes. But that is not enough for God's enduring love. We hope for exaltation too. Our hope stretches toward a future when even we shall be like God for we shall truly see God. "Give thanks to the LORD, who is good, whose love endures forever!"

Easter Common (1-2.16-17.22-23) [175]

This is the day the Lord has made; let us rejoice and be glad (24).

Psalm 118 is one of two psalms given for the Easter Common (see also

Psalm 66). The refrain and verses are the same as those for Easter Sunday (see above).

It is certainly appropriate that Psalm 118 be listed in the Common for Easter. The psalm is already used for the Easter Vigil, Easter Sunday, and the Second Sunday of Easter in all three cycles, as well as the Fourth Sunday of Easter in Cycle B. In the current Sunday Lectionary Psalm 118 is never used outside the Easter season. Its content makes it a fitting choice for the Easter Season. The thanksgiving of an individual rescued from death is taken up into the thanksgiving of the whole people. Easter celebrates the mystery that Jesus' resurrection has become the whole people's rescue from death. In him we all sing, "I shall not die but live and declare the deeds of the LORD" (Ps 118:17).

The psalm could well be used on any of the remaining Sundays of Easter. In the celebration of Easter's fifty days every Sunday is the day the Lord has made. Let us rejoice in it and be glad!

13. Psalm 138

Psalm 138 is a thanksgiving song of an individual. There is some disagreement whether the individual is the king, a priest, or an ordinary person. In any case, the song borrows traditional phrases to proclaim gratitude which reaches from heaven to earth.

The opening stanza (1-3) presents the declaration of thanksgiving and the reasons for thanksgiving. The psalmist sings to Yahweh in the presence of *'elohim*. The word *'elohim* can be translated "God" or "gods." It has been variously interpreted to mean the members of Yahweh's court (Ps 82:1; cf. Gen 6:2, 4; Job 1:6; 2:1), the pagan gods of the kings mentioned in verse 4 (cf. Deut 32:8; Josh 24:15; Ps 86:8), idols (cf. Isa 41:23; 42:17), or angels (see the Greek translation).[21] The basis for all these interpretations is the idea that although Yahweh is the only god for Israel, other gods do exist for the other nations. As the belief in only one god began to emerge, the other gods were demythologized and reduced to angels or scorned as empty idols. In Psalm 138 the psalmist is bearing witness to the highest imaginable powers concerning Yahweh's goodness.

Having reached to heaven, the psalmist bows low before God, whose presence (name) and promise are exalted over all. The wonder in the thanksgiving is that the exalted God bends down to answer the lowly sufferer.

The second stanza (4-8) consists of two parts. In verses 4-6 we hear God's praise sung now by earthly powers. All the rulers of the earth will proclaim

---

[21]For further discussion of *'elohim* in Psalm 138 see especially Kraus 2.1088–1089; Stuhlmueller 2.192; Dahood 3.276–277.

the greatness of this God who cares for the lowly. In verses 7-8 the psalmist returns to personal experience and expressions of trust. The thanksgiving continues because God's covenant love and fidelity (*hesed* and *'emeth*, 2, cf. 8) continue. The psalmist closes with a plea that such faith not be in vain.

5th Sun Year C (1-2.2-3.4-5.7-8) [76]

In the sight of the angels I will sing your praises, Lord (1).

All of Psalm 138 is used on the Fifth Sunday of Year C except verses 6 and 7. The two omitted verses refer to God's care of the lowly and the psalmist's own experience of rescue. The refrain is the announcement of thanksgiving in the presence of heavenly powers.

The overall theme for this Sunday is God's call. The psalm puts the experience of call in the context of thanksgiving. The first reading (Isa 6:1-2, 3-8) is the call of the prophet Isaiah. The prophet sees the temple's Holy of Holies transformed into a vision of God's heavenly court. Seraphim surround the throne and proclaim God's holiness. The divine presence is never described; it is symbolized by the train of the garment which fills the temple and by the earthquake and smoke (cf. the theophany at Sinai, Exod 19:16-19). The prophet anticipates death as a result of seeing God. Instead a seraph cleanses his lips so that he may proclaim God's word. Thus prepared the prophet volunteers for his ministry.

The refrain of the psalm suggests a connection between the *'elohim* of the psalm and the *seraphim* of Isaiah's vision. The seraphim, literally "burning ones," may be modeled on the flaming cobras of the Egyptian pantheon (cf. the seraph serpents in Num 21:6-9).[22] In the court of Yahweh they are the lesser gods whom later tradition will identify as angels. In their presence Isaiah receives his call; in their presence we sing for him a song of thanksgiving. Isaiah's ministry, which begins in the temple, will take him before earthly kings, Ahaz and Hezekiah (cf. Ps 138:4). His long ministry is witness to the fact that the Lord was with him to the end (cf. 138:8).

The gospel (Luke 5:1-11) is Luke's version of Jesus' call of the first disciples. After experiencing the miraculous catch of fish, Peter exclaims, "Depart from me, Lord, for I am a sinful man." His protest matches that of Isaiah who, after seeing the heavenly vision, declares that he is a man of unclean lips. The divine response is also parallel. Jesus says to Peter and his companions, "Do not be afraid; from now on you will be catching [people]." Like Isaiah, they left everything and followed him.

"The LORD is on high, but cares for the lowly and knows the proud from afar" (138:6). Confronted by the presence of God, those who are called

[22]J. J. M. Roberts, "Isaiah in Old Testament Theology," *Interpreting the Prophets,* ed. J. L. Mays and P. J. Achtemeier (Philadelphia: Fortress, 1987) 64.

recognize their weakness. Precisely at the point of weakness God enters their lives. No one knows this better than Paul. The second reading (1 Cor 15:1-11) is not the story of Paul's call, but rather his witness to Christianity's central belief, the resurrection of Christ. In presenting his testimony, however, the apostle states his qualifications: ". . . least of the apostles, not fit to be called an apostle . . . .But by the grace of God I am what I am." God's power works through his weakness.

Encouraged by the example of these faithful people, the psalm teaches us how to respond to our own call. "I thank you, LORD, with all my heart"; I bear witness before heavenly powers and earthly rulers. "The LORD is with me to the end"; the Lord's love endures forever.

17th Sun Year C (1-2.2-3.6-7.7-8) [112]

Lord, on the day I called for help, you answered me (3).

The verses of Psalm 138 chosen for the Seventeenth Sunday of Year C emphasize God's ongoing work of deliverance. Only verses 4-5, the reference to the praise of earthly kings, are missing. The refrain is the psalmist's introductory statement of the reasons for thanksgiving.

The readings center on the power and necessity of prayer. In the first reading (Gen 18:20-32) Abraham bargains with God over the fate of Sodom and Gomorrah. He works God down to a price of ten. For the sake of ten innocent people, God will not destroy the cities. But there are not ten innocent people, so destruction comes to Sodom and Gomorrah. On the one hand we see the power of Abraham's prayer and God's willingness to forgive all even for the sake of a few. On the other hand there is the inevitability of judgment if no one turns to God.

Our thanksgiving is filled with awe at the greatness of God's love and fidelity. God cares for the lowly. On the very day I cried out, God answered (3). "The LORD is with me to the end" (8).

Prayer is an important concept throughout the Gospel of Luke. In today's gospel reading (Luke 11:1-13) Jesus' teaching of the Lord's Prayer is followed by several sayings and short parables on prayer. The Lord's Prayer illustrates the simplicity and directness of genuine prayer. The story of the persistent friend teaches the power of persevering prayer. The final sayings emphasize God's willingness to answer prayer with goodness.

In the psalm we proclaim that it is all true. "When I cried out, you answered . . . .LORD, your love endures forever" (3, 8). The example of Abraham and the words of Jesus also teach us the necessity of prayer. If it is true that God answers our cry, that God cares for the lowly, then what is our responsibility for suffering, endangered people who may not have the power to cry out? God brought us to life through Christ when we were still powerless because of sin (cf. Col 2:12-14). Before we were able to cry out, God answered us with life. How great should be our thanksgiving! How fervent our prayer for those in need!

21st Sun Year A (1-2.2-3.6–8) [122]

Lord, your love is eternal; do not forsake the work of your hands (8).

The selection of verses from Psalm 138 for the Twenty-First Sunday of Year A focuses our attention on God. The verses referring to earthly kings (4-5) and even to the psalmist's own distress and rescue (7) are missing. The refrain, however, keeps before us our continuing need for God's deliverance.

The reading from Isaiah (22:15, 19-23) is a story of a shift in political power. Shebna, who has been a scribe under Hezekiah (cf. Isa 36:3) has exalted himself by preparing an elaborate tomb and has put his trust in military power (Isa 22:16-18). Therefore God will remove him from office and replace him with Eliakim, son of Hilkiah. Eliakim, however, is also warned that even if he is a "peg fixed in a sure spot," he too might fall (22:25). Power and authority come from God and belong to God. The proud who trust in themselves will discover that the Lord regards them from afar. The lowly, however, who cry out to the Lord, experience God's enduring love (cf. Ps 138:3, 6).

The gospel (Matt 16:13-20) presents Jesus' founding of the Church upon the disciples, Peter chief among them. Peter has been favored by God with the insight that Jesus is the Messiah. But in only a few verses Peter, trusting in human insight, will reject the idea of Jesus' passion (16:21-23). Jesus tells Peter that the gates of the netherworld will not prevail against the Church. However, the psalm reminds us of what Peter learns by experience, the ongoing need for God's faithful love.

At the end of a meditation on God's enduring choice of the Jews alongside the merciful call of the Gentiles, Paul bursts into rapturous praise of God's mysterious wisdom (Rom 11:33-36). "God delivered all to disobedience" in order to "have mercy upon all" (11:32). In unsearchable wisdom God chooses human beings to be the instruments of salvation for many. But power does not reside ultimately in any human institution, not even the Church. Power and authority belong to God. The human ministers of God's power may never forget the need to cry out: "LORD, . . . never forsake the work of your hands!" (8).

D. Psalms of Confidence

Like the songs of thanksgiving, psalms of confidence develop one of the elements of the lament, the expression of trust in God. Psalms of confidence are distinguished from laments only by emphasis. In the lament the focus is on the distress of the sufferer; in the psalm of confidence the emphasis falls on trust that God can and will protect the faithful.

There is no specific form for the psalms of confidence. Several themes predominate, however. Some psalms of confidence are quiet and gentle, rejoicing in the security that God's care can give. Other psalms of confidence reveal the awareness that danger is not far away, but nothing can shake the psalmist's trust in God. The advice to trust in God alone is repeated often. Only in God can peace and security be found. There is an unwavering assurance that God hears prayer, that God loves deeply, that God is more powerful than any creature.

1. Psalm 4

Psalm 4 is difficult to classify. It is interwoven with elements of both lament and confidence. The cry for help (2) and description of the enemies (3) are characteristic of lament. The expressions of confidence (2, 4, 8-9), however, predominate and give an overall tone to the psalm.

This short psalm may be divided into three stanzas: 2, 3-6, 7-9. The first stanza (2) is a reminder that confidence is not incompatible with the presence of danger. The psalmist is grateful for God's past help and prays for continued aid in the present.

The second stanza (3-6) is addressed to others. Verses 3-4 challenge idol worshippers (worthless lies = idols) who mock the psalmist's trust in Yahweh. The psalmist continues to assert God's loving fidelity to the faithful (*hasidim*). There is assurance that God will hear the cry of verse 2. Verses 5-6 exhort someone (the idol worshippers? or the listening congregation?) to reflect and live without sin; to offer just (*sedeq*) sacrifice to the just (*sedeq*) God (2).[1]

The final stanza (7-9) contrasts the grumbling of the faithless (7) with the joy of the psalmist who trusts in God. Perhaps the murmurers are those who trust in idols (cf. 3). The psalmist knows that Yahweh alone is the source of peace and security.

---

[1] *sedeq*, "righteous," is translated "saving" in verse 2, "fitting" in verse 6.

3rd Sun Easter B (2.4.7-8.9) [48]

Lord, let your face shine on us (7).

The verses chosen from Psalm 4 for the Third Sunday of Easter B represent only portions of the psalm. The description of the enemy (3) and the exhortation (5-6) are omitted from the second stanza, leaving only the expression of confidence. The murmurer's wish for better times (7) and the comparison of the psalmist's joy to a rich harvest are omitted from the third stanza. The result of this selection is that only with verse 2 do more than two consecutive lines of the psalm appear. This piecing together of psalm verses is apparently an attempt to improve the coherence of a somewhat confusing and disjointed psalm.

The refrain is a prayer for God's blessing: Show us the light of your face (cf. Num 6:24-26). In the psalm the prayer for God's blessing seems to be put in the mouth of the murmurers (7). There is a certain aptness then in the use of this verse with the readings for this Sunday. In each reading we see the fragility of human faith. We sing the psalm with all other people whose frailty teaches them that security comes from God alone.

The first reading (Acts 3:13-15, 17-19) is part of Peter's speech after the cure of the crippled beggar. Peter begins by asserting that in no way have he and John worked this miracle by their own power (12). It is through faith in Christ whom God raised from the dead that the man has been healed (16). Peter uses the occasion to point out the faulty human judgment of his listeners who condemned Jesus to death. He then points out to them the way of repentance and conversion, the way to new life.

Repentance and conversion are the way to better times which the murmurers seek. The blessing of God which brings more joy than grain and wine is life in Christ Jesus (cf. Ps 4:8). The psalm is a prayer for all of us whose faith is weak. "Know that the LORD works wonders for the faithful; the LORD hears when [we] call out!" (4).

The passage from 1 John (2:1-5) presents a paradox of weakness and strength. The author exhorts the hearers to avoid sin and to keep Christ's commandments. In the midst of the exhortation, however, is the recognition of the reality of sin. "But if anyone does sin, we have an Advocate with the Father, Jesus Christ the righteous one" (1 John 2:1). It is the Lord who "works wonders for the faithful" (Ps 4:4). The fitting sacrifice we are called to offer is obedience and trust (6).

The disciples to whom the risen Christ appears (Luke 24:35-48) are also examples of weakness turned to strength. The two who have returned from Emmaus have a story of discouragement turned to delight by the presence of Christ. His appearance in the midst of the group in Jerusalem is initially a cause for terror. But again the presence of Christ brings joy and strength to his disciples. "Many say, 'May we see better times!' LORD, show us the light of your face!'" (Ps 4:7).

2. Psalm 16

Psalm 16 is a difficult psalm for scholars and translators. There are serious textual problems, especially in verses 3-4. Translations and interpretations vary widely depending on the text corrections which are adopted. There is no agreement on the date of the psalm; proposals range from the pre-exilic to the intertestamental period (a span of five to eight centuries). Even the genre is debated. Some scholars consider the psalm a lament, but the majority classify it as a psalm of confidence.

For the worshiper, on the other hand, Psalm 16 provides a rich source for prayer. It is a strong statement of confidence in and love for God. The psalm may be considered in two stanzas: 1-6, the contrast between Yahweh's faithful and idol worshippers; 7-11, the rewards of trust in Yahweh.

The psalm opens with a plea that God guard the psalmist. The psalmist then moves to a statement of faith in Yahweh alone. Only Yahweh rules the psalmist; Yahweh is the only source of good. In contrast, those who worship false gods are only courting trouble.[2] The psalmist pledges never to join in idolatrous ritual. The stanza closes with an elaboration of Yahweh as the only good. In these verses (5-6) Yahweh is compared to the inheritance of the land which is the visible sign of the covenant (Lev 25). Since the Levites did not share in the division of the land (cf. Gen 49:5-7), Yahweh was considered their inheritance (cf. Num 18:20; Deut 10:9; Josh 13:14). These psalm verses echo the prayer of the Levites.

The second stanza (7-11) is an ecstatic song of joyful trust in God. God cares for the psalmist night and day. God's presence is protection and delight for the whole person—mind, soul, and body (literally "heart, liver, flesh"). This trust in God cannot be shaken even by death. The psalmist is sure that God will not let the faithful one (*hasid*) die. The original sense of these verses (10-11) seems to be an immediate rescue from a life-threatening situation. As belief in life after death began to develop, however, a deeper meaning could be found. The Greek translation of the psalm (second century BCE) points more clearly to eternal life. In the Acts of the Apostles (2:25-28) Luke cites the Greek translation as a prophecy of Jesus' resurrection.

[2]The interpretation of *qedoshim*, "holy ones," is part of the difficulty in translation. Here it is interpreted as "false gods" (cf. Dahood 1.87–88; Stuhlmueller 1.117). It could also refer to God's faithful people, the *hasidim*, or specifically to the Levites (so Kraus 1.264). These latter interpretations necessitate a different translation of the rest of the verse.

We may join in this psalm at all levels. We too have to make the choice between worshiping "the false gods of the land" and recognizing God as our only good. We too live under constant threat of death. Our cry of faith is a declaration that God will indeed show us the path to life, that the joy of God's presence is our life now and forever.

Easter Vigil 2 (5.8.9-10.11) [42]

Keep me safe, O God; you are my hope (1).

For the Easter Vigil the verses chosen from Psalm 16 are primarily from the second stanza, the song of joyful trust in God. This joyful trust is introduced by a verse from the first stanza in which the psalmist declares that the Lord is the best inheritance. The refrain is the first verse of the psalm, the plea for God's protection.

Psalm 16 is paired with the second reading of the Easter Vigil, Gen 22:1-18. God puts Abraham to the test by asking for the sacrifice of his beloved son. Abraham obeys without question, demonstrating radical trust in God. God, however, does not want the sacrifice of the boy but rather of Abraham's heart. God tests Abraham to see if the benefits of the covenant mean more to him than God, the covenant partner. Abraham is willing to sacrifice the only tangible sign of the covenant promise he has. God's response is a renewal of the covenant blessings, given explicitly this time because Abraham obeyed.

The psalm is a poignant reflection of Abraham's radical trust in God. God is his cherished inheritance; nothing else matters. The psalm also reflects Isaac's situation from the plea for protection to the confidence that God will rescue him from death. Isaac is a type of Christ, the son sacrificed by the father for the sake of the covenant, the son rescued by God from the power of death. The New Testament use of Psalm 16 as a reference to Christ's resurrection is linked here to Isaac's deliverance. We too pray in confidence, "Keep me safe, O God, . . . you will not abandon me to Sheol" (Ps 16:1, 10).

3rd Sun Easter A (1-2.5.7-8.9-10.11) [47]

Lord, you will show us the path of life (11).

Almost all of Psalm 16 is used on the Third Sunday of Easter A. The only verses missing are the two regarding false gods (3-4) and one of the verses referring to God as the psalmist's inheritance (6). The refrain is the joyful expression of confidence: "You will show me the path to life."

The first reading (Acts 2:14, 22-28) is part of Peter's speech on the first Pentecost. In constructing this speech of Peter, Luke uses several scripture passages to support his argument. Psalm 16 is used as a prophecy of the resurrection of Christ. The Greek translation, which Luke uses, points to life after death much more clearly than the Hebrew: "You will not abandon my soul to the netherworld, nor will you suffer your holy one to see corruption." Luke concludes that since David certainly died and was buried, he must have been speaking in the psalm about one of his descendants, the Messiah, who is Jesus (2:29-36).

The gospel story (Luke 24:13-35) relates one of the appearances of the risen Christ. The two disciples on the way to Emmaus (Cleopas and his wife?) are depressed because of Jesus' death. They do not believe the testimony of the women that angels have reported Jesus' resurrection. Jesus breaks open the scripture for them, pointing out the passages which allude to a suffering Messiah. This is a shift in Old Testament interpretation, which generally did not recognize suffering as part of the Messiah's mission. Luke may be interpreting the Servant songs of Isaiah as messianic, or referring to the psalms, especially laments. After opening the scriptures, Jesus breaks bread with the disciples. In this action they recognize him and rush back to tell the other disciples the news.

The First Letter of Peter (1:17-21) exhorts disciles to live as those who have been ransomed from idolatry. "They multiply their sorrows who court other gods" (Ps 16:4). They have been ransomed and given new life by the precious blood of Christ. This is the reason for Christian hope.

The readings for this Sunday remind us that the resurrection is not always obvious. David (or another psalmist) died long before his confident prayer was recognized as true on a deeper level than this present lifetime. The disciples on the way to Emmaus are slow to believe in the resurrection even with the risen Christ in their midst. The struggle to hope and believe in God's good news is a real struggle for us as well. We repeat our prayer with unrelenting hope, "Lord, you will show me the path to life; you will not abandon me to death" (cf. Ps 16:10-11).

13th Sun Year C (1-2.5.7-8.9-10.11) [100]

You are my inheritance, O Lord (5).

The verses of Psalm 16 chosen for the Thirteenth Sunday of Year C are the same as those for the Third Sunday of Easter A (see above). The refrain is a paraphrase of verse 5, claiming God as the only inheritance, the sole source of the psalmist's delight.

Singleness of heart is the demand of this Sunday. "I say to the LORD, 'You are my Lord; you are my only good' " (Ps 16:2). God is the only portion and cup who brings true joy. The first reading (1 Kings 19:16b, 19-21) tells the story of Elijah's call of Elisha as his successor. Elijah had been commissioned to do this by the "tiny whispering sound" that came to him at Mount Horeb (19:12, 16). Elijah ritualizes God's call of Elisha by throwing his mantle, sign of the prophetic office, over Elisha's shoulders. Elisha makes a rapid farewell to his people, cooks his oxen as a banquet for them, and follows Elijah. He has indeed "burned his bridges behind him" by destroying his means of livelihood, the oxen and the plow. From that day he is totally committed to the prophetic task.

The gospel (Luke 9:51-62) shows us Jesus abandoning everything, even vengeance, to hurry forward in his obedience to God. He has set his face toward Jerusalem, the scene of his passion. Those who follow him must recognize that no need, no other claim, may get in the way of that single-hearted journey of obedience. God is his inheritance, his only good.

Paul (Gal 5:1, 13-18) reminds us that to live by the desires of the Spirit is to be truly free. To live by the Spirit is to be free of the divisive works of the flesh (5:19- 21), free to love and serve one another (5:22-23). There is no law against the desires of genuine love. Rather love is the fulfillment of the Law. This is the freedom of Christ who is impelled by love to give his life for our sake.

Christ, Elijah, Paul sing to God as their inheritance, their only good. We, believing in the unbelievable sacrifice of Christ for our sake, can find no better way to express our thanksgiving and trust in God. It is true that God will not let us see the pit (Ps 16:10). God in Christ shows us the path to life (11). No other portion and cup can satisfy us; no other good may turn us aside from God, our inheritance, our true delight (5-6).

33rd Sun Year B (5.8.9-10.11) [159]

Keep me safe, O God; you are my hope (1).

The verses of Psalm 16 and the refrain chosen for the Thirty-Third Sunday of Year B are the same as those for the Easter Vigil (see above). The tension and exhilaration of the end-time are evident in this Sunday's readings. Psalm 16 steadies us in the hope that God will keep us safe even through the final catastrophe.

The reading from Daniel (12:1-3) is one of the very few clear statements in the Old Testament of belief in the resurrection of the dead.[3] This beginning concept of resurrection grew in the wake of an apocalyptic world-view which took hold during the persecution by Antiochus IV Epiphanes (175–164 BCE). The persecution was so severe that people began to believe that God's kingdom would come only after a catastrophic destruction of the

---

[3]The reference, however, may be only to the righteous. A belief in resurrection for the wicked also was much slower to develop.

whole world. Since even the righteous would die in this cataclysm, their vindication and glory would necessarily be in a life after death.

The gospel (Mark 13:24-32) also represents an apocalyptic world-view. Jesus describes the end of the world in which the Son of Man, an apocalyptic figure of judgment, comes to gather his chosen for the victory. The faithful are to be wise in recognizing the signs of the times, but they are not to worry about the exact day or hour. Their only duty is to watch.

The preparedness of the faithful consists in accepting the fruits of Christ's offering which has won the forgiveness of their sins (Heb 10:11-14, 18). Because of this single offering there is no longer reason to fear. God has made our destiny secure (Ps 16:5). With God at our right, we shall never be shaken (Ps 16:8), even in the final catastrophe. God will not abandon us to Sheol, but will lead us forever on the path to life (Ps 16:11). God, who keeps us safe, is our hope and our delight.

3. Psalm 23

Psalm 23 is a psalm of confidence and trust. It is a great favorite in the whole Christian tradition. If a person knows only one psalm, it will almost certainly be Psalm 23. Therefore it is fitting that Psalm 23 is used in the Sunday and feast day Lectionary a possible seven times. It serves for a wide range of needs. Psalm 23 is sung in both Lenten and Easter seasons, twice in Ordinary Time, on the feasts of Christ the King A and the Sacred Heart B, and as a possible response for All Souls Day.

The psalm falls into two major sections. The first section portrays God shepherding (1-4); the second section portrays God offering hospitality (5-6). God as the good shepherd gives the psalmist food, rest, water, and protection. As the host God provides food, anointing, and loyalty.

Shepherd is a frequent image in the Old Testament. It is an image of God (cf. Ps 79:13; 80:1; 95:7; 100:3; Isa 40:11; Mic 7:14) and of representatives of God, such as the king and the other leaders of Israel (cf. Jer 23:1-4; Ezek 34:1-31). The shepherd is required to be solicitous for the sheep because sheep are so helpless. Sheep need guidance. They also need the flock. A sheep left alone will die. Thus the absolute dependence of God's people on divine protection is well illustrated by the shepherd image. The confidence in this psalm is the confidence of one who knows real danger, but also real protection.

The figure of hospitality is a part of the shepherd imagery. In the desert, the shepherd's hospitality is necessary for the survival of travelers. This is evident even today with the Bedouin. According to the code of the desert, the host becomes responsible for the life of the stranger to whom hospitality and nourishment are given. God fed Israel in the desert; God invites the faithful into the tent, which is the temple. God is responsible for the life of the people. The psalm expresses confidence that God will honor that trust.

Shepherd is also a fitting image for the king. The king is responsible for the lives of all the people, especially those who are powerless—the orphan, the widow, the stranger. The king leads the people for their benefit. The psalm also refers to anointing. In the context of hospitality, the anointing simply indicates kindness to the guest who has been traveling through the desert. Anointing, however, also suggests kingship. The Hebrew word for anointed gives us our English word "messiah." The term "christ" comes from the Greek word for anointed. The complex of messianic traditions circles around the figure of David, an anointed king who was promised that a descendant of his would always sit upon his throne (cf. 2 Sam 7:8-16). According to its title, Psalm 23 is a psalm of David. This does not necessarily mean that David wrote the psalm, but that it is attached to the figure of David (see Ps 54 concerning psalm titles).

4th Sun Lent A (1-3.3-4.5.6) [31]

The Lord is my shepherd; there is nothing I shall want (1).

Psalm 23 is used in its entirety on the Fourth Sunday of Lent A. The first reading (1 Sam 16:1, 6-7, 10-13) tells the beginning of the story of David. Samuel, having reported God's rejection to Saul, has now been sent by God to anoint a king from Jesse's house. Samuel is certain that the eldest, a tall handsome man, is God's choice. But it is not so. God lets Samuel go through seven sons of Jesse without choosing any. Finally, Jesse sends for his youngest son, "who is tending the sheep." When David arrives, Samuel anoints him in the midst of his brothers; "and from that day on, the spirit of the LORD rushed upon David."

The other two readings emphasize light and vision (Eph 5:8-14; John 9:1-41). In the gospel Christ gives sight to the man born blind and accuses the Pharisees of being willfully blind. In the reading from Ephesians Christians are exhorted to live as children of light which they are because Christ has given them light.

A further element which is added to this Sunday is the Second Scrutiny for the Rite of Christian Initiation of Adults in which the community prays for wisdom and enlightenment for the catechumens.

The psalm provides an interesting unity for this wealth of images and concepts. In the psalm the community proclaims that God is the shepherd. There is an implication that David is shepherd only by analogy. David exercises the shepherd function for God. Within the psalm we sing, "you anoint my head with oil" (5). The community at that point is singing for

David as one anointed by God. The community also takes on messianic identity (Christian identity) as a group of people anointed in baptism. This messianic identity is the responsibility of the Christian community and the anticipation of the catechumens. We also declare with the psalmist that "even when I walk through a dark valley, I fear no harm for you are at my side" (4). Darkness and blindness lose their terror because of complete trust in the guidance of God. (Is it possible also to find Siloam, the quiet waters [cf. Isa 8:6] to which the blind man is sent, in the waters of verse 2?) Finally, both catechumens and faithful declare their hope: "I will dwell in the house of the LORD for years to come" (6).

4th Sun Easter A (1-3.3-4.5.6) [50]

The Lord is my shepherd; there is nothing I shall want (1).

The responsorial psalm for the Fourth Sunday of Easter A is the whole of Psalm 23.

The first reading for all the Sundays of the Easter season is from the Acts of the Apostles. The Easter use of Psalm 23 follows a part of Peter's speech on the occasion of Pentecost (Acts 2:14, 36-41). Peter declares: "God has made him both Lord and Messiah, this Jesus whom you crucified" (36). In the verses omitted on this Sunday (25-35) he asserts that Jesus is the descendant promised to David in 2 Sam 7. He goes on to inform his listeners that they must "repent and be baptized . . . in the name of Jesus Christ for the forgiveness of sins and . . . the gift of the Holy Spirit" (38). The story tells us that some three thousand were baptized that day.

The second reading (1 Pet 2:20-25) encourages Christians who are suffering to accept their affliction in the spirit of Christ who suffered for them. "By his wounds you have been healed. For you had gone astray like sheep, but you have now returned to the shepherd and guardian of your souls" (24-25). The gospel (John 10:1-10) is a complex of sheep-shepherd imagery. Jesus is the shepherd whom the sheep will follow; Jesus is the sheepgate, the safe entrance for the sheep.

Psalm 23 follows the reading in which Jesus is proclaimed both Lord and Messiah. It is through baptism in the name of Jesus that believers will find safety from the threat of sin and will receive the same Spirit which rushed upon David at his anointing. Christ is the true shepherd who protects the sheep, suffers for their sake, and leads them to life.

16th Sun Year B (1-3.3-4.5.6) [108]

The Lord is my shepherd; there is nothing I shall want (1).

The responsorial psalm for the Sixteenth Sunday of Year B is the whole of Psalm 23.

The first reading is part of Jeremiah's castigation of Judah's rulers (Jer 23:1-6). In the previous chapter the prophet has attacked the three previous kings; in the following chapter he will attack the reigning king, Zedekiah. In the passage for this Sunday he portrays the kings as evil shepherds who are challenged by God for not taking care of the flock. God promises to gather the remnant of the flock and appoint good shepherds for them. A descendant of David will arise who will be a good shepherd in contrast to these descendants of David who are not. The new king will truly be named "The LORD our justice," a play on the name Zedekiah.

In the gospel (Mark 6:30-34) Jesus and the apostles are attempting to get away from the crowds, but the people follow them. Jesus' "heart [is] moved with pity for them, for they were like sheep without a shepherd" (6:34). In the story which follows, five thousand are fed. In the Letter to the Ephesians (Eph 2:13-18) Christ is presented as the one who has reconciled all humans to one another and to God in his own body through the Cross.

Psalm 23 expresses our confidence that God indeed will care for us. God, the true shepherd, will provide just and wise leaders for the flock. God in Christ Jesus has shown compassion for the wandering flock, has gathered the sheep into one flock, has fed them with teaching, and has saved their lives. "The LORD is my shepherd; there is nothing I lack" (1).

28th Sun Year A (1-3.3-4.5.6) [143]

I will live in the house of the Lord all the days of my life (6).

Psalm 23 is used in its entirety on the Twenty-Eighth Sunday of Year A.

The readings emphasize God as host rather than God as shepherd. The first reading is from the apocalyptic section of Isaiah (Isa 25:6-10). On the Day of the Lord, the day of the final battle between good and evil, a victorious Yahweh will reign from Mount Zion. Then Yahweh will spread a banquet for all peoples, reminiscent of the sacred meal which sealed the Sinai covenant (cf. Exod 24:1-2, 9-11). Food and drink will be rich and abundant, symbolic of the fullness of the messianic age. In a dramatic reversal, Death, which is frequently portrayed as swallowing people (cf. Prov 1:12; Isa 5:14), will be swallowed up by God. All enemies will be destroyed and God's people will say: "Behold our God, to whom we looked to save us!"

The gospel (Matt 22:1-14) presents an ironic twist to this picture. People are invited to the great wedding banquet but they refuse to come! They even murder the servants of the king-shepherd. The king punishes them, but then invites everyone else to the banquet. In the second reading (Phil

4:12-14, 19-20) Paul informs the Philippians that he knows how to eat well or to go hungry. He closes with a prayer that God supply their needs in a way worthy of divine riches in Christ Jesus.

The refrain of the psalm comes from the last half of Psalm 23 which emphasizes the image of hospitality. The shepherd not only provides protection; the shepherd spreads the table and anoints the head of the guest. God provides abundantly for our needs, not only now (cf. Paul), but at the great banquet of the kingdom. We in turn must be prepared to respond to the divine invitation.

Christ the King A (1-2.2-3.5-6) [161]

The Lord is my shepherd; there is nothing I shall want (1).

Psalm 23 is used (except v. 4) for the Solemnity of Christ the King. This feast already by subject emphasizes the image of the shepherd-king. The first reading is from the prophet Ezekiel (34:11-12, 15-17). At the beginning of ch. 34 Ezekiel denounces the rulers of Israel because they have been bad shepherds, pasturing themselves rather than the sheep (cf. Jer 23:1-4). After the denunciation, God announces: "I myself will look after and tend my sheep" (11). God will be the good shepherd who nourishes the flock, gives it rest, and cares for the weak. Then God will separate the good sheep from the bad sheep (17-24) and appoint David as shepherd over the flock.

The gospel (Matt 25:31-46) is a parable of separation, good from bad. Jesus announces that the Son of Man will come in glory, sit upon his royal throne, and separate all people into two groups "as a shepherd separates the sheep from the goats" (32). The principle of separation is based on deeds of compassion and kindness toward the weak. Everyone has a responsibility for the weaker members of the flock. In them everyone finds Christ. Merciful treatment of the needy will be rewarded by Christ who is served in them. Hard-hearted neglect of the weak will be punished as the rejection of Christ which it is. Then, after the judgment, after everything has been subjected to Christ (cf. 1 Cor 15:20-26, 28) Christ will surrender all things to God, "so that God may be all in all."

Psalm 23 collects all the shepherd-king images. The Lord God is the good shepherd who cares for the sheep. The Lord Christ is the shepherd who separates good from bad sheep. The responsibility for the flock is shared by Christ with all the members of his body. All Christians are responsible to care for the weaker members of the flock, to guide and feed and welcome, to be host and shepherd for them. But in the end there is one shepherd-king. God will be all in all.

Sacred Heart C (1-3.3-4.5.6) [173]

The Lord is my shepherd; there is nothing I shall want (1).

On the Solemnity of the Sacred Heart the whole of Psalm 23 is used as the responsorial psalm.

The Solemnity of the Sacred Heart is a celebration of the great love and compassion of God, symbolized by the heart of Christ. The first reading (Ezek 34:11-16) is almost identical to the reading for the Solemnity of Christ the King A (see above). The verses concerning separation of the sheep are omitted (17-22). Two verses are added concerning return from Exile and settling upon the mountain heights of Israel (13-14). God is the good shepherd who cares for all in the flock, especially the weak.

The gospel (Luke 15:3-7) is one of the many parables about sheep and shepherds. Jesus presents three parables in Luke 15 about the joy of finding what was lost. The point in all three is that God is delighted when the sinner returns. The first of the three parables describes God's joy in terms of the joy of a shepherd who leaves ninety-nine sheep in order to find one which is lost. The second reading (Rom 5:5-11) declares directly the amazing truth that Christ died for us while we were still sinners. This proves God's love for us.

On this feast the shepherd is characterized primarily by care and compassion. The image of the shepherd-king who judges and separates is gone. This is the image of the shepherd who will do anything, even risk death, to care for the weakest sheep, the worst sinner. The sheep confidently declare: "The LORD is my shepherd; . . . I fear no harm for you are at my side" (Ps 23:1, 4).

All Souls (1-3.3-4.5.6) [791]

The Lord is my shepherd; there is nothing I shall want (1).

The readings and psalm for the Feast of All Souls Day are taken from the Common of the Dead. Psalm 23 is one of the possible choices for the responsorial psalm. Several of the readings which accompany Psalm 23 in the rest of the liturgical year are also given in the Common of the Dead: Isa 25:6-9 (cf. Twenty-Eighth Sunday of Year A); Rom 5:5-11 (cf. Sacred Heart C); 1 Cor 15:20-24, 25-28 (cf. Christ the King A); Matt 25:31-46 (cf. Christ the King A). If any of these readings are used for All Souls Day, Psalm 23 would be a good choice for the responsorial psalm. Psalm 23 might also be considered in the following cases: with John 6:37-40 in which Jesus says, "This is the will of the one who sent me, that I should not lose anything of what he gave me"; or with John 6:51-58 in which Jesus promises to give his flesh and blood for the life of the world.

4. *Psalm 27*

Psalm 27 is an expression of trust in God even in the most desperate situation. The psalm has two distinct parts: a prayer of confidence (1-6) and a lament (7-14). Some have considered it to be two psalms. The unity of the psalm, however, is supported by several factors. The meter in both sections is a consistent 3 + 2, a meter which often signifies a dirge. The overwhelming confidence in Yahweh is expressed at the beginning (1-3) and at the end (13-14), as is the desire for Yahweh's presence (4-5, 8-9). Both halves recognize the presence of enemies (2-3, 6, 11-12).

The two sections fall into two stanzas each (1-3, 4-6, 7-10, 11-14). In the first stanza (1-3) the psalmist makes the declaration of trust. Yahweh, who is light, salvation, refuge, is the only need even in the worst imaginable distress. No darkness can overcome this light. No destruction can conquer this salvation. No terror can penetrate this refuge. Yahweh is all.

Therefore the psalmist has only one desire, Yahweh's presence (4-6). The psalmist's whole delight is found in the Lord's beauty. But even in the midst of this tranquility the awareness of enemies is present. They are powerless, however, against the defense of God's sanctuary. The enduring gift of God's living among us is suggested by the ancient desert terms for the sanctuary: tabernacle/booth (*sok* or *sukkah*) and tent (*'ohel*). This dwelling place of God, now set on the rock of Zion, is protection against all danger. Therefore the psalmist offers the thanksgiving sacrifice with shouts and songs of joy.

The third stanza (7-10) begins with a cry for help characteristic of the lament: hear, pity, answer. The solution of the previous stanza returns immediately: "Seek God's face," God's presence. But the psalmist continues to plead in desperation, "Do not hide . . . from me;" do not abandon me. The unquenchable confidence is not shaken, however. The psalmist asserts that even if the closest human ties are broken, God will still be there.

The final stanza (11-14) again combines petition and trust, now in a calmer mood. The psalmist prays for God's direction, implying that obedience to God will protect against enemies. The threat of devouring enemies (cf. 2) is still present. Verse 12 reads, "Do not abandon me to the [throat] (*nephesh*) of my foes." The enemies now are witnesses who bring false accusation against the psalmist and threaten condemnation. For the last time the psalmist declares undying trust in Yahweh. Now in this life (the land of the living) the psalmist fully expects to enjoy the Lord's goodness.

The psalm closes with an exhortation (14). Either the psalmist encourages the hearers to imitate this boundless trust or a priest brings God's word to the psalmist, confirming the hope of this prayer. In either case the exhortation is a word to us. No matter how desperate the situation, the Lord is our light and our salvation.

2nd Sun Lent C (1.7-8.8-9.13-14) [27]

The Lord is my light and my salvation (1).

The verses of Psalm 27 chosen for the Second Sunday of Lent C come primarily from the second half of the psalm. The refrain and the opening stanza (1) introduce the psalm with its first verse, the declaration of unshakeable confidence. The remaining verses express the plea for help (7, 9), the longing for God's presence (8), and the confident assurance that God indeed is light and life (13-14). The expression of trust no matter what the danger (2-3, 5-6, 10), the single-hearted desire for God's presence (4-5), and the plea for God's teaching and protecting presence (11-12) are omitted.

The reading from Genesis (15:5-12, 17-18) describes the covenant making between God and Abraham. God has already promised Abraham descendants (12:2, 7), but it seems impossible to the childless man (15:2-3). God reassures him and repeats the promise (15:4-5). Abraham's trusting faith in God is credited to him as righteousness (15:6).

God then seals the promise to Abraham with a formal ceremony. In the ceremony animals are split and the covenanting parties pass between them as a sign that the party who breaks the covenant will be split like the animals. Abraham prepares for the ceremony and waits for God. He waits until sunset when a terrifying darkness overwhelms him. Then God appears in smoke and fire to pass between the carcasses. Thus God "cut a covenant" with Abraham.

Abraham's trust is echoed in Psalm 27. Abraham waits with courage for the Lord. His trust is rewarded. God is indeed his light.

The gospel for the Second Sunday of Lent in all three cycles is the story of the transfiguration of Jesus. This story (Luke 9:28-36) is an example of radical surrender to God and trust in the divine will. Jesus is so open to the will of God that he becomes transparent to the divine glory. Because he obeys in complete trust, the light and salvation of Yahweh shine clearly through him. Thus the disciples in his presence can see the light of God shining in his face (cf. 2 Cor 4:6). He himself has become the covenant bond which is our salvation, the light which the darkness of death cannot overcome. He is the goodness of the Lord, ours to enjoy in the land of the living. The voice of God instructs us, "Listen to him."

Paul tells us how to listen to Christ (Phil 3:17-4:1), by imitating Paul and embracing the Cross with trust. No other good is worthy of desire. "One thing I ask of the LORD: . . . to dwell in the LORD's house all the days of my life'' (Ps 27:4). Paul assures us that our citizenship is in God's house and that Christ will save us, even from the Death which devours our flesh (27:2). His final exhortation echoes the psalm: ''Stand firm in the Lord.''

7th Sun Easter A (1.4.7-8) [60]

I believe that I shall see the good things of the Lord in the land of the living (13).

On the Seventh Sunday of Easter A the responsorial psalm begins with the first verse of Psalm 27, the psalmist's confident expression of trust. The remaining verses emphasize the single-hearted longing for God's presence. The refrain is the psalmist's final cry of absolute trust.

The first reading (Acts 1:12-14) picks up the Christian story right after the ascension of Jesus. Most of the reading consists of a list of names, twelve names, including that of Mary the mother of Jesus. These are real people with real names who now have to carry on the business of ordinary life without the visible presence of Jesus. Their hearts say, ''Come, . . . seek God's face'' (Ps 27:8). In faith they must find the Lord's presence in the faces of their brothers and sisters—Peter and John, James and Andrew, Mary and the others. They must not lose the longing for God in the pressures and tedium of daily life. ''One thing I ask of the LORD; this I seek'' (Ps 27:4).

The gospel (John 17:1-11) is part of the last discourse of Jesus in the Gospel of John. Jesus prays for glory that he might glorify the Father. His obedience to the Father's will has allowed the light of divine glory to shine through him (see the discussion of the transfiguration above). Now the final work of that obedience is about to be accomplished. His work and his presence have revealed the face of God to his disciples. Those who surrender in trust to his revelation of God's presence are filled with life and the light of God's glory. They in turn become the revelation of God's face to the world in which they live.

This indeed is cause for rejoicing (1 Pet 4:13-16). Our share in Christ's work of obedience, in his suffering, is a sign of our share in his glory. Our identification with Christ reveals the Spirit of glory and of God within us. Therefore we do not fear; we trust in God's answer to our cry (Ps 27:1, 7). The Lord is our light, our salvation, our refuge. We believe we will see the Lord's goodness in our lives. We are the ministers of the Lord's glory.

3rd Sun Year A (1.4.13-14) [68]

The Lord is my light and my salvation (1).

The psalm refrain for the Third Sunday of Year A is the first verse of Psalm 27, the triumphant declaration that God is our light and our salvation. The verses include the rest of verse 1, the witness to fearlessness which comes from the Lord, and verses 4 and 13-14, the expression of longing for God's presence and of unshakeable confidence in the gift of God's goodness.

The political situation at the time of Isaiah's oracle (Isa 8:23–9:3) threatens annihilation for God's people. The Assyrians have piece by piece swallowed up the nations between them and the Mediterranean. In 733 BCE, near the time of this oracle, they have taken over the region of Galilee, territory traditionally assigned to the tribes of Zebulun and Naphtali. But Isaiah's vision is one of strong hope in God's deliverance. The Lord is the people's light and salvation (Ps 27:1). God will in the end deliver the people from all their enemies, even the world's superpowers. Isaiah tells his people: Do not fear. Be stouthearted. Wait for the Lord (cf. Ps 27:14).

Matthew presents Jesus as the fulfillment of Isaiah's vision, the one who brings God's salvation, the sign of God's deliverance from the superpowers of sin and death, sickness and ignorance (Matt 4:12-23). Jesus preaches the good news: The Lord's goodness is here (Ps 27:13); the kingdom of God is at hand. He calls for conversion, the single-hearted seeking of God's presence. He gathers disciples, "Come, . . . seek God's face" (Ps 27:8), and commissions them to gather others who wait for God's deliverance.

The demand on disciples, however, is for single-hearted dedication. Peter and Andrew, James and John signal this by leaving boats, nets, and father immediately. The Corinthians to whom Paul writes have become distracted from the one thing worth seeking by the demands of competition (1 Cor 1:10-13, 17). Factions among them are each claiming superiority because of the one who evangelized them. They have surrendered to the divisive power of the enemy, sin. Paul calls them back to seek the one thing necessary (Ps 27:4), the good news of Christ's victory over the enemy. It is the Lord who is their light (Ps 27:1); no one else is to be given power over them. It is the Lord whose goodness is their delight (Ps 27:13); no one else is worth waiting for.

For whom do we wait? What light gives us courage? Whose presence do we seek? What good news do we bring?

Year Common (1.4.13-14) [175]

The Lord is my light and my salvation (1).

The refrain and verses of Psalm 27 chosen for the Common of the Year are the same as those for the Third Sunday of Year A (see above).

Psalm 27 may be an appropriate response for several Sundays of the year. The gospel for the Fifth Sunday of Year A (Matt 5:13-16; see the fuller discussion with Ps 112) is Jesus' declaration that his disciples are the light of the world. The reading from Isaiah (58:7-10) promises light to those who care for the needy. The light promised in both readings is the light of the Lord, the power of God (Ps 27:1; cf. 1 Cor 2:1-5).

The story of a blind man's healing is the gospel for the Thirtieth Sunday of Year B (Mark 10:46-52; see Ps 126). The first reading (Jer 31:7-9) is a song of joy for the returning exiles who will see the Lord's goodness in their own land.

Psalm 27 echoes different themes from the three readings for the Sixteenth Sunday of Year C (see Ps 15). Abraham and Sarah (Gen 18:1-10) are certainly among the faithful who seek one thing, to dwell in the Lord's presence. They have also learned to wait for the Lord and to believe the promise. In the gospel (Luke 10:38-42) Mary is given us as a model who seeks the one thing necessary. Paul proclaims the revelation of God's glory, the light of God, in Christ (Col 1:24-28).

There are several variations on the light theme in the readings for the Thirty-Second Sunday of Year A (see Ps 63). Wisdom is the resplendent and unfading light of God (Wis 6:12-16). She gives life to those who seek her. The wise virgins of the gospel (Matt 25:1-13) are prepared to wait for the Lord and to carry the light. Paul tells us that God's light conquers even the darkness of death's sleep (1 Thess 4:13-18).

All Souls (1.4.7.8.9.13-14) [791]

The Lord is my light and my salvation (1).

The selection of verses from Psalm 27 for the Common of the Dead is the most thorough of all the Lectionary uses of this psalm. Verse 1, the introductory statement of fearless confidence, is still the only verse from the first stanza. There is also one verse (4) from the second stanza, expressing the longing for God's presence in the temple. Most of the third stanza is used (7-9a). The psalmist calls for help and turns to seek God's face. The selection concludes with the last two verses of the psalm, a final expression of confidence and the exhortation to persevere in trust (13-14).

In the Christian context of faith in the resurrection, Psalm 27 acquires a deeper nuance than the original meaning. The devouring enemy is death and our fearlessness comes from faith in the salvation won for us by Christ. The longing for God's presence and God's house suggests a longing for heaven. The confidence of the final verses can be interpreted as a hope for the Lord's goodness in eternal life.

Some Old Testament readings for which Psalm 27 would be appropriate are: Job 19:1, 23-27, Job's cry of longing to see God; Wis 3:1-9 and Dan 12:1-3 in which the just shine brightly like stars, like sparks. New Testament readings include: Rom 8:14-23, present sufferings are nothing compared to promised glory; Rom 8:31-35, 37-39, who can be against us if God is for us (cf. Ps 27:10); 2 Cor 5:1, 6-10 and Rev 21:1-5, 6-7, which speak of our heavenly dwelling and God's dwelling with us. Of the gospels, three have themes related to Psalm 27: Matt 5:1-12, blessed are the hungry, the single-hearted; Matt 25:1-13, the wise virgins with lighted lamps (see the Common of the Year above); John 17:24-26, Jesus' prayer that we might see his glory (the conclusion of the passage read on the Seventh Sunday of Easter A, see above).

5. Psalm 62

The strong message of Psalm 62 is that only God is worthy of trust. The psalmist maintains a tranquil peace in the midst of attack solely because of God. The psalm can be considered in three stanzas (2-5, 6-9, 10-13). The first two stanzas begin with the same assertion varied slightly. The third stanza is a wisdom reflection.

The first stanza (2-5) sets the tone for the whole psalm. The psalmist relies on God alone. God is rock, salvation, fortress. The enemies are questioned in verse 4 and described in verse 5. Their very existence is deceitful. They plot evil even as they speak sweetly. It is difficult to determine if the enemies are the sagging wall, ready to fall on an unsuspecting person, or if the psalmist is the sagging fence, beaten down by the enemy.

The second stanza (6-9) begins with a variation of the opening declaration. Instead of a statement there is a self-exhortation: "My soul, be at rest in God alone." The assurance carries through three verses of the stanza until finally the psalmist exhorts the people to have the same confident trust in God.

The final stanza (10-13) is a wisdom meditation on human powerlessness. Human beings who seem to be so influential really count for less than a puff of air. Wealth is not worth the devious means sometimes used to acquire it. The psalm ends with an oracle: power, faithful love (*hesed*), and reward belong to God.[4] God, whose covenant love for us is so strong, shares divine power with us so that our works may win the divine reward. The final message of the psalm is that God is indeed worthy of such trust; everything we have and do is a gift from our powerful, loving God.

8th Sun Year A (2-3.6-7.8-9) [83]

Rest in God alone, my soul (6).

The refrain for the Eighth Sunday of Year A is the psalmist's self-

---

[4]The oracle is in a common wisdom form: n,n+1. The form suggests a riddle, or the possibility of an endless list of God's attributes.

encouragement to rest in God alone. The selection of verses from Psalm 62 emphasizes total reliance on God. The opening declaration of trust (2-3) and its repetition (6-7) are both included. The third naming of God as rock and refuge leads into the exhortation to all people to trust God completely, to open their hearts to the Lord without reservation.

The first reading (Isa 49:14-15) gives an overwhelming argument for total reliance on God alone. Even if a mother should forget her baby, God will never forget us! Even if that closest of human bonds should break, God's bond of faithful love for us is stronger. To the Lord belongs love (Ps 62:13). The psalm is an almost perfect match to the reading. Where else do we rest with such security as in our divine mother's arms?

In the Sermon on the Mount Jesus too gives us an exhortation on trusting God (Matt 6:24-34). The first reading assured us with the image of God as tender mother. The gospel presents us with the image of God as father and creator. Just as the father clothes his children and the creator dresses the creature, so God takes care of us. The proof of this is God's care even for the plant and animal world. God has assured us that we are worth much more. How then can we worry? Rest in God alone, my soul!

God's gift to us, however, includes a share in divine power and responsibility. God will reward each of us according to our deeds (Ps 62:13). We are not to worry, but we are charged with the responsibility of seeking and spreading the kingdom of God. We are called to live in God's righteousness, a life-giving relationship with God and all of creation (Matt 6:33).

With Paul (1 Cor 4:1-5) our responsibility extends even to stewardship of the mysteries of God. Paul cuts through the illusion of human power from two directions (cf. Ps 62:10). He reminds the Corinthians, who are overly impressed by the apostles who have come to them, that power belongs not to human beings but to God (Ps 62:12). Paul, Apollos, Peter are simply stewards. But even as stewards they have an awesome responsibility to minister God's gifts in faithful love.

This Sunday calls us to a careful balance. The created world and the good news of God's kingdom have been entrusted to us. We have the responsibility to use the power God has shared with us in such a way that God's faithful love fills the world (cf. Ps 62:12-13). We may not surrender to exploitation and plunder to increase illusory wealth (Ps 62:11). The lilies of the field, the birds of the air, the children of God's kingdom depend on us to minister God's care. At the same time we may not succumb to the illusion that power belongs to us. God alone is our rock and salvation. God alone is mother and father, nurturer and sustainer. Seek first God's kingdom and everything else will be given us besides. "My soul, be at rest in God alone" (Ps 62:6).

6. Psalm 91

Psalm 91 is the prayer of someone who knows the protecting love of God and who wants to tell other believers how trustworthy God is. The psalm begins with a call to those who already live in the sanctuary of God's presence (1-2). God is named with ancient names, Elyon (Almighty), Shaddai (Most High). The ancient names suggest the enduring fidelity of divine love which is seen as far back as Abraham who called God Shaddai, as far back as the pre-Israelite sanctuary of Jerusalem where God was worshipped as Elyon. Those living in God's shelter are summoned to proclaim their abiding trust in this faithful God.

The second stanza (3-13) is a catalogue of all the situations in which God rescues the believer. There is no need to fear ambush or disease, demonic powers, enemy might, or wild animals. In the sanctuary God's presence, symbolized by the wings of the cherubim over the ark, is total protection. On the journey God's angels, ministers of God's power and will, defend believers from even the slightest injury. The psalmist has unwavering confidence in God's lifelong protection.

The confidence is rewarded by a divine oracle, God's response (14-16). God validates the exhortation to trust: "Whoever clings to me I will deliver, . . . [whoever calls] upon me I will answer." God promises honor to all who know the divine name, even the ancient names. God promises presence to the suffering. God promises life to all who embrace this total trust.

In spite of its fervent declaration of trust, Psalm 91 can be a problem. The psalm is not a promise that believers will not suffer. It is an exhortation not to fear and a promise of divine presence in the midst of the trial. The psalm is also not an encouragement to presumption: "It doesn't matter what risks I take, God will be with me." In the gospel account of Jesus' temptation, Satan attempts to distort the message of Psalm 91 in this fashion (Matt 4:5-7; Luke 4:9-12). But Jesus knows that trust is not a toy to be used for folly. His trust will prove the message of Psalm 91 in the mortal struggle with Satan which cost him his life and won life for us. He embodies the truth of this psalm as he says, "not my will but yours be done" (Luke 22:42).

1st Sun Lent C (1-2.10-11.12-13.14-15) [24]

Be with me, Lord, when I am in trouble (15).

The psalm refrain for the First Sunday of Lent C takes one of the promises of the psalm's oracle (14-16) and turns it into a prayer: "Be with me, Lord, when I am in trouble." The verses selected from Psalm 91 begin with the psalmist's exhortation to trust God (1-2). Part of the listing of occasions in which God proves trustworthy is included (10-13) and the selection concludes with more of the divine oracle (14-15). The description of God's rescue from plague and the demonic powers of the day and night is omitted, along with the final promise of life and the vision of God's power. The omissions are regrettable in the context of this Sunday when Jesus battles with Satan and trusts in the power of God to guard his life.

The message of this Sunday goes beyond trust to rejoicing. The first reading is from the Book of Deuteronomy (26:4-10). Deuteronomy, which was written on the verge of one crisis, the Babylonian Exile (587–539 BCE), presents itself as if the people were in the midst of another critical time, the exodus-wilderness period. The connection is clear. When we were powerless, God delivered us from Egypt and fed us in the desert. Even now God will continue to guard us in all our ways (Ps 91:11). The ritual described in today's reading calls for the offering of the first fruits of the harvest and the recital of God's saving deeds. The words and action signify ongoing trust that God will continue to protect and provide for the people. This trust leads inevitably to joy, the joy of those who have abandoned fruitless worry.

On the First Sunday of Lent the gospel always tells the story of Jesus' temptation (Luke 4:1-13). Jesus' experience follows the pattern of the ancient Israelites. Having passed through the waters of death in his baptism, he is led by the Spirit into the desert/wilderness to be tested by the devil. Just as the Israelites in the desert faced the need for absolute trust in God to provide food, protection, and a kingdom, so Jesus is confronted with the same need and the same temptation. The devil twists Psalm 91 to present Jesus with an alternative to trusting God, use of his own power. One by one, Jesus rejects the variations on this temptation. Instead he chooses radical trust in God which will lead ultimately to his death. But God keeps the promise of Psalm 91: "With length of days I will satisfy [him]" (16). His trust leads to life, both for him and us. The psalmist is right: Whoever clings to God will be delivered; whoever knows God's name will be set on high (cf. 91:14).

The message from the Letter to the Romans (10:8-13) puts us in the position of the believers in Deuteronomy. We are called upon to bear witness to God's saving deeds in Christ and to rejoice in our trust that God will save us along with him. We are caught between crises, Christ's victory and our own struggle with evil. We place our trust in God's power, not our own. We sing in joyful confidence: "Everyone who calls on the name of the Lord will be saved" (Rom 10:13; cf. Ps 91:14).

Lent Common (1-2.10-11.12-13.14.16) [175]

Be with me, Lord, when I am in trouble (15).

Psalm 91 is one of three psalms suggested for the Common for Lent (see also Pss 51, 130). The refrain and verse of Psalm 91 suggested for the Lenten Common are the same as those for the First Sunday of Lent C (see above), with one exception. The final verse of the oracle, promising life and the revelation of God's saving power, is included.

The psalm would be appropriate for the First Sunday of Lent A in which Matthew's story of Jesus' temptation is told (Matt 4:1-11; see the fuller discussion with Psalm 51). On the Second Sunday of Lent A, B, and C, both Abraham and Jesus are examples of radical trust (see Pss 27, 33, 116). The Third Sunday of Lent A contrasts lack of trust with persevering hope (see Ps 95). God's constant deliverance is the subject of the Fourth Sunday of Lent B (see Ps 137). New life and God's presence in trouble characterize the readings of the Fifth Sunday of Lent A, B, and C (see Pss 51, 126, 130).

7. Psalm 121

Psalm 121 is one of the fifteen Songs of Ascent (see Psalm 123). Like the other psalms in that collection, its imagery is simple and it is characterized by staircase repetition which intensifies its mood. Also characteristic of the Songs of Ascent is an interest in Jerusalem. Just as Psalm 120 appears to be a thanksgiving for safe arrival at the sanctuary, Psalm 121 appears to be a prayer for a safe departure.

The first stanza (1-2) is a dialogue. The pilgrim, contemplating the journey home, looks at the mountains which hold many dangers for the traveler. In danger from wild animals, robbers, rugged terrain, who will be there to help? The second verse is the confident answer: Yahweh, the creator God, will be your help. Who brings this answer? Is it the self-encouragement of the psalmist's own faith? Does a priest assure the departing pilgrim?

The remaining verses, a continuation of the assurance of verse two, take the form of a blessing. God who is the creator is also the guardian of Israel. As Israel's guardian God takes on the responsibility for every individual of the community. Thus God has the power to protect from all evil, even the demonic forces set loose by sun and moon. God will not let the pilgrim be moonstruck! God who has the power also has the desire to protect the individual believer. God's desire is so intense that nothing can distract from it. Unlike the gods of the other nations, Israel's God never sleeps, never fails to watch. This protective blessing extends to all of life, every coming and going now and forever.

The pilgrim's simple question has a simple answer. From where will my help come? From the Lord. The simplicity and the repetition give power to this psalm. There is no need to question further. There is only confident assurance.

29th Sun Year C (1-2.3-4.5-6.7-8) [148]

Our help is from the Lord who made heaven and earth (2).

The responsorial psalm on the Twenty-Ninth Sunday of Year C is all of Psalm 121. The refrain is the simple statement that captures the truth of the whole psalm: Our help comes from the Lord.

The main theme of the readings fits well with the psalm. It is the power of prayer. The first reading (Exod 17:8-13) portrays Moses as a powerful intercessor. The Israelites, under Joshua's command, engage Amalek in battle. This is the first battle of the wilderness wandering and a model for the battles to come as Israel takes the land. The lesson is strong: It is not the military power of Joshua and his army but rather the power of Moses' prayer which wins the victory. Moses' prayer is embodied in his posture, hands upraised to God in petition and praise. When his energy flags, his prayer is supported by others, Aaron and Hur. Moses witnesses to the statement of the psalm: "The LORD . . . will always guard your life" (Ps 121:7). His prayer, supported by other faithful people, is a living act of trust in the God who stands behind such a promise.

A favorite theme of the Gospel of Luke is prayer. In ch. 18 the evangelist gives us two of Jesus' parables on prayer (18:1-8, 9-14). Today's gospel is the first of them. The parable turns on the persistence of a widow who pesters a judge until he finally succumbs to her wishes. Jesus uses this common human example to emphasize his point. If such a judge, who cares nothing for anyone, finally hears the widow's plea, how much more so will God, who loves the chosen, answer them when they call. From where will my help come? From the Lord who neither slumbers nor sleeps (Ps 121:1-4).

The parable ends with a thought-provoking question: "When the Son of Man comes, will he find faith on earth?" (18:8). God will hear and protect those who cry out. That is a certainty. The question concerns the faith of God's people to believe that God will indeed guard their going and coming. The psalm is an expression of strong and peaceful trust in God. The challenge to us in the gospel is to make that trust the center of our lives, no matter how long we wait for the return of the Son of Man.

The exhortation to remain faithful to this trust opens the second reading (2 Tim 3:14–4:2). Timothy is reminded that the grounds for his trust come from what he has learned, especially from the sacred scriptures. In his turn he is to proclaim God's word incessantly, in good times and bad, so that others will have grounds for trust. The good news of God's word is that help beyond our comprehension comes from the Lord. God who never sleeps (Ps 121:3-4) has been so intent on guarding our lives that the beloved Son has been sent to die for our protection and to rise for our salvation.

How often do we neglect to trust the loving care of God? How often instead do we trust our own puny defenses while continuing to fret about the dangers of the road? How can we preach the good news of God's salvation if we do not embody it in our lives? How have we answered those who ask from where their help comes? When have we really trusted that our help comes from the Lord?

8. Psalm 131

Psalm 131 may well be the gentlest psalm in the psalter. Its stillness is striking, following as it does the psalm which begins "out of the depths." The peace of Psalm 131, however, is bought at a price. The first verse presents us with a series of negatives: not proud, not haughty, not busied with great matters, nor with things too sublime. The psalmist knows the cost and the emptiness of ambition and has rejected it. There is no longer an attempt to climb to the top in human society; there is no longer a greed to assume God's power (cf. Gen 3).

Rather there is an acceptance of the status of the ʿanawim, those who know their only hope is in God. The psalmist describes the peace of that surrender in the moving image of a weaned child on its mother's lap. The staircase parallelism characteristic of the Songs of Ascent (see Ps 123), heightens the imagery with the repetition of "weaned child" and the echo of "hushed"/"stilled." The peace of the weaned child is also bought at a price. The child has been forced to face the reality that the mother's breast is no longer available and has finally stilled desire to such a point that the proximity of the longed-for breast is no longer a source of distress. Even so is the psalmist's soul, no longer reaching for things too sublime, for matters too great.

God is not specifically mentioned in the image, but it is our mother-God who holds us in this psalm. With the psalmist we surrender in joyful trust to our Mother's care. The final verse exhorts the whole community of God's people to enjoy the delights of peaceful rest in the tender care of God our Mother.

31st Sun Year A (1.2.3) [152]

In you, Lord, I have found my peace.

Psalm 131 is used in its entirety for the Thirty-First Sunday of Year A.

The refrain is a summary of the theme of the psalm: In you, Lord, I have found my peace.

The reading from the prophet Malachi (1:14–2:2, 8-10) is part of a castigation of the priests. They are accused of offering the least valuable animals to the Lord in sacrifice. In the verse with which today's reading begins, the laity who bring the defective animals are accused as well. God declares that even if the chosen people offer paltry gifts, the Gentiles will honor God as the great king, the Lord of the whole cosmos.

The priests are further accused of offering the people poor instruction and leading them astray. They have violated God's special covenant with the tribe of Levi to minister to the people. God, therefore, will humble them since they have abandoned the honorable position they once held.

The reading ends with the rhetorical question: Have we not all the one Father? The psalm responds with the image of God also as Mother. The prophet has scolded those who dishonored their lofty position. The psalm is the response of one who seeks no honor but desires only to surrender to God's good pleasure. The contrast is striking. The psalm is a moment of relief after the stress of the prophetic denunciation.

The second reading (1 Thess 2:7-9, 13) combines themes of the first reading and the psalm in a powerful fashion. We see Paul as the example of a good minister of God's good news, in contrast to the priests of the first reading. Paul's own image of his ministry is that of a nursing mother, caring for her children, sharing her very self, working day and night for their sakes. This is his evidence that his ministry is truly from God. Like the psalmist, he is not interested in false honor or great things beyond him (cf. 1 Thess 2:3-6; Ps 131:1). Rather he took on himself the image of God, the gentle mother, so that the Thessalonians might receive the word of God without hindrance. Like a mother watching her children grow, Paul finds his delight in seeing the fruit of his work in the Thessalonians. This is the cause for his joyful thanksgiving to God.

In the gospel (Matt 23:1-12) Jesus takes the Pharisees to task for failing to minister God's love and compassion to the people. Like the priests of Malachi's time, they have become more interested in their own gain than their people's good. Unlike the psalmist, they have been more interested in the trappings of honor than in surrender to the gracious will of God who has given them such an awesome responsibility. They have missed the gift that would give them such peaceful joy.

The message to our world is overwhelming. Competition, climbing over others to the top, claiming what is coming to us, are all valued in modern society. What of the delight in surrendering to God? What of the courage in abandoning self-seeking to minister God's motherly care to those who have been entrusted to us?

E. Hymns

Praise is the goal of all biblical prayer.[1] The shape of the psalter itself indicates this movement toward praise. Most of the laments are in the first half of the psalter, most of the hymns in the second half. The hymn is disinterested praise, praise focused entirely on God with no notion of gain for oneself. The hymn springs from the recognition of God's great goodness and majesty. It is the response of wonder and awe; it is the song of a heart filled with gratitude that this great and wonderful God loves us so much.

The hymn always implies community. Such praise can only be expressed by the assembly of all the believers, even of all creation; a lone singer could never proclaim enough praise. The hymn focuses on God: who God is, what God does. God creates the whole world. God saves the chosen people. God gives the Law that the people might know how to live well. God is also the goal; it is the desire of the singers to live in God's kingdom.

The hymn is set in the continuing present. God's mighty deeds of creation and redemption are unending. The verb forms are often participles which indicate ongoing time. The hymns are a radical statement of faith that God is still the primary force in our modern world.

The structure of the hymn is simple. It begins with a *call to praise,* addressed either to oneself or (more frequently) to others—the believing community, all peoples, even all creation. Following the call to praise is the *body* of the psalm which gives reasons for praise. Or as Carroll Stuhlmueller points out, the body of the psalm gives us ways to continue the praise, to continue to be involved and hold God's greatness in our memory.[2] The body of the hymn frequently begins with the Hebrew particle *ki,* which is sometimes translated "for." It is more properly an exclamation: "indeed." We call everyone to join our praise of God and continue with a whole series of "indeeds." Sometimes the hymn concludes with a *recapitulation* of the call to praise. The simplest call is the exclamation "Hallelujah," which means "Praise the Lord!"

Praise is the goal of all our prayer. All our prayer reaches for Hallelujah!

1. Psalm 8

Psalm 8 is an ecstatic hymn of praise to God who has created the world in such splendid order. The psalm begins and ends with an exclamation of praise and delight that Yahweh (Lord), *our* Lord, is worthy of great honor

---

[1]See P. D. Miller (64–78) for an elaboration of this idea.
[2]Stuhlmueller 1.34–35.

throughout creation. The name of our God, Yahweh, is glorious in the heavens and on earth.

At the very center of the psalm is the proclamation of the paradoxical human condition, at once lowly and glorious (5). The two words for human beings both remind us of our lowly state. The first, *'enosh*, comes from a root that connotes weakness. The second, *ben-'adam*, signifies our descent from the first human creature formed out of the clay of the earth (*'adamah*). Yet it is precisely we weak earthlings whom the awesome Lord remembers and cares for.

The first section of the psalm (2b-4) proclaims the greatness of the creator who has placed the moon and the stars with careful fingers. Yet this creator has chosen the weakest instruments to defend the divine majesty. Even the babbling of infants, of weak human creatures, is enough to protect the divine honor.

The second section of the psalm (6-9) proclaims the exaltation of human beings. The glorious Lord has made them just a little less than gods themselves, "in the divine image [God] created them" (Gen 1:27). By divine decree they have been given dominion over and responsibility for all other creatures of land, sea, and sky (Gen 1:28).

Thus the first part of the psalm (3-4) telling God's greatness, and the second part of the psalm (7-9) describing creation, both revolve around human beings (5-6). Yet human beings have meaning only when surrounded by and carried in the glorious presence of God. "Human power is always bounded and surrounded by divine praise."[3] This is both our glory and our awesome responsibility. The mighty God acts through us!

Trinity Sunday C (4-5.6-7.8-9) [167]

O Lord, our God, how wonderful your name in all the earth! (2).

The refrain for Trinity Sunday C is the exclamation of praise that surrounds Psalm 8. The verses include the whole psalm with the exception of 2b-3 which are difficult textually. What is lost is the assertion that God uses even great weakness to build a defense against the enemy.

The readings for Trinity Sunday C describe the wonderful web of relationships through which God draws us into the inner life of the Trinity. The opening reading (Prov 8:22-31) is the Wisdom Woman's hymn describing her origin and her work. She is the firstborn of God, present before creation. Through her design all creation came into being. She is the Wisdom of God; she herself is God. She is the bridge between God and creation. She is God's delight and her delight is the human race. With creative

---

[3]Brueggemann, *Message*, 37.

energy she plays before God, plays on the surface of the earth. She joins God to creation, and her names are Play and Delight. This is the God who surrounds all creation with the glory of the divine name and whose delight is the human creature who has been set at its center (cf. Ps 8).

Paul (Rom 5:1-5) reminds us that our "access . . . to this grace in which we stand" has come through Jesus Christ. Through him we have peace with God. He is our bridge. Because of his union with us, we even boast of our afflictions, strengthened in hope by the knowledge that the Holy Spirit, the divine Love and Delight flowing between Father and Son, has now been poured out into our own hearts. Through the Spirit we have been swept up into the very life of God. Who are we, mere mortals, that God remembers us? Mere humans that God cares for us? Yet we have been filled with the very life of God (Ps 8:5-6).

In the gospel (John 16:12-15) Jesus himself tells us of this wonderful life which is his gift to us. What the Father has belongs to Jesus. What belongs to Jesus is given to us by the Spirit. The bridge between God and the favorite creature has been built. Wisdom has succeeded in her creative task. It is now our responsibility to use what has been given to us to complete the circle, to bring all creation back to God.

2. Psalm 29

The most obvious characteristic of Psalm 29 is its powerful use of repetition. The psalm is a parade example of staircase parallelism in which each line picks up an element from the previous line and carries the thought forward. The effect of this parallelism is a heightening of the tension and movement of the psalm. The two phrases repeated most often give shape to the first two stanzas of the psalm: "Give to the LORD" (1-2); "the voice of the LORD" (3-9). The final stanza (10-11) continues the repetition of the name "Yahweh" (LORD) which appears eighteen times in the eleven verses of the psalm. Only verse 6 is without it.

Psalm 29 seems to have been originally a Canaanite hymn to the god Ba'al. The staircase parallelism is a characteristic of Canaanite poetry. Even the sound of the poem supports the idea. If Ba'al is inserted instead of Yahweh there is striking alliteration of "b's" and "l's" throughout the psalm.

The Israelites transferred Ba'al's power to Yahweh, the God above all gods. The psalm begins with a call to all other gods (*bene-'elim*) to give glory to Yahweh, most powerful of all. The scene is the heavenly court. The lesser gods are Yahweh's courtiers (cf. Job 1–2). We are given a glimpse of the beginning of a heavenly liturgy.

The second stanza (3-9) gives evidence of the Lord's power and glory. The Lord's voice is heard in the thunder of the storm. In geographical terms the storm begins over the waters of the Mediterranean, moves through the mountains of Lebanon,[4] and strikes the Arabian desert. In the Canaanite hymn *midbar qadesh* probably meant "sacred desert," the place of superhuman powers. The place name Qadesh, however, signifies an important place in the Israelite desert period (cf. Num 20:1-21). Thus the verse came to mean this southern desert location. So the storm completely surrounds the promised land from the Mediterranean on the west, through Lebanon on the north, the Arabian desert on the east, to Qadesh in the south. God's earth-shaking power surrounds God's people. As a result of this awesome demonstration, all in the heavenly court cry, "Glory!" as they were called to do in the first stanza.

The final stanza (10-11) indicates that the Lord's power should be seen in cosmic terms. The Lord, whose word brought all things into being, sits enthroned above the flood, above the heavenly waters confined over the firmament (Gen 1:7) which were once released in Noah's time (Gen 6:17; 7:6, 10-11) to destroy the earth. The Lord has power, not only over creation, but over the watery chaos as well. It is this mighty king to whom we cry: "May the LORD give might to [this] people; may the LORD bless [this] people with peace." The Lord of such power cares about us. We beg the Lord of such power to bless us with the right order in which everyone has what is needed for a full life, everyone has *shalom*.

Baptism ABC (1-2.3-4.3.9-10) [21]

The Lord will bless this people with peace (11).

The refrain for the Baptism of the Lord ABC is the final petition of Psalm 29, asking the Lord, who has demonstrated such power over all creation, to give true peace to the people (see Isa 12 and Ps 104 for optional Masses for Years B and C). The verses begin with the opening call to prayer, summoning all the heavenly powers to worship (1-2). Two verses of the central stanza, describing the power of God's voice in the storm, are included (3-4). The psalm concludes with the heavenly beings' cry of praise and the declaration that the Lord reigns even over chaos (9-10). The verses which are omitted complete the description of the storm. One phrase of the final verse is also omitted, the prayer for a share in God's power (11a).

The gospel reading for all three cycles is the story of Jesus' baptism in the Jordan by John (Matt 3:13-17; Mark 1:7-11; Luke 3:15-16, 21-22). The images in the story suggest the cosmic dimension of the event. When Jesus rises out of the water, the Spirit of God, the mighty wind, splits the heavens and the voice of God, the creative word of God, declares Jesus the

---

[4]Sirion is the Phoenician name for Mount Hermon.

beloved son (cf. Gen 1:1-3). He is the new creation, emerging from the waters, summoned by the voice of God, given life by God's spirit. All in the heavenly court cry, "Glory!" (Ps 29:9).

But the concern of the mighty God whose voice shakes the earth is for the people who cry out for peace. Jesus, the new creation takes on the role of God's Servant, chosen and filled with God's spirit (Isa 42:1-4, 6-7). His commission is to bring justice to the nations. He is himself to be the covenant between God and the people. His manner contrasts with the thundering voice of the Lord which shatters mighty oaks (Ps 29:5, 9). He will not break even a bruised reed. But his power over chaos and death is no less. He restores the light of life; he delivers from the dungeon of death.

Peter puts the matter clearly in his speech to Cornelius (Acts 10:34-38): "He went about doing good and healing all those oppressed by the devil, for God was with him" (10:38). Through him God has proclaimed peace, the *shalom* which assures every person of all that is needed to live a full life. This is the prayer of the psalm: "May the LORD bless [this] people with peace." This is the responsibility we take up. We who share the baptism into Christ's death, immersion into the cosmic flood, share also in Christ's work of bringing justice and peace to all the earth. "May the LORD give might to [this] people; May the LORD bless [us] with peace!" (Ps 29:11).

3. Psalm 33

Psalm 33 opens with a call to prayer which echoes the closing verse of the preceding psalm (32:11). There is no title for this psalm, which is unique in a section (3–41) in which every other psalm is listed as "of David" (see Ps 54 for a discussion of psalm titles). Perhaps Psalm 33 was included at this place because of its echo of Psalm 32. The psalm may be considered in six stanzas (1-5, 6-7, 8-12, 13-15, 16-19, 20-22).

The first stanza (1-5) is bounded by the repetition of just (*sedeq*; 1, 5) and upright/true (1, 4). It is indeed fitting that the just and the upright praise the Lord who loves justice and whose word is upright. The Lord is even more: a source of truth, a lover of right, a giver of goodness. The Lord is worthy of a new song, accompanied with all musical skill.

The second stanza (6-7) begins to describe the specific reasons for praise. The Lord's true word (cf. 4) is the creative power which brought forth sky and sea. God's breath made the stars; God's command established order on the watery shores.

The earth and its people are called to reverent fear in the third stanza (8-12). The Lord's word brought forth the earth. The Lord's plan and design stand forever. The plans of God's enemies perish, but happy those who belong to this powerful God.

Both happiness and frustration stem from the fact that the Lord of all creation is attentive to the human race (13-15). The designer of the cosmos knows intimately the intricacy of the human heart. This is the delight of the righteous, the terror of the wicked.

The fifth stanza (16-19) describes the true source of power. Military might—armies, horses, physical strength—are ultimately useless defenses. Fear of the Lord, wonder-filled love of this God who knows the stars and our hearts, is the true source of power. The Lord saves those who hope in divine compassion.

The final stanza (20-22) is the application of the wisdom found in the rest of the psalm. The Lord saves those who wait; our soul waits for the Lord. The Lord knows our hearts; in God our hearts rejoice. The Lord fills the earth with goodness (*hesed*, 5); the Lord's eyes are upon those who hope for gracious help (*hesed*, 18). Therefore we pray with confident hope: "May your kindness (*hesed*), LORD, be upon us."

What is new about this song (3) which centers on an old idea, the creative power of the divine word? Egypt and Babylon too respected the power of the gods' word.[5] The new song praises the new creation. God's continued bringing forth of life never ends. The God who spoke "in the beginning" continues to use divine power to restore and recreate the people who trust in the holy name, who wait for the faithful loving Lord. "Rejoice, you just, in the LORD; [ongoing] praise from the upright is fitting!" (Ps 33:1).

2nd Sun Lent A (4-5.18-19.20.22) [25]

Lord, let your mercy be on us, as we place our trust in you (22).

The verses of Psalm 33 chosen for the Second Sunday of Lent A come primarily from the latter part of the psalm. Two verses from the first stanza are used, introducing the key words "upright" and "justice" as characteristics of the Lord, but the opening verses, in which "upright" and "just" people are called to praise the Lord, are omitted. The word of the Lord is also introduced, but the verses concerning its power are omitted. One key concept that is carried through, however, is that of *hesed*. The earth is full of the Lord's loving kindness (*hesed*). The eyes of the Lord are upon those who hope for gracious help (*hesed*). We pray that the Lord's kindness (*hesed*) will be upon us. Thus the primary focus of the responsorial psalm is the faithful love of God for those who persevere in hope.

Abraham is certainly one who hoped in the Lord. The reading for this Sunday (Gen 12:1-4) is the beginning of his story. The Lord, whose word

---

[5]Stuhlmueller 1.188–189; Kraus 1.411–413.

made the heavens and the earth (Ps 33:6-7), calls Abraham to leave all he knows and set out for a land known only to God. The Lord also promises blessing, blessing for Abraham, for his descendants, and for all those who bless him. Abraham himself will become a blessing for all the communities of the earth.

The promises are wonderful, but Abraham has nothing except the Lord's word. Yet he trusts that the word of the Lord is true (Ps 33:4). He puts his hope in the Lord and trusts in God's loving-kindness (22). Abraham's hope is not in vain. He waits for the Lord, whose plan stands forever (11). Happy indeed is he; happy his descendants, the nation whose God is the Lord, the people chosen as God's very own (12).

The Second Letter to Timothy (1:8-10) points out that we are all called as Abraham was. God has "saved us and called us to a holy life, not according to our works but according to his own design" (1:9). God's design for us in the great plan of creation was salvation through grace, the faithful love in which Abraham hoped, the loving-kindness for which the psalm prays.

This grace has been bestowed on us in Christ Jesus, who destroyed death and brought life to light. The gospel (Matt 17:1-9) shows us the light of God's life shining unhindered through Jesus. But this life is bought at a price. The letter reminds us to bear our share of hardship for the gospel (2 Tim 1:8). Jesus will not let the disciples build tents and simply bask in his glory. They must all come down the mountain and continue working through God's creative plan. For Jesus and all his disciples the way to life leads through the Cross.

Yet the psalm calls on us to rejoice in the Lord (Ps 33:1), whose word is true (4). We trust in the Lord who knows heaven and earth and the intricacies of the human heart (15). We wait for the Lord who is our help and our shield (20); with Abraham and Jesus we pray, Lord, may your loving-kindness be upon us; "we have put our hope in you" (22).

Easter Vigil Alt 1 (4-5.6-7.12-13.20.22) [42]

The earth is full of the goodness of the Lord (5).

Psalm 33 is an alternate choice for the responsorial psalm which follows the first reading of the Easter Vigil (Gen 1:1–2:2). With its strong emphasis on the creative power of God's word it is certainly an excellent choice. The verses chosen pronounce God's word true and effective. The Lord's word creates the heavens, confines the sea of chaos, and (by implication) fills the earth with goodness. Indeed God agrees. God looked at everything that had been made and said: How very good! (Gen 1:31). The pinnacle of God's creation is the human being, created in the divine image (Gen

1:27). The psalm describes the care of the creator for this favored creature: "From heaven the LORD looks down and observes the whole human race." How happy the people whose God is the Lord (Ps 33:13, 12).

The closing verses of the psalm remind us that this is not only a story of the very dawn of time but that it has impact on our lives as well. We too are the people called into being by the Lord's word, chosen as God's very own (Ps 33:12). Our task is to live in hope, to wait for the Lord, to trust in God's protection and love. Our task also, we who are made in the divine image, is to extend God's protection and love to the rest of creation. Then we can sing with happy hearts: "The earth is full of the goodness of the Lord" (Ps 33:5).

5th Sun Easter A (1-2.4-5.18-19) [53]

Lord, let your mercy be on us, as we place our trust in you (22).

The verses of Psalm 33 chosen for the Fifth Sunday of Easter A are taken primarily from the first stanza of the psalm, the call to the just and upright to praise the Lord who loves justice, whose word is upright. The final verses are from the fifth stanza which reveals where true power lies. Those who fear the Lord can count on God's attentive care to deliver them from all harm, even death. The refrain is our own appropriation of this good news as we pray that the Lord's loving-kindness surround us too.

The amazing news of today's gospel (John 14:1-12) comes in the final verse. Jesus promises that whoever believes in him will do the works that he does, and even greater ones than these (14:12)! How is this possible? How is it possible even to do his works, not to mention those greater than his! Jesus begins his discourse by calling for faith, faith in God, faith also in him. He goes on to say that he is in the Father and the Father in him. His works are not his own, but the Father's. Now the news is even more amazing. In doing his works we are doing the Father's!

God's works, we sing in Psalm 33, are trustworthy, and the Lord's word is true (Ps 33:4). It is the Lord's word and work which create the heavens and earth. It is this work of creation we are called to share. How? Through Jesus working in us. When Thomas asks, Jesus promises "I am the way and the truth and the life" (John 14:6). Later he says, "Whatever you ask in my name, I will do" (14:13). Why? So that the Father may be glorified in the Son, and also in us. "Praise from the upright is fitting" (Ps 33:1).

It is this work of Jesus that the disciples are doing in the passage from the Acts of the Apostles (6:1-7). The work, however, is too much for them. The work needs order and they need help. Order is a primary characteristic of God's work, and it is our glory that God has chosen to share the responsibility for that work with us. Thus the Twelve follow the divine example in ordering and sharing the work. As a result the work prospers. "The LORD's eyes are . . . upon those who hope for . . . gracious help" (Ps 33:18).

The foundation of all our work, however, is Christ. He is the cornerstone; we simply contribute to the structure (1 Pet 2:4-9). It is his work we do. For this we were chosen and consecrated, so that we might announce the praise of God who called us and all creation out of darkness into wonderful light. "Rejoice, you just, in the LORD; praise from the upright is fitting . . . .For the LORD's word is true; all [God's] works are trustworthy" (Ps 33:1, 4). By this word we have been created; with these works we have been entrusted. Lord, "we have put our hope in you" (Ps 33:22).

19th Sun Year C (1.12.18-19.20.22) [118]

Happy the people chosen as God's very own (12).

The selection of verses from Psalm 33 for the Nineteenth Sunday of Year C is scattered throughout the psalm. After the opening call to prayer (1) the responsorial leaps to verse 12, the conclusion of the third stanza which blesses those who fear the Lord, i.e., God's own people. The remainder of the selection is the conclusion of the psalm with the exception of verse 21. True salvation comes, not from human power but from God's watchful care. Therefore we hope in the Lord. The refrain echoes the happiness of the chosen who put their trust in God.

The readings present three examples of waiting for God in trust. The first reading (Wis 18:6-9) is part of a long discourse on how Wisdom saves her followers while their enemies perish: "By the things through which their foes were punished they in their need were benefited" (Wis 11:5). The exodus-wilderness experience is the primary example, with comparisons drawn from the plagues, the manna, and the water from the rock. Today's reading contrasts the death of the Egyptian firstborn with the rescue of the Israelites from Egyptian genocide. The plagues are a witness to the power of God's word (cf. Ps 33:4-9). Through Moses God warned the Israelites of the threat to the firstborn and prescribed the ritual of Passover to protect them (Exod 12). "The people chosen as [God's] very own" (Ps 33:12) were offering the Passover sacrifice on the very night the Egyptian firstborn were slain (Wis 18:9). Even though they were helpless, they waited for the Lord, trusting their help and their shield (Ps 33:20).

The Letter to the Hebrews (11:1-2, 8-19) lists many examples of people who waited for the Lord, who rejoiced in being God's chosen. Today's reading centers on the faith of Abraham who obeyed God in what seemed impossible conditions. His faith was not misguided. He received one son back from the dead, and through him descendants as numerous as the stars. His descendants sing: "Happy the nation whose God is the LORD, the people chosen as [God's] very own" (Ps 33:12).

Today's gospel teaches us, Jesus' disciples, how to wait for the Master's return (Luke 12:32-48). Jesus assures us that we are chosen as God's very own (Luke 12:32; cf. Ps 33:12). But this does not relieve us of all responsibility. The household of the Church has been entrusted to us. We bear the charge to serve the hungry who come (12:42). We have been entrusted with much; much will be required of us (12:48). The reward for faithful waiting, however, is very great. The master himself will serve us! Happy indeed are those who wait for the Lord.

Do we wait? Does our awesome responsibility ever cross our minds? Or are we like those servants who think the master will never come? Happy are those who wait.

29th Sun Year B (4-5.18-19.20.22) [147]

Lord, let your mercy be on us, as we place our trust in you (22).

The refrain and verses chosen from Psalm 33 for the Twenty-Ninth Sunday B are the same as those for the Second Sunday of Lent A (see above). The central section is from the fifth stanza (16-19) concerning true power. The stanza begins with the images of king and warrior depending on human military might. The contrast is found in those who fear the Lord. The latter are the ones who escape death because of the Lord's gracious help. The refrain emphasizes trust in God's loving-kindness.

The passage from Isaiah (53:10-11) is a taste of the fourth Servant song (see Passion Sunday ABC). In this final song the Servant is portrayed as one who willingly accepts suffering and even death for the guilt of others. The section assigned to this Sunday announces the Servant's reward: he shall see his descendants in a long life; he shall see the light in fullness of days. The will of the Lord is accomplished through him; through his suffering many are justified. The real victory of the Lord, salvation for those who fear God, is accomplished not by military might but by the Servant's silent acceptance of suffering (cf. Ps 33:16-19).

The early Christians saw the Servant as an image of Jesus, the sinless one whose suffering takes away our guilt. Today's gospel (Mark 10:35-45) is in the midst of a section in which Jesus announces his passion to the disciples. They, however, are unable to comprehend the reality of his words. They cannot believe that he will really suffer and die. Right after the third of these announcements (10:32-34), James and John ask for the chief places of honor in the kingdom. Jesus reminds them that they do not know what they are talking about. Can they share in his suffering? When they declare their willingness, Jesus agrees that they will indeed share his suffering. But places of honor are not his to give. God has prepared them for those who wait (cf. Ps 33:20)

There are two levels of trust in this gospel: The unlimited trust that Jesus has in God and the somewhat blind trust the disciples have in Jesus. They are both models for us as we hope in the Lord whose eyes are upon us (Ps 33:18). It is the Lord who will deliver us from death, who will enable us to drink the cup and endure the baptism. Our support in this blind trust is Jesus, one who can sympathize completely with our weakness (Heb 4:14-16). He is the Servant who takes on our guilt, the high priest who makes sacrifice for our sin. He is God's loving-kindness come to fill the earth, come to be upon us who put our hope in God.

This Sunday confronts us with the cost of waiting for the Lord, trusting in God's word. The cost may take us even into death; the reward is life. "May your kindness, LORD, be upon us; we have put our hope in you" (Ps 33:22).

Trinity Sunday B (4-5.6.9.18-19.20.22) [*166*]

Happy the people chosen as God's very own (12).

The verses selected from Psalm 33 for Trinity Sunday B emphasize the power of God's word (4-6, 9). All things came into being by the word of the Lord. But the powerful creator turns with tender care toward the reverent and hopeful (18-19). Those who wait for the Lord are saved (19-20, 22). Happy indeed are they (12)!

Deuteronomy presents Moses exhorting the people to fear the Lord who has chosen to speak to them (Deut 4:32-34, 39-40). Fear of the Lord is the reverent wonder of those who have experienced God's great love. Its natural response is loving obedience to this awesome God who has deigned to care so much for us.

The psalm echoes Moses' exhortation. The Lord's word is true; the Lord's eyes are upon the reverent (the God-fearers). The Lord delivers them from death (Ps 33:4, 18, 19). The word of the Lord which created the heavens has also given us the life-giving Law. The Lord who delivered Israel from Egypt now looks with care upon those who hope for gracious help. How happy are we, chosen as God's very own (12).

The New Testament readings (Rom 8:14-17; Matt 28:16-20) expand the wonder. Not only does God look upon us with care, Jesus who shares our very flesh has promised to be with us until the end of time. Paul tells us that the Spirit, Jesus' gift to us, makes us God's own children along with him. The Lord who created us by a word and who watches us with saving help, has caught us up into the divine life of love, the *hesed* for which we hope (Ps 33:18). Our response of loving obedience compels us to spread the good news to others. God's word in our mouths retains its creative power. As we now make disciples, baptizing them in the name of the Father and of the Son and of the Holy Spirit, more and more children of God are created and welcomed into the awesome life of God. "Did anything so great ever happen before? Was it ever heard of?" (Deut 4:32). Happy indeed the people chosen as God's very own (Ps 33:12).

4. Psalm 47 (Enthronement)

Psalm 47 sweeps us into a great procession. The ark of the covenant, sign of the presence of God, is being carried in solemn procession into the temple.[6] There is much discussion about the original occasion for such a procession. Was there an Enthronement festival, modeled on the enthronement of kings or on the Babylonian New Year's festival at which the god was again declared king?[7] Was there a re-enactment of David's bringing the ark into Jerusalem (cf. 2 Sam 6)? No certainty about the specific occasion can be achieved. But without a doubt the psalm describes a ritualization of Yahweh's kingship over the chosen people and over all the earth. Thus it belongs to the category of Enthronement Psalms (see also Psalms 93, 96, 97, 98).

The first stanza (2-5) begins with a call to all peoples to praise God with hand-clapping and shouting. The mood is one of victory and national pride. Clapping and shouting mark events like the defeat of Jericho (Josh 6:5, 16, 20), the designation of Saul as king (1 Sam 10:24), and the accession of Joash to the throne (2 Kgs 11:12). In this psalm the popular delight results from the renewed celebration that Yahweh, the Most High God, is the great king of all the earth. This great king has chosen this people, given them a land and dominion over other nations. The mood fits the period of David when the kingdom was at its largest extent and the surrounding nations were subject and paying tribute.

The second stanza (6-7) describes the main event. God, enthroned upon the ark, ascends to the place of honor as the trumpets sound and the people continue to shout. The trumpet (*shophar*) is also associated with the accession of the king (2 Sam 15:10; 2 Kgs 9:13) and with special celebrations such as New Year's (Num 29:1) and the announcement of the jubilee year (Lev 25:9). A new call to praise (Ps 47:7) flows from this glorious occasion.

The final stanza (8-10) proclaims the extent of God's reign. God is king of all the nations, of all the earth. Rulers of the other nations join for the

[6]See Stuhlmueller (1.244) for a description of the probable route and ritual.
[7]See Kraus 1.503–504.

celebration with the people covenanted to God through Abraham. The vision has expanded from David's kingdom to the great Day of the Lord when all nations will assemble in Jerusalem to acknowledge Yahweh as the great king, God Most High.

Ascension ABC (2-3.6-7.8-9) [59]

God mounts the throne amid shouts of joy; a blare of trumpets for the Lord (6).

Most of Psalm 47 is used for the Solemnity of the Ascension. The verses omitted all treat directly or indirectly the subjection of other peoples to God's chosen people (4-5, 10). The refrain is the central verse of the psalm and describes the central event, God's ascent to the throne and the people's jubilant response.

The readings for this solemnity always begin with the story of the ascension of Jesus from the Acts of the Apostles (1:1-11). Jesus instructs his disciples, commissions them as witnesses, and is lifted up to the heavens out of their sight. The juxtaposition of Psalm 47 with the images of this event is rich in new insight. Jesus has been instructing the disciples about the kingdom of God (1:3) and they, not quite clear yet, have asked him if he will restore the kingdom now (1:6). His answer reserves that time to God, and we sing: "God is king over all the earth," over all nations (Ps 47:8-9).

Jesus is taken up into heaven in a cloud, a common sign of God's presence. When Solomon dedicated the temple, the cloud filled it to such a degree that the priests could no longer continue the ritual (1 Kings 8:10-11). The psalm celebrates a renewal of that event, a procession of the ark into the temple. The ark is Israel's primary sign of the presence of God. Now as we celebrate this feast we see Jesus, our sign of the presence of God, surrounded by a cloud as he ascends to his throne at the right hand of God (cf. Eph 1:20-23).

The disciples are promised the gift of the Spirit to strengthen and enlighten them (Acts 1:5, 8). The passage from the Letter to the Ephesians (1:17-23) is a prayer that we may be enlightened specifically concerning the great hope that is ours. Our hope springs from God's great power which raised Christ from the dead and seated him in the heavens. This power is now exercised for us who believe. God is king; God raises Jesus to the throne and through him brings us all into the glorious kingdom of his inheritance. "Sing praise to God, sing praise!" (Ps 47:7).

But even shouts of praise and applause are not enough. Jesus commissions the disciples to be witnesses that the peoples of the whole earth might know the good news that they belong to God, who is enthroned on high (cf. Ps 47:10). The gospel readings for each of the three years emphasize the importance of bearing witness (Matt 28:16-20; Mark 16:15-20; Luke 24:46-53). The signs of the kingdom for which the disciples asked are already present in the defeat of the powers of evil (Mark 16:17-18). Jesus has been given the full authority of the kingdom (Matt 28:18). The disciples are entrusted with the good news. Their joy overflows into continual praise of God (cf. Luke 24:52-53). With Psalm 47 we enter into their joy and accept the awesome responsibility of continuing to bear witness. "God is king over all the earth; sing hymns of praise" (Ps 47:8).

Ascension Common (2-3.6-7.8-9) [175]

(see above, the Solemnity of the Ascension).

5. *Psalm 66*

Psalm 66 is a wonderful example of the power of liturgical memory to bring past events into the present and to layer all God's awesome deeds into one grand occasion for praise. The psalm also weaves together community praise (1-12) and the thanksgiving of an individual within the community (13-20). In addition, not only are God's people called to give praise, but so too all the nations on earth (1, 4, 8). Thus the psalm effectively dissolves the ordinary boundaries of space and time.

The first stanza (1-4) is an extended call to prayer. Worshipers are summoned to shout, sing, and praise. Then the text of the prayer is provided: "Say to God, 'How awesome your deeds!'" (3). All people on earth are called to praise the mighty deeds of God.

The second stanza (5-12) begins with another summons, "Come and see." God's awesome works are made present in the liturgical action. God's liberation of the people in the exodus happened not only for the people of the thirteenth century BCE. It is happening now for us. "Come and see!" Let us rejoice! In mid-stanza there is yet another call to praise (8). This call introduces praise for a more recent liberation by God who has kept us alive, who after distress has led us out to freedom. The trial is accepted from the hand of God; the deliverance is also accepted. The context for recalling the whole event is praise.

The third stanza (13-20) switches the focus to an individual who has also experienced God's deliverance. This individual now summons all God-fearers to "come and hear." The individual follows the same liturgical pattern, telling the story and doing the action. The story brings God's rescue into the present. The action gives flesh to the thanksgiving. Lavish gifts accompany the praise of God who hears. The final verse is the individual's thanksgiving to God who is lavish with the gift of *hesed*, loving-kindness.

6th Sun Easter A (1-3.4-5.6-7.16.20) [56]

Let all the earth cry out to God with joy (1).

The refrain for the Sixth Sunday of Easter A is the opening call to praise of Psalm 66, calling all peoples on earth to shout joyful praise to God. The verses are taken primarily from the beginning and end of the psalm. All of the extended call to praise from the first stanza is used with the exception of the half verse portraying God's enemies cringing before the divine strength (3b). The liturgical recollection of the exodus is included up to the dismissal of rebels. The responsorial ends with two verses from the individual thanksgiving, the summons to come and hear and the prayer of gratitude for God's *hesed*. The second half of the community praise, recalling a more recent deliverance, is omitted along with the description of the individual sacrifice.

The readings for this Sunday are an invitation to come and see the works of God. The story of Philip in Samaria (Acts 8:5-8, 14-17) follows a notice that the disciples scattered throughout the countryside because of the persecution which broke out in Jerusalem following the martyrdom of Stephen. Thus Philip found himself in Samaria and proclaimed there the awesome deeds God has done in Christ. The people responded by receiving the word in great joy. When the apostles who had remained behind in Jerusalem heard the good news, they came to confer the Holy Spirit on the new believers. The word of God is already crossing the boundaries which separate people.

In the psalm we sing with the voice of Philip calling the Samaritans to believe: "Shout joyfully to God, all you on earth!" (Ps 66:1). The Samaritans too join the song: Come and see God's awesome deeds for us! (Ps 66:5). The overflowing of joy to all the nations on earth begins because of the effects of persecution, but ends in joyful praise. "We went through fire and water; then you led us out to freedom" (Ps 66:12).

The element that transforms suffering is hope, hope in the God who never fails. The author of 1 Peter (3:15-18) exhorts us not to abandon hope. Rather even in the midst of suffering we must be ready to explain this extraordinary perseverance in hope. Even in suffering we can bless God who has kept us alive (Ps 66:8-9). Even in suffering we can proclaim to others: Come and see God's awesome deeds for us! (Ps 66:5). The word of God transcends the boundaries of human experiences.

What is the work of God that sustains such joyful hope? It is the Father's gift of the Spirit, promised us by Jesus (John 14:15-21). The Samaritans receive the gift of the Spirit through the disciples. Jesus promises us too that we will not be left orphans. God's awesome deed done for us in Christ will not be locked into the first century but will transcend time through

God's Spirit who continues to live in the Father, we in him, and he in us (John 14:20). How awesome God's deeds!

In our own liturgical memorial we dissolve the boundaries of time and through the power of memory bring God's glorious deeds into our present. We call to the whole earth to shout joyfully to God. We praise God for deliverance past and present. As a community we celebrate; as individuals nourished in that community we give thanks for God's deeds for each of us. We proclaim God's goodness that the praise may spread to the ends of the earth. Come and hear, all who fear God, what has been done for me! (Ps 66:16).

14th Sun Year C (1-3.4-5.6-7.16.20) [103]

Let all the earth cry out to God with joy (1).

The refrain and verses from Psalm 66 chosen for the Fourteenth Sunday of Year C are the same as those for the Sixth Sunday of Easter A (see above).

Joy in the Lord's power is the theme that characterizes this Sunday. The reading from Isa 66:10-14 is a summons for all God's people to rejoice. The new Jerusalem has given birth to God's children. Those who thought her dead now delight in her motherly comfort. She is God's new creation. Her joy overflows to all her people. With the prophet we cry out to all the earth: "Shout joyfully to God . . . who rules by might forever" (Ps 66; 1, 7).

In the gospel (Luke 10:1-12, 17-20) we hear of the rejoicing of the seventy-two disciples whose missionary journey has been very successful. Their work of preaching the good news is a share in God's power, establishing the kingdom, bringing the new creation. As seventy-two, the symbolic number of the Gentile nations (Gen 10), they suggest the spread of the kingdom even to the Gentiles. Human boundaries dissolve. Satan, the power of evil and chaos, has fallen from the sky. Come and see the works of God who has kept us alive and delivered us from the enemy! (cf. Ps 66:5, 9-12).

Paul teaches us the cost of the victory which brings us such great joy (Gal 6:14-18). It is through the Cross of our Lord Jesus Christ that the new creation has been born. Our share in the Cross marks our share in the joy. Paul has made the Cross his only boast. With the psalmist he can say, "You tested us, O God, tried us as silver tried by fire . . . then you led us out to freedom" (Ps 66:10, 12). An individual immersed in the life of the community, Paul brings his own thanksgiving. Like the psalmist he calls us to come and hear what God has done for him (Ps 66:16).

We reap the benefit of all who have gone before us. The boundaries of time and space are transcended in the workings of God's new creation. We are brought the good news by the missionary disciples. Through baptism we are marked with the sign of the Cross. We share in the prosperity of the new Jerusalem. Blessed be God, whose loving-kindness does not fail for all generations (cf. Ps 66:20). Shout joyfully; sing God's praise (Ps 66:1).

Easter Common (1-3.4-5.6-7.16.20) [175]

Let all the earth cry out to God with joy (1).

Psalm 66 is one of two psalms suggested for the Easter Season (see also Psalm 118).

The refrain and verses of Psalm 66 selected for the Common of Easter are the same as those for the Sixth Sunday of Easter A (see above).

Psalm 66 is well suited to any of the Sundays of the Easter season because of its spirit of joy, its summons to praise, its focus on the mighty works of God which transcend space and time. Specific themes which are echoed in the Sunday readings include the relationship between community and the individual (Second Sunday of Easter A, B, C [see Ps 118]; Seventh Sunday of Easter A, B, C [see Pss 27, 103, 97]), the actualization of God's mighty deeds in liturgical worship (Third Sunday of Easter A [see Ps 16]), God's rescue after testing (Third Sunday of Easter B [see Ps 4]; Fourth Sunday of Easter A, C [see Pss 23, 100]; Fifth Sunday of Easter B [see Ps 22]), the summons for all the earth to join God's people (Fourth Sunday of Easter B [see Ps 118]); Fifth Sunday of Easter C [see Ps 145]).

6. Psalm 93 (Enthronement)

Psalm 93 is a hymn to Yahweh's kingship (cf. also Pss 47, 96–99). The psalm is powerful in its brevity and staircase repetition (see Ps 123). The mood is one of celebration that the Lord who made covenant with Israel is the ruler of all creation.

The psalm can be considered in two brief and balanced stanzas (1-2, 3-5). The first stanza presents an enduring image of Yahweh, unshakeable and glorious. Power and dignity clothe the divine ruler who serves and defends the fragility of creation against the dissolution of chaos. Above it all the Lord reigns as far back as the beginning, as far ahead as eternity.

The second stanza (3-5) presents a vivid display of the Lord's victory over the waters of chaos (see also Ps 29). The Lord who defeated the roaring, rushing chaos in creation has also established decrees for the people as their defense against the same chaos. Holiness, being drawn out of chaos and set apart for new life, is the gift to these who belong to Yahweh. It signifies especially the temple service, the model of new creation.

The psalm is a prayer of joyful hope for us. Faced with the chaos of famine, violence, greed, and threatened nuclear destruction, we sing with unbelievable confidence: The Lord is king; the world will not be moved (1). God has given us the key to the power that sustains creation. It is the Law, the decrees firmly established. Our challenge is to live by them.

Christ the King B (1.1-2.5) [162]

The Lord is king, robed with majesty (1).

The refrain and verses from Psalm 93 for the Solemnity of Christ the King B emphasize the stability of God's rule. The verses which present the dynamic image of Yahweh's active and continuing dominion over chaos (3-4) are omitted. The omission is regrettable in an age in which our awareness of the need for Yahweh's power over chaos becomes more and more acute. Since the psalm in its entirety is so short, it would be preferable to use the whole thing.

In today's readings there is a rich and paradoxical interplay between creation and the future kingdom of God, between the Son of Man and God's people, between Jesus and Yahweh. Daniel's vision (7:13-14) is political as well as eschatological. The four world kingdoms of the ancient world and especially the immediate persecution of Antiochus IV (175-164 BCE) inspire the author's vision of four beasts emerging from the sea of chaos (7:1-8). God, the Ancient One, mounts the throne for judgment (7:9-12). Then a fifth figure appears, coming not from the sea but on the clouds of heaven. This last figure is not a beast but one in human likeness (= like a son of man). To him is given everlasting dominion, an indestructible kingship. In the interpretation of the vision the fifth figure, the Son of Man, is identified as "the holy people of the Most High" (7:27). In succeeding centuries, however, the Son of Man becomes an individual figure who will come to judge the living and the dead at the end of time.

We sing Psalm 93, holding in tension the declaration that Yahweh is king, more powerful than the chaos from which the beasts emerge, and the vision of kingship being given to the Son of Man, who represents both God's people and their final judge.

In the gospel (John 18:33-37) Pilate confronts Jesus directly with the question, " Are you the king of the Jews?" Jesus responds, "My kingdom does not belong to this world." The interplay between political reality and God's eternal kingdom is again put before us. Jesus continues with a description of his real mission, of real kingship. "I came . . . to testify to the truth." Jesus himself is the Truth (John 14:6). He bears true witness to the Father (5:31-40; 8:39-47). His disciples are characterized by their acceptance of the truth he brings. They are consecrated in the truth (17:17-19). They bear the holiness of God's people (cf. Ps 93:5).

The whole story is overshadowed by the chief representative of chaos, death. Jesus is on trial for his life and Pilate will condemn him to death.

His death itself will be his final great witness to the Father. God is victorious over chaos, even death. "More powerful than the breakers of the sea . . . is the LORD" (Ps 93:4). The truth that Jesus brings is God's purpose for us, God's firmly established decree (Ps 93:5). The goal of Jesus' witness, the goal of God's decree is life, life for us and life for the world.

The reading from Revelation (1:5-8) shows us Daniel's vision transformed. Jesus Christ is the one in human likeness coming on the clouds to receive the kingdom in the name of all God's people. He is the faithful witness to God's truth, the firstborn creation drawn from the sea of death. He loves us and draws us into new creation with him to become the people of the great king, Yahweh, the Alpha and Omega, the beginning and the end, who rules forever.

7. Psalm 95 (Enthronement)

Psalm 95 is an enthronement song (see Psalm 93). The psalm suggests a great procession into God's sanctuary. During the procession a leader encourages the people to sing praise. The first two stanzas balance each other, each repeating the hymnic pattern of call to praise and reasons for praise. The final stanza is an oracle warning the people to obey in sincerity.

The first stanza (1-5) begins with an insistent call to praise: come, sing, cry out, greet God. The mood is one of joyful celebration. The reasons for praise follow. The Lord is the God over all gods, the God who formed and holds all of creation.

The second stanza (6-7a) develops the first. The procession has now reached the sanctuary. The call is to enter and worship this great God of creation. The motivation turns from the cosmic to a personal viewpoint. This great God is our God. We belong to the Lord who made us. The divine hands that hold land and sea also care for us as a shepherd cares for the flock.

The oracle (7b-11) is a warning against complacency. To be God's people entails responsibility. The celebration of liturgical worship in the temple brings into the present God's saving deeds of the past. The memory of the past also includes the murmuring of the ancestors in the desert. For forty years they tested God, failing to believe in God's creative care for them. Condemned by their own lack of hope, the exodus generation failed to reach the land of promise (cf. Num 14:26-30). Their situation is brought into the present as a warning to the current generation. "Oh, that today you would hear [God's] voice; do not harden your hearts" (Ps 95:7-8).

The present time of the psalm continues into our time. We too are called out of our complacency to listen to God's voice, to believe in God's new plans for us, and to act on them. The Lord who holds the depths of the earth cares for us like a flock. Oh, that today we would hear God's voice.

3rd Sun Lent A (1-2.6-7.8-9) [28]

If today you hear God's voice, harden not your hearts (7-8).

The refrain for the Third Sunday of Lent A is the turning point of Psalm 95. It shifts the emphasis slightly from the prayer that we might hear God's voice to the plea that we harden not our hearts. The selected verses juxtapose the double call to prayer (1-2, 6) omitting the motivation of vv. 3-5 that God is great king and creator. The only motivation included is the proclamation that the Lord is our God and our shepherd. The oracle is introduced and the situation of the ancestors described (7b-10). The conclusion, God's judgment, is omitted.

The reading from Exod 17:3-7 describes one of the incidents of murmuring in the desert. The story follows a common pattern. When the people experience a genuine need they abandon all faith in God to take care of them and begin to complain about the very exodus itself. Moses, in near despair himself, turns to the Lord who teaches him a way to answer the people's need. Thus through Moses, God tends the needs of the people. The place, however, is named for the murmuring.

The connection with the psalm is obvious. The same incident at Massah or Meribah seems to be recalled. The message, however, is deeper. The people murmur because they lose faith in God's power to provide for them. But this God holds the whole earth with creative care (Ps 95:4-5). Their failure in trust leads to hardness of heart. God's encouragement to risk taking possession of the promised land is met by craven despair (Num 14:1-4). They do not hear God's voice, but God hears theirs. "They shall never enter my rest." The psalm describes a liturgical actualization of the desert incident. Our liturgy too brings God's saving actions into the present. Oh that we now might hear God's voice!

The Samaritan woman who meets Jesus at the well (John 4:5-42) is an example of one who hears. From the beginning of the encounter she never ceases to listen, even when she doesn't understand, even when she does! She does not harden her heart; her reward is the revelation of the Messiah. Not only that, she receives a commission to preach the good news to her townspeople. She becomes the crier who calls out, "Come, let us sing joyfully to the LORD. . . . For this is our God, whose people we are" (Ps 95:1, 7). In contrast to the Israelites in the desert who despaired because they had no water, she gives water and receives back eternal life for herself and many more.

The paradox of the chosen who failed and the outcast who succeeded disappears in the light of the announcement in the second reading (Rom

5:1-2, 5-8). None of us dares boast on our own. While we were all still sinners Christ died for us. This is the tender care of the creator whose hand holds all things (Ps 95:4-5). How can we fail to trust? Today, if you hear God's voice, harden not your hearts! (7-8). Rather rejoice and sing; call your neighbors to worship this great God who made us, whose we are (6-7).

Fourth Sun Year B (1-2.6-7.7-9) [72]

If today you hear God's voice, harden not your hearts (8).

The refrain and verses of Psalm 95 chosen for the Fourth Sunday of Year B are the same as those for the Third Sunday of Lent A (see above).

The refrain and the readings for this Sunday teach us how to listen well. The refrain counsels us to listen with open hearts, vulnerable to God's voice. The first reading (Deut 18:15-20) warns us also to listen wisely. God, out of consideration for our weakness, sends prophets to us. The words of the true prophet are the words of God. Whoever refuses to listen to the prophet has hardened the heart against God. Such prophets follow in the line of Moses, the friend to whom God spoke face to face (Num 12:6-8). Care must be taken, however, to discern the true prophet. The people together must learn how to listen well.

What the people hear in the gospel (Mark 1:21-28) is the authority of Jesus. The word of God flows through him with no hindrance. No moment of self-interest clouds the message. The Law is clear from his mouth; the spirits of evil flee at the sound of his voice. He is the prophet like Moses *par excellence*. Come, let us sing to the Lord who speaks to us with such care.

Paul's concern in his letter to the Corinthians (1 Cor 7:32-35) is that we be free to listen. Any preoccupation, good as it is in itself, which distracts us from opening our hearts fully to God's voice, is better avoided. Paul indicates that marriage may be such a distraction. Marriage, on the other hand, may open the heart and celibacy build a selfish wall against God's call. Paul's point is that nothing, however good in itself, should be allowed to hinder our listening hearts.

Oh, that today we would hear God's voice; oh, that today we would open our hearts. The people together must learn to listen well. Where indeed is God's voice to be heard today?

18th Sun Year C (1-2.6-7.8-9) [115]

If today you hear God's voice, harden not your hearts (7-8).

The refrain and verses of Psalm 95 chosen for the Eighteenth Sunday of Year C are the same as those for the Third Sunday of Lent A (see above).

The readings for this Sunday tell us where to set our hearts, where to direct our attention. The first reading and the gospel present the negative side, the second reading the positive. The first reading is from the Book of Qoheleth (Qoh 1:2; 2:21-23). This third-century sage struggled with the seeming emptiness of all human effort. Without a belief in life after death, the sage was forced to conclude that death destroys everything: pleasure, wealth, learning. The section chosen for today centers on work. At death all the fruits of one's labor go to another. As the popular proverb says, "You can't take it with you." Qoheleth does not end in complete despair, however. He exhorts his readers to enjoy the present moment, and to fear God whose gift it is.

The sage gives us great wisdom. The present is the only time we have in which to live, enjoy, love, and praise God. Today, while we have the moment, let us hear God's voice (Ps 95:7). Let us cry out to God with joy and kneel before the Lord who made us (Ps 95:1, 6). This moment, this day, are the gifts of the God who is our shepherd, the God to whom we belong (Ps 95:7).

Jesus is confronted with a similar situation in the gospel (Luke 12:13-21). The problem of leaving one's wealth to others at death is presented from the other side. The heirs fight over the inheritance, the wealth for which they did not labor. In response Jesus tells a parable which echoes Qoheleth's wisdom. The rich man of the parable remembers only half of Qoheleth's advice: "Eat, drink, be merry!" He forgets the other half, however: "Remember your creator; fear God" (cf. Qoh 5:6; 7:18; 12:1). He allowed wealth to harden his heart so that he did not hear God's voice (Ps 95:7-8). He set his heart on the wrong good.

The Letter to the Colossians (3:1-5, 9-11) advises us to set our hearts on Christ, not on earthly goods. We have already died in Christ. But we know what the sage did not. Our life is not ended but hidden with Christ in God; all is not vanity. The sage knew only half: Make use of the present and fear God. To that Christ adds: Your treasure is kept in heaven. What a gift this news is! Come, let us sing joyfully to the Lord who made us (Ps 95:1). Let us abandon all the defenses which harden our hearts and put on the new self in which we are renewed in the image of the Lord who made us (Col 3:8-10, cf. Ps 95:6). We can risk vulnerability to the present moment which is God's gift. We do not have to waste our energy defending our small hoard against one another. It is all kept by our God, if only we use this day to hear the divine voice with open hearts.

23rd Sun Year A (1-2.6-7.8-9) [128]

If today you hear God's voice, harden not your hearts (7-8).

The refrain and verses of Psalm 95 chosen for the Twenty-Third Sunday of Year A are the same as those for the Third Sunday of Lent A (see above).

The art of listening is again the subject for this Sunday. The warning in Ezek 33:7-9 outlines the heavy responsibility of the person called to be a prophet. The prophet's mission is twofold. First of all, the prophet must listen to God with tender and open heart. But that is not enough. The prophet must also carry God's message to the people. To fail in this second task is to be responsible for whatever happens to the people. On the other hand, the prophet who carries out this twofold task is absolved of responsibility for those who do not listen. This is the second warning in the reading. Those who fail to listen to and act on the words of God's prophet will die for their guilt. The statement is simple and without exception: Listen and live; harden your heart and die.

The gospel situation is more complex (Matt 18:15-20) but the truth is the same: hear God's voice and live. In the gospel God's voice comes through the believing community, the Church. The Church is represented first in the individual member who is offended, then in two or three members, and finally in the assembled community. In each case the offender is urged to listen to God's voice, to abandon hardness of heart. If none of these attempts work, the offender is cut off from the life of the community, left like the unheeding ancestors to die in the desert (Ps 95:10-11).

The additional news at the end of the gospel is that God also listens. Whenever two or three gather together to pray, God hears. The overwhelming love of the Lord who made us is revealed to us in this, that wherever we are gathered in Christ's name, Christ is in our midst. God's heart lies completely open to us, who have God's own Word incarnate among us. Our challenge is to follow the direction of that Word, to be completely vulnerable, not only to God, but to each other. "Owe nothing to anyone, except to love one another; . . . love is the fulfillment of the law" (Rom 13:8, 10). Only in this love is it possible to carry or hear the prophetic message. Only in this love is it possible to confront an offender and make a genuine peace. May we harden not our hearts, so that today we may indeed hear God's voice wherever it is to be found.

27th Sun Year C (1-2.6-7.8-9) [142]

If today you hear God's voice, harden not your hearts (7-8).

The refrain and psalm verses from Psalm 95 chosen for the Twenty-Seventh Sunday of Year C are the same as the Third Sunday of Lent A (see above).

This Sunday's readings describe the faith which underlies true listening. Habakkuk (Hab 1:2-3; 2:2-4) prophesied in the troubling time when the Babylonian empire was rising to power. The prophet complains that God is allowing the chosen people to sink into violence and discord. The wicked prosper and the righteous suffer (1:2-4). God responds with a terrifying message: God is raising up the Babylonians as a judgment against Judah (1:5-11). The prophet then responds by bemoaning the terrible cruelty of the Babylonians (1:12-17).

In spite of the paradox of God's actions, the prophet sets himself to await God's answer in faith (2:1). God responds that the one who waits in faith will live. God's justice will prevail in its own time. Trust in God is the way to salvation. If today you hear God's voice, no matter how paradoxical its message, you will prevail (Ps 95:7-8).

Perseverance in faith requires courage. The author of the Second Letter to Timothy exhorts ministers of the gospel to bear witness bravely even in the midst of hardship (2 Tim 1:6-8, 13-14). The strength for this witness is the Spirit given by God. God's Spirit is one of "power and love and self-control." The challenge to us is the daily willingness to heed God's Spirit, the daily willingness to be open to God's gifts.

The apostles in today's gospel story do not seem to be aware of the power that they already have been given by God (Luke 17:5-10). Faith in God the size of the tiniest seed is powerful enough to uproot trees. The faith to keep our hearts listening to God allows God's power to flow through us. Both the faith and the power, however are God's gift. Jesus does not give the apostles a minute to exult in their own strength. He reminds them that whatever they do is only the common obligation of the servant. The very best they can do is carry out the will of the master.

It is not easy to wait for God's will. It is not easy to keep our hearts open and to trust in God's power. Most of all it is not easy to surrender even our satisfaction in having done well, of having listened perfectly and obeyed completely. But we have a perfect example in Christ, "who, though he was in the form of God, did not regard equality with God something to be grasped" (Phil 2:6). He is the Servant who did the Master's will in every way. Because of his total obedience he is the perfect revelation of God in human flesh. God longs to be revealed in us as well. Christ gives us courage; God's Spirit gives us strength. How good it is to hear God's voice; let us open wide our hearts! (Ps 95:7-8).

Year Common (1-2.6-7.8-9) [175]

If today you hear God's voice, harden not your hearts (7-8).

Psalm 95 is one of eight psalms suggested for the Common of the Year (see also Pss 19, 27, 34, 63, 100, 103, 145). The refrain and verses are the same as those chosen for the Third Sunday of Lent A (see above).

There are several Sundays for which this psalm might be appropriate. The readings for most of them refer to Israel's sojourn in the desert (cf.

Ps 95:8-11). Several of them emphasize listening. The first reading for the Eleventh Sunday of Year A (Exod 19:2-6; see the fuller discussion with Ps 100) introduces the Sinai covenant. God promises that Israel will be a chosen people if they listen to God's voice. In the gospel (Matt 9:36–10:8) the disciples are sent out to proclaim the good news of God's salvation to the wandering sheep. Listening is also the theme for the Fifteenth Sunday of Year C (see Ps 69). The command to heed God's voice is proclaimed in Deut 30:10-14. The gospel (Luke 10:25-37) illustrates the two great commandments. Mark's version of Jesus' teaching on the two great commandments (Mark 12:28-34) is the gospel for the Thirty-First Sunday of Year B (see Ps 18). The first reading is the Shema ("Hear, O Israel" from Deut 6:2-6). A passage from Deuteronomy exhorting the people to listen (Deut 4:1-2, 6-8) also opens the Twenty-Second Sunday of Year B (see Ps 15). The Letter of James (1:17-18, 21-22, 27) emphasizes what a gift God's word is. In the gospel (Mark 7:1-8, 14-15, 21-23) Jesus points out the superiority of God's word to human tradition.

Two Sundays describe Israel's murmuring in the desert. The first reading for the Eighteenth Sunday of Year B (see Ps 78) tells the story of the manna and quail (Exod 16:2-4, 12-15). In the gospel (John 6:24-35) Jesus announces that he is the bread sent by God. On the Twenty-Fourth Sunday of Year C (see Ps 51) the story of Israel's sin with the golden calf is told (Exod 32:7-11, 13-14). Moses prays and God relents. In the gospel (Luke 15:1-32) Jesus tells three parables about God's mercy toward sinners who repent. Paul is presented as an example of God's forgiving mercy in 1 Tim 1:12-17.

The importance of hearing God's word with an open heart is the theme of the Twenty-Eighth Sunday of Year B (see Ps 90). God's word penetrates to our depths. God's wisdom is more valuable than all treasure (Wis 7:7-11), but the rich man cannot see that (Mark 10:17-30). His heart is hardened by his riches.

Dedication Lateran (1-2.3-5.6-7) [*703*]

Let us come before the Lord and praise him (2).

The readings for the Feast of the Dedication of St. John Lateran are taken from the Common of the Dedication of a Church. Psalm 95 is one of four suggested Psalms (see also Pss 84 and 122). The verses selected represent the first two stanzas of the psalm, the call to praise of the creator God and the call to come into God's presence. The stanza which refers to Israel's murmuring in the desert is omitted.

Old Testament readings for which Psalm 95 is appropriate are: 1 Kgs 8:22-23, 27-30, the great king of all gods cannot be contained in any temple;

and Gen 28:11-18, the God who holds the whole earth will protect the covenant people wherever they go. New Testament readings include: Eph 2:19-22, we are God's people, strangers and aliens no longer; and Heb 12:18-19, 22-24, we have been called to praise God our shepherd. The gospel of the Samaritan woman (John 4:19-24) emphasizes the worship of the God of the whole earth (see above, the Third Sunday of Lent A).

8. Psalm 96 (Enthronement)

Psalm 96 is another enthronement psalm (see Pss 47, 93, 95, 97-98). Themes common to enthronement psalms appear: a new song, praise to the God who is creator and judge of the world, proclamation of God's greatness to all the nations on earth. Psalm 96 is also similar to the ancient Ps 29. Both psalms are characterized by staircase parallelism in which successive lines repeat the same phrase. Both psalms demand fitting praise of God. Psalm 96 also echoes Ps 47, the procession to Mount Zion. The story in 1 Chr 16 of David's establishment of the ark of the covenant in Jerusalem describes the ministers singing Psalm 96 between sections of Pss 105 and 106.

The psalm may be approached in four stanzas (1-3, 4-6, 7-10, 11-13). The first stanza (1-3) is an ecstatic call to praise. Six times the psalmist exhorts God's people and the whole earth to sing (3x), bless, announce, proclaim. Their new song tells God's glorious work of salvation to every nation. The final verb (*basar*) means "to proclaim good news." This new song is the forerunner of the gospel, God's good news.

The reasons for praise are in the second stanza (4-6). Yahweh, Israel's God, is greater than the gods of all other nations. There is no comparison. The other gods do nothing, but Yahweh made the heavens. Our delight in the works of our God shines through this stanza and leads to a new call to praise.

The third stanza (7-10) consists almost totally of this renewed summons to praise. Again the imperatives pile up: give (3x), bring, enter, bow down, tremble, say. Verse 7 echoes Psalm 29, but in Psalm 96 praise is demanded of human beings whereas the heavenly beings were summoned to give praise in Psalm 29. The whole earth is called to proclaim God's righteous rule.

The final stanza (11-13) extends the call to the whole earth. Sky and land, sea and plains, even the trees rejoice because God comes to establish lifegiving order. In this new song creation is restored. God's justice brings true peace.

Christmas Midnight ABC (1-2.2-3.11-12.13) [14]

Today is born our Savior, Christ the Lord (Luke 2:11).

The refrain for Christmas Midnight ABC is taken from the angels' proclamation in the gospel. Psalm 96 continues as a fitting announcement of God's transformation of the whole world through the kingdom made flesh in Christ. The verses from the psalm include the first and last stanzas, the opening call to prayer, and the final results of God's righteous judgment. The two middle stanzas, the reasons for praise, and the second summons to the whole earth to give praise, are omitted. Thus some sense of the vast scope of God's glorious kingdom is lost and the insistence on giving praise is weakened.

The first reading (Isa 9:1-6) is a coronation song. The prophet introduces the song by describing the distress of the northern tribes who were plundered by the Assyrians. He encourages them with the news that God's salvation is indeed on the way. The joy which comes to them surpasses any comparison they can make—abundant harvest, great victory, exhilarating liberation. Their joy comes at the accession of a new king who assumes the rule over David's kingdom. Like David he is proclaimed a child of the people and a son of God. His titles express the hope that his reign will be prosperous, peaceful, and just. To his people he is a representative of God, to God a representative of the people.

On this day we see Christ as the new king assuming David's throne, our child and Son of God. He is our representative who sings a new song to God and announces who comes to bring God's just and faithful rule, delight for the earth and peace for its peoples. Let all creation sing for joy!

The gospel (Luke 2:1-14) announces Jesus' birth in Bethlehem, David's city. The angels are the first to sing the new song: "Glory to God in the highest!" They begin the proclamation of God's glory to all nations by telling the news to the shepherds of that region. They proclaim "good news of great joy": The Lord has come to govern the earth with justice and faithfulness. He is found as a child wrapped in swaddling clothes and lying in a manger. This is the marvelous work of the great God who is above all gods.

The Letter to Titus (2:11-14) reminds us that we are still awaiting the fullness of God's kingdom, "the appearance of the glory of the great God and of our savior Jesus Christ" (2:13). We are called not only to sing the new song but to live in justice and faithfulness as people of the new kingdom. The Lord continues to work in us to announce salvation by the witness of our lives. The joy of our song is both the sign of our hope and the proclamation of God's glory.

2nd Sun Year C (1-2.2-3.7-8.9-10) [67]

Proclaim God's marvelous deeds to all the nations (3).

The refrain and verses from Psalm 96 chosen for the Second Sunday of Year C are from the first and third stanzas of the psalm. Thus the whole responsorial psalm for this Sunday is an insistent joyful call to praise. The reasons for praise and the final establishment of God's kingdom are omitted. All we need to remember on this Sunday is to sing praise. We see the signs of God's salvation right before our eyes.

The prophet of the final section of the Book of Isaiah sings joyfully about the restoration of Zion (Isa 62:1-5). He refuses to be silent until God's salvation is accomplished. Then the city of God's people will be glorious in the eyes of all nations. Then it will be revealed how very much God loves this people.

We borrow the prophet's words to shout our joy at the beginning of Jesus' ministry. The first of his signs, according to John, is performed at a wedding in Galilee (John 2:1-12). God, who loves the people as a bridegroom loves his bride, has come in Christ to restore them to life. The new wine of God's kingdom has already been poured.

The sign of the kingdom is the Spirit poured out on each of God's people with gifts for the common good (1 Cor 12:4-11). The proclamation of this Sunday is the announcement that God's salvation has begun (Ps 96:2). The kingdom is at hand! This is why our whole response is a call to praise. Only if the whole earth joins the song can our praise begin to be adequate. Only if all nations see our joy have we succeeded in giving the Lord fitting honor. Sing to the Lord a new song! Sing the Lord who comes!

29th Sun Year A (1.3.4-5.7-8.9-10) [146]

Give the Lord glory and honor (7).

The verses and refrain from Psalm 96 to be used for the Twenty-Ninth Sunday of Year A represent three of the four stanzas of the psalm. Only the final stanza which reports the rejoicing of all creation is completely missing. One verse is omitted from each of the first two stanzas: verse 2, part of the call to praise; and verse 6, one of the reasons for praise.

The readings for this Sunday deal with the question of power. Who has real power? What is its source? The sixth-century prophet, ministering to a people in Exile, introduces the Persian king Cyrus as a Messiah of God (Isa 45:1, 4-6). Cyrus will defeat the Babylonians and allow the Jews to return to Jerusalem and rebuild the temple. The prophet declares that Cyrus is an agent of God's plan to restore the people. Power, however, belongs to God; there is no other. The psalm gives us a fitting response: Give to the Lord glory and praise (Ps 96:7).

Jesus extricates himself from a sticky discussion with a wise, witty answer: Repay to Caesar what belongs to Caesar and to God what belongs to God (Matt 22:15-21). It is again a question of power. The Pharisees attempt to trap Jesus by setting up an opposition between political power and God's power. Jesus avoids their categories and recognizes the legitimate function of human power in its proper relation to God's power. Real wisdom is found in knowing what it is that belongs to Caesar and what belongs to God. What is the relationship between secular authority and God's power?

Paul teaches us that power is found in the gospel (1 Thess 1:1-5). The Thessalonians were moved by the power of the gospel and of the Holy Spirit to change their lives. Today's gospel challenges us also. Daily we meet the demands of human power—political, economic, religious. Which demands are legitimate? When is obedience to human power also submission to God's power? When is resistance to human power obedience to God? It requires wisdom and courage to sing today's new song. The gods of the nations are nothing (Ps 96:5). Human power exists only as a share in the power of God who made heaven and earth. To God belong glory and praise.

9. Psalm 97 (Enthronement)

Psalm 97 is another of the enthronement psalms (see Pss 47, 93, 95-99). The psalm portrays God as the mighty king coming to Mount Zion in triumphant procession. The setting seems to be the final judgment. God comes to establish justice.

The first stanza (1-6) begins with the announcement of the enthronement. God's kingship gladdens the earth even to the distant islands. God's throne is surrounded by cloud and darkness, reminiscent of the theophany at Mount Sinai (Exod 19:16-19) and of the cloud that filled Solomon's temple at its dedication (1 Kings 8:10-12). The true manifestations of God's magnificent power, however, are the justice and right which support the throne. Against these no other power can prevail.

As God goes forth in procession (3-6) all creation responds to divine glory. Fire sets out in advance to consume the enemies. Storm and lightning strike fear in the earth. The mountains melt, the heavens proclaim. All peoples are awed by God's glory.

The second stanza (7-12) describes the result of this theophany. Those who serve other worthless gods are disgraced and defeated. The Lord's servants, on the other hand, are filled with joy. The Lord, the Most High God, establishes true justice on the earth. The psalm closes with a call for the just to rejoice and give praise.

Christmas Dawn ABC (1.6.11-12) [15]

A light will shine on us this day: The Lord is born for us.

The refrain for the Christmas Mass at Dawn ABC announces the theme of light. At midnight Christ's birth is proclaimed (see Psalm 96 above); the light of this dawn liturgy will enable the whole world to see God's salvation in the Mass During the Day (see Psalm 98 below). The verses from Psalm 97 for the Dawn Mass include only the enthronement, the disgrace of idol worshipers, and the joy of God's just ones. The theophany is omitted. Perhaps its images are considered too violent. The great joy of Zion and Judah is also omitted. The emotion of the psalm has been muted to fit this early morning hour.

The readings juxtapose the news of Jesus' birth in Bethlehem (Luke 2:15-20) with the hope for the Lord's restoration of Zion (Isa 62:11-12) and of our own hope for salvation given to us through baptism (Titus 3:4-7). With the psalm these readings are an excellent example of the liturgical use of memory, pulling past, present, and future together into one present time.

The hope of the sixth-century prophet is a hope for restoration of God's city in the prophet's own lifetime and a description of the final glory of God's people on the great Day of the Lord. The gospel tells a single event which reflects in both directions: back to the prophet's hope, forward to our own longed-for salvation at the end of time. In Luke's story of the first witnesses to the good news of Jesus' birth, the shepherds follow the directions of the angel and find Mary and Joseph with the infant lying in a manger. Seeing leads them to proclamation and praise. The Letter to Titus describes the pledge of salvation which we have received in baptism and points forward again to the hope of eternal life.

The psalm in its eternal present ties all these times together: The Lord is king, now and forever. The Lord's justice, the right relationship which sustains all creation, brings salvation to all peoples in all ages. The ancient prophets glimpsed the dawn of salvation. The shepherds found God's light in the infant Christ, and we hope for the fullness of day promised through our baptism. The center of all this hope is Christ, whose birth we celebrate on this day. For us all time focuses on his life, death, and resurrection. Remembering that event, we pull the past and future time of God's salvation into our present and sing for joy: "A light will shine on us this day; today the Lord, the king, is born for us!"

7th Sun Easter C (1-2.6-7.9) [62]

The Lord is king, the Most High over all the earth (1, 9).

The psalm refrain for the Seventh Sunday of Easter C announces two titles of Yahweh: King and Most High. The verses from Psalm 97 tell us the scope of God's domain: king of the whole earth, most high above all gods. At this news the earth rejoices, the heavens proclaim the Lord's justice, the peoples see God's glory, and the gods fall prostrate in the divine presence. The Lord reigns supreme. The missing psalm verses describe the awesome theophany, the shame of idol worshipers, the joy of God's people at their salvation.

This Sunday between the celebration of Ascension and Pentecost emphasizes the exaltation of Christ and his continued care for his disciples. At the Ascension we sang, "God mounts the throne" (Ps 47:6). Now we proclaim, "The Lord is king, the Most High over all the earth" (Ps 97:1, 9).

The vision of Stephen (Acts 7:55-60) confirms our proclamation. At the conclusion of his eloquent witness to Christ, Stephen describes a vision of Christ standing at God's right hand. Christ is exalted over all the earth. But Stephen also recalls Christ's road to glory, the agonizing death that preceded the resurrection. In his own death, Stephen models himself on Christ: "Lord Jesus, receive my spirit. . . .Do not hold this sin against them" (cf. Luke 23:34, 46). Stephen dies in faith that "the LORD loves those who hate evil, protects the lives of the faithful" (Ps 97:10).

In his final prayer for his disciples, Jesus asks his Father to bring his disciples to see and share in his glory (John 17:20-26). He and the Father are one. He prays that his disciples may share in that oneness, that they may live by the love which unites Father and Son. The Son of the mighty God, the Lord of all the earth (Ps 97:5), shares the very life of God with his disciples. What light dawns for the just (Ps 97:11)! Stephen is our first witness to this great gift.

The vision of Jesus' glory is described in the Book of Revelation (22:12-14, 16-17, 20). Jesus, "the Alpha and the Omega, the first and the last, the beginning and the end," comes soon to reward his disciples. When he comes, cloud and darkness will surround him and fire will go before him to consume his enemies (Ps 97:2-3). The mountains will melt like wax at his advance and we will all see his glory (Ps 97:5-6). Then may we all together be among those who rejoice because of his judgments (Ps 97:8). May we all together share in the forgiveness won for us by Christ's death and resurrection. May we all together sing praise: "The LORD is king; let [all] the earth rejoice" (Ps 97:1).

Transfiguration (1-2.5-6.9) [614]

The Lord is king, the most high over the earth (1, 9).

The psalm refrain for the Feast of the Transfiguration is the same as that for the Seventh Sunday of Easter C (see above). The verses of Psalm 97 are also similar to that Sunday, with a slight variation. More of the imagery which surrounds God's coming is included (5-6). Nature's power melts before the divine king. Heaven and earth sing praise to the Most High God.

This feast celebrates the glory of God shining on the face of Christ. Jesus, completely open to the will of his Father, is transparent to the Father's glory (Matt 17:1-9; Mark 9:2-10; Luke 9:28-36). The cloud which signals the presence of God surrounds him. The voice of God proclaims him the beloved Son. The vision echoes the experience of Daniel who saw the glory of the Ancient One seated upon the throne (Dan 7:9-10, 13-14). Fire and light surrounded the divine judge (cf. Ps 97:3). The final action of the Ancient One was the conferral of kingship on "one like a son of man," one in human likeness. In Jesus the glory of God takes up residence in human flesh. The Second Letter of Peter (2 Pet 1:16-19) presents the vision of Jesus' transfiguration as evidence of the reliability of the Christian message. The vision of Christ in glory is the lamp which guides us through the darkness.

In the midst of all these visions the psalm we sing is our awed acknowledgment of God's glory. We believe the message of Christ, that God in all splendor is present in him. So we bind together God and Christ in the shout: "The Lord is king!" The Jesus of the gospels who in all things but sin is like us is now revealed as the image of God. Before him the mountains melt like wax; around him the bright cloud gathers (cf. Ps 97:2, 5). The good news is that through his resurrection we too will share in the glory of God.

10. Psalm 98 (Enthronement)

Psalm 98 is an enthronement psalm, a hymn celebrating Yahweh as king over all creation (see Pss 47, 93, 95-97). The kingship theme, however, is subordinated in this psalm to the witness that Yahweh has acted to save the chosen people.

The first stanza (1-3), after the call for a new song, proclaims the Lord's great victory. All the nations have seen God's mighty deeds for the favored people. God has kept the covenant with faithful love (*hesed, 'emunah*).

Insistent calls to praise this great God and king seem to interrupt one another in the second and third stanzas (4-6, 7-9). The second stanza is a summons to the liturgical musicians; the third stanza calls all creation to join the song. The liturgical action encompasses all space and time, embracing all creation, including God's saving deeds of the past and the final great victory to come.

This psalm echoes Psalm 96. The last three verses are virtually identical except that Psalm 96 calls field and forest to join the song while Psalm 98 summons rivers and mountains. There is also a slight variation in the final word of the psalm. The similarity reveals that the "new song" may be an old song in its outward form. Stock phrases and patterns may be repeated over and over. What is new is the moment we bring to it. Each liturgical occasion renews the saving acts of God in our own time and place. "Sing a new song to the Lord!"

Christmas Day ABC (1.2-3.3-4.5-6) [16]

All the ends of the earth have seen the victory of our God (3).

At the third Mass of Christmas we celebrate in the full light of day. The psalm refrain announces: "All the ends of the earth have seen the victory of our God." The verses consist of the first two stanzas of Psalm 96. The third stanza, calling nature to join the song is omitted. The third stanza would add the reason for celebration: The Lord comes to bring justice and truth to the whole world!

The delight of seeing the Lord's work is the focus of this liturgy. The sixth-century prophet preaching to the exiles proclaims a vision of the Lord restoring Zion (Isa 52:7-10). The sentinels shout for joy because they see. Indeed all the ends of the earth will see. Now we know the good news: The Lord, the King, comes (Ps 98:7-9)! He has won the victory (Ps 98:1-2)!

The Letter to the Hebrews (1:1-6) confirms that now indeed we do see. In times past God spoke in fragmentary ways through the prophets. But now the revelation of God comes through the Son, a perfect reflection of the Father. Through the Son, the Word, all creation came to be. Now all creation celebrates the just rule of the true king.

The gospel (John 1:1-18) continues the announcement of Christ as God's word of creation from the beginning. The life that came to be through him was born into light, the light no darkness could diminish. Now the light comes into the world that we all might see. What we see is the wonderful victory of God's faithful love, the Word of God clothed in our flesh, the only Son coming from the Father full of faithful love. God has remembered faithful love; "all the ends of the earth have seen the victory of our God" (Ps 98:3)!

6th Sun Easter B (1.2-3.3-4) [57]

The Lord has revealed saving power to the nations (2).

A shortened version of Psalm 98 is used for the Sixth Sunday of Easter B. Only the first stanza and one verse of the second are included. The effect of the selection is to surround the proclamation of God's mighty deeds with two summons to praise (1, 4). The emphasis falls on God's faithful love for the chosen people. The song of the musicians joined by the voices of creation is omitted.

The wonder of God's faithful love is also a focus of the readings. The amazing news in the passage from Acts (10:25-26, 34-35, 44-48) is that God's love extends even to the Gentiles. Even those thought to be outside the believing community are given the gift of the Holy Spirit. Cornelius is the patron saint of all who are not born into the chosen people. We sing the new song in Cornelius' voice. God has won the victory over the prejudice and separation caused by sin. All the ends of the earth have seen this triumph. All nations are embraced by God's faithful love (Ps 98:3).

The two New Testament readings (1 John 4:7-10; John 15:9-17) expand on the theme of God's love and instruct us regarding our necessary response. The love of God has been revealed to us through God's only Son who was sent "so that we might have life" (1 John 4:9). It is God who has loved us. Jesus tells us that his love for us compares even to the love of the Father for him (John 15:9). What can we possibly do in response? Both letter and gospel tell us: love one another. Jesus' demand is total: love one another as I have loved you, even to death. The response to God's faithful love is to become ministers of that love to one another, to bear the fruit of faithful love.

God's gift of the Spirit to Cornelius came through the ministry of Peter. At the risk of his reputation (see Acts 11:1-3) Peter entered the house of a Gentile and ate with him. He ignored the boundaries of the community in order to extend those boundaries. Christ died outside the community, outside the city walls, in order to eliminate the boundaries between the chosen and the outcast, between God and sinners. This is the great triumph of God's faithful love for a chosen people, for all people. The challenge for us who sing the new song is to continue Christ's work of eliminating division, to continue to be open to the surprising movement of God's lifegiving Spirit even to the ends of the earth.

28th Sun Year C (1.2-3.3-4) [145]

The Lord has revealed saving power to the nations (2).

The refrain and verses of Psalm 98 assigned to the Twenty Eighth Sunday of Year C are the same as those for the Sixth Sunday of Year B (see above).

The beginning of Psalm 98 praises God's mighty deeds for the house of Israel. But God's faithful love cannot be limited to any one group of people. It continues to break out of any confinement and embrace all peoples everywhere. The prophet Elisha's experience with Naaman (2 Kgs 5:14-17) is an example. Naaman is a Syrian army commander who is struck with leprosy. On the advice of his wife's maid, a little Israelite girl, he goes to the prophet Elisha in search of healing. Elisha gives him a simple formula which, with a little persuasion, he follows: Plunge into the Jordan seven times. He is healed, so that he may know "that there is a prophet in Israel" (2 Kgs 5:8). Naaman offers to pay the prophet, but as a true prophet Elisha refuses. So Naaman returns to Syria carrying earth from Israel, the land that belongs to Yahweh who healed him.

In the words of Psalm 98 we sing, The Lord "has revealed [the] triumph for the nations to see" (Ps 98:2). The psalm speaks of God's saving deeds for Israel which are witnessed by the nations. But in Naaman's case God's saving act is for a non-Israelite. Not only the vision of salvation, but salvation itself overflows to all peoples. God's faithful love fills the whole earth (Ps 98:3).

Luke's story of the grateful Samaritan (Luke 17:11-19) gives us another example of one who seems to be outside the covenant and yet acts with covenant virtue. Only the Samaritan returns to give thanks for his healing. Only the Samaritan has learned to sing the new song. Jesus uses the Samaritan's goodness to chide those who are so complacent in their chosenness that they fail to give praise to God who is the source of their salvation. The ends of the earth have seen, but the children of the house have forgotten.

"The word of God is not chained" (2 Tim 2:8-13). The author of 2 Timothy shows us Paul who suffers "for the sake of those who are chosen, so that they too may obtain the salvation that is in Christ Jesus." Naaman and the Samaritan show us that the chosen are a bigger group than we had imagined. All those who persevere and die with Christ are chosen. "All the ends of the earth have seen the victory of our God" (Ps 98:3).

This is a day for gratitude. Even the psalmist deserves our thanks for giving us the words so we will not forget. In typical Hebrew fashion we do not attempt to give thanks alone. Rather we summon the whole world to hear of God's wonderful works and to sing with us (Ps 98:4). God's faithful love has won the victory (Ps 98:2-3).

33rd Sun Year C (5-6.7-8.9) [160]

The Lord comes to rule the earth with justice (9).

In contrast to the other uses of Psalm 98 the refrain and verse chosen for the Thirty-Third Sunday of Year C represent the last half of the psalm. The liturgical musicians are called to begin the new song to the Lord. Sea and land, rivers and mountains are exhorted to join the celebration. The Lord comes to establish justice and fairness on the earth.

On these final Sundays of the year we turn to face the future, the return of Christ in glory to judge the living and the dead. Psalm 98 corresponds perfectly with its theme of the arrival of God who will grant justice to all peoples.

The prophet Malachi (Mal 3:19-20) presents a slightly different picture of the Day of the Lord. That day will come, blazing like an oven. The fire will mean destruction for the wicked but the healing light of the sun for the righteous. The Day of the Lord will be a great and terrible day (Mal 3:23).

Each of the synoptic gospels presents Jesus' description of the Day of the Lord. The signs of that day will indeed be great and terrifying: wars, earthquakes, famine, and plague. Nature too will be shaken by mighty signs.

No one knows when that day will come. What Jesus' disciples need to know is that they will be cared for throughout the calamity. They will be hated, persecuted, even killed, but paradoxically not one hair of their heads will be destroyed.

Luke emphasizes the need to live faithfully day by day since we do not know the day when this will happen (Luke 21:5-19). Paul finds it necessary to remind the Thessalonians to do just that (2 Thess 3:7-12). Some of the community, believing as Paul himself did that Christ would return during their lifetimes, had ceased working and were simply waiting. Paul's rule of thumb is simple: as long as you do not need to eat, you do not need to work. Speculating about the day of Lord's coming is not the Christian's most important business. Persevering in righteousness is.

How can we reconcile the variety of images of the Day of the Lord? How can we stir up our own generation which has ceased to expect anything at all? The key lies in the psalm refrain: "The Lord comes to rule the earth with justice." What is this justice (*sedeq*)? It is the faithful response to the demands of each relationship. For the unjust, who have violated the rights of others, the Lord's fire will be destruction. For the slothful, who have not served others' needs, the day will mean shame. But for those who have put their trust in God and tried to answer the demands of every day, the Day of the Lord will mean singing and shouting for joy. Then nature, which always shares the fate of God's people, will respond not with destruction but with delight. The Lord comes! May we be found singing the new song!

Christmas Common (1.2-3.3-4.5-6) [175]

All the ends of the earth have seen the saving power of God (3).

Psalm 98 is the only psalm suggested for the Common during the Christmas season. The refrain and verses are the same as those for Christmas Mass During the Day (see above). The psalm could certainly be used for all three Masses of Christmas since the enthronement psalms have such similar themes (see Pss 96 and 97). Perhaps the proper refrains should be retained, however. Psalm 98 would also be appropriate for the Second Sunday after Christmas ABC, again with the proper refrain (see Ps 147 for a fuller discussion).

Immaculate Conception (1.2-3.3-4) [689]

Sing a new song to the Lord, who has done marvelous deeds (1).

The verses of Psalm 98 chosen for the Solemnity of the Immaculate Conception ABC are the same as those for the Sixth Sunday of Easter B (see above). The refrain, however, is different. The refrain is the opening verse of the psalm which summons us to sing the new song of the redeemed, to praise our God who has done amazing things to rescue us from sin and death. The verses elaborate on God's wonderful works.

The readings for this celebration are a challenge. Read superficially, they give us a false picture. The Genesis reading is not a simple description of "original sin." The gospel story of Jesus' conception can be confusing at this celebration of Mary's own conception in the womb of her mother.

What richness can we find in these readings? The marvelous deed of the Lord is the faithful love poured out upon generation after generation of God's people (Ps 98:3). The story of the human beings in the garden (Gen 3:9-15, 20) tells us of our own need. Because of our limited vision the great gift of freedom allows us sometimes to make wrong choices. The consequence of choosing to turn away from God is always separation. The garden story illustrates it perfectly. Human beings hide from God and blame each other. Even creation suffers because of this disruption of natural bonds.

God, however, never gives up. God chose us before the foundation of the world (cf. Eph 1:3-6, 11-12). "In love [God] destined us for adoption . . . through Jesus Christ" (1:5). God's choice precedes our failures. God's love triumphs over our weakness (cf. Ps 98:1-3). The triumph of God's faithful love is Jesus. His very name, Yeshua, means "salvation," "victory" (Ps 98:1, 2, 3).

The depth of God's love for us is demonstrated in divine respect for human freedom. The age-old plan of God waits for the consent of a young Jewish woman (Luke 1:26-38). The story is told in the standard pattern for an announcement of birth: objection, reassurance, and sign (cf. Gen 17:15-22; 18:1-15). The very formality of the pattern gives weight to the moment when the whole of our history hung on a woman's word. The incarnation is the Lord's triumph, a double triumph: the will of God and the consent of God's beloved human beings.

Mary stands as the first of us to say yes. The son born to all of us because of her consent heals our weakness and destroys our sin. Here too she stands as the first of us. The Lord has indeed won a marvelous victory. Come, sing the new song! (Ps 98:1-2).

11. Psalm 100

Psalm 100 is a perfect little hymn. What it lacks in poetic grace it redeems by theological depth. The heart of biblical faith is here: we belong to God because it is God who made us. God is the shepherd who cares for us (cf. Ps 23). God's enduring love is the cause of our great joy and praise.

The psalm outlines a procession to the temple. It is punctuated by two summons to praise (1-2, 4). The worshipers are called to come, enter, and give thanks to the Lord whose love (*hesed*) endures forever.

4th Sun Easter C (1-2.3.5) [52]

We are God's people, God's well-tended flock (3).

All of Psalm 100 is used for the Fourth Sunday of Easter except verse 4 which calls the worshipers to enter the temple with praise and thanksgiving. Perhaps the reference to the temple in such close proximity to the Jews' rejection of Paul and Barnabas (Acts 13:45, 50) seemed too paradoxical.

The readings illustrate both exclusion and inclusion. The flock of God is larger than we might initially suppose; but there are those who choose to remain outside. In the gospel Jesus presents himself as the good shepherd (John 10:27-30). He knows his own sheep; he gives them eternal life. No one has the power to snatch them away. The passage is set in the midst of a controversy between Jesus and the Jews. Immediately preceding today's passage, Jesus accuses them: "You do not believe, because you are not among my sheep." Following today's passage they pick up rocks to stone him. Clearly not everyone belongs to the flock (cf. Ps 100:3).

The experience of Paul and Barnabas indicates that some unexpected sheep *do* belong to the flock (Acts 13:14, 43-52). The two begin their preaching in the synagogue and many of the Jews follow them. However, when the crowds of Gentiles begin to believe, some of the Jews stir up a persecution to drive Paul and Barnabas from their city. But God's salvation will not be limited; it extends to the ends of the earth.

The flock of God envisioned by the author of the Book of Revelation is a huge multitude beyond counting (Rev 7:9, 14-17). These people are included because they have washed their robes in the blood of the Lamb. Now we see that the one who shepherds them is also the Lamb who shed his blood for them. They know the fullness of peace. They know how good the Lord is (Ps 100:5).

We claim their joy and join their worship. We too are God's people, God's well-tended flock (Ps 100:3). We recognize the danger of trying to exclude others. We shout joyfully in thanksgiving for the gift of being included among God's people. "Good indeed is the LORD, whose love endures forever" (Ps 100:5).

11th Sun Year A (1-2.3.5) [92]

We are God's people, God's well-tended flock (3).

The refrain and verses from Psalm 100 for the Eleventh Sunday of Year A are the same as those for the Fourth Sunday of Easter C (see above).

The readings show us the gradual gathering of the sheep of God's flock. The Exodus passage (19:2-6) tells the beginning of covenant making between God and Israel at Sinai. The essence of the promise is here. Through Moses God reminds the people of the tender care they have already experienced. God has delivered them from Egyptian slavery and carried them as a mother eagle carries her young. Knowing the tenderness of God they are able to hear the divine proposal: "If you hearken to my voice and keep my covenant, you shall be my special [people]." God presents the possibility of a binding commitment between them. The people will be bound to listen and obey; God will be bound to care for them as a special chosen people. The effect will be to make them holy, like the God to whom they are bound, and priestly, ministering God's tender care to the rest of the world.

These people are the first sheep of God's flock (Ps 100:3). These people are the first witnesses of God's faithful love (Ps 100:5). They are the first to know that the Lord is God (Ps 100:3).

Jesus initially confines his ministry to this chosen flock (Matt 9:36–10:8). He pities them because they are like sheep without a shepherd. In his ministry of God's faithful love he sends twelve chosen apostles, numbered for the twelve chosen tribes, to care for their needs and to bring them the news of God's kingdom.

But God's faithful love is without limit. The gift of the good news overflows beyond the boundaries of the first flock, the first chosen people. At the appointed time Christ died for all of us (Rom 5:6-11). Not even sin can block this overwhelming love. We have been reconciled with God by the death of Christ. Now we are also saved by his life.

What a gift we have in Psalm 100 which gives us words to clothe our praise and thanksgiving. We call the whole world to join our joyful worship. All of us who claim to be God's creatures now celebrate also the gift of God's salvation. God, whose faithful love endures forever, has gathered us safely into the chosen flock. "Good indeed is the LORD!"

Year Common (2.3.5) [175]

We are God's people, God's well-tended flock (3).

Psalm 100 is designated as a possible selection for the Common of the Year. (See also Pss 19, 27, 34, 63, 95, 103, and 145). Only verses 2, 3, and 5 are used: the call to praise; the acknowledgment of Yahweh as God, Creator, and Shepherd; and thanksgiving for God's faithful covenant love. This psalm would be appropriate for any Sunday on which the theme is covenant, God as shepherd, or gratitude that we are God's people.

Two Sundays are particularly apt. On the Sixteenth Sunday of Year B (see Ps 23) the primary image is sheep. In Jer 23:1-6, God declares, "I myself will gather . . . my flock." In Eph 2:13-18 we learn that the flock includes us "who once were far off" but have now been brought "near through the blood of Christ." The gospel (Mark 6:30-34) shows us Jesus pitying the crowds who are "like sheep without a shepherd."

Christ the King A has similar images (see Ps 23). God will tend the cho-sen sheep (Ezek 34:11-12, 15-17). All people will come to life in Christ (1 Cor 15:20-26, 28). On the last day Christ will separate the sheep from the goats on the basis of their service to him in the little ones of the flock (Matt 25:31-46).

12. Psalm 103

Psalm 103 is a hymn of deep gratitude to God for the gift of *hesed*, faith-ful covenant love (see Ps 136). The word *hesed* occurs four times in the psalm (4, 8, 11, 17). The psalm traces the workings of God's *hesed* from the per-sonal experience of the psalmist, through the history of God's people, to the witness of the whole cosmos. All of reality is given life through the strong and tender love of God.

The psalm can be considered in four stanzas (1-5, 6-10, 11-18, 19-22). The psalm begins with personal experience (1-5). The psalmist addresses the *nephesh*, the center of one's being. The root meaning of *nephesh* is "throat," and so it conveys both life and longing. To reinforce the call to the essential core of one's life, the psalm goes on, "all my being, bless God's holy name." Three times the injunction to bless the Lord is repeated. To bless is thankfully to return to God the share in divine life and power that we human beings enjoy. The final imperative enjoins us not to forget. The reasons for this intense call to praise follow. God removes every danger from us, forgives all our sins, heals all our ills, delivers us from the grave. God also gives us everything good, life, love, the vitality of youth. We are sur-rounded by the *hesed* and tender compassion of the Lord.

The second stanza (6-10) elaborates the vision of God's love by show-ing it in action for Israel. It is the Lord who creates righteousness, the right relationship with Israel. That righteousness is demonstrated through love. Moses is the primary witness to the workings of God's saving love. In the story of Moses we find the little creed that is repeated here: "Merciful and gracious is the Lord, slow to anger, abounding in kindness" (Ps 103:8; cf. Exod 34:6-7; Ps 145:8-9). Because this is the heart of the divine nature, God does not deal with us as our sins deserve. What was true on the indi-vidual level, is also true on the national level.

The third stanza (11-18) calls on nature itself to witness the wonder of God's love. Three comparisons stretch us to imagine God's compassionate love. It is as expansive as the heavens; it is as tender as a father's love. There-fore our sins have been removed to the ends of the earth. Why? Because God remembers how frail we are, dry dust, withering grass. Fragile as we are, we are sustained by the everlasting love (*hesed*) of the Lord. Those who keep the covenant can count on this faithful covenant love.

The fourth stanza (19-22) calls on all creation from heaven to earth to join in blessing the Lord who rules over all with love. Finally, lest we forget, the psalm returns us to the beginning: "Bless the LORD, my soul!"

3rd Sun Lent C (1-2.3-4.6-7.8.11) [30]

The Lord is kind and merciful (8).

The refrain and verses from Psalm 103 chosen for the Third Sunday of Lent C are primarily from the first two stanzas. Only one verse of the third stanza is used, the comparison in which the whole universe is called upon as example of God's overwhelming love. The other verses describe the individual experience of God's love and the action of that love for God's chosen people. The refrain is the opening phrase of the little creed, describing the nature of the Lord.

The readings reverse the direction of the psalm by moving from God's saving acts for the people to the individual experience of forgiveness. The call of Moses (Exod 3:1-8, 13-15) testifies to God's care for the chosen people who suffer under Egyptian oppression. God has heard their cry and knows their suffering. Therefore God has come down to rescue them and to give them a land of milk and honey. This act in itself gives God a new name. The God of Abraham, of Isaac, and of Jacob, will now be known forever as Yahweh, not only the one who *is* but the one *who will be there* when we are in need. God's very name pledges fidelity to covenant love. "Merciful and gracious is the LORD, slow to anger, abounding in [*hesed*]" (Ps 103:8). Moses is the bearer of this divine love, the one who will bring it to action in the exodus.

Paul, however, will not let us forget that God's overwhelming love demands a response (1 Cor 10:1-6, 10-12). The covenant demands love and fidelity from God's people also. Those who experienced God's mighty deeds in the exodus nonetheless forgot God's gifts. They turned to other gods to save them; they grumbled against the Lord in their lack of trust. God indeed knows how we are formed, remembers that we are dust (Ps 103:14), but even God's compassion cannot save us if we turn away. We cannot be so foolish as to trust in our own strength: Let those who think they are standing, take care not to fall! We have been warned. With the psalmist we turn in joyful confidence to the Lord who is merciful and gracious, slow to anger and rich in love.

Jesus repeats both the warning and the promise of compassionate love (Luke 13:1-9). The sight of others' suffering should not lead us to think that they are sinners while we are safely just. We are dust, like the grass swept away by the wind (Ps 103:15-16). Still we have cause for joy. God's love towers over us as the heavens tower over the earth. "As far as east is from west, so far have our sins been removed from us" (Ps 103:11-12). God is like a man who had a fig tree which bore no fruit. Even though he considers cutting it down as useless, he can be persuaded to leave it yet one more year to see if it responds to cultivation. The contrast between this story and the story of the fig tree in other gospels is instructive. In Matthew and Mark Jesus curses the fig tree that has no fruit; it withers and dies (Matt 21:18-22; Mark 11:12-14, 20-21). Luke does not have that story. Rather he relates this parable, found only in this gospel. The fig tree is not cursed but given yet another chance. Those who fear God are healed and restored over and over again. How merciful and gracious is the Lord! "Bless the LORD, my soul; all my being, bless [God's] holy name!" (Ps 103:1).

7th Sun Easter B (1-2.11-12.19-20) [61]

The Lord's throne is established in heaven (19).

After the initial call to praise (1-2), the responsorial psalm for the Seventh Sunday of Easter B is drawn from the last two stanzas of Psalm 103. The cosmic expanse of God's love is emphasized. The verses include the two comparisons between God's forgiving love and the vastness of creation, the testimony to the universality of God's rule, and the summons to the angels to join the praise. The refrain shows us the Lord who rules over all.

The cosmic witness may be chosen for this Sunday between Ascension and Pentecost to remind us that the story of Jesus leads from death in a little province of the Roman empire to a universal kingdom of love. God's overwhelming love for us is the theme which permeates the readings as well as the psalm.

The reading from the Acts of the Apostles (1:15-17, 20-26) reminds us that God's love for us is worked out at specific times in specific places. God works within our human history. After the ascension of Jesus and before the descent of the Holy Spirit the disciples choose another to replace Judas and fill out the number of the twelve. God's love is given flesh through the ministry of human beings to one another. The little Christian community acts in faith that God works in their midst. They nominate two candidates and then give God the final choice. When they drew lots, the choice fell to Matthias who was counted with the eleven apostles.

The selection of Psalm 103 to follow the story of Judas' replacement leads to another consideration. A thread that weaves throughout the psalm is the faith that God's surpassing love leads directly to forgiveness. God "pardons all your sins, heals all your ills, delivers your life from the pit"

(103:3-4). "God does not always rebuke, nurses no lasting anger, has not dealt with us as our sins merit, nor requited us as our deeds deserve" (103:9-10). "As far as the east is from the west, so far have our sins ben removed from us" (103:12). It is impossible to sing this psalm with the memory of Judas in our minds and not ask if Judas too has experienced the unbelievable forgiveness of this tender God. We cannot know, but we can ask.

The gospel (John 17:11-19) is Jesus' prayer for his followers. He has guarded them with the holy name of God, the one who will be there for us. He pleads for protection for them from the evil one. He asks with faith in the Lord who surrounds the faithful with love and compassion, who delivers their lives from the pit. In his prayer he reports that while he was with them not one was lost, "except the son of destruction." Does this mean that Judas is indeed lost? Is this a warning to us? The Lord's love is forever toward those who fear God (Ps 103:17). Did Judas abandon fear of the Lord? Or trust in the overwhelming compassion of God?

The First Letter of John (1 John 4:11-16) forces us to continue to consider that love which is beyond our understanding. But the letter also gives us a sign by which to recognize that love. If we love one another, God's love is brought to perfection in us. The greatness of God's love calls us to love one another. The demand is greater: to love one another *with God's love*! This is how we can know and believe in the love God has for us. We experience it in the love we have for one another. Matthias is chosen to carry on the ministry of love which Judas abandoned. Can we consider the possibility that even if he abandoned God, the God who knows that we are dust did not abandon him? Can his witness be a warning to us to cling to God's great love, never to forget all God's gifts? "Bless the Lord, my soul!" (Ps 103:1-2).

7th Sun Year A (1-2.3-4.8.10.12-13) [80]

Merciful and gracious is the Lord (8).

The psalm refrain for the Seventh Sunday of Year A is part of the little creed from Psalm 103. This statement of God's nature is repeated throughout the Old Testament. God is merciful and gracious, slow to anger and abounding in love (cf. Exod 34:6-7; Joel 2:13; Jonah 4:2; Pss 86:15; 145:8). The verses include portions from the first three stanzas: the repeated call to prayer which opens the psalm along with most of the motives for prayer from the first stanza; the little creed and a statement of God's forgiveness from the second stanza; and two of the comparisons from the third stanza which illustrate the greatness of God's forgiving love. The emphasis of the selection is forgiveness and compassion.

The link between readings and psalm on this Sunday is the command: "Be holy, for I, the LORD, your God, am holy" (Lev 19:2: cf. Matt 5:48). The first reading is a selection from the chapter headed by that command (Lev 19:1-2, 17-18). Throughout the chapter there are reminders that the basis of the Law is to be like God. Be just because God is just; be compassionate because God is compassionate. Often the reminder consists simply in the statement: "I am the LORD." In verses 17-18 we find the command of love of neighbor sealed with that simple statement.

The psalm follows immediately with the creedal statement: The Lord is gracious and merciful. The command from Leviticus is to be holy as the Lord is holy. The psalm tells us that the holiness of the Lord is expressed in mercy and compassion. Thus the love of neighbor is a way to be holy as God is holy. The psalm continues by calling our attention to all the gifts God has showered on us, especially the gift of forgiveness. We sing in thanksgiving for God's compassion to us. Can we fail to offer that same compassion and forgiveness to others?

The gospel (Matt 5:38-48) is Jesus' interpretation of the passage from Leviticus and of the law of retaliation (Exod 21:23-25; Lev 24:19-20; Deut 19:21). As a true rabbi, Jesus quotes the law and offers an interpretation. The law of retaliation—an eye for an eye—was originally meant as a limitation on revenge. Jesus subordinates it to the command to be like God, to "be perfect as your heavenly Father is perfect." We have proclaimed in the psalm that God does not return injury for injury. God "nurses no lasting anger, has not dealt with us as our sins merit, nor requited us as our deeds deserve" (Ps 103:10). Jesus calls us to act in the same fashion: offer no resistance, turn the other cheek, go two miles, don't turn away from the borrower.

Jesus uses the same method with the command to love one's neighbor. The prevailing interpretation of the Leviticus passage stated that love of one's own people implied hatred of enemies (which is not found in Leviticus). Jesus reverses the interpretation of his day. Love your enemies, pray for your persecutors. This is what it means to be perfect as God is perfect. "Merciful and gracious is the LORD, slow to anger, abounding in kindness" (Ps 103:8).

Paul gives us a different perspective on being like God (1 Cor 3:16-23). Our glory is that we are the temple of God, the sign of God's presence; the Spirit of God dwells within us. This is our wisdom; this is the support of our lives. Everything is ours because we belong to Christ, and Christ to God. If we are to be truly who we are, the sign of God's presence in the world, then we must act as God acts—mercifully, graciously, forgiving one another, surrounding one another with love and compassion. This is who God is; this is who we are called to be.

7th Sun Year C (1-2.3-4.8.10.12-13) [82]

The Lord is kind and merciful (8).

The refrain and verses from Psalm 103 chosen for the Seventh Sunday of Year C are the same as those for the Seventh Sunday of Year A (see above).

The Seventh Sunday of Year A presents Matthew's version of the command to be like God. This Sunday presents Luke's version of the same command: "Be merciful, just as your Father is merciful" (Luke 6:36). An Old Testament example of such compassion is David (1 Sam 26:2, 7-9, 12-13, 22-23). Saul, consumed by jealousy of David's rising power and popularity, has driven him from the court and is now pursuing him through the Judean desert. In the account of this pursuit there are two similar stories of David sparing Saul (see also 1 Sam 24). In today's version David and Abishai walk unhindered into Saul's camp and find Saul and Abner, his army general, lying asleep and apparently unguarded. Abishai offers to kill Saul. David stops him and instead takes a sign that he had the opportunity to kill Saul and did not. He will not harm the Lord's anointed. Whatever David's motivation, he has acted with compassion toward a man whose purpose is to kill him. He has imitated the Lord who is gracious and merciful, slow to anger and abounding in kindness. He has not dealt with his enemy according to his crimes (cf. Ps 103:8, 10).

In the Sermon on the Plain Jesus spells out the implications of being compassionate as God is compassionate (Luke 6:27-38). "Love your enemies, do good to those who hate you. . . . Do to others as you would have them do to you." David is an example. He, like Saul, is the Lord's anointed; David hopes for the same compassion from Saul that he has shown him.

To be like God is to love even those who hate you, to lend without expecting repayment. To be like God is to forgive rather than to judge. The reward for this is life without measure. God has forgiven us, loved us even when we have not deserved it. The psalmist calls us to remember all the gifts of God (Ps 103:2). Remembering God's gifts with gratitude will lead us to be like God, forgiving, loving, compassionate.

Paul tells us that we are indeed like God (1 Cor 15:45-49). Just as we resemble Adam, so we are also like Christ. Like Adam, we are made in the image of God and yet have the weakness of human nature. But we have also been given likeness to Christ, and so we will share in his resurrection. God, who "knows how we are formed, remembers that we are dust" (Ps 103:14), has delivered our lives from the grave, filled us with all good things (Ps 103:4-5). We sometimes cover our faults by claiming to be "only human." Jesus calls us to be truly human, made in the image and likeness of God. Merciful and gracious is the Lord. If we are truly human, we too are merciful and gracious.

8th Sun Year B (1-2.3-4.8.10.12-13) [84]

The Lord is kind and merciful (8).

The refrain and verses from Psalm 103 for the Eighth Sunday of Year B are the same as those for the Seventh Sunday of Year A (see above).

The mystery of old and new is the theme of this Sunday: old covenant and new, old wineskins and new wine. The mystery is that the new is like the old. The difference is that the old has been allowed to grow rigid and static, whereas the new is still full of life.

The end of chapter two of Hosea is one of the first prophetic suggestions of a new covenant (Hos 2:16-17, 21-22). The chapter begins with a divorce trial. God is divorcing Israel because she has been unfaithful. She has consorted with Ba‘al rather than with Yahweh, her true husband. But God will not give up. God decides to take everything away from her so that she will return to him, her first husband. He will lead her back into the desert where she will be completely dependent upon him in hopes that the honeymoon love of her youth will return. God's solution is painful. Israel will lose everything and go into captivity in order that she may recognize that it is God who gives her all good gifts. She has let her love grow stale and forgotten the living love of God. But God promises that after the stripping there will be a new beginning, a new covenant. The wedding vows will be renewed, the promise between the spouses of love, mercy and faithfulness to their relationship. The marriage will be consummated again: "You shall know the LORD."

The ordinary law regarding a divorced wife who has married another is that the first husband may not take her back (Deut 24:1-4). But God's love supersedes the law. God does not deal with us as our sins deserve (Ps 103:10). Rather, the Lord is slow to anger and abounding in love (103:8). As far as east from west does God remove our sins from us (103:12). Even though the covenant has been broken and God has divorced Israel, yet will he take her back in compassionate love. This is the living covenant, the same covenant kept alive through love.

Paul describes the new covenant as one not of law but of spirit (2 Cor 3:1-6). It is this covenant that is written on the living flesh of our hearts. It is this new covenant that shows through our lives, making us all a letter of Christ to the world, a witness that God lives, that God perseveres forever in love and compassion. Paul is in difficulty because others have come to the Corinthians claiming to be true apostles with letters of recommendation to prove it. They are attempting to convince the Corinthians that salvation lies in a rigid following of the letter of the Law. Paul argues against rigidity and for life.

Jesus is faced with a similar problem (Mark 2:18-22). His disciples are not keeping the rigid fast advocated by the Pharisees, the pious among the Jews. Jesus responds with two arguments: The wedding is just now taking place. The renewal of the living covenant with God is being celebrated in him. This is not a time for fasting but a time for feasting. Fasting will come in its own time. The second argument is an explanation of the first. A true keeping of the Law of the covenant is to be truly like God. God is a god of the living, not of the dead. To keep the Law in truth is to respond to each moment with the living flexibility of love and compassion, to be able to stretch to the moment as the new wine skins stretch to the wine. To be new wine skins is to be ready for whatever gifts God sends, to respond to every moment of life as God responds. "Merciful and gracious is the LORD, slow to anger, abounding in kindness" (Ps 103:8).

24th Sun Year A (1-2.3-4.9-10.11-12) [131]

The Lord is kind and merciful; slow to anger, and rich in compassion (8).

The refrain from Psalm 103 used for the Twenty-Fourth Sunday of Year A is the whole little creed found in the second stanza of the psalm (cf. Exod 34:6-7; Joel 2:13; Jonah 4:2; Pss 86:15; 145:8). The verses are chosen from the first three stanzas of the psalm: the emphatic call to praise and the reasons for praise from the first stanza; the assertion of God's great forgiveness from the second stanza; and two of the comparisons used in the third stanza to describe the immensity of God's love and the extent of God's forgiveness. The reference to Israel's experience has been omitted. The psalm moves immediately from individual experience to cosmic truth.

God's forgiveness is set out as a standard for us in our relationships with one another. Sirach, a second-century BCE Jerusalem sage, introduces the concept which Jesus will incorporate into the Lord's prayer (Sir 27:30–28:7): As we forgive one another, so will God forgive us. The sage emphasizes the opposite truth: If we are vengeful, we in turn will suffer the Lord's vengeance. The measure for our own forgiveness is the forgiveness that we extend to one another. The psalm response is both encouraging and challenging. We sing our hope in God "who pardons all [our] sins, heals all [our] ills" (Ps 103:3); at the same time we recognize that if God treats us with such compassion, that same compassion is what we owe to one another. If we hope for God's forgiveness, we may nurse no lasting anger, nor deal with others as their sins merit (cf. Ps 103:9-10). Rather we must set our memory of their offenses as far away as east is from west (cf. Ps 103:12). Then when we pray, our own sins will be forgiven (cf. Sir 28:2).

Peter gets the same answer from Jesus (Matt 18:21-35). Peter is ready to extend forgiveness the generous number of seven times. Jesus says, multiply your generosity to such an extent that you lose count—say, seventy times seven. Jesus' story illustrates the principle of the Jerusalem sage. The king is willing to forgive the servant a large debt; the servant is merciless in regard to a petty amount. God is willing to forgive all our sins; we are tempted to hold a grudge over a small slight. The king's response to the unforgiving servant is a warning to us. Unless we forgive one another from the heart, we too will be held to impossible repayment. Our persistent hope is in the Lord who is merciful and gracious, slow to anger and rich in love (Ps 103:8). But the Lord, whose love is greater than heaven's height (Ps 103:11), puts only one condition on forgiving us: that we forgive one another.

In the Letter to the Romans Paul exhorts the Christian community to be very careful not to scandalize one another but rather to be sensitive to other's consciences. The issue is food sacrificed to idols: those who feel free to eat anything should not offend others by their freedom. The heart of Paul's reasoning is found in today's reading (Rom 14:7-9). We do not belong to ourselves; rather, we belong to the Lord. Christ's death and resurrection have won dominion for him over both the dead and the living. We are not our own. In the context of this Sunday's readings Paul's message gives reason for our forgiveness of one another. If we are not our own but belong to God, then offenses against us are really not our concern but are God's. God, we know, is slow to anger and quick to forgive. If God, to whom we belong, forgives, then how can we, mere flesh, hold a grudge. What a gift of freedom this is, to be allowed to let go of the burden of anger and revenge! "Bless the LORD, my soul; do not forget all the gifts of God" (Ps 103:2).

Sacred Heart A (1-2.3-4.6-7.8.10) [171]

The Lord's kindness is everlasting toward the faithful (17).

The psalm refrain from Psalm 103 for the Solemnity of the Sacred Heart A is the psalm's final declaration about Yahweh's *hesed*. The psalmist has followed this great love from individual experience, through Israel's history, and finally to the expanse of the universe. The conclusion is: Yahweh's *hesed* is forever. Those who fear the Lord can depend on it. The verses include the opening call to prayer and the reasons for praise: the great gifts of God's love. The little creed follows, which declares that God's essence is love: "Merciful and gracious is the LORD, slow to anger, abounding in [*hesed*]" (8). The result of that great love is forgiveness. God does not deal with us as our sins deserve. The citation indicates that verses 6-7 are also included, which describe God's *hesed* toward Israel. Lectionaries in common circulation, however, do not include those two verses.

The Solemnity of the Sacred Heart celebrates the greatness of God's love which takes flesh in Jesus. The readings explore God's love from Israel's experience throughout history and into ongoing Christian hope. Deuter-onomy continually reminds God's people of this great love. The passage chosen for today is particularly tender (Deut 7:6-11). God chose a people for a special possession, not because they were so great, but simply out of love. This love was pledged first to the ancestors, Abraham and Sarah and their children. This love became visible in their redemption from Egyptian slavery. The great joy of God's people throughout the ages is that this great love never fails. God faithfully keeps the covenant down to the thousandth generation for those who respond with love. What other response could there be to this faithful God than love and obedience?

The First Letter of John tells us how to give flesh to this loving obedience: let us love one another (1 John 4:7-16). God's love has been revealed to us now through the coming of Christ into the world in order that we might have life. God is the source of love. Love has no meaning apart from God. If we understand the greatness of God's love, we must have the same love for one another. Our mutual love is the pledge that the loving God lives in us.

Jesus praises his father for revealing this great truth to us, mere children (Matt 11:25-30). No one knows the Father except the Son, but the Son has willed to reveal the Father to us! The revelation is this: God is love. This lightens the yoke and eases the burden of life. Bless the Lord, who fills us with good things, renews our youth like the eagle's. Bless the Lord who is so rich in love (Ps 103:5, 8)!

Year Common (1-2.3-4.8.10.12-13) [*175*]

The Lord is kind and merciful (8).

Psalm 103 is one of several choices for the Common of the Year (see also Pss 19, 27, 34, 63, 95, 100, 145). The refrain and verses are the same as those for the Seventh Sunday of Year A (see above). The psalm would be appropriate for any Sunday on which the love and forgiveness of God are primary themes. Some particular Sundays on which the psalm could be used are: the Sixth Sunday of Year C (see Ps 1), which emphasizes trust in the Lord rather than human beings (Jer 17:5- 8), the importance of hope in the resurrection (1 Cor 15:12, 16-20), and the compassion of God illustrated in the Beatitudes (Luke 6:17, 20-26); the Eighth Sunday of Year A (see Ps 62), which includes the tender description of God's mother love (Isa 49:14-15) and the importance of trust in God (1 Cor 4:1-5; Matt 6:24-34); the Eighth Sunday of Year C (see Ps 92), which again emphasizes hope in the resurrection (1 Cor 15:54-58) and the call for us to be like our compassionate God, especially in speech (Sir 27:4-7; Luke 6:39-45); and the Fourteenth Sunday of Year A (see Ps 145) on which the gospel is the same as that of the Sacred Heart A (Matt 11:25-30) and the other readings proclaim God's great love in redeeming the chosen people (Zech 9:9-10; Rom 8:9, 11-13).

All Souls (8.10.13-14.15-16.17-18) [791]

The Lord is kind and merciful (8).

Psalm 103 is one of the choices for the Common of the Dead (see also Pss 23, 25, 27, 42-43, 63, 116, 122, 130, 143). The refrain is part of the little creed, emphasizing God's love and mercy. The verses are chosen from the last half of the psalm, emphasizing the cosmic greatness of divine compassion for frail human beings. God remembers that we are dust, that we wither like the grass, and so God is as tender with us as a father is with his children. In contrast to the love of a human father, however, God's love is from age to age.

Some readings which share themes with Psalm 103 are: Lam 3:17-26, in which the mourner is consoled by recalling that God's mercies are renewed each morning, so great is divine faithfulness; Acts 10:34-43, which describes the ministry of Jesus and announces the good news that everyone who believes in him has forgiveness of sins through his name; Rom 5:17-21, which proclaims the surpassing grace which has come to us through Jesus; Rom 6:3-9, which reminds us of the great gift of our baptism which is the pledge of our resurrection; 1 Cor 15:51-57, which expresses our gratitude to God who has saved us through Jesus Christ; and 1 John 3:14-16, which defines love through Christ's willingness to die for us.

Psalm 103 would be especially appropriate with three gospel passages: Luke 7:11-17, Jesus' compassion toward the widow of Naim and her son; Luke 23:33, 39-43, the story of Jesus' death and the women's finding of the empty tomb; John 17:24-26, Jesus' prayer for his disciples that God's love for Jesus may live in them.

13. Psalm 104

Psalm 104 is a hymn of delight in God's creation. The psalmist revels in poetic descriptions of nature and returns in wonder to praise of the Creator. At the beginning and end of the psalm is the same call to praise which enclosed Psalm 103: "Bless the LORD, my soul!" The seven stanzas echo the order of creation described in Genesis 1.

The creation of the heavens is the subject of the first stanza (1-4). The creator God, clothed in light, spreads out the heavens like a royal tent. Clouds, winds, fire serve the mighty God. Attention turns to the earth in the second stanza (5-9). First the earth is settled firmly on its foundations.

Then, reflecting the ancient myth of divine conquest of the waters of chaos, the waters flee at God's roar and are confined within controlled limits; thus the dry land can appear.

The third stanza (10-18) celebrates the creation of living beings. Cattle and birds, trees and grass drink the water of life provided by the creator. Every creature finds a home; every creature is given food. Human beings enjoy bread and wine and oil, staples of life. All creation lives in balance; peace and joy abound. The fourth stanza (19-23) introduces times and seasons. God creates the moon to mark the larger rhythm of months, the sun for the smaller rhythm of night and day. Even these rhythms create a balance for living things. The night is the time for beasts of prey. They too are part of God's creation. When day comes they yield the earth to God's human creatures who work until night falls again.

The fifth stanza (24-26) opens with an exclamation of praise for God's wisdom which brings forth such variety. Then the psalmist's attention turns to the sea, traditional symbol of chaos. But even the sea is a part of God's great design of creation. Like the earth, it is full of living creatures. Human beings tame its power too. Even the sea monsters, which seem to be the ultimate personification of chaos, are part of the great variety and balance.

The sixth stanza (27-30) celebrates the power of God in sustaining all these creatures. It is God who feeds every one of them; it is God who, moment by moment, gives them the breath of life. God's withdrawal from creation would bring death and destruction. God's constant care renews the earth with every breath.

In the final stanza (31-35) the psalmist turns again to awe at the great majesty of the Creator God. God's power can overwhelm the earth; in contrast to fragile creation, God's glory lasts forever. Yet with the psalmist we pray that God may delight in creation, may say day by day, "How good!" (cf. Gen 1:4, 10, 12, 18, 21, 25, 31). For our part we pledge to continue the song of praise as long as God gives us life. Our delight mirrors that of the creator. The final phrase is a prayer that good will finally overcome evil, that creation may flourish in all its richness. "Bless the LORD, my soul!"

Baptism of the Lord C [opt] (1b.-2.3-4.24-25.27-28.29-30)

Bless the Lord, my soul! (1).

The tone for the Feast of the Baptism of the Lord C is set by Psalm 104. God's ongoing creation is the focus of today's liturgy. In the beginning God created the world and everything in it. In the sixth century when the Israelites seemed to be dead in Exile, God conquered the chaos again and brought out the people, a new creation. Jesus, baptized by John, is the Word of God who saves us from the chaos of death and gives us life. Our way to share in that life is through our own baptism through which the Spirit of life is given to us. God's creative power continues to conquer the chaos of sin and death. The psalm refrain gives words to our grateful response: Bless the Lord, my soul! (Ps 104:1).

The beginning of the story is told in Psalm 104. The verses chosen for this feast come from the first, fifth, and sixth stanzas of the psalm. After the call to praise, the first stanza extols the great majesty of the Creator God, clothed in light, riding the clouds, sending wind and fire as messengers. The fifth stanza is an exclamation of praise for God's wisdom. Even the sea, symbol of primeval chaos, is subject to God's wisdom. The sixth stanza celebrates the care of the Creator for creation. God feeds every living creature. God gives all of us the breath of life.

The power of the Creator God becomes a focus of hope for the people in the Babylonian Exile. The sixth-century prophet whose work is found in the latter part of the Book of Isaiah (chs. 40-55) wrote to encourage the people with the news that God both could and would restore them to their own land. God as Creator had the power to recreate them and the compassion to heal their misery. The reading for this feast (Isa 40:1-5, 9-11) is the introduction to this prophet's work. God calls the prophet to proclaim to the people that the time for mercy has come. All creation will rejoice in God's deliverance of this special people. Their own city, Jerusalem, will rise up like a herald to announce God's arrival. The mighty and powerful God comes like a shepherd to care for the needy sheep. The mighty and powerful God comes to give the people new life.

The evangelists announce the beginning of the good news with the prophetic words from Isaiah celebrating God's arrival. John the Baptist comes as the one preparing the way (Luke 3:15-16, 21-22). He is not the Messiah; he is his messenger, his prophet. His mission is to introduce the Messiah. He baptizes the one who is to come, Jesus. The baptism scene is a new creation with the Spirit of God brooding over the waters of chaos. The waters are parted by Jesus, Word of God, who brings the new creation. God saw how very good it was: "You are my beloved Son; with you I am well pleased."

The Letter to Titus (2:11-14; 3:4-7) announces clearly what good news we have in Jesus. "The grace of God has appeared, saving all." Through him we are trained to reject the chaos of evil and to be open to the goodness of life. We are brought to this life out of the water, "through the bath of rebirth and renewal by the holy Spirit." Our merciful God has given us this pledge that we might await the fullness of life in hope, believing in Jesus Christ who surrendered himself that we might become a new creation through him. "How varied are your works, LORD! In wisdom you have wrought them all. . . . Bless the LORD, my soul!" (Ps 104:24, 35).

Easter Vigil 1 (1-2.5-6.10.12.13-14.24.35 [42]

Lord, send out your Spirit, and renew the face of the earth (30).

Psalm 104 is well chosen as a response to the opening reading of the Easter Vigil. The formal recital of the creation story of Genesis 1 is echoed in the poetic celebration of the psalm. The refrain interprets the final verse of the sixth stanza, praise of God who sustains all creation. The psalm refers to the breath of life which comes from God and re-creates living things moment by moment. The Hebrew word, *ruah*, means breath, wind, spirit. The psalmist may well be referring to the western winds which bring the life-giving rain to the land. The verse also suggests the breath of life breathed into the human creature in the creation story of Gen 2:7. At the Easter vigil we understand *ruah* at a deeper level, the Spirit of God through whom we share the divine life.

The verses are a sampling from every stanza except the fourth which refers to the balance of times and seasons (and the sixth from which the refrain comes). We sing the praise of God who creates heaven and earth, who nourishes living beings with water and food. The final verses represent the exclamation of praise from the fifth stanza, which proclaims the wisdom of God in creating such variety, and the closing call to prayer which repeats the opening: "Bless the LORD, my soul!"

Together Genesis 1 and Psalm 104 are a powerful beginning for the great re-telling of the story of our salvation by the awesome and tender God who created us. "May the LORD be glad in these works!" (Ps 104:31).

Pentecost Vigil (1-2.24.35.27-28.29.30) [63]

Lord, send out your Spirit, and renew the face of the earth (30).

Psalm 104 is the psalm chosen for all the celebrations of Pentecost. The selected verses lead rapidly to the sixth stanza, the celebration of God's power in sustaining all creation. God's gift of food nourishes every living being; God's life provides every breath. We join the psalmist in proclaiming praise for God's great wisdom.

The refrain captures the sense of the feast. It is God's Spirit, God's *ruah* (see above, Easter Vigil), which gives life to all that is. The *ruah* of God is the mighty wind sweeping over the abyss at the beginning (Gen 1:2). In the second creation story God breathes life into the human creature (Gen 6:3; cf. 2:7). At the exodus God sends a strong east wind to dry up the sea so that the people may cross on dry land (Exod 14:21; cf. 15:8). In the Babylonian Exile, when the people seem to be dead, God sends the wind to bring life to their dry bones (Ezek 37:1-14). The prophet Joel sees a vision of the Day of the Lord on which God's spirit will be poured out on all people, filling them with prophetic gifts (Joel 3:1-5).

Jesus announces that faith in him is the condition for the gift of God's Spirit (John 7:37-39). Whoever is thirsty and comes to him will be filled with rivers of living water; whoever believes in him will receive the Spirit. Jesus continues the work of creation, giving drink to sustain every living creature (cf. Ps 104:10-18). Paul reminds us that creation is not ended, that "all creation is groaning in labor pains even until now," struggling to give birth to the new creation for which we hope (Rom 8:22-27). The feast for which we keep vigil is a pledge of the new creation. The Spirit of God still moves over chaos. The Spirit of God still comes to the aid of our weakness. God continues to renew the face of the earth.

The other possible Old Testament readings for the vigil emphasize different aspects of Pentecost. At Pentecost the disciples are able to preach so that people of every language can understand them; this reverses the alienating consequence of sin at Babel when the confusion of languages separated all peoples (Gen 11:1-9). The Jewish celebration of Pentecost commemorates the making of the covenant on Mount Sinai (Exod 19:3-8, 16-20) just as the Christian celebration commemorates the birth of the Church. These two events are different expressions of the great variety worked by the wisdom of God.

Pentecost Sun (1.24.29-30.31.34) [64]

Lord, send out your Spirit, and renew the face of the earth (30).

The verses of Psalm 104 chosen for the Solemnity of Pentecost represent a selection from several stanzas. The responsorial psalm opens with the call to prayer (1). The exclamation of praise for God's wisdom from the fifth stanza follows (24). Two verses of the sixth stanza (29-30) suggest the central theme of the feast, the gift of God's life-giving breath, the Spirit. The final two verses come from the seventh stanza (31, 34): the psalmist's double prayer that God's glory will last forever and that the poem of God's fragile creature will be pleasing. The prayer is ours too: may our worship be pleasing to the Lord.

The gospel for this solemnity repeats a portion of the gospel for the Second Sunday of Easter (John 20:19-23). The events we celebrate are one event; the gift of the Spirit seals the redemption won for us through Jesus' death and resurrection. On that first Easter evening, Jesus comes to tell the disciples this good news. He brings the Easter gift of peace; he breathes the new life of the Spirit into them. Then he commissions the disciples to continue his mission. They are to carry Easter peace and the reconciling gift of God's Spirit to the rest of the world. The new creation has begun. God has sent forth the life-giving breath that renews the face of the earth (Ps 104:30). The news is this: this time God relies on human beings to spread the gift of new life! "How varied are your works, LORD; in wisdom you have wrought them all" (104:24).

The Jewish feast of Pentecost, the celebration of God's giving of the Law on Mount Sinai, is the setting for the story of the coming of God's Spirit on the disciples (Acts 2:1-11). Men and women, the community who believed in Jesus as the new Law of God, were gathered together on the feast. Suddenly God's new creation was evident in signs reminiscent of the beginning. The psalmist had praised the Creator God: "you make the winds your messengers; flaming fire, your ministers" (Ps 104:4). Now on this day of new creation the Spirit came as a mighty wind and appeared as tongues of fire resting on every believer. The alienation of Babel is reversed as the Spirit-filled disciples preach the good news in words understandable to every people. The life-giving breath of new creation begins its journey to renew the face of the whole earth.

This time God relies on human beings to spread the gift of new life. Paul describes the way in which this happens (1 Cor 12:3-7, 12-13). The gift of the Spirit has given us life as one body. As one body the different members have different gifts with which to nourish the life of the whole body. Through every person life is sustained and the body flourishes.

How wonderful are the works wrought by God's wisdom (cf. Ps 104:24). We see God's care for all living things through the gifts of food and water (cf. 104:10-18, 27-28). We recognize God's power in the gift of breath, moment by moment (104:29-30). But these works, glorious as they are, are only signs of the truly great work of God, the new creation which is our share in the life of God forever. The Spirit of God within us is the gift of God's life. The Spirit is the water which gives us drink, the food which fills us in due time. Without the Spirit we "perish and return to the dust from which [we] came" (104:29). Today we celebrate the amazing news that God sends forth the Spirit to create us, to renew the face of the earth (Ps 104:30). May we sing praise to God as long as we live (cf. 104:33).

Pentecost Common (1.24.29-30.31.34) [175]

Lord, send out your Spirit, and renew the face of the earth (30).

Psalm 104 is the choice for the Common of Pentecost. The refrain and verses are the same as those for Pentecost Sunday. For a discussion of the psalm and its relationship to the Pentecost season, see above under Pentecost Sunday.

14. Psalm 113

Psalm 113 is the first of the Hallel psalms (113-118) which are sung on the three great feasts of Passover, Weeks, and Tabernacles, as well as on

Hanukkah and the New Moon. The psalm falls easily into two stanzas: 1-3, 4-9.

The first stanza (1-3) is an extended call to praise. The servants of the Lord may be the temple priests, called to lead the community's worship, or the call may be to all God's people. The praise centers on God's proper name, Yahweh. The gift of the name, Yahweh (cf. Exod 3:13-15), is Israel's great treasure. The name is a sign of God's presence, a revelation of God's identity. The gift of the name signifies the bond between God and the people. Many scholars and saints have pondered the meaning of the name. There is general agreement that the root of the name is the verb "to be." Our God is signified by a verb not a noun; our God is living. The central meaning of the name is more than existence. The central meaning is presence. Our God is the one who will be present; our God is the one on whom we can count to be there. It is this reality which is praised in Psalm 113. For all time and in all places we call for praise of this name, this reality that our God will always be with us.

The second stanza (4-9) describes the activity of this ever-present God. This God, who is our God, is more exalted than all other reality. Yet this exalted God is characterized by care of the lowly. God enthroned on high bends down to raise up the needy. The primary example of lowliness is the barren woman. She is under a curse because she cannot give sons to her husband. No comfort can be found for her (cf., e.g., Sarah, Rebekah, Rachel, and especially Hannah in 1 Sam 1). She even becomes an image of the whole people in Exile (Isa 54:1). Even this desperate woman enjoys the care of Yahweh. Like Hannah and the matriarchs, she is given children and status by this gracious God.

Psalm 113 is a song which praises the essential nature of our God, the one who is present to save even the least and lowliest among us.

25th Sun Year C (1-3.4-6.7-8) [136]

Praise the Lord who lifts up the poor (1, 7).

The refrain from Psalm 113 for the Twenty-Fifth Sunday of the Year captures the essence of the psalm. It is the Lord, our God whose name we know, that we praise. Praise is due because it is the very nature of our exalted God to lift up the lowly. The verses represent most of the psalm. Only verse 3, the call to praise God's name in all places from east to west, and verse 9, the barren woman as the example of the lowly person, are omitted.

The psalm holds up God's care for the poor; the readings focus paradoxically on the human struggle to share material resources. The merchants to whom Amos preached (8:4-7) are anxious for the day of rest to be over and the work week to begin. They have reduced the size of the product and raised the price. They have no concern for the poor whom they are exploiting. Their only concern is profit. But they have forgotten that the poor have a powerful advocate. The Lord who lifts up the poor swears, "I will never forget." The mighty God who is exalted above the heavens will demand an accounting from the greedy merchants who destroy God's beloved poor.

It is dangerous to sing Psalm 113 after hearing the reading from Amos. By so doing we acknowledge that we indeed know of God's preference for the poor. By singing Psalm 113 we take the responsibility on ourselves to give flesh to the divine concern.

The gospel is the paradoxical and difficult parable about the servant who seems to cheat his master for the benefit of his master's debtors (Luke 16:1-13). A servant who has been accused of dishonesty apparently changes the bills recording the amount owed his master. In fact, the servant may simply be lowering the interest rate radically or eliminating the interest altogether. Does the interest payment represent the servant's commission? Or is it the master's profit? That seems impossible to determine. The message of the parable, however, is clear. The master praises not his methods but his cleverness in solving his own situation. The wisdom sayings appended to the parable (9-13) elaborate on the prudent use of material goods. This world's wealth is to be used to gain everlasting treasure in heaven. How can we do this? By sharing this world's goods with others. The elusive wealth that we have now has been entrusted to us by the real owner. Only if we prove trustworthy will we be given wealth of our own. How to prove trustworthy? By following the master's wishes regarding material wealth, by sharing it with those who have less. The final message has to do with wisdom in discerning true value. We must choose between God and money. We cannot dedicate our lives to both.

Psalm 113 gives us God's attitude toward riches. The all-powerful God, who is enthroned above all nations, devotes loving attention not to those who can give something in return but to the bottom of the heap, to the poor and lowly and outcast. This is a signal to us of what to do with the gifts we have been given, with the wealth entrusted to us.

In every society the persons who bear the greatest responsibility for the care of all, especially the needy, are political leaders. They face daily the situation of the servant entrusted with managing the master's affairs. They most of all are in need of wisdom. The Letter to Timothy (1 Tim 2:1-8) exhorts us to pray for all people, but especially for those in authority. Thus all of us may lead quiet and tranquil lives.

This Sunday faces us with a modern challenge. How can we, a wealthy nation, raise the needy from the dust and give the outcast a place in society (cf. Ps 113:7, 9)? Where can we find the wisdom to make friends for ourselves through our use of this world's goods? Will we choose leaders, "the princes of [our] people," who are willing to sit with the poor (cf. Ps 113:7-8)? The challenge should drive us to prayer, prayer of petition for all of us, prayer of praise for the Lord who lifts up the poor.

15. Psalm 117

Psalm 117 is a perfect hymn. In just two short verses it expresses the form: call to praise, reasons for praise, reiteration of the call (Hallelujah = praise the Lord). The content is the heart of covenant faith. Yahweh, Israel's God, keeps the covenant virtues of binding love (*hesed*) and lasting fidelity (*'emeth*). The covenant is given to Israel as a ministry. God's faithful love longs to enliven all nations. Thus all nations are called to praise this gracious God.

9th Sun Year C (1.2) [88]

Go out to all the world and tell the good news (Mark 16:15).

The whole of Psalm 117 is used on the Ninth Sunday of Year C with the exception of the final Hallelujah. The Hallelujah is suggested, however, as an alternate refrain. It also appears, of course, in the gospel acclamation. The refrain for the psalm is taken from the longer ending to the Gospel of Mark. The risen Christ commissions the disciples to spread the good news of redemption to the whole world. There is a good fit between refrain and psalm. The psalm calls all nations to praise God because they experience God's faithful covenant love. The supreme expression of that love is our redemption in Christ.

The amazing fact that there is only a single item of good news for all people is the subject of this Sunday's readings. No people have an exclusive claim on God's faithful love; no other good news can replace the wonder of God's salvation. The first reading (1 Kgs 8:41-43) is a tiny snippet of Solomon's long prayer at the dedication of the temple in Jerusalem. Brief as this section is, it contains a very important truth. Even in the building which symbolizes the heart of Israel's faith there is no claim to exclusive enjoyment of God's saving presence. God keeps the bond of covenant love with the descendants of Abraham and is faithful to the promise to David (1 Kgs 8:23-24), but this same God cannot be contained by any one structure or any one people (1 Kgs 8:27). Israel's God is God of all the earth. Israel's God cares for all nations. Therefore God's ears are open to the foreigner as well as to the covenant people. God's faithful love is strong for other peoples as well as for the chosen (cf. Ps 117:2). This is good news for the whole world.

In the gospel (Luke 7:1-10) Jesus points out that sometimes the stranger can be an example to those who think they are God's own. The Roman centurion at Capernaum is recognized as a good man by the people of his city. He is seen as a friend even though he represents an occupying nation. His conversation with Jesus reveals a man of humility and faith. He believes in Jesus' power; he does not consider his status worth any inconvenience to Jesus. His humble faith wins a great reward: high praise from Jesus and the favor he requested, the health of his servant. God's faithful love not only envelops him; he himself reflects the holiness of a life shaped by covenant virtues. Praise the Lord, all you nations, and tell the good news!

The Galatians to whom Paul writes are suffering from confusion regarding the good news (Gal 1:1-2, 6-10). Is God's covenant love available only to those who follow one specific set of religious customs? Or is the good news that God's salvation in Christ is now extended to all peoples? Some preachers have come telling the Galatians that they must follow all the prescriptions of Jewish law. This was a great challenge throughout early Christianity as Gentiles accepted the gospel. Paul's message is that it is not the letter of the Law that saves, but rather the following of Christ. The demand of following Christ is not satisfied only by ritual but must be demonstrated through the keeping of the heart of the Law: Love your neighbor as yourself (Gal 5:14). This challenge is extended to all peoples; salvation in Christ is open to all nations. The test of God's covenant people is the observance of the Law. The goal of the Law is to be like God. God's love for all nations is strong; God is faithful to all peoples forever. This is the good news! This is the challenge today to any of us who are tempted to rest on the structures of our faith and to neglect the demand of extending and accepting God's covenant love in every stranger, in any foreign nation.

21st Sun Year C (1.2) [124]

Go out to all the world and tell the good news (Mark 16:15).

The refrain and the verses of Psalm 117 are the same for the Twenty-First Sunday of the Year as those for the Ninth Sunday of Year C (see above).

What are the criteria for inclusion in God's people? That is the question posed by this Sunday's readings. The prophet of the final section of Isaiah, preaching to the people who returned to Jerusalem from the Babylonian Exile, reminds them that God's choice is often wider than the limitations we humans would impose (Isa 66:18-21). In the final great Day of the Lord when God's kingdom will reach its fullness, there will be people there whom none of us would have guessed. People from the most out of the way corners of the earth, people speaking the least familiar languages, will come to proclaim God's glory. Some of these strangers will be chosen as priests and ministers to God's covenant people. The prophet proclaimed this message to a people who were tempted to think that their salvation lay in rigid rules of separation. They considered the possibility that only in avoiding other nations could they be faithful to God. The prophetic message is a reminder that their status as a chosen people is for the purpose of ministry. They are to give flesh to God's covenant. Their mission is to spread the good news of God's faithful love and to call all nations to give praise (cf. Ps 117:1-2).

The gospel (Luke 13:22-30) is a warning that having our names listed in the register is not sufficient to be counted among God's people. Membership is measured by the demands of covenant love, not by circumstances of birth or association. God is open to all peoples. God welcomes anyone who surrenders to the working of faithful love. Our claim to share in the heavenly banquet must be based on the same demand. The Letter to the Hebrews (12:5-7, 11-13) reminds us that any special claim we may have to be God's children also subjects us to God's paternal discipline. Our honored status as children of God brings with it the responsibility to act like God's children, to bring forth "the peaceful fruit of righteousness" (Heb 12:11). "The LORD's love for us is strong; the LORD is faithful forever" (Ps 117:2). We are God's children, God's special people, when we are known by that faithful love. We are God's children when we rejoice in sharing our honored status as God's children with everyone throughout the world, when there are no enemies, no outcasts. Then all nations will praise the Lord. Then all nations will proclaim the good news.

16. Psalm 145 (Acrostic)

Psalm 145 is an alphabetic psalm. Each verse begins with a successive letter of the alphabet. The psalm praises the creator who cares for everything in the world from A-Z. Blessing threads its way through the psalm. In verse 1 the psalmist promises to bless God's name forever. In verse 10, God's faithful people, the *hasidim* bless God. In the final verse (21) we see all flesh blessing the holy name of God.

The universality of God's goodness is signaled by the use of the word "all." "The LORD is good to *all*, compassionate to [*all*] creatures" (9); so *all* the LORD's works give thanks (10). God's goodness encompasses deeds of rescue and the daily work of feeding everything. "The LORD supports *all* who are falling and raises up *all* who are bowed down" (14). "The eyes of *all* look hopefully" to God who satisfies "the desire of [*all*] living things" (15-16). God acts justly in every relationship: "You, LORD, watch over *all* who love you, but *all* the wicked you destroy" (20). Our praise extends, not only over space, but also over time. We pledge praise of God *all* our days (2). One generation tells the next about the mighty works of God (4). God's reign is a reign for *all* ages, God's dominion for *all* generations (13). God is the center of our praise: "You, LORD, are just in *all* your ways, faithful in *all* your works . . . near to *all* who call upon you, to *all* who call upon you in truth" (17-18; cf. 13b[8]). . . . "*all* flesh will bless your holy name forever" (21).

Psalm 145 is a late psalm. It borrows phrases and ideas from many other psalms. Because it is an alphabetic psalm each verse tends to stand independently. The repetition of independent assertions emphasizes the main point of the psalm's content: the great and mighty God is powerful in every place and faithful for all time. The praise of this psalm is as pertinent now as it was two thousand years ago. "All flesh will bless [God's] holy name forever" (21).

5th Sun Easter C (8-9.10-11.12-13) [55]

I will praise your name forever, my king and my God (1).

The verses chosen from Psalm 145 for the Fifth Sunday of Easter C run through the middle of the alphabet. They begin with the little creed, Israel's statement of faith in the nature of Yahweh: gracious and merciful, slow to anger and abounding in love (8; cf. Exod 34:6-7; Joel 2:13; Jonah 4:2). The following verses exhort all creatures to praise God's faithful love and great power. Let all people know the good news that God's kingdom, which extends over all time and space, is a kingdom ruled by the power of compassionate love. In the refrain each of us is given a chance to join this great song of unending praise.

The readings set before us the timeless character of God's kingdom. The travels of Paul and Barnabas (Acts 14:21-27) take us back to the beginnings of Christian faith. Three actions of the apostles outline this early missionary effort. They set out to proclaim God's wonderful deeds to people who had never heard it before: They make known to all people God's power and the glorious splendor of God's rule (cf. Ps 145:11-12). They return to the newly established communities to encourage them to persevere in faith even in the face of trials: They remind them that God is good to all; God raises those who are bowed down (Ps 145:9, 14). Then they return to the community which sent them out in order to report God's mighty

---

[8]The Hebrew text we have does not have a verse for the letter *nun* ("n"). A Qumran Psalm scroll from Cave 11 does, however, have a *nun* verse which is also found in the Greek and Syriac translations: "The LORD is trustworthy in every word, and faithful in every work."

works accomplished through them (cf. Ps 145:5-6). Thus the circle is complete and all God's faithful ones join in blessing the great king (Ps 145:1).

The reading from Revelation (21:1-5) is a vision of the final goal, the new creation in which everything comes to fullness. In the new Jerusalem the covenant bond will be consummated. The union between God and the people, closer than the union between husband and wife, will be complete with no threat of separation. They will be God's people and the Lord will be their God who is always with them. The compassionate love which characterized their relationship from the beginning will finally achieve its goal—no more tears or pain, no more grief, no more death. God, who is good to all, makes all things new. This is the end toward which the psalm strives, God's glorious kingdom which endures for all ages.

The gospel (John 13:31-33, 34-35) bridges the gap between the other two readings. How are we to live between the moment when we first heard the good news and the arrival of the kingdom in all its glory? We must live as citizens of that kingdom. God's kingdom is characterized by God's faithful love. God rules by raising the downtrodden, feeding the hungry, hearing those who call, satisfying the desires of the needy (cf. Ps 145: 14-19). God's people must extend the rule of God's kingdom by doing the same. Jesus captures the demand in one commandment: Love one another as I have loved you. Love one another even to the point of laying down your life for the other—as I do for you. This is how all will know we are Jesus' disciples, citizens of God's kingdom: our love for one another, our love for all God's creatures. "The LORD is gracious and merciful, slow to anger and abounding in love; the LORD is good to all, compassionate to every creature" (Ps 145:8-9). So too must the Lord's people be.

14th Sun Year A (1-2.8-9.10-11.13-14) [101]

I will praise your name forever, my king and my God (1).

The verses of Psalm 145 chosen for the Fourteenth Sunday of Year A begin with the psalmist's declaration of intent to praise God the King every day and forever. The reasons for praise follow. As the little creed states, God is "gracious and merciful, slow to anger and abounding in love." God's compassionate love extends to every creature and every generation, but with special attention to the needy (Ps 145:9, 13-14). This is the subject which leads God's faithful people to praise and proclamation. The praise must be heard and joined by all people, because all people are supported by God's compassionate love. Then all people can join the refrain: "I will praise your name forever, my king and my God" (Ps 145:1).

The readings portray the compassionate love of God given flesh in God's Messiah. The last part of the Book of Zechariah is the work of an unknown prophet who envisions the glory of God's kingdom to come in future times. The short passage assigned to this Sunday (9:9-10) describes the arrival of the Messiah, the anointed king. He will come as Solomon came, riding on an ass (cf. 1 Kgs 1:38). Solomon is the beginning of God's fulfillment of the promise to David that his descendants should sit on his throne forever (cf. 2 Sam 7:8-16). Solomon rode to his anointing on an ass, the transportation of peace, rather than on a horse, the "vehicle" of war. In the prophet's vision this new king will also ride an ass as a symbol of peace. The new kingdom will be a kingdom of peace. Chariots and horses, the ancient war machines, will be banished along with armaments. The kingdom of peace, the domain of the new king, will extend throughout the world, even to the ends of the earth.

Psalm 145 sees through the reign of the new king to God who is the true and lasting king. The peace of the new kingdom is sustained by the Lord who is compassionate toward all creatures, who supports the falling and raises up the needy. The new King-Messiah of the prophet's vision is a forerunner of the glorious kingdom of God.

Christians see Jesus as the fulfillment of the hope for a King-Messiah, a descendant of David, who would bring a kingdom of peace. Through him God's kingship shines most clearly. This Sunday's gospel (Matt 11:25-30) presents him as the true revelation of God. Through him we come to know as much as human nature can ever know the true nature of God. It is not the powerful who understand this revelation but the weak, the merest children. The weak understand the revelation of God's nature because they experience it: God "supports all who are falling and raises up all who are bowed down" (Ps 145:14). The weak understand when Jesus describes the nature of God's kingdom: "Take my yoke upon you and learn from me, for I am meek and humble of heart; and you will find rest for yourselves" (Matt 11:29). They know the weariness and the burdens; they know the refreshment of God's compassionate love. They understand the kingdom of peace, the peace which lasts because every creature has what is needed for a full life. They best of all can proclaim the glory of God's kingdom.

In the new kingdom God's people live by God's Spirit within them (Rom 8:9, 11-13). In Christ, God's Spirit delivers God's people in their greatest need, raises them up when they are bowed down in death (cf. Ps 145:14). Thus through God's Messiah they are given new life in the kingdom. Now they are called to live as members of that kingdom, to live according to the Spirit which gives them new life. The new kingdom is a kingdom of peace, ruled by God's compassionate love. The new life to which we are all called is a life of peace. As messianic people (Christ-ians) we now give flesh to God's peace, to God's faithful love.

17th Sun Year B (10-11.15-16.17-18) [111]

The hand of the Lord feeds us and answers all our needs (16).

The refrain and the verses of Psalm 145 designated for the Seventeenth Sunday of Year B emphasize God's care of the hungry. The mighty Lord of creation feeds every living thing. Verses 15-16 of the psalm have been a traditional table prayer for centuries. Today in the Eucharist we remember that everything which nourishes our lives comes to us from the compassionate God who listens to all who call.

The readings also recall the fact that all our food is a gift from God. The prophetic legends of Elijah and Elisha which are told in the Books of Kings portray the prophets as miracle workers. Several of their miracles serve the purpose of feeding those in need. Because of the presence of Elijah, the widow in whose house he stays is supported for a year on a little jar of flour and a jug of oil (1 Kgs 17:7-16). Elisha purifies some poison stew so that the guild prophets in his company may eat (2 Kgs 4:38-41). In today's story (2 Kgs 4:42-44) the prophet feeds over a hundred people on twenty barley loaves and some fresh grain. Not only is there enough; there is some left over! The hand of the Lord feeds all people (Ps 145:16).

The gospel story (John 6:1-15) mirrors the prophetic legend. A vast crowd has followed Jesus and the disciples worry about how to feed them. Human resourcefulness is inadequate in the face of such numbers. As Philip says, not even two hundred days' wages can pay for food for such a crowd. Jesus, however, sees the situation from a different perspective: God feeds every living thing. Jesus collects the food that is available—five barley loaves and a couple of fish—and gives instructions for the people to be seated. He then says the table prayer and distributes the food. Not only is there enough; there are twelve baskets left over. "The eyes of all look hopefully to [God who] gives them their food in due season" (Ps 145:15).

The people recognize the event as a sign. It is Passover time and they see Jesus as the prophet like Moses who will again lead them out of oppression and feed them in the desert. But their understanding of his mission is too narrow. He will indeed lead them to life, but not in the way they anticipate. The life he brings is sustained by the Spirit of God (Eph 4:1-6). This life unites all believers in one body supported by one hope. This life is the gift of God "who is over all and through all and in all" (Eph 4:6). All God's ways are just; all God's works are faithful (Ps 145:17). The eyes of all look hopefully to God for sustenance. Not only does God give food to sustain their mortal lives; God satisfies the desires of the faithful by giving them a share in the divine life. Not only is there enough; there is an abundance overflowing into eternity. "The hand of the Lord feeds us and answers all our needs" (Ps 145:16). The Lord gives us life.

18th Sun Year A (8-9.15-16.17-18) [113]

The hand of the Lord feeds us and answers all our needs (16).

The refrain for the Eighteenth Sunday of Year A is the same as that for the Seventeenth Sunday of Year B (see above). The verses from Psalm 145 emphasize God's gift of food and life to all creation. The little creed is included which describes the nature of God: "gracious and merciful, slow to anger and abounding in love." This is who God is; God's compassionate actions spring from abiding love.

What sustains our lives? That question focuses the readings for this Sunday. Just as the Babylonian Exile was ending, a prophet whose work is included in the scroll of Isaiah (chs. 40–55) encouraged the people to believe that their God not only had the power to restore them but also the will to do so. The whole message of this prophet is a passionate exhortation to abandon despair and to believe again. Today's passage (Isa 55:1-3) summons the hungry and thirsty to come without worrying about the cost. The food which sustains their hearts is not bought with money. The food of life is given away free. The gracious and merciful God satisfies the desire of every living thing (Ps 145:16).

The action of Jesus in the gospel is a sign of God's gracious care (Matt 14:13-21). Jesus pities the crowd that has followed him and gives freely what he has. He cures their sick until evening. Then the disciples, worrying about supplies, encourage Jesus to send the crowd away that they might provide for themselves. Jesus shifts the responsibility back to the disciples: Feed them yourselves! The disciples panic: We have nothing but five loaves and a few fish. But Jesus is showing them that it is God who feeds all people. He takes the loaves, says the table prayer, and gives them to the disciples to distribute. Everyone ate their fill; God satisfies the desires of every living thing (Ps 145:16). The number does not matter; God always provides more than enough.

We have a greater need, however, than the need for food. We cannot live without faithful, supporting love. In a soaring poetic passage (Rom 8:35, 37-39) Paul assures us that nothing, absolutely nothing, can separate us from the overflowing love of Christ. Just as the prophet dismissed the worry about money, Paul dismisses the fear of every power, even the power of death. Nothing, absolutely nothing, can "separate us from the love of God in Christ Jesus." "The LORD is gracious and merciful, slow to anger and abounding in love" (Ps 145:8). This is the God who sustains our lives, who satisfies our every desire. This is the God who feeds us.

25th Sun Year A (2-3.8-9.17-18) [134]

The Lord is near to all who call (18).

God's ways are not our ways; God's ways are beyond our understanding. That is the subject of the verses selected from Psalm 145 for the Twenty-Fifth Sunday of Year A. What is specifically beyond our understanding is God's compassion. It is the very nature of God to be "gracious and merciful, slow to anger and abounding in love" (145:8). Therefore God is compassionate to every creature, hears every person who cries out. These ways are beyond us. Yet we know that God's way, not our way, is truly just; it is God's work that is truly faithful.

The prophet whose work is found in the latter part of the Book of Isaiah (chs. 40–55) exhorted the people to trust God's ways (Isa 55:6-9). The possibility that the Babylonian Exile could end, that they could be restored as a people, was beyond their understanding. Yet that restoration was precisely God's design. The prophet calls the people to forsake the short-sighted ways by which they think they will survive and to turn to God for mercy. Their survival depends not on their own cunning and skill but rather upon the gracious love of God. God does not act as we do; God is generous in forgiving. The hope for new life is found in seeking the Lord, in crying out while God is near. We affirm the hope as we sing: Indeed the Lord is near to all who cry out in truth (Ps 145:18).

The gospel strikes at our human sense of justice (Matt 20:1-16). At the end of the workday all the workers are paid the standard daily wage, regardless of how long each worked. It is true, each agreed to the daily wage. It is also true that we expect more pay for more work. Our economic system does not run on "distribution according to need." Presumably every worker needed the daily wage to survive. But we strive for a different kind of equality: pay equal to work. God, however, gives food according to need. God hears all who call, is compassionate to every creature (Ps 145:18, 9). "You open wide your hand and satisfy the desire of every living thing" (Ps 145:16). God's ways are just, but God's ways are beyond us (cf. Ps 145:17, 3).

Paul has reached a point of surrender to God's ways (Phil 1:20-24, 27). Even death has lost its terror because through death he hopes to gain life with Christ. He is willing to accept whatever comes from God's hand, death or life. The only goal is to live "in a way worthy of the gospel of Christ." Paul has based his life on the conviction that God is just in all ways, faithful in all works. He believes, even when he cannot understand, how great is the compassionate love of God.

31st Sun Year C (1-2.8-9.10-11.13.14) [154]

I will praise your name forever, my king and my God (1).

The verses of Psalm 145 chosen for the Thirty-First Sunday of Year C are the same as those for the Fourteenth Sunday of Year A (see above).

The readings for this Sunday expand on the universality so well expressed in the psalm. "The LORD is good to all" (Ps 145:9). The Book of Wisdom was written in Greek sometime during the first century BCE and reflects the breadth of Greek philosophy as well as the heart of Jewish teaching. The Greek notion of God as all-knowing, all-powerful, and above all things is superimposed on the biblical vision of a God who works within human history and is attentive to the life of every creature. Today's reading (Wis 11:22–12:1) illustrates that combination. It is part of a discussion of God's care of Israel during the exodus-wilderness period. After considering God's treatment of the Egyptians and the Israelites, the author pauses to consider God's universal mercy. God who is all-powerful uses that power for forgiveness and mercy. God who has created all things also loves and cares for all things. Everything that exists lives because of God's spirit within it.

The psalm approaches the same truth from the opposite direction. God feeds all things; God is compassionate to all creatures. God raises up the most desperate (Ps 145:15-16, 9, 14). Therefore God must be all-powerful; "God's grandeur is beyond understanding" (Ps 145:3).

The gospel (Luke 19:1-10) provides a lesson for us in compassion toward all people. Jesus again suffers disapproval because he associates with social outcasts. Zacchaeus is a tax collector and a wealthy man. Tax collectors in first-century Israel were despised because they cooperated with the occupying power, the Romans. They were often suspected of cheating and exploiting the people from whom they collected taxes. Jesus not only speaks to Zacchaeus, he invites himself to dinner at the tax collector's house. At this point we find the social judgment of Zacchaeus, "He has gone to stay at the house of a sinner." But nothing in the text indicates that Zacchaeus is in fact a sinner. Actually he has a very tender conscience. Not only does he offer to give half his wealth to the poor, he declares that if by chance he has defrauded anyone, he will restore four times the amount. Jesus does not seem to consider him a sinner either. There is no mention of forgiveness. He includes Zacchaeus as a descendant of Abraham, a righteous man who honors the demands of relationships. He also identifies him as lost. Is that because the rest of his society has excluded him? And what about us? "The LORD is good to all" (Ps 145:9). Are we?

Zacchaeus would easily sing Psalm 145: "I will extol you, my God and king; I will bless your name forever. . . . [The LORD] raises up all who are bowed down" (1, 14). The second reading (2 Thess 1:11–2:2) might also be addressed to Zacchaeus: "We always pray for you, that our God may make you worthy of his calling and powerfully bring to fulfillment every good purpose and every effort of faith." God is praised by our perseverance and by our trust. Fear of the Day of the Lord, even fear of judgment, is a failure of trust in the God who is "slow to anger and abounding in love" (Ps 145:8). God loves "all things that are" (Wis 11:24); the Lord is "compassionate to every creature" (Ps 145:9). It is our responsibility to help each other follow God's ways and sing God's praise. "The LORD is good to all." So must we be.

Year Common (1-2.8-9.10-11.13-14) [175]

I will praise your name forever, my king and my God (1).

The verses of Psalm 145 chosen for the Common of the Year are the same as those for the Fourteenth Sunday of Year A (see above).

Psalm 145 is a good all-purpose hymn. Because the connection between verses is loose, many standard ideas about God are found in the psalm. The central idea is the little creed in verse 8: "The LORD is gracious and merciful, slow to anger and abounding in love." This compassion extends to all creatures. Thus any set of Sunday readings which emphasize God's compassionate love would be complemented by Psalm 145.

Psalm 145 could be used on Sundays in which the theme is trust in God's providence. For example, on the Eighth Sunday of Year A the gospel (Matt 6:24-34) is the exhortation to stop worrying about food and clothing but rather to seek the kingdom of God (see Ps 62 for a fuller discussion). The first reading (Isa 49:14-15) reveals the image of God more tender than a nursing mother. The Eighteenth Sunday of Year C approaches the same topic from a different angle (see Ps 95). In the gospel Jesus tells the story of the rich fool who feels secure because he has provided for himself (Luke 12:13-21). Qoheleth proclaims such activity vanity (Qoh 1:2; 2:21-23). The Letter to the Colossians (Col 3:1-5, 9-11) reminds us that we must set our hearts on what is above because now we belong to Christ. Psalm 145 provides the foundation for such trust. The Lord cares for all creatures, satisfies "the desire of every living thing" (Ps 145:16).

The Twenty-Eighth Sunday of Year C focuses on God's care of all peoples and on our need to be grateful (see Ps 98). Naaman the leper (2 Kings 5:14-17) and the Samaritan leper (Luke 17:11-19) are outside the people of Israel yet they are cured by God. Both men return to offer thanks. Their praise might well be Psalm 145: "The LORD . . . raises up all who are bowed down . . . all flesh will bless your holy name forever" (145:14, 21).

17. Psalm 146

Psalm 146 begins the final Hallel collection of the psalter (Pss 146–150). Hallel psalms begin (or end) with Hallelujah, "Praise the LORD." The other collections are Pss 113–118 and the long litany of Ps 136. Psalm 146 doubles the call to praise the Lord (*Hallelujah halleli* . . . *'eth-YHWH*) and addresses the call to the self. The call is followed by an enthusiastic pledge to praise God throughout life.

The two stanzas which follow the call to praise (3-4, 5-10) use a contrast to give the reasons for praise. The contrast deals with the question of whom to trust. Human beings are too frail to be trusted (3-4). Even those who appear to be the most powerful are only mortal. They will die and their power turn to dust.

God, on the other hand, is worthy of all trust (5-10). This section begins with a beatitude: those who are wise enough to hope in God are truly happy. Their security is in the God whose power over all creation never diminishes; they trust the God who uses power to care for the powerless. The most needy have the most assurance of divine protection and deliverance. The hungry and the blind, the oppressed and imprisoned, the most helpless in the society (stranger, orphan, and widow) are the special subjects of God's concern. This is the sign both of God's power and of God's fidelity. Only one group of people should worry, the wicked, those who have broken the relationship with God. God loves the righteous who maintain the covenant relationship, but God "thwarts the way of the wicked." That single dark note does not detain the psalmist, however. The psalm closes with a glorious shout: "The LORD shall reign forever, your God, Zion, through all generations! Hallelujah!" All the faithful are drawn home to Jerusalem, to the everlasting kingdom of our God.

3rd Sun Adv A (6-7.8-9.9-10) [7]

Lord, come and save us (cf. Is 35:4).

On the Third Sunday of Advent A we sing the final verses of Psalm 146 which praise the trustworthy Lord who cares especially for the helpless. The refrain takes a declaration from the reading and turns it into a plea. God, you have promised to save us; you are the God who cares for the weak and needy; come now!

The passage from Isaiah (35:1-6, 10) builds a bridge between the work of the eighth-century prophet from whom the book takes its name and the nameless prophet of the sixth century who proclaimed the return from Exile. The prophet envisions a new exodus. Just as Israel came through the desert in the thirteenth century on the way to the land of promise, so now Israel will return to the land. The desert itself will rejoice in their return; it will forget its dryness and will bloom abundantly. The people who have become a desert of apathy are called to forget their despair and to bloom with energy and song. God comes with salvation; God will repay for the years of sorrow. God, the next-of-kin who is responsible to ransom from slavery, comes to lead the people home again. Joy overflows.

The responsorial psalm gives voice to our mixed emotions. The psalm verses declare that what we have heard in the reading is indeed true of our God. God does feed the hungry and free the prisoners (Ps 146:7). But we also know the distress and despair that threatens our lives daily. Oppression rages in too many places; too many hungry and homeless fill our cities. So even as we sing the praise of the faithful God who does these things, we plead, "Come, save us now!"

The overlapping of different times continues through the New Testament readings. In the gospel (Matt 11:2-11) Jesus demonstrates to his questioners that God's deliverance has taken flesh in him. The prophet's vision has been fulfilled. "The blind regain their sight, the lame walk, lepers are cleansed, the deaf hear, the dead are raised, and the poor have the good news proclaimed to them." The desert, however, is nonetheless real. John the Baptist is the prophet in the desert exhorting the people to be ready for the arrival of God's salvation, to abandon their weakness and to accept God's strength. Both realities emerge: our salvation has arrived but the desert is still with us. We continue to sing of God's faithful love and at the same time to plead: "Lord, come and save us."

The Letter to James tells us to "be patient . . . until the coming of the Lord" (James 5:7-10). The farmer knows that the seed is growing even when he cannot see it. We too must know that the coming of the Lord is at hand. We are given the prophets as an example of persevering in trust. Neither the Baptist nor the prophet of the first reading saw the full accomplishment of their vision. Yet their message does not falter: "Be strong, fear not! Here is your God" (Isa 35:4). It is hard to persevere in hope but we must. Only then can we begin to bring the messianic vision to our society. We continue to cling to the truth of God's saving love. We continue to cry out: "Lord, come and save us."

4th Sun Year A (6-7.8-9.9-10) [71]

Happy the poor in spirit; the kingdom of heaven is theirs! (Matt 5:3).

On the Fourth Sunday of Year A the verses of Psalm 146 are the same as those for the Third Sunday of Advent A (see above). The refrain is taken from the gospel. The beatitude echoes the beatitude of the psalm: "Happy those whose help is Jacob's God, whose hope is in the LORD, their God" (Ps 146:5). The poor in spirit are happy because they are the recipients of God's special attention. It is the poor and hungry, the oppressed and imprisoned, who are saved by God's faithful love and brought into God's kingdom (Ps 146:7-10). Those who know their only hope is in God have the best reason to rejoice. Happy are they!

It is the prophet Zephaniah who begins to point out the special status of the *'anawim*, those whose hope is only in God (Zeph 2:3; 3:12-13). Zephaniah preached in the years preceding the Babylonian Exile. He proclaims the arrival of a Day of the Lord which will be a day of great distress and destruction. It seems that no one will be saved. But perhaps there is one group that has hope, the humble. The only way to escape the terrible doom is to seek humility and to keep the Law. That is true righteousness, living by the right relationship to God. God responds to the prophet's "perhaps" with an "indeed." God will leave a remnant, those who trust in God alone. They shall prosper in peace.

We sing the psalm with hope in the prophetic "perhaps." Bravely we declare God's faithfulness to the helpless. Bravely we proclaim the beatitude. There may be a twinge in our hearts, however. Are we the oppressed and the bowed down? Can we acknowledge the truth that our only hope is in God? Can we abandon our reliance on our own power (cf. Ps 146:3-4)? The psalm challenges us to that surrender.

The gospel (Matt 5:1-12) is the charter statement of Jesus' law which begins the Sermon on the Mount. This initial declaration sets out the radical reversal which characterizes the message of Jesus. It is precisely those who are of least account who can anticipate the highest places in God's kingdom. They are the truly happy, not because poverty or sorrow or hunger are good, but because they are the ones who can count on God to deliver them. Those who have no need of God may miss the experience of God. Happy those who recognize their true situation and abandon themselves to the care of the God who is faithful forever (Ps 146:6).

Paul reminds us that we all belong to the category of the weak and lowly (1 Cor 1:26-31). He punctures the pride of the Corinthians by pointing out that whatever they have is God's gift. Their only cause for boasting is God. Their own worth is of no account. How hard it is to let God give us worth. How hard it is to be the poor in spirit. Yet happy are they; the whole of God's kingdom is theirs! Happy those whose only hope is in the LORD their God! (Ps 146:5).

23rd Sun Year B (6-7.8-9.9-10) [129]

Praise the Lord, my soul! (2).

The verses of Psalm 146 chosen for the Twenty-Third Sunday of Year B are the same as those for the Third Sunday of Advent A (see above) with one exception: The LORD who keeps faith forever is identified as the God of Jacob (cf. Ps 146:5a). The refrain is taken from the verse immediately following the opening Hallelujah. It is the call to praise addressed to the psalmist's own self which becomes in turn our own.

The first reading (Isa 35:4-7) is also taken from the same passage as the Third Sunday of Advent A (above). Only one verse (7) is included on this Sunday which is not used for the Advent Sunday. The new verse repeats the image of the fruitful desert, watered by rivers and springs (cf. Isa 35:1-3).

The gospel (Mark 7:31-37) is the acting out of Jesus' declaration from the Advent Sunday. Isaiah 35 proclaims a day of God's arrival when weaknesses will be healed: blind will see, deaf will hear, lame will leap, dumb will sing. In Matt 11:2-11 (3rd Sun Adv A) Jesus recites the same list as proof to the messengers from John that he is the one who is to come. In today's gospel Jesus heals a deaf and dumb man. The gospel miracles are the sign that God's day has arrived, that evil has lost its grip on human life. The power of Satan is broken; the kingdom of God has burst through. The man in today's gospel is freed from the evil which afflicts him, the isolation of the deaf and dumb. God's kingdom has arrived in his life, opening him to all God's creation. He himself becomes a sign of God: God is indeed faithful; God does heal the afflicted and attend to the most needy (cf. Ps 146:6-9). The healed man's response is the same as that of the psalmist: "Praise the LORD, my soul" (Ps 146:2).

The Letter of James (2:1-5) contrasts the ways of God with our human tendencies. Like the first-century Christians, we are tempted to give the most attention to the wealthy, well-dressed person. God, on the other hand pays special attention to the blind, the hungry, the oppressed, the helpless. As Christians we are called, like the healed man in the gospel, to be signs of God's arrival in the world. If we cannot be completely like God, who specifically chooses the poor to be "rich in faith and heirs of the kingdom," then the author of this letter says at the very least we should even out our treatment of rich and poor. Psalm 146 may catch in our throats as we praise the God who sustains the most impoverished and remember at the same time the wealth we enjoy.

26th Sun Year C (6-7.8-9.9-10) [139]

Praise the Lord, my soul! (2).

The verses of Psalm 146 chosen for the Twenty-Sixth Sunday of Year C are the same as those for the Third Sunday of Advent A (see above). There is, however, a mistranslation in the Lectionary in the first verse (6): "Happy he who keeps faith forever." The psalm verse refers to God, "who keeps faith forever." The previous verse of the psalm (5) states: "Happy those whose help is Jacob's God, whose hope is in the LORD, their God." The opening of the responsorial psalm for this Sunday mistakenly indicates that it is this happy, trusting person who "keeps faith forever, secures justice for the oppressed, gives food to the hungry." It is rather the Lord "who keeps faith forever"!

The psalm emphasizes the fidelity of God who tends the needs of the poor. The readings for this Sunday point out the difficulty we have in imitating our generous God. The prophet Amos preached to prosperous Israelites in the eighth century (Amos 6:1, 4-7). Archaeologists have discovered wonderful ivory inlays from the king's palace in eighth century Samaria. Times were good, at least for some people. True, the rich were getting richer and the poor poorer, but life seems always to be that way. The prophet, however, stabs at the complacency of the well-to-do. He cries "Woe," the equivalent of singing a dirge over them. Their good life has insulated them from the cries of the poor. They have failed in their covenant responsibility to care for each other; they will be the first to lose the covenant gift of the land.

Psalm 146 is both frightening and comforting. To those of us who have forgotten the poor, the psalm is a painful reminder that precisely the poor are God's special people. To those who know their only hope is in God, even those of the first reading who face Exile, the psalm proclaims the hope that the Lord will again set prisoners free and raise up those who are bowed down (Ps 146:7-8).

The gospel sets out the reversal even more clearly (Luke 16:19-31): a rich man enjoying his life, a poor man longing for the rich man's leftovers. The rich man's wealth insulates him from the desperation of the poor man. The poor man's poverty makes him invisible to the rich man. But at death their situations are reversed. Now the rich man sees. He begs first for relief for himself. When he realizes the impossibility of that, he begs for his brothers who are still alive. The answer is devastating: "They have Moses and the prophets." They have the covenant law; they have the preaching of God's word. They have what the rich man had and failed to heed. "No," says the rich man, "if someone from the dead goes to them, they will repent." Abraham replies, "If they will not listen to Moses and the prophets, neither will they be persuaded if someone should rise from the dead." And what of us? We have all of that. We have Moses and the prophets; we have the witness of one who has risen from the dead. We sing the praise of the God who gives special care to the beggars who sit at our doors. How do we have the courage?

The Letter to Timothy lays out the demands of Christian life (1 Tim 6:11-16): "righteousness, devotion, faith, love, patience, and gentleness." We are called to persevere in those virtues until the coming of our Lord Jesus Christ. In that way we take firm hold on the life which has been promised us in baptism. Alone we cannot do it; our own resources are far too inadequate. Our only hope is in the God who raises up those who are bowed down, who sustains the helpless (Ps 146:8-9). "Happy those whose help is Jacob's God, whose hope is in the LORD, their God. Praise the LORD, my soul!" (Ps 146:5, 2).

32nd Sun Year B (6-7.8-9.9-10) [156]

Praise the Lord, my soul! (2).

The verses from Psalm 146 for the Thirty-Second Sunday of Year B are the same as those for the Third Sunday of Advent A (see above). The refrain is the call by which we summon ourselves to join the psalmist's praise.

The readings focus our attention on the most helpless people of Israelite society, the widows. Without the help of their families or the charity of the society at large they have no means at all to support themselves. They are the first to suffer when the economy declines. The prophet Elijah is called by God to proclaim a drought because God's people have gone over to the worship of Ba'al. The prophet spends the first months by a brook, being fed by ravens. But when the brook runs dry, God sends the prophet to Zarephath: "Stay there; I have designated a widow there to provide for you" (1 Kgs 17:9). The most helpless person of the society is called to provide for God's prophet.

Today's reading tells the story of Elijah and the widow (1 Kgs 17:10-16). She is indeed destitute when Elijah arrives. She has only a handful of flour and a little oil, only enough for a final meal for herself and her son. Elijah asks her to share even that little bit with him. He promises that the God who gives food to the hungry (Ps 146:7) will not let the jar of flour go empty or the jug of oil run dry until the rains come again. The prophet's word is true. The prophet, the widow, and her son eat for a year on the little handful of flour and the little bit of oil. The LORD "keeps faith forever, . . . gives food to the hungry" (Ps 146:6, 7). The woman, a non-Israelite, mirrors the action of Israel's God who protects the stranger. Israel's God responds by sustaining the orphan and the widow (Ps 146:9).

The gospel (Mark 12:38-44) provides both a contrast and a parallel. The scribes, who are accused by Jesus, are far from Elijah's situation. They are not in need; rather they enjoy the perquisites of their office. The widow, on the other hand, parallels the widow of Elijah's time. She too is destitute. She too is being asked for the last little bit that she has to live on. Jesus condemns the system that can make a demand like this on the widow. By his presence Elijah supports the widow who supports him. He brings the gift of God to repay her gift. In contrast, the religious leaders of the gospel devour the widow's savings and provide her nothing in return. They have lost the vision of the God whose special love is for the widow (Ps 146:9).

The Letter to the Hebrews (9:24-28) portrays Christ as the true religious leader, the one who truly images the compassionate God. Rather than devouring the life of others, Christ offers his own blood to take away our sins and win life for us. Christ is the perfect image of the God who feeds the hungry, protects the stranger, sustains the helpless (Ps 146: 7, 9). How happy are we whose hope is in the Lord, our God (Ps 146:5). "Praise the Lord, my soul!" (Ps 146:1).

18. Psalm 147

There are really three hymns in Psalm 147. Three times there is a call to praise (1, 7, 12); three times reasons are given for praising God (2-6, 8-11, 13-20). In the Greek and Latin translations Psalm 147 is divided into two psalms, vv. 1-11 numbered as Psalm 146 and vv. 12-20 as Psalm 147.[9] The psalm is a general praise of God the powerful creator. The specific references to Israel's own history are minimal.

The first stanza (1-7) begins with an exclamation of delight: "How good to celebrate our God in song!" The rebuilding of Jerusalem's walls under Nehemiah (cf. Neh 12:27-43) is suggested in verse 2. The psalm moves rapidly to generic praise of God. God is great in power, great enough to control the stars who represent the Mesopotamian gods. This powerful God is known especially for care of the brokenhearted and wounded. Only the wicked suffer God's wrath.

The second stanza (7-11) begins with a renewed call to sing God's praises. The focus is on God's power in creation, especially the gift of rain which makes the land fertile so that it produces food. All of creation is ordered

[9]The numbering of the Hebrew psalter and the Greek psalter differ by one number throughout most of the book, beginning at Psalm 9-10. What is 9-10 in the Hebrew psalter is only 9 in the Greek psalter. The difference is made up here in Psalm 147 (or 146-147).

so that every creature has what it needs. But God's special delight is found in people who recognize their dependence and trust in God's loving care.

The third stanza (12-20) calls Jerusalem to praise God. The rebuilding of the walls is again suggested (13). Attention moves swiftly to God's power in creation, especially in the gift of moisture. God's creative word is the source of this gift (cf. Isa 55:10-11). The psalmist wonders at the variety of forms this moisture takes: snow, frost, hail, ice. The winter imagery may come from Canaanite psalmody north of Israel. But the focus is the word of God. This wonderful word which brings life-giving moisture has been given to Israel in the life-giving Law. Other nations will learn it only through Israel.

2nd Sun after Christmas (12-13.14-15.19-20) [19]

The Word of God became flesh and lived among us (John 1:14).

The refrain for the Second Sunday after Christmas ABC presents the content of the readings. It is the climax of the prologue to the Gospel of John. God's own word, by which all things were created and which has been given to Israel as the Law, has become flesh and pitched a tent among us! Twenty centuries of meditation is not enough to understand that fully. The verses of Psalm 147 are from the final stanza which sings the praises of God's word. The verses omitted are the psalmist's wondering about all the forms of moisture: snow and hail, frost and ice.

The reading from the Book of Sirach (24:1-4, 8-12) is well chosen. Throughout the wisdom tradition Wisdom is personified as a wonderful woman. The Book of Proverbs introduces us to the Wisdom Woman (see especially Prov 8). She calls to the unlearned and offers them life (Prov 1:20-23; 9:1-6, 11). She is herself the tree of life (Prov 3:18). She was present at creation as God's designer (Prov 8:30). Her delight is in human beings; God delights in her (Prov 8:30-31). Ben Sira builds on this tradition. Wisdom came forth from the mouth of the Most High. Thus Wisdom is God's word and/or God's spirit. God chose the spot for her tent, the holy city of the chosen people. The sage comes to the exciting conclusion that Wisdom herself is the Law (Sir 24:22). It is the Law which teaches human beings how to be fully human, to grow into their creation as image of God (cf. Gen 1:26-27).

The responsorial psalm leads us from Sirach to the gospel (John 1:1-18). Wisdom, who is the Law and the Word of God, has not only pitched a tent among us but has taken on our own flesh and become human with us. Now we who are made in the image of God see God in our human flesh. The gospel introduces this amazing action of God by rehearsing what we already know about the Word of God. The Word was present at creation; all things came into being and found life through God's Word. But for God even this was not enough. God's love longed for a complete sharing of life with us: The Word became flesh and pitched a tent among us!

The hymn from the Letter to the Ephesians (Eph 1:3-6, 15-18) gives us words of response: "Blessed be the God and Father of our Lord Jesus Christ, who has blessed us in Christ with every spiritual blessing in the heavens!" (1:3). God's gift is even greater. Now we too are caught up in Christ to be God's children. Paul prays that wisdom may come to help us know clearly what God has done for us, what God has planned for us. May God's word sink into our hearts like rain that we may know the riches of our hope!

5th Sun Year B (1-2.3-4.5-6) [75]

Praise the Lord who heals the brokenhearted (3).

The truth which gives hope to the readings of the Fifth Sunday of Year B is found in the refrain from Psalm 147: "The Lord . . . heals the brokenhearted." The verses are the whole little hymn which forms the first stanza of the psalm. The heights and the depths are juxtaposed in the verses. God is great, powerful, and wise. God numbers the stars and gives them their names. But this mighty God uses power precisely for the powerless. The God of the stars heals the brokenhearted and tends their wounds.

Job's speech (Job 7:1-4, 6-7) is a reply to the first of his friends who has exhorted Job to repent of the sins which have caused his misery. Job insists that he has done nothing to deserve the tragedy which has befallen him. He sets the blame for his pain squarely on God. His suffering is part of the human condition. Everyone has known nights when it seemed the day would never come; everyone has known days when the fragility of life was all too obvious. Job gives us a model for dealing with those days and nights. Even when it seems he has given up all hope—"I shall not see happiness again"—he continues to struggle with God. He knows that only God can relieve his misery.

We must respond to Job's suffering very carefully. It is easy, when we are well and happy, to join Job's friends in saying, "Just relax, it's God's will." But Psalm 147 does not say that. The psalm recognizes the reality of pain and despair. In the psalm we have an opportunity to join Job in acknowledging that only the powerful God can really heal the wounds of human tragedy. "Praise the Lord who heals the brokenhearted" (Ps 147:3).

The gospel (Mark 1:29-39) shows Jesus as the minister of God's compassion for the brokenhearted. From the beginning of his ministry (represented in today's reading) to the very end, Jesus recognizes the reality of human pain and spends a great deal of energy in alleviating it. Today's gospel gives us a specific instance, the healing of Simon's mother-in-law, and a general summary of Jesus' typical activity. He cured many and expelled the demons who represent the evil of suffering. He also preached the good news. His miracles bear witness to the fact that the power of Satan is broken, the power of suffering and sin and death is crushed. The kingdom of God has arrived. The God who heals the brokenhearted reveals divine power in gentleness and healing for the needy but in violence toward the evil and suffering which afflicts people.

This is the good news that Paul is compelled to preach (1 Cor 9:16-19, 22-23). God has come in Christ to heal the brokenhearted. Paul takes the message into his own flesh. Just as God in Christ took on the weakness of human flesh in order to heal our suffering, so Paul becomes weak in order to win the weak. Today's readings face us with the enormity of our own need. Praise the Lord who heals the brokenhearted! (Ps 147:3).

Corpus Christi A (12-13.14-15.19-20) [*168*]

Praise the Lord, Jerusalem (12).

The refrain and verses of Psalm 147 chosen for the Solemnity of Corpus Christi A are all from the final stanza of the psalm which celebrates the power of God's creative word. God's word brings the moisture which makes the land fertile. Thus by means of the word God provides finest wheat to nourish the chosen people. The refrain is the call to praise of this final little hymn. Jerusalem is personified as a mother gathering her children. She is called to praise God for giving her peace and prosperity. The verses describing snow and frost, hail and ice, are omitted.

The readings for Corpus Christi A focus on the gift of bread. In the sermon from Deuteronomy (8:2-3, 14-16) the people are reminded that God provided everything for them when they were most helpless. God fed them and gave them water. God guided them to a good land. God also tested them to see if they were committed to the covenant. The reality of the desert period is that they lacked nothing even though they had absolutely no resources. But the greatest gift God gave them was the living word. God's word creates and sustains all things. God's word in the Law teaches people how to live a full life. All the other gifts are only symbols of this essential gift.

In the psalm we agree that God's word is the best gift. God's word comes swiftly, bringing peace and nourishment. God's word is the special gift to Israel, the sign of God's special love. For this gift we give thanks.

Paul deepens our understanding of the reality of God's gift (1 Cor 10:16-17). The word of life which nourishes us is a sharing in the body of Christ. Through sharing the bread, the symbol of the living word, we share in reality in the life of Christ. Through sharing the bread we share life with one another, thus becoming ourselves the body of Christ. This is the bread by which we live, the "word that comes forth from the mouth of the LORD" (Deut 8:3). God's word runs swiftly to the earth, bringing the finest wheat to fill our hunger (Ps 147:14-15).

In the gospel (John 6:51-58) Jesus states the reality clearly: "I am the living bread that came down from heaven; whoever eats this bread will live forever; and the bread that I will give is my flesh for the life of the world." This is the true bread of life, the living word of God. The response to Jesus' announcement echoes the murmuring of the desert period, but the greatness of the gift outweighs the petty murmuring.

The message of this solemnity is stunningly simple. God feeds us with a share in the divine life itself. The Word which created us becomes our very life. Praise the Lord, Jerusalem; your God has "filled you with finest wheat" (Ps 147:12-14). The Lord has sent the Word that we might know the true source of our life.

F. Liturgies

Almost all of the psalms have a liturgical setting. Biblical prayer is primarily the prayer of the assembled community. A few psalms, however, show such a connection to liturgical worship that they are categorized simply as liturgies. Like other categories which are distinguished by content rather than form, the category of liturgical psalms is fluid. There is no general agreement on how many or which psalms belong to this genre.

The psalms included here under the category of liturgy may be considered under three headings: entrance liturgy, covenant renewal, and procession.

Psalms 15 and 24 are entrance liturgies. They outline the ceremony at which the worshipper seeks entrance to the sanctuary. A cultic official lists the requirements for participation. The requirements are an outline of Israel's Law, and so these psalms are sometimes called *torah* liturgies.

Psalms 50 and 81 seem to reflect a ceremony at which the covenant was renewed. The existence of a regular covenant renewal ceremony in Israel is debated. However, it is certain that from time to time the community did renew the covenant. Such a ceremony is described in Josh 24. These psalms also refer to Israel's Law, especially the Ten Commandments.

Psalm 68 is very difficult to classify. The subject of the psalm seems to be a grand procession, symbolizing the procession of God from Sinai to Jerusalem.

These psalms give us an opportunity to reflect on our own liturgical worship. How have we kept the Law, the conditions for participation? How often do we remember that every Eucharist is a renewal of our covenant with God? Do we recognize our processions as the sign of God's journey with us? Such reflection is the value of the liturgical psalms.

1. Psalm 15

Psalm 15 is an entrance liturgy. The worshipper, seeking to participate in the temple liturgy, asks the entrance requirements and receives the answer from the attending priest or minister. The ceremony functions somewhat like the penitential rite in the Eucharistic liturgy. It is both instruction and an examination of conscience. To participate in worship of Yahweh one must agree to live by Yahweh's Law. This little list is both a summary and a sample. Other examples of loyalty to Yahweh's covenant could be listed.

There are three brief sections to the psalm (1, 2-5ab, 5c). The seeker's question opens the psalm: "Who may abide in your tent? Who may dwell on your holy mountain?" (1). "Tent" and "holy mountain" are names for the Jerusalem temple. The temple replaces the tent of the desert as the meeting place of God. The tent is the sign of God's sojourning with the people. The holy mountain is Mount Zion, the site of the temple. It is also the mythological mountain which is the home of divinity. The questioner seeks entrance to the divine presence. The two verbs, however, indicate that the questioner knows that this admittance to God's home is temporary. Who may be a sojourner (*ger*) with you; who may tent (*shkn*) on your mountain?

There are ten parts to the answer, suggesting a kind of decalogue (2-5). The opening response is a general summary of the other nine: "Whoever walks without blame, doing what is right." Such a person lives by God's Law, honoring the demands of relationships (*sedeq*) and steering clear of evil through every step of daily life. Specific examples of this upright life follow. The responses all illustrate right relationships. The recognition that worthiness for cultic celebration depends on relationships within the community reflects the message of the prophets. Ceremonies are useless if love of one another is absent.

The final statement is a promise: "Whoever acts like this shall never be shaken." Not only is such a person admitted to worship; this person enjoys the fullness of life.

The psalm may lead us to despair. Who could ever be admitted to worship if such perfection is demanded? The demand of the psalm is rather one of acceptance and commitment. Do you agree to live like this? Then you are one of Yahweh's covenant people and may enter the holy tent. The focus is on present and future rather than on the past.

16th Sun Year C (2-3.3-4.4-5) [109]

Whoever does what is right will live in the presence of the Lord (1-2).

The refrain for the Sixteenth Sunday of Year C is the summary answer to the question in Psalm 15: "Who may abide in your tent." The answer is simple: "Whoever does what is right." That may seem too vague to us, but the word *sedeq,* "right" or "just," has very specific connotations. The person who is just is the one who honors the demands of each relationship. Righteousness cannot be measured simply by a list of regulations; it is a living thing which is tested every day in the interactions with other people. Every person has a right to something from us; every right is just a little bit different. The person who does what is right heeds each of those demands daily. The verses of the psalm continue with examples: speaking truth, avoiding slander and harm; keeping oaths, avoiding actions that exploit the needy; avoiding association with the wicked who scorn God, honoring those who honor God. The specific examples set the tone. We could add others.

The readings show us people who honor the demands of various relationships. When Abraham sees three men near his tent, he immediately turns to the task of hospitality (Gen 18:1-10). His care for their needs knows no bounds—water to wash, a rich feast, good conversation. Abraham does this for three fellow human beings. His response, however, is worthy even of God who has come to visit him. Abraham is rewarded by God's keeping the demands of the relationship too. God has promised Abraham descendants; now the promise is about to be fulfilled. Abraham's example teaches us how to receive one another, as if we were receiving God. God abides in Abraham's tent.

The story of Martha and Mary (Luke 10:38-42) can be interpreted at many levels. The juxtaposition with Genesis 18 suggests a focus on the element of hospitality. Martha is busy with all the details of hospitality. She is, however, neglecting the central element: presence. Mary is supplying that gift to their guest. Mary is rewarded with the status of disciple, one who sits at the Lord's feet and listens to his words.

Psalm 15 presents an interesting reversal. The questioner in the psalm asks for hospitality in God's tent. Hospitality is granted to those who heed the demands of the relationships in their lives. The people in this Sunday's readings heed precisely the demands of hospitality. What they give will be given back to them. They offer hospitality to fellow human beings. In reality the recipient of their hospitality is God. How could they be refused a return of hospitality when they seek admittance to God's tent? "Whoever does what is right will live in the presence of the Lord."

The Letter to the Colossians (1:24-28) reveals the mystery to us that whenever we receive another as a guest we are receiving Christ. Christ is in us, our "hope of glory." We have been raised with Christ; we live in Christ. What we do to others we do indeed to Christ. That is why those who honor the demands of each relationship are welcome in God's tent. God honors the demand of hospitality in return.

22nd Sun Year B (2-3.3-4.4-5) [126]

Whoever does what is right will live in the presence of the Lord (1-2).

The refrain and psalm verses from Psalm 15 for the Twenty-Second Sunday of Year B are the same as those for the Sixteenth Sunday of Year C (see above).

What is the meaning of the Law? That is the question of this Sunday's readings. The passage from Deuteronomy (4:1-2, 6-8) reminds Israel of what a great gift the Law is. The Law teaches what human beings have longed for from the beginning: how to be like God. Observance of the Law is true wisdom, because observance of the Law leads to a happy and full life. Keeping the Law is the visible sign of keeping the covenant. Therefore the promises of the covenant are fulfilled: land, descendants, blessing.

Psalm 15 describes the person who keeps the Law, a person who does what is right. This person is not simply keeping a set of rules but is accepting the guidance of God in daily affairs. Whoever does this honors the demands of the various relationships of life. Thus this person is truly just. The consequence is the ultimate fulfillment of covenant law: life in the presence of God.

The Pharisees in the gospel (Mark 7:1-8, 14-15, 21-23) have been distracted by the letter of the Law. The prescriptions and customs have become more important than the goal of the Law: to be like God, to share life with God. Such an attitude makes it possible to keep the shell of the Law and forget the longing for God that is at the heart of the Law. Jesus responds that it is what is internal that matters. Attention to details is no substitute for the love of God. The psalm keeps the balance. External observance is still necessary. Love of God and neighbor must be acted out in daily life. External observance gives expression to the internal disposition. "Whoever does what is right lives in the presence of the Lord."

The Letter of James (1:17-18, 21-22, 27) states the principle clearly. The Law is a great gift of God. This word of God is already rooted in our hearts. It has the power to save us, but only if we live by it. Assent is not enough; we must commit ourselves to give flesh to the Law of God in our lives. Our treatment of other people, especially the weakest among us, reveals the presence of God in our lives. It is the one who does what is right who lives in the presence of the Lord.

The greatness of God's gift of the Law is sometimes lost on us. We see the law as a hindrance or restriction rather than as a key to freedom. We have the mistaken notion that if the law did not limit us we could be completely happy. Try this: reverse the statements of the psalm: one who speaks falsehood, slanders a neighbor, defames a friend, honors the wicked, disdains the good. Is this really the way to happiness? Or is it really true that whoever does what is right shall never be shaken, shall live in the presence of the Lord?

2. Psalm 24

Psalm 24 is a processional hymn. Perhaps it was used as a re-enactment of David's bringing the ark of the covenant to the temple (see 1 Sam 6). There are three distinct parts to the psalm (1-2, 3-6, 7-10). The first stanza (1-2) defines God's relationship to creation. Everything that exists belongs to God who created it. Like the gods of the Ancient Near Eastern myths, Yahweh conquered the sea of chaos and established the world upon it. The world is then dependent upon God's power to hold chaos in check and thus maintain the order of creation.

The second stanza (3-6) resembles Psalm 15. Like that psalm this is an entrance liturgy. Who is allowed to enter and worship before the presence of God? It is those who have kept the Law. Psalm 24 lists specifically cultic purity: no idol worship. The other stipulations show the interrelatedness of faithfulness to God and to one another. "Clean of hand" suggests both ritual purity and freedom from acts of violence which fill the hands with blood. "Pure of heart" indicates single-hearted devotion to God and right relationships with other people. True oaths respect God by whom one swears and the neighbor who trusts the word. Those who in this way keep their part of the covenant will receive covenant blessings in return. God too remains faithful to the covenant. The final verse summarizes the stanza: These characteristics identify the covenant community, the people who live in faithful relationship with the covenant God.

The final stanza (7-10) describes the procession with the ark. The gates of the city are personified as ancient guardians, bowed down by the years. At the arrival of God they rise up with attention and joy. God arrives enthroned upon the ark, the war palladium of Israel. God the Warrior who defeats all enemies arrives to take possession of the city. The image of God as warrior is problematic for us. The image, however, reflects Israel's experience. God has protected them, delivered them from slavery, given them a land. This is the same God who defeated the powers of chaos to establish the world. The faithful people celebrate the divine victory.

4th Sun Adv A (1-2.3-4.5-6) [10]

Let the Lord enter, the king of glory (7, 10).

The processional refrain from Psalm 24 is the psalm response for the Fourth Sunday of Advent A. The mighty God arrives to take possession of temple and city. The verses represent the first two stanzas of the psalm. God has defeated chaos and established the world. Those who wish to worship this mighty God must be faithful to the covenant. This fidelity is their identification and their glory. The final stanza is missing except for the refrain.

The readings set before us the paradox of the incarnation, the arrival of the mighty God. Ahaz, eighth-century king of Judah, is threatened by two nations who have laid siege to his capital city of Jerusalem. They intend to depose him and replace him with a king who will do what they want. Isaiah the prophet reassures the king that God will continue to be faithful to the promise to David that there would always be a son of David on the throne. The king, however, is frightened and would rather rely on the power of Assyria than on the power of God. So God offers the king a sign (Isa 7:10-14). The king does not want the sign because he does not want to heed the message. But God intends to give the sign anyway. We would expect at this point that God would give a sign of great power, perhaps a plague to strike the invading armies. But God's sign that city and king will be saved is a child. Before the child grows up, the two invading nations will have disappeared. The child may be a son of Ahaz, signaling that the Davidic dynasty is indeed safe. Or it may be any child, because every child is a sign of hope. The child carries the message: God is still with us. The mighty God has not abandoned the people.

When he begins to tell the story of Jesus' birth, the evangelist Matthew re-interprets the message of Isaiah (Matt 1:18-24). The mighty God comes in order to deliver the people from the besieging armies of sin and death. Again the powerful message is carried by a child. God comes, clothed in our own flesh, truly God-with-us. Who can recognize the divine presence: Those who are "clean of hand and pure of heart" (Ps 24:4). Let the mighty LORD enter, the king of glory (Ps 24:7, 10).

Paul announces this good news in the beginning of his letter to the Romans (1:1-7). This is the good news of God's son, "descended from David according to the flesh, but established Son of God in power according to the spirit of holiness through resurrection from the dead." This is the paradox of power clothed in powerlessness. God has remained faithful to the promise to David. God has arrived hidden in the person of a child. God has released again the mighty power that defeated chaos and established creation. The chaos of death is now defeated forever; the new creation in the resurrection has arrived. "Who is this king of glory? The LORD, a mighty warrior" (Ps 24:8). Who is this king of glory? Our faithful God. Let the king of glory enter.

Presentation of the Lord (7.8.9.10) [524]

Who is this king of glory? It is the Lord! (8).

The last stanza of Psalm 24 is the responsorial psalm for the Feast of the Presentation of the Lord. This stanza describes the procession of the ark into the temple. God takes possession of the holy dwelling place. God ascends the throne. The city gates rise up in delight to admit the mighty God. The people proclaim the great power of this God who protects them from all their enemies.

The readings for the feast present the paradox of the incarnation. The mighty God comes to defeat the greatest enemy, death. Yet this mystery is hidden in the presence of a child. The first part of the Liturgy of the Word concentrates on the images of power. The prophet Malachi describes the arrival of the messenger of the covenant and then of the Lord (Mal 3:1-4). It is a vision of the Day of the Lord. God comes for the final victory. Wickedness will at last be crushed; the just will be purified and will delight in God's rule. The Day will be announced by a messenger. In the period after the Babylonian Exile a belief emerged that the prophet Elijah would come back to announce the Day of the Lord. The story of Elijah suggests that the prophet did not die; he was taken to God in a fiery chariot (2 Kgs 2:11-12). Thus he might be chosen to be God's messenger again (cf. Mal 3:23-24). The Day he announces is a day of terror and of victory: the God whom we have sought through the centuries will arrive in the temple.

Psalm 24 is a brave response. We celebrate this arrival of God, announcing the divine presence, calling out to the city gates to join our celebration. The reading from the Letter to the Hebrews (Heb 2:14-18) confirms our courage and soothes our fear. The one who comes does not come to help angels but rather human beings. Therefore he becomes like us in every way, tempted in every way that we are. Through his suffering he becomes a fitting minister of God's mercy. The arrival of the powerful God demonstrates the gentleness of God.

The gospel is the story of the feast (Luke 2:22-40). Mary and Joseph bring the child Jesus to the temple in order to redeem this firstborn son (cf. Exod 13:1-16). God in human flesh has arrived to take possession of the temple. Two holy people announce his arrival. They are the people who have gone up the mountain of the Lord, who can stand in the holy place (cf. Ps 24:3). They are the clean of hand and the pure of heart who lead the procession (Ps 24:4). They recognize the king of glory and announce his arrival. "Who is this king of glory? It is the Lord!"

All Saints (1-2.3-4.5-6) [667]

Lord, this is the people that longs to see your face (6).

The first two stanzas of Psalm 24 are used for the responsorial psalm on the Solemnity of All Saints. The first stanza celebrates the great power of the God who defeated chaos and founded creation upon it. The second stanza is an entrance liturgy, describing the characteristics of God's worshipers, those who maintain right relationships both with God and with other people. These are the people who are rewarded with the presence of God whom they have longed to see.

The readings are three visions of the same reality. Who are these people that are the saints? Are we counted in this great community? The refrain of the psalm keeps returning to the central meaning of the feast: "Lord, this is the people that longs to see your face." In the Book of Revelation (7:2-4, 9-14) the visionary sees a great crowd of God's servants: one hundred and forty-four thousand from the tribes of Israel and a huge throng from all the other peoples of the earth. These are the people who have entered the holy place (Ps 24:3). Who are they? They are "the ones who have survived the time of great distress"; who have "washed their robes and made them white in the blood of the Lamb." They are the people whose hands are clean and whose heart is pure, not through their own doing, but through the blood of Christ. They have remained faithful to Christ through every trial. Through him they stand confidently in God's holy place.

The readings work backward to our present time. The passage from the First Letter of John (1 John 3:1-3) is an exclamation of delight that we have been numbered among the children of God, that we can be found in the huge throng seen by the visionary. How can this be so? We are God's children, not by our own merit, but by the gift of God. It may not be easy to see at present, but the glory that awaits us is beyond our imaginations! We are already God's children; later we shall be found even to be like God. Then we will know, for we will see God. We hold to this vision in faith. We strive to keep ourselves pure, faithful to God and truthful to one another, because we long to see God's face (Ps 24:4, 6).

The gospel is too familiar. It is too easy to forget how shocking is the reversal of the Beatitudes (Matt 5:1-12). How can it be that the hungry and the lowly are blessed? How is it that the merciful and the peacemakers end up on top? The list of the happy may look like a list of losers in our day. It is hard to see, but these are the children of God. Now. These are the people who will be found to be like God. These people form the huge throng who stand before the throne of God. These are the people who know that it is all gift. Who may go up the mountain of the Lord? Those who trust the God who holds the earth firm over chaos. Who may stand in the holy place? Those who are faithful to God and to one another. These are the people that long to see God's face. Their blessing is what they long for: These people shall see God as God is.

3. *Psalm 50 (Covenant Renewal)*

Psalm 50 is a lawsuit in which God accuses the chosen people of breaking the covenant. The psalm may belong to a covenant renewal ceremony. It is a liturgy of the courtroom. The psalm has four stanzas: 1-6, in which the court convenes; 7-15, in which God declares that sacrifice is not the issue; 16-21, in which the real issue is outlined; and 22-23, the declaration of judgment.

The first stanza (1-6) opens with a glorious theophany. God appears in beautiful majesty. Fire and storm accompany the divine presence. God summons the witnesses, heaven and earth, and calls the accused, those who are covenant partners. God is both accuser and judge.

In the second stanza (7-15) God dismisses an issue which may become a distraction from the real matter of the trial. Liturgical correctness is not the point. Sacrifices are neither part of the accusation nor a way out for the accused. God acknowledges that the sacrifices are there, but declares forcefully that they are not a need. God owns the whole world; God is not indebted to the people for sacrificial meat. What God desires is something more: genuine praise and thanksgiving. God looks for the people's acknowledgment that they are the ones who are dependent, not God. When they recognize their dependence, God in turn will grant them what they need.

The third stanza (16-23) turns to the main issue: keeping the covenant. Lip service to the commandments is not enough. The people who know the commandments by heart mock the covenant by ignoring the Law. There are two tablets to the Law, one regarding relationship to God, the other regarding relationship to one another. God cannot be bought off with sacrifice if one's neighbors are being injured at the same time. The final insult to God's honor is the assumption that God is made in the worst human image, ignoring evil and thus allowing it to grow. God will maintain the covenant even if the human partners do not. God will protect the weak who are suffering even as the covenant partners prey upon them. The exploitation of others is the substance of God's accusation.

The final two verses state God's judgment. To renew the covenant both relationships must be restored. The relationship with God, enacted through sacrifice, must be acknowledged as a relationship of dependence. Praise and thanksgiving are the appropriate attitude. The relationship with other people must be characterized by care and respect. Obedience to the Law is the guide for such relationship. The health of both relationships signals the health of the covenant. Life within the covenant is salvation for the people.

10th Sun Year A (1.8.12-13.14-15) [89]

To the upright I will show the saving power of God (23).

The refrain for the Tenth Sunday of Year A is part of the statement of God's judgment at the end of the trial scene in Psalm 50. The double judgment in verse 23 refers first to the issue of sacrifice and then to the issue of obedience to the Law, especially the law regarding relationship to the neighbor. Today's psalm refrain is the second half of the judgment, referring to obedience to the Law. The verses chosen for this Sunday represent the first issue, that of sacrifice. After the opening of the trial (1), God clarifies the usefulness of sacrifice. Sacrifice does not satisfy a divine need for food, rather it satisfies a human need to acknowledge dependence on God and gratitude for God's gifts. Sacrifice offered in a spirit of praise and thanksgiving opens the worshiper to God's continued care.

Both issues, genuine obedience and trust in God, permeate this Sunday's readings. Hosea preached to people in eighth century Israel who had turned away from both relationships which constitute the covenant. They were worshipping Ba'al and at the same time attempting to placate Yahweh with sacrifices. They had succumbed to "false swearing, lying, murder, stealing and adultery" (Hos 4:2). Because of this God withdraws from them. Today's passage (Hos 6:3-6) describes their attempt to renew the covenant without genuine conversion of heart. God, however, sees not only the externals of the sacrifice but also the interior of the heart (cf. Ps 50:13-14). God desires a genuine embracing of the covenant virtue of *hesed*, faithful love for God and for each other which is demonstrated through their way of life (cf. Ps 50:16-20). Their actions show that they do not truly know God. They think that God is like them, satisfied with external compliance (Ps 50:21). God's demand rather is obedience from the heart and grateful praise of the divine compassion. God's demand is for true humility which recognizes that God is God and we are not.

Abraham (Rom 4:18-25) is an example of that true humility. Abraham knew his dependence on God. He knew that God's fulfillment of the promise had to be an act of God's own power. "He did not doubt God's promise in unbelief; rather, he was empowered by faith and gave glory to God" (4:21). Abraham knew what it meant to offer praise as a sacrifice (Ps 50:14).

His trust in God was "credited to him as righteousness" (Rom 4:22). God grants salvation to the obedient Abraham (Ps 50:23).

The gospel (Matt 9:9-13) gives us contrasting examples of the situation described in Psalm 50. The self-righteous are interested in the externals of the Law. They are especially interested in judging others by their observance. The Pharisees condemn Jesus for eating with those whom they judge to be sinners. Jesus points out that those supposed sinners may have a better relationship with God because they know their need for God. Sick people know their need for a doctor. Their response to God is the covenant love which praises God's goodness to them. This is the *hesed* God desires rather than external sacrifice. These people who know their need can call upon God in time of distress and expect rescue (Ps 50:15). These people hope against hope and their faith is credited to them as righteousness (cf. Rom 4:18, 22). This is the true conversion which forms a contrast to the attempt made in the time of Hosea. To the obedient God shows salvation (Ps 50:23). The tax collectors of the gospel teach us who the obedient, the upright, really are.

4. Psalm 68

This long psalm is one of the most poorly preserved in the psalter. W. F. Albright even suggested the possibility that the psalm is a kind of Table of Contents listing the first line of several other psalms. Because of its confusing condition, the lines of verses 10-14 and of 31-32 are rearranged in the *Revised Psalter of the New American Bible*. Commentators outline the general flow of the psalm. As it stands, the psalm describes a grand procession from Sinai to Jerusalem. The first stanza (2-4) announces the procession. God arrives in battle array to scatter the enemy and vindicate the just. The call to prayer is found in the second stanza (5-7). The content is familiar from many hymns: Sing to the powerful God, the cloud-rider who stoops to care for the helpless.

The following stanzas describe the procession and the great battle by which God wins a land for the people and a holy place for the divine presence. Stanza three (8-11) recalls the great theophany at Sinai. The God of Sinai is now the God of Israel who has claimed a land for the chosen people. The victory provides rich spoil for everyone (12-15). The fifth stanza (16-19) challenges the other mountains to recognize the greatness of God's new dwelling place on Mount Zion.

The sixth stanza (20-24) moves our focus to the present time. God who has won these great victories is the God who can be counted on to save us now from our enemies. The liturgical procession recalling God's victory march comes into view in the seventh stanza (25-28). When the community arrives, the prayer for the future begins (29-32). God is called to summon the divine power again to subdue war-mongering nations and gather tribute.

The final stanza (33-36) is a renewed call to praise. All the kingdoms of the earth are called to praise the mighty God who rides on the clouds and who protects the chosen people. This powerful God gives power to the people.

The blatant rejoicing in military victory and the subjection of other peoples makes this psalm difficult for us to pray. It is not that blood-thirsty delight in crushing our enemies has been wiped out of our society. It is rather that we know our need of God's strength to help us love our enemies. Perhaps we can pray this psalm begging the powerful God to smash the violent tendencies in our own hearts and to win for all people a holy place where we may be free and at peace.

22nd Sunday Year C (4-5.6-7.10-11) [127]

God, in your goodness, you have made a home for the poor (11).

The refrain and verses of Psalm 68 chosen for the Twenty-Second Sunday of Year C come from the opening stanzas of the psalm and emphasize God's use of divine power for the helpless. Because of the difficulties with the text and because the selection for the responsorial psalm omits parts of several verses, the revised translation of the verses in question is printed here (RNAB):

4 Then the just will be glad;
    they will rejoice before God;
    they will celebrate with great joy.
5 Sing to God, praise the divine name;
    exalt the rider of the clouds.
  Rejoice before this God
    whose name is the LORD.

6 Father of the fatherless, defender of widows—
    this is the God whose abode is holy,
7 Who gives a home to the forsaken,
    who leads prisoners out to prosperity,
    while rebels live in the desert.

10b You claimed a land as your own, O God;
11a   your people settled there.
10a There you poured abundant rains, God,
11b   graciously given to the poor in their need.

The two verses omitted from the third stanza (8-9) describe the powerful advent of the mighty God of Sinai before whom the earth quakes and the heavens shake. It is this powerful God who cares for those who have no other hope.

The second reading for this Sunday (Heb 12:18-19, 22-24) picks up the paradox of the psalm. The God whose power inspires fear has finally found a way to convince us of the divine gentleness which that power supports. We have not drawn near to Mount Sinai, scene of the great and terrible theophany. We have come to the new Jerusalem. We have been given courage to come through Jesus who has led us to believe in the great love that our God has for us. Just as the psalm moves from Sinai to Zion, so have we.

The other two readings remind us of our obligation to act toward others as our covenant God acts toward us. Whatever power we may have must be used to support the gentle compassion which we extend to other people. In the gospel (Luke 14:1, 7-14) Jesus turns ordinary social etiquette upside down. We think it is an honor to have the highest place; Jesus shows us that taking the lowest place may lead to greater honor. We expect to be invited back by those whom we invite to a meal or a party. Jesus advises that we invite those who cannot repay. The amazing news is that God picks up the social obligation. If the poor cannot invite us to dinner, God will at the heavenly banquet. One of Jesus' fellow guests understands him perfectly and exclaims: "Blessed is the one who will dine in the kingdom of God" (Luke 14:15). God not only provides a home for the forsaken; God takes on their debts, even the social ones! (cf. Ps 68:7). The message for us is to care for those who are so special to God. Even our greatest generosity will be outdone by God.

We find the same practical advice in the words of the sage (Sir 3:17-18, 20, 28-29). God loves the lowly. Therefore it is to our advantage to humble ourselves when we are strong, and to accept our situation when we are weak. God cares for the poor (cf. Ps 68:11). The sage goes even further. Our own care for the poor atones for our sins just as water quenches a fire. Our attention to the helpless confronts us with our own need for God. We rejoice in the great power of the holy God whose might is mustered to win a peaceful home for the powerless (Ps 68:5-7).

The psalm is a battle psalm. If we face honestly the struggle to be compassionate even toward those who are sometimes called "the dregs of our society," we know that we need a warrior God to help us. Only a God who can "crush the skulls of the enemy" (Ps 68:22), can enable us to defeat the enemies of selfishness and complacency. "Summon again, O God, your power;" give power and strength to this people (Ps 68:29, 36).

5. *Psalm 81*

The first stanza of Psalm 81 (2-6) suggests the liturgical ceremonies surrounding the autumn feasts of the seventh month, Tishri (September-October). The first day of the month, the new moon, is to be a festival day announced by the trumpet (Num 29:1-6; Lev 23:24-25). This celebration is the New Year even though the count of the months still follows the older calendar in which Nisan (March-April) was the first month of the year. At the full moon, the fifteenth day of the month, the Feast of Tabernacles is to be celebrated (Num 29:12; Lev 23:34). The Israelites are instructed to live in shelters made of branches (booths or tabernacles) in order to commemorate the sojourn in the desert. The instruction closes with a statement reminiscent of the psalm: "I, the LORD, am your God" (Lev 23:43).

The second stanza (6b-17) begins with the announcement of an oracle, probably by priest or prophet present at the ceremony. The oracle gathers together past, present, and future. God's past deliverance of the people in the exodus event is recalled. God rescued them from slavery (7), spoke to them at Sinai (8), and made covenant with them, demanding their exclusive loyalty (9-10). The whole covenant law is contained in the first commandment of the decalogue (11): "I, the LORD, am your God, who brought you out of the land of Egypt, that place of slavery. You shall not have other gods besides me" (Exod 20:2-3; cf. Deut 5:6-7). Verses 12-13 recount Israel's infidelity to the covenant. They followed other gods; their God abandoned them to their own desires. Verses 14-17 move to the present time and give hope to the future. Even now, if the people turn and obey, God will again rescue them from their enemies and satisfy them with the best food.

Psalm 81 echoes both Psalm 50 and Psalm 95. In Psalm 50 God summons the people and calls them to listen (Ps 50:7; cf. Ps 81:8-9). The covenant commandments are recalled (Ps 50:16-20; cf. Ps 81:11). The sense of judgment is stronger in Psalm 50, however. Psalm 81 reveals God's own desire to renew the people. Psalm 95 recalls the testing at Meribah (Ps 95:7-9; cf. Ps 81:8-9). Psalm 95, however, ends with God's anger, Psalm 81 with God's promise of renewal. Listening is important in all three psalms. The word for "listen" or "obey" (= listen to the voice of) occurs four times in Psalm 81 (9 [2x], 12, 14), and at the turning point in Psalm 50 (7) and Psalm 95 (7).

Psalm 81 is a good illustration of the function of liturgy. The people are assembled for the great celebration, using all their musical skill and all their strength for worship. They remember and thus make present God's saving actions of the past. They also recall their own failures. Their repentance draws God to renew them, once more to save them and give them life. It is a good model for our own liturgy.

9th Sun Year B (3-4.5-6.6-8.10-11) [87]

Sing with joy to God our help (2).

The refrain for the Ninth Sunday of Year B is the call to the liturgy which opens Psalm 81. The verses continue with the summons to celebrate with great ceremony. The celebration centers on the Law—the command to commemorate God's saving acts and the gift of the covenant law itself. The verses conclude with the recollection of the exodus event and the command to have no other God but Yahweh. The remembrance of the people's past infidelity and God's renewed promise in the present are omitted.

The Law is the focus of the readings also. Special attention is given to the law which is the sign of the Sinai covenant, the keeping of the Sabbath (Deut 5:12-15). The Sabbath is a sign of the people's liberation. God has delivered them from Egypt, relieving their shoulders of the burden (Ps 81:7). They must not succumb to another slavery. They are free to rest one day a week; God will support them. They must not forget that in reality it is always God's power and not their own which supports their lives. Just as God gives them rest, they must give their slaves and all their dependents rest as well.

The psalm celebrates the people's freedom. The responsibility which comes with freedom is to worship Yahweh alone. They must not surrender their freedom to any other god. In the gospel (Mark 2:23–3:6) Jesus is involved in two controversies with the Pharisees concerning the Sabbath. The question turns again on freedom. The Law has become an idol, a false god, which enslaves the people. Jesus points out that this is a perversion of the gift of the Law, which is intended to give life and freedom. The Law was given for the sake of God's people; people were not made for the sake of the Law. The Sabbath especially is a gift of life. For one day a week life is free, simply a gift of God. Preoccupation with deadly details obscures the saving action of God. The disciples pick standing grain; God's intent is to feed the people with finest wheat (Ps 81:17). Jesus heals a man with a shriveled hand; God's intent is to relieve people of their burdens (Ps 81:7).

The Sabbath is a sign of creation. God's first act was the creation of light. Paul shows us how that initial creative gift is the foundation of God's saving act in Christ (2 Cor 4:6-11). God's glory shines through Christ and thus through us. We know our own weakness. We are like the darkness of chaos before creation. But through Jesus' death we have been delivered from the chaos of death and given the light of life. We know that the power comes from God and not from us. It is God who relieved our shoulders of the burden (Ps 81:7). The Sabbath is a celebration of God's rescue. Yahweh alone is our God who brought us up from the land of death (Ps 81:11). "Sing joyfully to God our strength!" (Ps 81:2).

G. Wisdom Psalms

Wisdom psalms share content and form with the biblical wisdom literature, especially the books of Proverbs, Qoheleth, Job, Sirach, and the Wisdom of Solomon. There is general agreement that there are wisdom psalms in the psalter; there is almost no agreement concerning which psalms belong to this category or on the method by which they should be distinguished. Many psalms have wisdom elements. How many elements of form or content are necessary to include a psalm in this genre?

Several wisdom forms are evident in the psalms. The most evident is possibly the acrostic form in which every verse (or section of verses as in Psalms 37 and 119) begins with the next letter of the Hebrew alphabet. Beatitudes or "happy" sayings are also frequent in these psalms. Some wisdom psalms include "better" sayings: "Better the poverty of the just than the great wealth of the wicked" (Ps 37:16). Other proverbs are also found.

The content of wisdom is also found in these psalms. There are the questions of suffering and justice: Why do the wicked prosper and the innocent perish (Pss 37 and 73)? The two ways of the just and the wicked are outlined clearly (cf. Psalm 1). The goal of wisdom is the good life. The way to live well is to observe the Law, the *torah*. The wise person is characterized by the attitude of "fear of the Lord," the awe which recognizes God's greatness and mercy. Creation is a favorite topic of wisdom writers. God is praised for the wisdom manifested in creation; God's people can enjoy the benefits of creation's order by keeping the Law. Often wisdom psalms are written in an autobiographical style (cf. Ps 73). The sage shares the fruit of long pondering with us.

The tone of wisdom psalms, like the rest of wisdom literature, is reflective. There is an emphasis on instruction. There is also, however, a sense of awe at the mysterious workings of God. Wisdom psalms require time. They must be "chewed," in the ancient sense of meditation. The wonder is that wisdom psalms do not wear out; the flavor does not diminish with age.

1. Psalm 1

Psalm 1 (along with Psalm 2) is the introduction to the psalter. It is a late addition, put in this position by the final editor of the book. Psalm

1 sets the whole psalter in the context of wisdom. This psalm tells us how to live well. This psalm suggests that to keep the whole Book of Psalms in our minds and hearts is to live well.

The psalm clearly sets out two ways to live. The first stanza (1-3) describes the life of the righteous. They do not *follow* the advice of the wicked. They do not *stand* on the way of sinners. They do not *sit down* in company with scoffers. The progressive way to possible disaster is obvious in the verbs: follow (literally "walk"), stand, sit down. The righteous reject the way of sin. Rather they set their hearts on God's Law. The Law becomes their delight. Day and night the Law is their constant companion. The result is life. They become like well-watered trees, prospering through all seasons. The image is powerful in the Middle East where water is a precious commodity.

The second stanza (4-6) turns to the wicked. Their way is not described. Presumably it consists of ignoring and breaking God's Law. The result of their way is directly opposite that of the righteous. The wicked become like chaff which is blown away. The righteous are rooted in the Law; the wicked have nothing to which to cling. They cannot survive judgment.

The psalm concludes with a summary of the consequences of the two ways. The contrast is not perfect, however, and thus it leads us to further meditation. The way of the wicked leads to ruin. That was clear from the preceding verses. We might suppose that opposing statement would be that the way of the righteous leads to life. That statement would follow from verse 3. We already know that, however. The psalm leads us one step further: "The LORD watches over [knows] the way of the just." Their whole attention has been turned to God through the Law. Now we learn that God's attention is turned toward them as well. This is the reason that the way of the righteous leads to life. Their way is surrounded by the presence of God. How happy they are!

6th Sun Year C (1-2.3.4.6) [79]

Happy are they who hope in the Lord (Ps 40:5).

The refrain for the Sixth Sunday of Year C is taken not from Psalm 1 but from Psalm 40. It is a beatitude like the opening verse of Psalm 1. Psalm 1 begins with a negative, what the righteous person does not do; the verse from Psalm 40 states the positive side of the same truth. All the verses of Psalm 1 are used for this Sunday except verse 5 which states the inability of the wicked to withstand judgment.

"Trust" is the key word for this Sunday. Jeremiah (17:5-8) echoes the main image of Psalm 1 and also reverses it. Happy the person who trusts in God; that person is like a well-watered tree. In contrast, the one who trusts in human beings rather than God is like a barren bush in the salty desert. There is no hope for such a one. The contrast in attitudes and results is clear.

Jesus also pronounces beatitudes and curses (Luke 6:17, 20-26). Where does each group put its trust? The poor, the hungry, the mourners, the outcasts are all declared happy. Why? Their only hope is in God. The circumstances of their lives have taught them that trust in human beings is folly. Even trust in their own power is useless. Only God can reverse their situation. Happy are they because God cannot resist such unconditional trust. The other group—the rich, the satisfied, the honored—are always tempted to trust in their own strength. Life is good; how could it be otherwise. In good times it is too easy to forget God. This, however, is the ultimate folly. Unless they are rooted in God they have no hope for help when bad times come. Woe to them; the center of their lives is blowing away.

Paul brings us to the center of our hope: the resurrection of Christ (1 Cor 15:12, 16-20). If our hope is not rooted in his resurrection, we have no hope. No human power can save us. We are the most pitiable of people. If, on the other hand, we believe in him whose resurrection is the pledge of our own, then we are indeed like well-watered, fruitful trees.

This Sunday sets before us happiness and misery with no ambiguity. Trust in God is our happiness; God's presence is our life. Nothing can disturb us if we delight in God's Law; nothing can make us happy if we turn away from God.

2. Psalm 19

Psalm 19 is a celebration in two acts. The juncture between the first stanza of the psalm (2-7) and the rest is so clear that it is often suggested that the psalm originated as two separate compositions. Both subject and rhythm shift dramatically at verse 8. The juxtaposition of the two halves, however, provides a whole message: The God of all creation is the Lord who shows us the way of life.

The first stanza (2-7) is a hymn to the sun. The scene opens with the heavens announcing God's glory. Day and night take up the perpetual song. The message fills all creation, even to the ends of the earth. The world trembles with excitement waiting for the splendid sun to spring from his tent and run from one end of the earth to the other. In this mythological picture we see the sun as the image of God, gloriously reigning over the whole earth, bringing life and warmth everywhere. Creation responds by proclaiming the message without ceasing.

Human senses, however, are too insensitive to grasp the message in its fullness (4). Thus the great God of the universe in gentle mercy reveals the divine name which is a revelation of the divine identity. Yahweh, Lᴏʀᴅ, is the one who will be present with the people. The Lord's gift to people is the Law, the light which is our guide to life. What the sun does for creation, the Law does for us. The second stanza (8-12) is a litany singing the praises of the Law. The Law teaches us how to be like God, how to be fully human. Thus the Law refreshes our lives and brings joy to our hearts. The Law is wisdom, worth more than any other good. The Law fills us with life.

The final stanza (13-15) looks at the shadows cast by the light of the Law.[1] Clumps of death still cling to us. We cannot bear the purity of God's light. We beg to be delivered from willful sins. Even then, however, we know the inadvertent failings that no human being can fully escape. Only God can enlighten us, can rescue us from every darkness. We end our prayer by calling on the Lord who is our redeemer, our next-of-kin whose obligation it is to ransom us from slavery.

The psalm moves from a focus on the universal God of creation to the Lord who chooses a special people. Then the focus shifts from God to us, and we end with a prayer for help to the Lord who is our special God.

3rd Sun Lent B (8.9.10.11) [29]

Lord, you have the words of everlasting life (John 6:68).

The responsorial psalm for the Third Sunday of Lent B is taken entirely from the second stanza of Psalm 19. The whole litany of praise to the Law is included. Only the closing verse of the second stanza is omitted, in which the psalmist acknowledges the reward of obedience to the Law. The first and third stanzas are also omitted. The double image of sun and Law is lost as is the recognition of our own sin. Holding the whole of the psalm in our imaginations will enrich our praise of the Law in today's response.

The readings for this Sunday lead us to the deeper meaning of the Law. By its juxtaposition of images the psalm shows us the Law as God's sun which gives light and life to the earth. Today's readings teach us that the Law, the word of God, is the gift of God's life-giving presence with us. The commandments (Exod 20:1-17) are the charter of the Sinai covenant. They are given in the midst of the theophany in which God makes covenant with the people. The covenant is a bond in which each party pledges to share life with the other. Israel found marriage an apt symbol for this life-sharing bond. The commandments show the people how to share life with God. A life characterized by this Law is a life in which God is present.

Psalm 19 is our way of bringing the message of the first reading into our lives. We hear the covenant charter and we sing: "Lord, you have the

---

[1]See Stuhlmueller, 1.137.

words of everlasting life." The litany of praise is our whole-hearted acceptance of the goodness of God's Law.

The gospel (John 2:13-25) considers God's presence from another angle.
First the ark of the covenant and then the temple which housed it became
the visible sign of God's presence with the people. The people, however,
had forgotten the gift of God's presence and become more interested in
their business ventures. Like a fiery prophet of old, Jesus drives the business-
men out of his Father's house. When they ask for a sign of his authority,
he gives them another sign of God's presence, the temple of his body.

Paul shows us how misguided our search for God's presence can become
(1 Cor 1:22-25). Some demand signs, some look for wisdom. Both have
been given us in Christ. Jesus is now the sign of the presence of God. Jesus,
the Word of God, is our covenant charter. Jesus is the gift of wisdom, our
guide for sharing life with God. But sometimes the message is too profound
for us. The glorious God of creation has chosen to take on our flesh in order
to bring us the news. The covenant God has come to share our lives and
even our death that we might share the divine life more fully. This is the
word of everlasting life!

Easter Vigil 6 (8.9.10.11) [42]

Lord, you have the words of everlasting life (John 6:68).

The verses from Psalm 19 and the refrain for the sixth reading of the
Easter Vigil are the same as the Third Sunday of Lent B (see above).

The sixth reading for the Easter Vigil is a hymn to wisdom from the
Book of Baruch (Bar 3:9-15, 32–4:4). This book circulated with the Greek
translation of the Hebrew Scriptures, but when the rabbis decided on a
canon for the Hebrew Bible, Baruch was not included. Thus it is found
in the Roman Catholic Bible, but not in Jewish or Protestant scriptures.
The book was written sometime during the last centuries BCE; the author
took as a pseudonym the name of Jeremiah's secretary (cf. Jer 45:1). The
book is intended to be an encouragement for the Jews who lived in the
Diaspora, i.e., outside of the homeland. The hymn to wisdom personifies
her as the Wisdom Woman and equates Wisdom with the Law. The Wisdom of God is inaccessible to human beings, but God has given her to us
through the Law. Now she has appeared on earth and moves among us.
To walk by her light is to find life with God. "Blessed are we, . . . for
what pleases God is known to us!" (Bar 4:4). The Lord has taught us the
words of everlasting life!

On this night when we keep vigil through the darkness of death awaiting the rising of the Sun of Life, Psalm 19 is an encouraging companion.
The sun will come forth like a bridegroom (19:6). The light of God will

dawn for us. God's Law will give us wisdom (19:8). The Word of God will rise to bring us life.

3rd Sun Year C (8.9.10.15) [70]

Your words, Lord, are spirit and life (John 6:63).

The responsorial psalm for the Third Sunday of Year C includes part of the litany in praise of the Law and concludes with the final verse of Psalm 19 which pleads with God to save us and to keep us in the divine presence. The Law is God's gift to us, teaching us how to live. Only through God's presence with us can we take this gift fully into our lives.

The refrain borrows a verse from the controversy which followed the Bread of Life discourse in the Gospel of John (John 6:63). The disciples are shocked by the discourse, but Jesus assures them that the words that he has preached to them are indeed spirit and life. The juxtaposition of this statement of Jesus with Psalm 19 equates Jesus' words with God's Law. The words of Jesus mediate to us God's Law which gives us life. Jesus is the presence of God with us who enables us to take the Law fully into our lives.

Both the first reading and the gospel show us crowds of people hearing the word of God proclaimed to them. Ezra reads and interprets the whole book of the Law, probably the Pentateuch, to a solemn assembly of all the people (Neh 8:2-4, 5-6, 8-10). This is a renewal of their commitment to the covenant through acceptance of covenant law. The Exile is over, the new temple has been dedicated, the city walls have been rebuilt. Now the community is reconstituted as God's covenant people. Ezra declares the day a holy day of rejoicing. The people are exhorted to eat rich foods and drink sweet drinks. Everyone must have a share. Everyone's joy must be complete in this new embrace of the covenant bond with God.

We join the people in their rejoicing as we sing Psalm 19. God's Law refreshes our lives and gives joy to our hearts. God's word is good and wise. But even as we proclaim that the word of God is life, we know our own frailty. We plead with God to look on us with favor, to be the stable element in our lives, to be the one who saves us from danger and death.

The gospel (Luke 1:1-4; 4:14-21) actually presents us with a double layering of proclamation of God's word. The evangelist presents his purpose in writing. He has done careful research in order to proclaim the story and message of Jesus in order that future disciples might know that the preaching they hear is reliable. Within the evangelist's presentation is Jesus' proclamation of God's word. Jesus reads Isaiah 61 in the Nazareth synagogue: the good news of a jubilee year in which all debts are canceled, all slaves are free, all property returns to the original owner (cf. Lev 25:8-22). The jubilee year is a year in which everyone gets a fresh start with no hindrance. Jesus' homily is one sentence: "Today this scripture passage is fulfilled in your hearing." Today this fresh start is announced and begun. Thus in today's gospel we really have a triple proclamation of good news! Jesus announces the beginning of the jubilee year, God's establishment of a fresh start for us all. Luke tells the good news of what God has done for us in Jesus, God's saving act through his death and resurrection. Today in our liturgical assembly we hear the word read again, the proclamation that today—this very day—God's word presents us with the gift of new life. Truly the word of God is spirit and life!

Only through God's presence with us are we able to take this good word into our lives. Paul tells us the amazing news that God's presence is not only with us but within us (1 Cor 12:12-30). Through baptism we have become one body, the Body of Christ. We have been given to drink of the one Spirit, which gives the body life. We then are the body of Christ! We together are the sign of God's presence in the world. We have not only received the word of life; through baptism the Word of God has taken up residence within us. The Word of God is now our life. The Word which became flesh to live with us, is now visible in the world through our flesh. We find this as hard to believe as the disciples who heard the Bread of Life discourse (John 6:60). With them we say: Lord, to whom shall we go? Your words are spirit and life (John 6:68, 63).

26th Sun Year B (8.10.12-13.14) [138]

The precepts of the Lord give joy to the heart (9).

The refrain and verses of Psalm 19 chosen for the Twenty-Sixth Sunday of Year B are taken from the second and third stanzas of the psalm. All of the litany in praise of the Law is represented except for verse 11 which compares the value of the Law to a heap of the finest gold. The third stanza is the confession of human frailty, so visible in the clear light of the Law. Only God can keep us from willful sin, can cleanse us from unknown faults. The Law is the gift to show us the way; the compassion of God is the strength by which we live it.

The readings teach us the breadth of God's acceptance. We human beings set limits on membership. There are those who are *in* and those who are *out*. There are requirements for belonging. But God is without limits. God's Law and God's compassion are open to all people. During the desert wandering Moses complains to God about the intolerable burden the people have become. Moses is so weary that he prays for death. But God's solution is that Moses' responsibility and his gifts be shared (Num 11:25-29). Seventy elders are chosen to receive a share of the spirit. The seventy follow directions: they come to the meeting tent, receive the spirit, and prophesy and the spirit comes to rest on them. But two of the chosen men do not go out to the meeting tent. By human standards, since they do not follow the process, they should not receive the spirit. God, however, is not hindered by human standards. They are chosen; the spirit comes to rest on them too. They prophesy just like the seventy. Joshua cannot bear what he sees to be a flaunting of Moses' authority. Moses, however, reflects the openness of God: "Would that all the people of the LORD were prophets! Would that the LORD might bestow his spirit on them all!"

The goal of the Law is to teach us to be like God. Moses has lived with the Law long enough to reflect God's way. Would that all the people of the Lord might live the Law like Moses! "The law of the LORD is perfect, refreshing the soul, . . . giving wisdom, . . . enduring forever" (Ps 19:8, 10). Lord, teach us to keep your precepts; teach us to be like you (cf. Ps 19:12-15).

The beginning of the gospel story (Mark 9:38-43, 45, 47-48) is an almost perfect parallel to the desert story. Jesus' disciples are outraged because someone outside the group is driving out demons by means of Jesus' name. How dare he! Jesus uses the opportunity to clarify what "with us" and "against us" means. "Whoever is not against us is with us." Judgment with regard to people must always be biased in their favor. God accepts again and again those who certainly seem to be opponents. Too often we ourselves might be included among those who seem to be against God. The goal of the Law is to teach us to be like God, to be open again and again. On the other hand, there are things as close to us as our own bodies which may truly be "against us." Whatever leads us to sin, whatever leads us to break the Law, must be cut off. Jesus is not talking about bodily mutilation. Jesus is using the body as a shocking metaphor to teach us that attitudes and actions that we think impossible to live without may indeed be "against us." It is those attitudes and actions, not other people, which must be rejected. The Law is trustworthy, giving us wisdom (Ps 19:8). God's word will teach us how to discern what is for us and what is against us; God's compassion will give us the strength to act on that wisdom.

The Letter of James gives one example of what might be against us: greedy attachment to wealth (Jas 5:1-6). The passage is a merciless attack on those who have preferred wealth to other people. Their wealth has meant the deprivation of others. It is a frightening word to our comfortable society. How can we endure the evils of homelessness and hunger, insufficient wages and unemployment? The wealth that causes such inequality should inspire our anger, not the human distinctions regarding who belongs and who does not. Everyone belongs; everyone is dear to God. Our sense of helplessness in the face of such injustice leads us to cry out: "Who can detect heedless failings? . . . From willful sins keep your servant; let them never control me" (Ps 19:13-14). Lord, you are our rock and our redeemer (Ps 19:15); fill us with the spirit of your Law.

Year Common (8.9.10.11) [175]

Lord, you have the words of everlasting life (John 6:68).

The verses from Psalm 19 and the refrain for the Common of the Year are the same as the Third Sunday of Lent B (see above).

Psalm 19 would be appropriate for any Sunday in which the theme is the gift of God's Law. Here are some suggestions.

The Sixth Sunday of Year A: The gospel is Jesus' interpretation of the Law from the Sermon on the Mount (Matt 5:17- 37; see Ps 119 for a fuller discussion). Sir 15:15-20 declares that we are free to choose to keep the Law; Paul (1 Cor 2:6-10) discusses the wisdom revealed to us through the Spirit.

The Fifteenth Sunday of Year C (see Ps 69): In the gospel (Luke 10:25-37) a scribe asks Jesus to interpret the two great commandments. In the first reading (Deut 30:10-14) Moses declares that God's command is already very near to us. Col 1:15-20 presents Jesus as the image of God, the goal of the Law.

The Thirtieth Sunday of Year A (see Ps 18): The gospel (Matt 22:34-40) is Jesus' presentation of the great commandments. The first reading (Exod 22:20-26) is the legislation concerning care for the most helpless in the society. In the second reading Paul presents himself as an example (1 Thess 1:5-10).

The Thirty-First Sunday of Year A (see Ps 69): This Sunday describes the abuse of the Law. The post-exilic priests cause others to falter by their instruction (Mal 1:14–2:2, 8-10). Jesus accuses the Pharisees of failing to live by their own teaching (Matt 23:1-12). On the other hand, Paul preaches the true word of God and lives by it (1 Thess 2:7-9, 13).

See also the following Sundays in which the gospel comes from the continuous reading of the Sermon on the Mount: the Fourth Sunday of Year A (Ps 146); the Fifth Sunday of Year A (Ps 112); the Seventh Sunday of Year A (Ps 103); and the Ninth Sunday of Year A (Ps 31).

3. Psalm 112 (Acrostic)

Psalm 112 is a companion piece to Psalm 111. Both psalms begin with Hallelujah. They share the same vocabulary: "fear the Lord," "righteous," "gracious and merciful," "endure forever." Psalm 111 focuses on God; Psalm 112 is directed toward the righteous person. The happiness of the righteous person in Psalm 112 is a consequence of the righteousness of God in Psalm 111.

Like Psalm 111, Psalm 112 is an acrostic. Each half-line of the psalm begins with a successive letter of the Hebrew alphabet. The content of the psalm is as ordered as the form. As Browning says, "God's in his heaven; all's right with the world." The psalm begins with a beatitude (cf. Ps 1) which is a summary of the whole psalm: "Happy are those who fear the LORD, who greatly delight in God's commands." Fear of the Lord is the loving awe of the great and compassionate God which is expressed in obedience. Fear of the Lord is the recognition that God is in control of the world and that our delight is to live by the divine will. The assertion of the psalm is that the people who live this way are the truly happy.

The happiness of the God-fearers is revealed both in good times and bad times. They receive the blessings of wisdom: prosperity, good children, everlasting remembrance (2, 3, 5-6). Even in bad times they are not shaken. They shine through the darkness; they do not fear slander and gossip. They trust that they will eventually be victorious over any enemy (4, 7-8). Fear of the Lord and obedience to the Law has made them truly images of God. As God is gracious, merciful, and just (Ps 111:4, 7), so are they (Ps 112:4). As God is generous (Ps 111:5), so are they (112:5, 9). Their generosity is rewarded with lasting prosperity and fame. Even in a society in which there is no real belief in life after death, they live on in memory.

The only dark note in this psalm is in the last verse. The wicked see the unshakable prosperity of the righteous and waste away in anger. "The desires of the wicked come to nothing."

The psalm may be over-simplified. The picture it paints may be too black and white. There is certainly no ambiguity here. Nonetheless the message of the psalm is true. Genuine and lasting happiness comes only from a right relationship with God and thus with other people. That is true righteousness. That is true wisdom: how to live well. Nothing else can give us real joy.

5th Sun Year A (4-5.6-7.8-9) [74]

The just are a light in darkness to the upright (4).

The refrain and verses for the Fifth Sunday of Year A are taken from the center of Psalm 112. All that is missing is the opening beatitude and the promise of the blessings of wealth and descendants. The final verse, referring to the envy of the wicked, is also omitted. The Lectionary, however, has re-interpreted v. 4. The Hebrew verse says literally: "He shines in the darkness. . . ." "He" is commonly understood to be the one "who fears the Lord," who has been the subject of all the verbs throughout the psalm (cf. the refrain which has simply replaced the pronoun with the subject).

The Lectionary reads, "The Lord dawns through the darkness . . .," echoing the faith statement of Psalm 111 that the Lord is gracious and merciful (Ps 111:4). The change weakens the connection between the psalm and the first reading (Isa 58:10).

The image of light links the readings and the psalm for this Sunday. Where is light to be found? The reading from the sixth-century prophet (Isa 58:7-10) is a description of true righteousness in God's eyes. Righteousness is always judged by the demands of the relationship. The truly righteous person shares with those who are more needy. "Lavishly they give to the poor" (Ps 112:9). But this generosity does not impoverish anyone. The givers discover that "their prosperity shall endure forever" (Ps 112:9). God will be present to them, even before they cry out. Darkness can not overcome them. Their light breaks forth like the dawn; the gloom shall become like midday (Isa 58:8, 10). They themselves shall become light to others (Ps 112:4).

Jesus makes the same startling announcement to his disciples (Matt 5:13-16). They are salt and light for the world. He does not say they have salt or reflect light, but they *are* salt and light. Both salt and light are recognized in relationship. Salt is always used in connection to other things. It enhances the flavor of other foods and preserves them. Light too is useful because it illuminates other things. Neither is valued simply in isolation. Both are good images for righteousness which is always judged by relationship. The righteous are generous and just toward others; they are obedient and loving toward God (Ps 112). In these relationships their true value is recognized.

To live well is the goal of wisdom and the consequence of righteousness. Paul exposes the limitations of human wisdom and preaches the true wisdom of God (1 Cor 2:1-5). Jesus Christ crucified is the revelation of God's mysterious wisdom and the expression of God's boundless righteousness. God has gone to such lengths for the sake of relationship with us. Lavishly God gives to the poor (cf. Ps 112:9), thus our prosperity endures! "Happy are those who fear the Lord, who greatly delight in God's commands" (Ps 112:1).

4. Psalm 119 (Acrostic)

Psalm 119 is the longest psalm of the psalter. It is ingeniously constructed. Not only is it an acrostic with verses beginning with successive letters of the alphabet, but it is an expansive acrostic. Each letter of the alphabet is represented by eight verses. Thus verses 1-8 begin with 'aleph, the first letter of the Hebrew alphabet, verses 9-16 with *beth*, the second letter, and so on. As if this were not enough, there are eight synonyms for Law which are woven throughout the poem: teachings, decrees, precepts, laws, commands, edicts, words, promises. Only a very few verses do not have one of them.

The subject of the psalm is the Law. The attitude toward the Law, however, is not one of legalism. Rather the Law is the source of life and delight. Only in God's Law can happiness be found. Meditation on God's word gives joy to the heart and peace to the soul. To live a life immersed in the Law is to be truly wise. Law in this psalm is the whole of God's ongoing revelation, the gift to help us live well day after day.

The structure of the psalm convinces us of the reliability of the Law. Just as we know that *beth* follows *'aleph*, we know that God's Law will always be there to guide us. Just as we know that A-Z comprises the whole of the alphabet, we know that the Law supports the whole of life.

The great attention to external structure and the length of the psalm sometimes masks the profundity of its content. The verses and stanzas are not linked together in any progressive thought pattern. Each verse stands alone in its statement about God's Law. This characteristic may be the value of the psalm. One verse may be chosen for meditation without destroying the sequence. One or two stanzas may be used for prayer without disrupting the fabric of the whole. In the monastic tradition the stanzas are spread over two weeks for midday prayer. The repetition of ideas without sequence or plot can also lead to deeper meditation, somewhat in the way the repetition of the rosary does. This is a mantra prayer for the Law of God.

6th Sun Year A (1-2.4-5.17-18.33-34) [77]

Happy are they who follow the law of the Lord (1).

The refrain and verses for the Sixth Sunday of Year A are chosen from the first several stanzas of Psalm 119. Following the principle that each verse can stand alone, these verses are chosen in pairs rather than in an extended sequence. The verses are united by shared vocabulary. The first two verses are the double beatitude which begins Psalm 119: How happy are those who live by God's Law. Of the eight synonyms for Law, *torah*, which means properly instruction or teaching,[2] appears three times, in verses 1, 18, and 34; *hoq*, "law," appears twice (5, 33). "Decree," "command," "precept," and "word" each appear once. "Way" (*derek*) is found in verses 1, 5, and 33. There are two words with similar meaning, "keep" (*shamar*) and "observe" (*nazar*) which appear in these verses: "keep" 4, 5, 17, 34; "observe," 2, 33, 34. The phrase, "with all [the] heart" appears twice (2, 34). There is a request both for sight (18) and insight (34). After the double beatitude and a statement of God's command, every verse is a prayer to

---

[2]It is translated "teaching" in the *Revised Psalter of the New American Bible*.

God for help in keeping the Law. The message of the juxtaposed verses is that keeping the Law is a very desirable thing; therefore we beg God to help us do it.

The second-century Jerusalem sage Ben Sira advises that we can indeed keep God's Law if we choose to do so (Sir 15:15-20). The choice is between life and death. We are free to choose. If evil and death come to us it is the consequence of our own choice and not to be blamed on God. We need the verses of Psalm 119 to provide a nuance to Ben Sira's stark alternatives. We agree with his assessment of the Law; it is indeed what we long for (Ps 119:1-2). But we know too well our own frailty. Thus we beg God to help us make the wise choice (Ps 119:5, 17-18, 33-34).

Paul continues to direct our attention to wisdom (1 Cor 2:6-10). The wisdom of which he speaks has now been revealed to us not only as the word of God's Law but as the living Word of God who has taken on our flesh. This Word has come as a pledge to us of what we cannot even imagine, what God has prepared for those who love God. Only through God's Spirit can we glimpse this revelation. May God "open [our] eyes to see clearly the wonders of this teaching" (Ps 119:18).

Jesus, God's living Word, has come, not to abolish the Law, but to teach the Law to us (Matt 5:17-37). His teaching centers the Law in our hearts where it becomes the source of our lives. He himself is the answer to our prayer: "LORD, teach me the way of your laws; . . . give me insight to observe your teaching, to keep it with all my heart" (Ps 119:33, 34).

We sometimes see law as the limitation of our freedom or the inhibition of our desires. But the reason for our freedom, the goal of our desires, is life. We long for life. God longs to give us the Law that we might know how to live well. How happy we are if we walk by God's teaching!

17th Sun Year A (57.72.76-77.127-128.129-130) [110]

How I love your teaching, Lord! (97).

The responsorial psalm for the Seventeenth Sunday of Year A is selected from the middle stanzas of Psalm 119. The independent verses of this psalm are chosen singly or in pairs. The verses emphasize the desire for what is precious. God's teaching is more precious than heaps of silver or gold (72), worth more than finest gold (127). Thus the psalmist loves God's commands (127, cf. 97), delights in God's teaching (77), finds God's decrees wonderful (129). God is the psalmist's inherited share (57). God's faithful love (*hesed*) can be trusted (76); God's revelation enlightens even the most simple. By contrast every wrong way is hateful (128).

The wisdom to know where the real treasure is and to know how to obtain it is the subject of this Sunday's readings. The psalm gives us the clue that God's word is the most precious treasure we could hope for. Solomon becomes the patron saint of wisdom because he seeks this treasure. Instead of asking for wealth or long life, he asks for a listening heart to know what is right (1 Kgs 3:5, 7-12). He asks for wisdom; he asks for the revelation of God's Law. Because he has the insight to ask wisely, wisdom is given to him. Along with wisdom comes every good gift because the goal and the end of wisdom is life. Solomon knows where the real treasure is and knows who can and will give it to him. His precious share is the Lord; God's teaching is his delight (Ps 119:57, 77).

Jesus teaches that the treasure worth more than everything we have is the kingdom of God (Matt 13:44-52). For the sake of that treasure we rejoice in selling everything else that we have. That treasure is priceless because it is life. If we lose the kingdom we will be thrown away like the worthless flotsam and jetsam pulled up by the dragnet. The way to gain that treasure is through the teaching of God. God's teaching is more precious than heaps of silver and gold (Ps 119:72). Therefore it is our delight (77).

Paul assures us of God's fidelity in keeping the treasure and in pouring it out for us (Rom 8:28-30). Just as all things came to Solomon with wisdom, all things work together for good for those who love God. God is our portion; God's word is our delight; God's teaching is our treasure. What a wonderful gift is God's Law, God's wisdom.

5. Psalm 128

Psalm 128 is one of the Songs of Ascent (see Psalm 123). There are fifteen psalms with that title (120-134). They may form a collection of psalms used by pilgrims on their way to Jerusalem. In the context of such a pilgrimage, Psalm 128 may be the blessing before returning home.[3] The psalm celebrates the joys of daily life. Satisfying work provides prosperity. Family life brings true happiness.

These joys are God's blessing for the righteous. The psalm is a simple statement of belief in the theory of retribution: the obedient are blessed, the disobedient are cursed. Thus those who fear God enjoy the simple and nourishing delights of daily life.

The final verses (5-6) extend the view to include the whole nation. God's generous blessing on each family is a share of the covenant blessing to the whole people. By the same token, the prosperity of each righteous family is the peace of the nation.

The picture is simple and beautiful. Psalms 1 and 119, which praise the wisdom of God's Law directly, both begin with a beatitude. This little psalm

[3]So Stuhlmueller 2.168.

also begins with a beatitude, but instead of encompassing the whole search for wisdom it gives us a portrait of one moment in the life of a wise person. Psalms 1 and 119 present the promise and the search. Psalm 128 shows us the fruits of wisdom.

Holy Family ABC (1-2.3.4-5) [17]

Happy are all who fear the Lord, who walk in the ways of God (1).

All of Psalm 128 except the last verse is used for the responsorial psalm for the Feast of the Holy Family ABC (see Pss 105 and 84 for optional Masses for Years B and C). Omitted are the prayer to see one's grandchildren, and the prayer for peace upon Israel. This psalm which is a celebration of the joys of family life is a fitting choice for this feast.

During the Christmas season when our society places such emphasis on family life, the Church directs our attention to the source of family joy: the blessing of God. The readings consider family life from several angles. Sir 3:2-6, 12-14 advises us of the true meaning of the fourth commandment: care for our parents as long as they live, especially when they are elderly. The fourth commandment (Exod 20:12) is the only commandment to carry a promise of reward. The sage elaborates on the blessings which result from honor to parents: forgiveness of sins, long life, good children. Parents are deserving of reverence, even in the weaknesses of old age. Honor to parents is rewarded with life.

The Letter to the Colossians (Col 3:12-21) describes the virtues that bring about a happy family life: compassion, kindness, humility, gentleness, and patience. Every member of the family has a right to expect gentle forgiveness for faults and weaknesses. Each member of the family receives special attention. Husbands and wives must love each other and surrender to one another.[4] Children must obey; parents must instruct with gentleness and respect. A family in which such virtues reign will live in peace.

Such happy family life, however, is a gift from God (cf. Ps 128). It cannot be taken for granted. Every day we must sing gratefully to God for the loving companionship of those with whom we live. We are happy who have such blessings. Our happiness is God's gift.

---

[4]The author of the Letter to the Colossians wrote from his social perspective. Wives were expected to submit to their husband's authority. His advice is that wives should accept this social situation in the context of their obedience to God. He makes a further demand, however. Husbands must not lord it over their wives. Rather they must love them. This will make the unequal social situation bearable. At the end of the twentieth century our social situation is different. Husband and wife are seen as equal partners in marriage. Love and submission are demanded of each of them toward the other.

The gospels for the three years (Matt 2:13-15, 19-23; Luke 2:22-40; Luke 2:41-52) give us glimpses of the family life of Joseph and Mary. It is a paradoxical example. Psalm 128 tells us that prosperity and peace are the blessings which righteous people can expect. Each of these three gospels presents a situation of distress. The family is forced to flee into exile because Herod wants to kill their child. Simeon casts a cloud over the happy event of the child's redemption as the firstborn son. The parents lose the twelve-year-old boy and are frantic with worry. But each gospel ends with a moment of peace. The family settles in Nazareth. The child grows in wisdom and strength, and is obedient to his parents. This final glimpse of peace suggests the harmony of their relationships with one another even in the sorrows of their lives. Family life will not be without suffering; some families will suffer terribly. But no suffering is worse than that of disharmony within the family circle. No blessing is greater than love of one another. May the Lord bless our families all the days of our lives (Ps 128:5).

27th Sun Year B (1-2.3.4-5.6) [141]

May the Lord bless us all the days of our lives (5).

The whole of Psalm 128 is the responsorial psalm for the Twenty-Seventh Sunday of Year B. God blesses the righteous with the blessings of daily domestic life.

The multi-faceted relationships that attach to what we call "family" appear in the readings for this Sunday. Both the gospel and the first reading focus on the primary relationship of marriage. The Genesis account (Gen 2:18-24), which is part of the second account of creation, is perhaps our most beautiful story of the longing for and delight in union between man and woman. God has created the *'adam*, the human being, from the clay of the earth. Nothing in the story indicates gender for this human being. It is alone. But God declares that it is not good for the human being to be alone. Human beings were made for companionship. No animal is suitable. Only an equal partner can satisfy the longing of the human heart. So God puts the human being to sleep, and from the flesh of one human being God creates two equal but different human beings. Only in recognizing the difference and complementarity do the two human beings become "man" (*'ish*) and "woman" (*'ishshah*). In the moment of recognition the man declares ecstatically: "This one, at last, is bone of my bones and flesh of my flesh." Thus the two who once were one long to become one again. This longing for unity in diversity is the foundation of marriage.

In the gospel (Mark 10:2-16) Jesus faces the difficult question of what to do when the union of marriage fails. The issue of divorce was just as difficult in Jesus' time as it is in ours. The ideal of marriage is described in the Genesis story. In no generation has it worked perfectly every time. Jewish men in Jesus' time were allowed to divorce their wives by simply presenting them with a decree of divorce. Jesus declares divorce to be a failure of God's plan of creation. His explanation to the disciples is also a subtle judgment on the double standard of his time. Jesus puts the wife on equal footing, with equal rights and equal responsibility. A husband who divorces his wife and marries another commits adultery against his wife. In Jesus' time adultery was usually seen as an offense against the husband; seldom did anyone see it as an offense against the wife. On the other hand, a woman who divorces her husband (unheard of!) and re-marries commits adultery against him. Equal rights and equal responsibility.

A further reflection is required. Jesus assumes, as his society would, that a divorced person would re-marry. A woman without husband or sons was incapable of supporting herself in the economy of the time. A man would marry again in order to have children to carry on his name and inherit his property. It would be rare for either to live alone.

Our social situation is different from that of Jesus. Two principles endure from his teaching. Both the man and the woman in marriage have equal rights and equal responsibility. The failure of unity which brings about divorce is a failure of God's good creative plan. It is not good for the human being to be alone. Happy family life is a gift and blessing of God (Ps 128). May God grant us this blessing!

Ordinarily the family extends to include children. Children can often be a source of annoyance to adults. Jesus scolds the disciples who are annoyed by children who press around him, and even uses them as an example for the righteous life. This too was unheard of! Childhood was not as romanticized in Jesus' time as it is today. But Jesus sets the lowly, helpless child as an example for his "wise," grown disciples. Only those who know their dependence on God their Father can enter the kingdom. Jesus came to teach us how to live that dependence (Heb 2:9-11). Made for a little while lower than the angels, he endured all that we endure—suffering and death. He became our brother in order to show us our Father.

The happy family is a living symbol of the relationship between God and the covenant people. Israel's best images of the covenant are the relationships between husband and wife and between parent and child. The happiness of family life is also a gift of God. We may never take it for granted. May the Lord grant us this blessing all the days of our lives!

33rd Sun Year A (1-2.3.4-5) [158]

Happy are all who fear the Lord (1).

The verses of Psalm 128 selected for the Thirty-Third Sunday of Year

A are the same as those for the Feast of the Holy Family (see above). The refrain is the first half of verse 1, the refrain for that same feast.

Where can we find the wisdom to survive the last days, the end of the world? That is the question of today's readings. Paul tells us that we tend to worry about the wrong things, to look for the answer in the wrong places (1 Thess 5:1-6). We think that if we knew the day or the hour we might be ready. But Paul tells us that we cannot know the answer to that question. Even so, we are not left helpless. We are children of light; we have been given wisdom if we only watch for it.

The search for wisdom is absolutely essential. We have been entrusted with someone else's riches, the gifts of God, and we will be called to account for them (Matt 25:14-30). If we have buried our blessings and refused to risk sharing them with others, even the little that we have will be taken from us. The stakes are life and death. We must find the wisdom that shows us the way to life.

The beginning of the Liturgy of the Word tells us that the place to find wisdom is at home. The psalm suggests that the blessings for those who fear the Lord are in the ordinary joys of human life: work and family. The first reading uses the image of a good wife to describe the Wisdom Woman herself (Prov 31:10-13, 19-20, 30-31).[5] Verse 30b may be translated: ". . . the woman, Fear of the Lord (i.e., Wisdom herself), is worthy of praise." It is Wisdom who brings us good and not evil all the days of our lives. It is Wisdom who is the treasure beyond pearls. She whose name is Fear of the Lord is the one worthy of praise. We find her at home, in the ordinary moments of our lives; her gift to us is life. How happy are those who find her; how happy are those who fear the Lord!

6. Psalm 139

Psalm 139 is a wisdom psalm. It sings of a wisdom born of personal experience. This psalmist knows the meaning of "fear of the Lord," even though the term is not used in the psalm. This psalmist lives in the all-knowing presence of God (cf. *Rule of Benedict* 7.10–13).

The psalm can be divided into five stanzas: 1-6, 7-12, 13-16, 17-22, 23-24. It begins and ends with the concept of God's testing and knowing (the device of inclusion, see Ps 86). The psalmist's whole being lies open to the knowledge of God (1-3). Because God's knowing is life-giving, the psalmist continues to pray, "Probe me, God, know my heart" (23-24).

---

[5]See Thomas P. McCreesh, "Wisdom as Wife: Proverbs 31:10-31," *Revue Biblique* 92 (1985) 25–46.

The first stanza (1-6) is a meditation on God's knowledge of all the psalmist does. All thoughts and actions are present to God. In the second stanza (7-12) the psalmist considers God's inescapable presence. Flight from God is impossible. God is present above and below and in every direction. The dawn and the sea suggest east and west, and, in a society which calculated direction by facing east, the right hand connotes south and the other hand north.[6] Not even darkness is impenetrable to God. Not even in Sheol, the land of death, does one leave God's presence![7]

Stanza three (13-16) moves from activity to essence. God knows our inner being better than we know ourselves. From the moment of creation, beginning with the fashioning of humankind from the earth (cf. Gen 2:7), through the delicate formation of the child in the womb, God knows.

Throughout the psalm God's wonderful knowledge leads the psalmist to awe and praise (cf. 6, 14). The recurring exclamation of wonder opens the fourth stanza (17-22). God's knowledge is beyond human imagination. But God's knowing is filled with the tender concern of the creator, and so the psalmist turns to two practical concerns. In reality the two concerns are the same: Deliver us from evil! The psalmist pleads with God to destroy the godless. The psalmist becomes an ally of God in rooting out evil. But the psalmist is a realist and knows that no human being is free of faults. Thus the prayer ends with a petition that God find the evil in the psalmist's own life and root it out as well.

The prayer against evil is difficult for believers. But we must remember our own commitment to spread the kingdom of God in the world. Christ has won the victory, but poverty and war, sickness and death still hold sway over millions of people. They are enemies of God, deceitfully posing as the will of God or as themselves the All-Powerful. "Do I not hate, Lord, those who hate you? . . . With fierce hatred I hate them, enemies I count as my own?" (Ps 139:21-22).

Birth of J Baptist (1-3.13-14.14-15) [587]

I praise you, for I am wonderfully made (14).

The verses chosen from Psalm 139 for the celebration of the Birth of John the Baptist focus on God's intimate knowledge of human beings from the beginning of life in the womb. After three verses from the opening stanza, all the rest are from the third stanza, the tender knowledge of the creature by the creator. The refrain celebrates this knowledge: "I praise you,

---

[6]Dahood 3.287–288, 289–291.

[7]The suggestion that God is present even in death (cf. Pss 23:4; Job 26:6; Prov 15:11) contrasts with the assertion that God is absent from Sheol (Pss 6:6; 30:10; 88:6, 11-12).

so wonderfully you made me." It would be well to ponder the final stanzas of the psalm as well (19-24) in the light of John's ministry to prepare the way by preaching a baptism of repentance. Much of John's message, as reported to us by the gospels (cf. Matt 3:7-12; Luke 3:7-20), has to do with the eradication of evil.

The first reading (Isa 49:1-6) is the second Servant song from Second Isaiah.[8] The Servant describes his call in a manner reminiscent of the prophet Jeremiah (cf. Jer 1:4-10). God called him from birth, formed him in his mother's womb. God commissioned him to bring Israel back to God. But that is not enough! He is to be a light to the nations, bringing God's salvation to the ends of the earth. Only God fully understands the Servant's mission. In his own eyes his labor seems in vain. But God, who holds his reward, makes him glorious.

Psalm 139 repeats the image of God's knowledge and power even in the womb. God who sees knows how wonderfully the human being is made. We sing in John's voice, praising the wonder of his call and mission. John teaches us to look also at ourselves, at how God knows us, at what God calls us to be, at how wonderfully we are made.

The other readings (Acts 13:22-26; Luke 1:57-66, 80) continue the mood of awe at the God who knows our days before one comes to be (Ps 139:16). In the reading from Acts John insists that he be known for what he is, as God knows him. He is not the Messiah; he is the one who goes before, the one who introduces the message of salvation. That is his glory. The gospel tells the story of John's birth and naming. It is truly an occasion for awe. The mother was thought to be barren; the father has been dumb since the conception. The child has a name before birth, a name only reported by the parents. At the moment of naming the speechless father begins to sing God's praises. It is no wonder that "fear came upon all their neighbors." They understood that the hand of the Lord was with this child. They know that God's knowledge is too lofty to reach, God's thoughts too numerous to count (Ps 139:6, 18). They are aware that God knows the inmost being and they are led to fear of the Lord.

H. Royal (Messianic)

In 2 Sam 7 Nathan brings a promise from God to David that his throne and his kingdom will last forever. That promise is the foundation of Israel's royal theology and ultimately of the messianic hope. That promise underlies the royal psalms.

[8]The others are 42:1-4; 50:4-11; 52:13–53:12.

The king is the anointed one, in Hebrew *mashiach* (messiah), in Greek *christos* (christ). At his coronation the king becomes the adopted son of God (cf. Pss 2 and 110). Thus he can be addressed as "god" (Ps 45:7) and "Most High" (Ps 89:28). The king is the representative of God to the people and the representative of the people to God. The king sits at God's right hand (Ps 110:1). Through the king divine blessings come to the people (Ps 72).

The royal psalms are distinguished by content rather than by form. Some are prayers for the king or prayers of the king; some are celebrations of the institution of monarchy. The royal psalms represent various forms. In this book Psalm 18, thanksgiving for the king's victory, is included with the songs of thanksgiving and Psalm 78, which sets the Davidic monarchy as the goal of Israel's history, is included with the historical psalms. Psalm 45 is a celebration of a royal wedding. Psalms 72 and 110 are coronation psalms. Psalm 89 is a lament over the disgrace and suffering of the king.

The royal psalms have a special significance for Christians. We see Christ as a special fulfillment of God's promise to David. Christ is the Son of God who sits at God's right hand, whose kingdom endures forever. Christ is the king whose wedding to his bride, the Church, is our cause for celebration. Christ is our representative before God through whom divine blessings continue to sustain our lives. We will be doubly enriched if we can hold two realities in our minds: Israel's historical experience of monarchy and our own experience of God's saving rule in Christ.

1. Psalm 45

Psalm 45 is a wedding song for the king. Its origin is unknown. There are indications that it was written in the northern kingdom for the marriage of Ahab to Jezebel in the ninth century. She was a princess of Tyre and Sidon (1 Kgs 16:31; Ps 45:13); Ahab had an ivory palace in Samaria (1 Kgs 22:39; Ps 45:9). Some of the Samaritan ivories can still be seen in the Israel Museum in Jerusalem. The psalm also seems to echo the royal theology that begins with God's promise to David (2 Sam 7:8-16) and develops into a full-blown theology of the ideal messianic king ruling a kingdom of peace from God's city, Jerusalem (cf. Isa 9:5-6; 11:1-9).

Wedding imagery is also used to describe the relationship between God and the covenant people (Isa 54:1-8; 62:1-5; Jer 2:2; Hos 1-3). So Psalm 45, a piece composed for the celebration of human love, can become a way to describe the bond of love uniting God with the people (cf. Song of Songs). In the New Testament marriage is interpreted as a symbol of the relationship between Christ and the Church (Eph 5:21-33). The final day, when the kingdom arrives in its fullness, will be the wedding day of the lamb (Rev

19:6-8). At the end, the new Jerusalem, God's people, will appear as a bride prepared for her husband (Rev 21:2).

Psalm 45 opens with an introductory remark of the poet announcing the theme of the song (2). The second stanza (3-10) is in praise of the king. Favored by God, he is the most handsome of men. He is eloquent in speech and mighty in battle. His cause is God's cause. He inherits the promise to David that his throne will stand forever (2 Sam 7:13, 16). As king, he is the son of God, representing God to the people and the people to God (cf. 2 Sam 7:14; Pss 2:7; 110:3). Therefore he is called by the title "god," *'elohim* (Ps 45:7). He is the anointed one, the Messiah. The celebration of his wedding is marked by rich splendor.

The bride is addressed in the third stanza (11-16). She has left her own country and her own people. She must forget them and become part of the king's family. She must leave the gods of her father's house and accept the covenant God of Israel. Her wedding party is richly adorned and stunningly beautiful. The final verses (17-18) are addressed again to the king. The promise of a lasting dynasty and enduring fame is repeated.

In the New Testament the psalm is applied to Jesus, the messianic king who is higher than the angels (Heb 1:8-9; Ps 45:7-8).

Assumption (10.11.12.16) [622]

The queen stands at your right hand, arrayed in gold (10).

The responsorial psalm for the Solemnity of the Assumption of Mary is taken from the wedding song of Psalm 45. The refrain, which is repeated in the verses, is the concluding verse of the praise addressed to the king. He is honored because "a princess arrayed in Ophir's gold comes to stand at [his] right hand" as his queen. The remaining verses are from the stanza addressed to the bride. She must abandon the house of her origins and become part of the king's family; she must become totally devoted to him. Her bridesmaids follow her with joy as the whole wedding party enters the royal palace.

The use of this psalm for the Assumption is rich with paradox. The king in the psalm is the anointed ruler, the Messiah. In the symbolism of the feast is the king Christ? Does Mary as the bride stand for the Church, the whole people of God? Is this feast the wedding day of the lamb? What are the origins which are to be forgotten? Earthly life plagued by sin, suffering, and death? The queen stands at the king's right hand. Are we her bridesmaids, allowed to enter the palace too because we are part of the wedding party? The psalm alone is a rich feast for our meditation on this day.

The readings present the central mystery of our salvation in images ranging from the mythological to the ordinary. The passage from the Book of

Revelation (Rev 11:19; 12:1-6, 10) begins with a vision of God's temple, opened so that the ark of the covenant is visible to all. The ark and the temple which housed it were the sign of God's presence among the covenant people. This vision of the new reality will be a revelation of God's presence with the people. The sign which then appears symbolizes the birth of the Messiah, the one who will rule the nations with an iron rod (cf. Ps 2:9). He is given birth by the Woman. She is the people of God, Israel, the Church. She is crowned with twelve stars, the totality of her people represented by the twelve tribes, the twelve apostles. She is threatened by the dragon, the personification of evil which plagues God's people. She gives birth to the Messiah; the moment of God's salvation has arrived.

The gospel (Luke 1:39-56) presents a parallel event in homely terms. A young pregnant woman goes to help her older pregnant cousin. What could be more ordinary? But in this simple scene the salvation of the whole human race can be glimpsed. This is the meeting of the woman who is to give birth to God's Messiah and the woman whose son will announce his arrival. The moment of God's salvation has arrived. Mary sings the good news for all of us. "The Mighty One has done great things for [us]!"

Paul tells us in plain terms what the good news is (1 Cor 15:20-26). The resurrection of Christ is the pledge of resurrection for all of us. The dragon of sin and death has been defeated once and for all. The moment of God's salvation has arrived; the Messiah has been given the kingdom.

Christ has gone before us as our pledge of resurrection. In order to give us hope another sign has been given to us, a Woman, the Bride, taken into the king's palace. The train of bridesmaids is still being led in with glad and joyous acclaim (Ps 45:16). At the end, when we are all assembled in God's presence, Christ will hand over the kingdom to God the Father. Then the party will really begin!

2. Psalm 72

Psalm 72 is a royal psalm which may have been composed for a state occasion such as the enthronement of the king. It is both a prayer for the king and a blessing on his reign. The high hopes of the psalm match other enthronement passages (Isa 9:1-6; 11:1-9). The anointed king is God's representative to the people. He has the responsibility of carrying out God's rule, especially care of the weaker members of the society. He is also the mediator of God's blessings to the people. Psalm 72 presents the ideal of this royal theology.

The first stanza (1-4) is the prayer that the king may exercise the royal function of carrying out God's rule and mediating God's blessing. The king belongs to the favored dynasty of David. By that very fact he is already a sign of God's fidelity. Justice for the weak and prosperity for the land will be further signs of God's presence with the people during the king's reign. The two signs are really one. The word *shalom*, which is commonly translated "peace," really means the situation in which everyone has what is needed for life. In verses 3 and 7 it is translated "bounty." The word *sedeq*, "righteousness/justice," signifies right relationships. The hills yield *sedeqah* when they yield abundance (3); *sedeq*, "abundance," will flourish during the king's reign (7).

The second stanza (5-7) raises the hope to mythological standards. May the king reign as long as sun and moon endure. May the king himself be the giver of prosperity to the people as the rain is the giver of fertility to the earth.

In the third stanza (8-14) the political realm is the focus. The prayer is that the borders of the king's land will reach the ideal limits: Egypt to the Euphrates, the Mediterranean Sea to the Arabian desert. This empire will be supported by tribute of kings from far-flung lands, from Tarshish in Spain to the Arabian peninsula to Seba (Ethiopia) in Africa. The empire will be ruled in justice. The sign of this, repeated again, is that the weak in the society have what they need.

The final stanza of the psalm (15-17) summarizes the prayer. The reign of this king will be marked by prosperity—both from the land's fertility and the tribute of nations. His fame will endure through many generations in many lands. He will be prayed for and blessed continually. The blessing of Abraham, that all nations would find blessing in him (Gen 12:2-3), will be continued through this king.

The psalm is rooted in the real world, in real time and place. This is a prayer for political peace and economic security. But as the representative of God, the messianic king also functioned as a symbol of God's kingdom which is yet to arrive in its fullness. After the monarchy ended in the sixth century, the hope for God's kingdom and God's anointed did not die. The images of peace and prosperity increased in intensity. Christians find this psalm an expression of their hope in Christ, an extension of their prayer, "Your kingdom come!"

There are two verses (18-19) at the end of Psalm 72 which form the conclusion to Book Two of the psalter (Pss 42-72) and to the large collection of Davidic psalms in Books One and Two (Pss 3-41, 51-72). Each of the five books of the psalter ends with a doxology (cf. Pss 41:14; 89:53; 106:48; 150). The doxology at the end of Psalm 72 is a fitting conclusion to the psalm as well as to the book. It is God who is the source of all peace and prosperity. All the wonderful things hoped for in the reign of the king are gifts of God. The fame of the king is a reflection of God's honor. It is God's name which endures forever; God's glory which fills the earth.

2nd Sun Adv A (1-2.7-8.12-13.17) [4]

Justice shall flourish in his time, and fullness of peace forever (7).

The responsorial psalm for the Second Sunday of Advent A samples each of the stanzas of Psalm 72. The refrain concludes the mythological picture of a perfect society in which justice and peace, bounty and abundance, flourish forever. The beginning of the enthronement ceremony is represented by the first two verses of the psalm in which the king is given the responsibility to be the mediator of God's justice and blessing to the people. The political boundaries of the king's empire are drawn and the significant situation in which the poor receive what they need is described. The psalm ends with the final verse, the prayer that the blessing of Abraham continue through the king's reign.

The polyvalent imagery of the psalm which portrays both the earthly king and the longed-for Messiah is matched by the multiple imagery of Advent. We commemorate the birth of Jesus; we wait for the coming of the messianic king in all his glory at the end of time. The complexity of this season should not be simplified. Through our celebration we hold together the already and the not yet. What continues to be true is that we are still waiting.

Each of the readings contributes to the complex picture. Isaiah sings of the ideal Davidic king, filled with God's spirit at his anointing (Isa 11:1-10). The gift of the spirit endows the king with the attributes of God: wisdom, understanding, and knowledge. Thus endowed, he enacts God's justice by caring for the weak and destroying wickedness. The consequence is perfect peace. Even the animals abandon the demands of their nature and co-exist in perfect harmony. The reign of the king has become the kingdom of God. The psalm reinforces the portrayal of the ideal king. During his reign the people will enjoy justice and peace, bounty and abundance.

After the Babylonian Exile this ideal picture seemed farther and farther from reality. There was no king; hardly ever was there peace. Throughout most of the period the people were under foreign domination. Rather than abandon their hope, however, the people clung to belief in God's fidelity. They used "whatever was written previously" as instruction for their hope (cf. Rom 15:4). Thus when John the Baptist arrived preaching "The kingdom of heaven is at hand," they had the imagination with which to clothe his words (Matt 3:1-12). John seemed to be Elijah, announcing both the Day of the Lord and the Kingdom of God. People flocked to him, repenting of their sins in anticipation of the great day. John reminds the religious leaders among them that their imagined picture might not be large enough. The ideal kingdom might belong not only to the children of Abraham. The righteousness of which they are proud might not be sufficient. The king who is anointed by the spirit will baptize in the Holy Spirit and fire. Only those who reform their lives can survive the day of his coming. Only those who recognize their poverty and affliction can hope for his rescue (Ps 72:12-13).

But Jesus did not look like the picture John painted either. No matter how vivid the portrayal of the king, God's Messiah, human imagination is not sufficient. We have the benefit of hindsight for our picture of the coming of Jesus in history. What do we have to sustain our imaginations as we hope for his coming in glory at the end of time? Paul tells us that, like the people of Jesus' time, we have "whatever was written previously," which has been given us for our instruction, "that by endurance and by the encouragement of the scriptures we might have hope" (Rom 15:4-9). God is faithful; the promise to Abraham endures. Whatever image we have, however, must fall woefully short. What we have is hope. What we must do is continue the growth of the messianic kingdom now, the kingdom of justice for the poor, abundance for the needy. That is how we will know the kingdom of God when it arrives in its fullness: justice shall flourish, and fullness of peace forever.

Epiphany ABC (1-2.7-8.10-11.12-13) [20]

Lord, every nation on earth will adore you (11).

The refrain and most of the verses of the responsorial psalm for the Solemnity of the Epiphany ABC come from the section of Psalm 72 which describes the political power of the messianic king. The boundaries of the empire expand to the fullest possible extent. Surrounding nations bring tribute and approach the king with reverence. This political dominion is just because the king enacts the rule of God. Righteousness flourishes. Even the poorest people receive everything they need for a good life. There is an abundance of good things for all God's people.

The Solemnity of the Epiphany represents the transformation of the political-theological vision of one small nation into the hope of the whole world for salvation. God works in human history. The image of the ideal king preserved by one people special to God becomes God's plan for the full realization of the hopes of all creation (Eph 3:2-3, 5-6). God's plan unites all peoples. The author of the Letter to the Ephesians expresses the depth of this unity by coining words with the prefix, *syn-* ("together" or "co-"). The Gentiles are now "co-heirs" with the Jews, members of the same body ("co-bodies"), "co-partners" in the promise. The kingdom is bigger than people imagined!

The prophet of the final section of Isaiah, who is trying to give hope to the people as they rebuild after the Exile, paints a glorious picture of the new Jerusalem (Isa 60:1-6). God's light shining upon it, within it, makes the city itself light for the other nations. All the exiles begin to return; all the people of God, unimagined in their number, stream toward the city. An abundance of good things flows in for the benefit of God's people. The little city of Jerusalem, still bearing the marks of Nebuchadnezzar's devastation, seems a poor symbol for all this richness. But the kingdom of God is greater than the people can possibly imagine!

The psalm presents the king who rules over this ideal kingdom. He governs with justice; he cares for the poor. His kingdom is a kingdom of enduring peace and prosperity. All nations bow down before him. But God's ways are beyond our imagination. The gospel (Matt 2:1-12) reinterprets the image of Psalm 72 in the birth of Jesus. There are two kings in the gospel and some very rich and powerful men who have come to pay homage. The king on the throne is disturbed at the news of the king announced by the star. The wise men leave the king in the palace and worship a child in a house with his mother. God's ways are paradoxical. The establishment of the ideal kingdom does not come in human power but in weakness. The king who provides for the poor knows their need from his own experience. Every nation comes, not because they are coerced to offer tribute, but because they rejoice to be included in this wonderful kingdom. The kingdom of God is greater than we have ever imagined!

Epiphany Common (1-2.7-8.10-11.12-13) [175]

Lord, every nation on earth will adore you (11).

See the Solemnity of the Epiphany above.

3. Psalm 89

Psalm 89 is a complex psalm which portrays both the blessings and the trials of the Davidic king. The psalm is woven together like a symphonic work with a series of repetitions. The theme that permeates the whole is God's love (*hesed*; 2, 3, 15, 25, 29, 34, 50, cf. 20)[1] and faithfulness (*'emunah*; 2, 3, 6, 9, 25, 34, 50; cf. 15, 29, and 38), which are each repeated seven times, the biblical number signifying completeness. The two words "covenant" (*berit*; 4, 29, 35, 40) and "forever" (*'olam*; 2, 3, 5, 29, 37, 38, [53]) appear only slightly less often. The overall impression given by the repetition is that God's faithful love, demonstrated in the covenant with David, will last forever. The fact that this does not seem to be true is the problem of the lament at the end of the psalm (39-52).

---

[1]*Hesed* is translated "promise" in vv. 2 and 50.

There are three main divisions in Psalm 89 (2-19, 20-38, 39-52); the first section may be subdivided into two stanzas (2-5, 6-19). Verse 53 is a doxology which concludes Book Three of the psalter. As such it is really not part of the psalm. It is worth noting, however, that Book Two also ends with a royal psalm, Psalm 72.

The first section (2-19) which is a hymn, gives three reasons to sing God's praise: God has made an everlasting covenant with David (2-5); God's faithfulness is demonstrated through creation (6-15) and through love for a chosen people (16-19). Creation is used as the witness to support the other two statements.

The covenant with David is the promise that his dynasty will continue forever (cf. 2 Sam 7:8-16) That promise can be trusted because the God who made the promise is like no other god. The awe-filled question of who is like God (7, 9) alternates with statements of Yahweh's supremacy over all the other gods (6, 8). Yahweh is praised and feared in the assembly of heavenly powers (holy ones). No one in that council can match Yahweh's loyalty.

At this point the psalmist's praise of God moves to direct address. The emphatic "You" is the favorite word of the next several verses (10 twice, 11, 12, 13, 18). The psalmist praises God's power in conquering chaos—the sea and its monster Rahab—and in founding the whole world including the four sacred mountains named in verse 13. Everything belongs to and is supported by this mighty creator. Verse 15 returns to the theme of God's fidelity manifested both in creation (6-15) and in care of the people who know the Lord (16-19). These people rejoice in full security because their God, the true king who maintains all of creation, has given them a king (2-5) and protection from their enemies (18-19).

The second section (20-38) is the report of God's oracle to David (cf. 2 Sam 7:8-16). The section begins by echoing verse 4: David, my chosen one, my servant. God has chosen and sealed David with holy oil. David has thus become God's anointed, i.e., Messiah. The rest of the section lists God's promises (acts of *hesed*, cf. 2) to David. Almost every verse begins with "I" or a first-person verb. God has promised. God has the power. God is faithful. David will have protection from enemies and dominion over vast territory. He will call God, "Father," and God will make him the first-born. He will honor the Most High God, and God will make him Most High over all kings. His dynasty will last forever. If his descendants break God's Law, they will be punished, but the throne will not be taken away from David's house. God will be faithful to the covenant promise: David's throne will last as long as the sun, moon, and sky.

The final section (39-52) is a lament, a complaint to God that this everlasting covenant with David seems to be broken. Does this mean that the covenant with creation is broken too? The language of the hymn and the oracle return, but now they are used in accusation. The stanza begins with the emphatic "you." "You have rejected your anointed, . . . renounced the covenant with your servant" (39-40). "You . . . hurled his throne to the ground" (45). "Where are your promises of old, Lord, the loyalty sworn to David" (50)? The plea is that God will remember: remember how frail all humans are and remember especially the suffering of the anointed (48, 51).

There is no agreement on the situation which inspired this lament. The king has apparently been defeated in battle. The most plausible suggestions are the threat to the monarchy at the time of the Syro-Ephraimite war (733–732 BCE) or the defeat and death of Josiah in 609 BCE. In the eighth-century crisis King Ahaz of Judah is besieged by his neighbors, Syria and Israel, in an attempt to force him to join a coalition against Assyria. The coalition partners plan to depose him if he refuses, thus ending the Davidic dynasty. The prophet Isaiah encourages Ahaz to stand firm, with a word from the same root as *'emunah*, "loyalty," which weaves Psalm 89 together (Isa 7:9), and promises a child named Emmanuel, God-with-us, as a sign of hope for the Davidic dynasty. The other suggestion relates the psalm to the death of King Josiah. Josiah had gone out to Megiddo to meet Pharaoh Neco. The Pharaoh was on his way to help the Assyrians against the Babylonians. In the ensuing battle Josiah was killed. It was a great blow to the people. Josiah was a good king and had carried through a reform of worship and a renovation of the temple. How could God allow him to die so young!

The specific situation of the psalm, however, does not matter. The challenge it presents is ongoing: how to maintain faith in God's wonderful promises even when the human structures that seem to embody those promises are crumbling. The psalm teaches us to stand firm in the midst of the paradox, to shout joyfully to all the world the greatness of God's love and fidelity, and at the same time to cry out to God boldly in every place where the Messiah, the Body of Jesus, still suffers.

4th Sun Adv B (2-3.4-5.27.29) [11]

Forever I will sing the goodness of the Lord (2).

The psalm refrain for the Fourth Sunday of Advent B is the opening verse of Psalm 89 which announces the theme of the psalm: God's faithful love throughout the ages. The verses highlight the psalm's primary example of God's fidelity: the promise to David that his dynasty will last forever. The entire first stanza of the psalm is included in the selection along with two verses from the second section which emphasize the strong bond between David and God. The lament is totally omitted.

The readings develop the theme of God's faithfulness to David. The first reading (2 Sam 7:1-5, 8-11, 16) is the narrative version of God's promise of a lasting dynasty. The passage turns on a play between three words all from the same root: "house" (*bayit*) which refers both to temple and dynasty, "build" (*banah*), and "son" (*ben*). David plans to build a house, a temple for God. Through the prophet Nathan, however, it is revealed that God will build a house, a dynasty, for David. David's son, the first successor in the promised dynasty, will build a house for God. The element in the reading which is not in the psalm is the connection of David's house with the temple. The element in the psalm which is not in 2 Sam is the emphasis on God's faithfulness to the promise.

The gospel (Luke 1:26-38) reveals the amazing creativity of God's faithfulness. It seems that God has indeed renounced the covenant with David (Ps 89:40). There has been no Davidic king since the Babylonian Exile in the sixth century BCE. Various dreams center around the promise to David— hopes for another king like David who will drive out the Romans, or for an eschatological judge who will inaugurate the kingdom of God. God, in loving fidelity, sends an angel to a young woman to announce the birth of her child, a child who will inherit David's throne, who will be called "Son of the Most High," whose reign will last forever. Here is the Son of David; here is the lasting dynasty. Here is the one who cries to God, "You are my Father," the one of whom God says, "I myself make him firstborn, Most High over the kings of the earth" (cf. Ps. 89:27-28). Here is the son of David's house who will build the house for God. God's faithful love has not failed.

The second reading (Rom 16:25-27) is the doxology concluding Paul's Letter to the Romans. Paul encourages his readers by reminding us of God's faithfulness, so much greater than the recipients of the promises could imagine, so much greater than we can imagine. The gospel reveals the mystery. Our response is the obedience of faith and a commitment to sing the goodness of the Lord forever (Ps 89:2). God's love is built (*banah*) forever (Ps 89:3)!

Christmas Vigil ABC (4-5.16-17.27.29) [13]

Forever I will sing the goodness of the Lord (21).

The refrain for the Vigil of Christmas ABC is the introduction to the theme of Psalm 89. The verses are selected from the first two main sections of the psalm. The lament is not represented. The verses highlight God's promise to David and the happiness of God's people. The reference to creation is also omitted.

God's promises are worked out in human history and continue through their expression in different places at different times. God's faithfulness is manifested precisely in this variety. The gospel for this day (Matt 1:1-25) is a statement of God's promise carried through the muddy history of David's family. The genealogy is just a list, but with every name there is a story. Each story is an incarnation of God's promise. The final story in the list is told: "Joseph, son of David, do not be afraid to take Mary your wife into your home. For it is through the holy Spirit that this child has been conceived in her" (Matt 1:20). God has sworn to David to make his dynasty stand forever. This is the story of the ages through which the promise has been fulfilled. Now as the fulfillment culminates in the conception of Jesus, the evangelist recalls the promise to Ahaz, afraid that he would lose his throne (Isa 7:1-16): "Behold the virgin shall be with child and bear a son, and they shall name him Emmanuel." Little did Ahaz or Isaiah realize the shape this promise would take in the coming ages. Little do we as we continue to sing the promises of the Lord.

Both the prophet in the final section of the scroll of Isaiah (Isa 62:1-5), and the apostle Paul (Acts 13:16-17, 22-25), present the good news of God's promises fulfilled in different ages. The prophet encourages a sixth-century audience, only lately returned from Exile, saying that God will indeed restore David's city, Jerusalem. The people of God who live there will be God's delight, God's bride. The promises of the Lord will stand forever. Even through the destruction and desolation of the Exile, God has not forgotten (cf. Ps 89:39-52). As Paul begins to carry the good news to the ends of the earth he tells the story, beginning with the exodus, to illustrate God's faithfulness. He quotes Ps 89:20-21 concerning God's promise to David and presents Jesus as the fulfillment of that promise.

Through all ages God's promise takes root in different peoples. In us the Christ, Son of David, takes flesh anew and establishes the everlasting kingdom. How are we the messengers of God's amazing fidelity? To whom do we proclaim the promises of the Lord?

Chrism Mass ABC (21-22.25.27) [39]

Forever I will sing the goodness of the Lord (2).

The verses from Psalm 89 chosen for the Chrism Mass are all taken from the second section of the psalm, the oracle promising David a lasting dynasty. The oracle begins with the anointing of David as king, sealing him as God's servant. The refrain celebrates God's faithfulness to the promise to David.

Anointing with oil is a rich symbol in biblical literature. Oil is a sign of gladness and strength, of healing, and of consecration (cf. Ps 45:8; Lev

14:15-18, 26-29; Isa 1:6). Kings, priests, and sometimes prophets were anointed, stones and altars as well (cf. 1 Sam 16:1, 13; Exod 30:26-29; 1 Kgs 19:16; Gen 28:18). Frequently there is a mention of the outpouring of God's spirit in connection with anointing (1 Sam 16:13). The Hebrew and Greek terms for "anointed" have given us our English words messiah and christ. The readings and the psalm turn our attention to various facets of the theme of anointing.

The reading from Isaiah (61:1-3, 6, 8-9) is part of the center section of the post-exilic part of the book (chs. 56–66). It opens with the call of the prophet who has been anointed, filled with God's spirit, and commissioned to bring good news to God's people on Zion. The people too will be anointed with the oil of gladness and clothed with the mantle of God's spirit. The inhabitants of Zion, struggling to rebuild after the Babylonian Exile, will be named priests, as the whole people were so named at Sinai (Exod 19:6). God will renew the covenant with them and they will carry out the mission foretold to Abraham (Gen 12:3) to bring God's blessing to the world.

The psalm puts before us the image of David, the anointed king, the bearer of the promise that one of David's descendants would always sit upon his throne. The gospel (Luke 4:16-21) binds both images together. Jesus, Son of David, fulfillment of the messianic promise, announces his mission in the words from the Book of Isaiah. Jesus is now the anointed prophet, filled with God's spirit, commissioned to bring good news to God's people.

The reading from Revelation (1:5-8) shows us the fulfillment of Jesus' mission. Having by baptism led us into his death and filled us with life by the anointing of the Holy Spirit, he has made us all "a kingdom, priests for his God and Father." God who is Alpha and Omega, beginning and end, has brought the plan of salvation full circle. The oil of anointing for kings, priests, and prophets has been poured out on God's people. It is indeed an oil of gladness. Forever we will sing the goodness of the Lord (Ps 89:2).

13th Sun Year A (2-3.16-17.18-19) [98]
Forever I will sing the goodness of the Lord (2).

The psalm verses for the Thirteenth Sunday of Year A are all from the two stanzas of the first section. The general announcement of God's faithful love which supports the covenant with David opens the selection. The responsorial then moves to the end of the second stanza, the description of the happy people, chosen and supported by the powerful creator God. The specific references to David, the oracle and the lament, are omitted. The hymn in praise of the creator is also omitted. Thus the major focus of the original psalm has been lost.

The readings remind us that God's presence, God's goodness, is often found in unlikely people and situations, a theme underlying the main event of the psalm: David too was an unlikely king (1 Sam 16). The woman of Shunem who entertains Elisha finds the presence and blessing of God in the prophet (2 Kgs 4:8-11, 14-16). God's blessing always overflows in life. She is rewarded by the birth of a son. The God whose power supports all creation (cf. Ps 85:6-14), whose love gives life to a whole people (Ps 89:15-19), also cares for any individual whose generosity is extended toward God's servants.

The gospel (Matt 10:37-42) confronts us with a paradox. Human relationships chosen in preference to God are condemned; human interaction chosen because of God is rewarded. Not even life is to be preferred to Christ, but life poured out for his sake will be regained. God's faithfulness is the only reliable foundation upon which to build a life. God's "love is established forever; [God's] loyalty will stand as long as the heavens" (Ps 89:3).

Our witness to the truth of God's faithful love is Christ who was "raised from the dead by the glory of the Father" (Rom 6:3-4, 8-11). We who through baptism share in his death are also granted a share in his life. We are the people who sing joyfully in the name of the Lord, who shout for joy at his victory (Ps 89:17).

This is the ultimate goal of Psalm 89, a people gathered into God's kingdom by an anointed son of David. God's ways, however, lead through darkness to light. The anointed king suffers defeat (Ps 89:39-52). The woman of Shunem endures barrenness. The prophets are reduced to dependence on the generosity of others (Matt 10:40-42). We are baptized into Christ's death and buried with him (Rom 6:4). But God's faithfulness endures forever. All creation is on its way to new life. Every unlikely person, every unlikely event, may be the sign of the fulfillment of God's promise. "Forever I will sing the goodness of the Lord!" (Ps 89:2).

4. Psalm 110

This short psalm is perhaps the most difficult psalm in the psalter to translate and interpret. The text is corrupt and there are disagreements in the early versions, especially regarding verse 3. Thus there is a great variety of translations. To add to the complications, Psalm 110 is the Old Testament psalm which is most frequently cited in the New Testament. Thus not only is there variation in translations, there is a rich abundance of traditional interpretation.

Psalm 110 is a psalm for the enthronement of the king. Two prophetic oracles are pronounced at the coronation (1-3, 4-7). The first is introduced by the messenger formula common in prophetic texts: "Thus says the

LORD." Psalm 110:1 begins literally, "the oracle of Yahweh (LORD) to my lord" (*'adonai*). In post-exilic times the sacred name of Yahweh ceased to be pronounced and the term "lord," *'adonai*, was substituted for it. The double use of "lord" contributes to the confusion in understanding the first verse of Psalm 110 (cf. Matt 22:45 par.). The first "LORD" in the verse refers to Yahweh; the second "lord" refers to the king.

The king is invited to take his throne at the right hand of God. From the coronation of Josiah we infer that kings had a special place in the temple "by the column" (2 Kings 23:3).[2] This may have been to the right of the Ark of the Covenant which symbolized God's presence. Whether or not the reference is to an actual physical place, the meaning of the verse is that the king's authority comes from God; the king is God's "right-hand man." God will give him power over all his enemies. They will be subdued enough to be used as a footstool. In verse 2 the king receives the scepter, the symbol of his authority. His rule will extend outward from Zion, his capital city.

In verse 3 the king is acknowledged as God's son, the representative of God to the people (cf. Pss 2:7; 89:27-28). The coronation day is thus the day of the king's "birth." God has begotten him mysteriously like the dew (cf. Job 38:28). The revised NAB translation of this difficult verse is:

> [The LORD says:]
> "Yours is princely power from the day of your birth.
> In holy splendor before the daystar,
> like the dew I begot you."

The second section (4-7) begins with a new prophetic announcement: "The LORD has sworn and will not waver" (4). The new king receives the titles of the pre-Davidic kings of Jebusite Jerusalem. Like Melchizedek, king of Salem, the new king is declared priest of *El-Elyon*, God Most High (Gen 14:18). The Lord God is now at the king's right hand, winning victories for him and judging nations in the final judgment. The final verses can also be interpreted with the king as subject, crushing kings, crushing heads. The last verse may refer to part of the enthronement ceremony having to do with water. Solomon was declared king at the Gihon spring (1 Kings 1:33, 38). The Jerusalem temple was the mythological source of the water of life (Ps 46:5; Ezek 47:1-12).[3]

The dual authority of priest and king presents several problems. The relationship between political and religious authority is difficult for God's people throughout their history. Saul disobeys Samuel and is stripped of the kingship (1 Sam 13:10-14). David, on the other hand, has the authority to ap-

[2] Cf. Stuhlmueller 2.129.

[3] For a suggested outline of the enthronement ceremony, see Stuhlmueller 2.129.

point Zadok as high priest (2 Sam 8:17). Kings continued to exercise some priestly functions (cf. 1 Kings 3:4). But after the limitation of the priesthood to descendants of Levi, or of Aaron specifically, the Davidic kings could not legitimately hold the official position of priest since they were descended from the tribe of Judah. The same limitation applies to Jesus. The author of the Letter to the Hebrews names Jesus as a priest according to Melchizedek, the only way he, a Judahite, could be considered a priest in Jewish tradition (Heb 5:5-10).

Corpus Christi C (1.2.3.4) [170]

You are a priest forever, in the line of Melchizedek (4).

The first four verses of Psalm 110 are used as the responsorial psalm for the Solemnity of Corpus Christi C. The verses describe the enthronement of the king at God's right hand, his adoption as God's son, and his appointment as priest. Omitted are the verses referring to the violent victories over the king's enemies (5-7).

Each celebration of Corpus Christi in the three-year cycle emphasizes a different element of the mystery. The readings of Year A focus on the bread of life; Year B centers on the blood of the covenant. Year C has a subtle emphasis on the ministers of the covenant meal. The refrain of the psalm highlights this emphasis with its reference to priesthood.

Chapter 14 of the Book of Genesis is almost as difficult to interpret as Psalm 110. Melchizedek, the king of Salem, appears only in this chapter and in Psalm 110 and in the Letter to the Hebrews. Because of his sudden appearance and disappearance, Hebrews describes him as "without father, mother, or ancestry, without beginning of days or end of life" (Heb 7:3). Genesis 14 presents him as the priest-king of Salem. Abraham, on his way home from a victory over the Canaanite kings, camps near Melchizedek's city. Melchizedek comes to Abraham with a peace offering of bread and wine, presumably to prevent Abraham from attacking his city. Then he blesses him by the God of Salem, El-Elyon, God Most High. Abraham responds by giving the same name to his own God, Yahweh (Gen 14:22).

On a literal level the Genesis reading has little to do with today's feast. It is rich, however, on a symbolic level. Psalm 110 suggests the direction. Melchizedek, priest-king of Salem, is a type of the Messiah, king of Jerusalem. The Messiah is what Melchizedek's name means: the legitimate (just) king. Melchizedek offers the peace offering of bread and wine. Christian tradition thus sees him as a type of Christ, the messianic king, priest of the new covenant, who offers the bread and wine of his body and blood.

The gospel (Luke 9:11-17) is another symbolic foundation of today's celebration. Jesus feeds thousands of people with no resources except a few loaves and fishes. But he does not feed them without the involvement of his disciples. The disciples come, worried about what the people will eat, and he says to them: "Give them some food yourselves." They know they cannot do it, but after Jesus blesses the loaves and fishes he gives them back to the disciples to distribute to the people. The event is a symbol of the Eucharist in which the Body and Blood of Christ, the food of life, is ministered to us by other human beings, Jesus' disciples. The description of the event gives the vocabulary for our celebration of Eucharist: Jesus takes, blesses, breaks, and gives the food to the disciples for distribution.

The passage from 1 Corinthians (11:23-26) is the oldest narrative of the institution of the Eucharist that we have. Paul presents it in the formal way that tradition is passed on: "I received . . . what I also handed on to you." The event described in this text is the foundation of the celebration of Corpus Christi. It is the Eucharist in which Christ gives us his body and blood. It is this share in his life which constitutes us as a community, the Body of Christ. This is the event we celebrate and renew with every Eucharist.

Psalm 110 is related to this feast only tangentially by the mention of Melchizedek and the presentation of the Messiah as priest-king. It provides a clue for our interpretation, however, by suggesting to us that the only way to approach this feast is on the symbolic level. Then we see Christ, the true priest king, offering us the bread and wine of his body and blood. Then we see the Eucharist as our pledge of membership in the kingdom of God.

I. Songs of Zion

The Songs of Zion are related to the royal psalms. God chose David and promised him an everlasting kingdom. God also chose David's city; David's bringing the ark to Jerusalem (Zion) made that city also the city of God (2 Sam 6). The Songs of Zion celebrate the glory of the city of David, city of God. There God is present with the people. There all the tribes gather to worship (Ps 122). There all God's people are at home (Ps 87).

The mythology which surrounds the idea of the dwelling place of the gods is found in the Songs of Zion. Zion is the highest mountain, the center of the universe. A stream flows from Zion, or from Zion's temple, which gives life to all creation (Ps 46; cf. Ezek 47). Zion is the place of God's great and final victory over all the nations, the place where God's kingdom will be established once and for all (Pss 46, 48, 76).

Jerusalem is the site of pilgrimage. God's people are required to celebrate the three great festivals there. This theme is found in the songs of Zion and also in a related and overlapping category, the Songs of Ascent (Pss 120-134), which are specifically pilgrimage psalms. Jerusalem/Zion is also the goal of the final pilgrimage of God's people. There all people long to be.

The new Jerusalem is our symbol for the kingdom of God (cf. Rev 21). There God will dwell with us forever. There true peace and prosperity will be found. There we will at last be home. These are our hopes as we sing the Songs of Zion (cf. Ps 137:3).

Psalm 84

Psalm 84 is a prayer of great faith and longing. It describes the yearning of a pilgrim to arrive in the Holy City and to enter God's temple. The predominance of the image of water suggests that the pilgrimage feast is Tabernacles, celebrated at the time of the first fall rains. The psalm can be divided into four stanzas (2-5, 6-8, 9-10, 11-13). The first stanza (2-5) begins with an exclamation of praise for the temple. The temple is called God's dwelling, God's tenting-place. This is the home of the Lord of hosts. "LORD of hosts" is the title of God whose special presence is signified by the ark of the covenant housed within the temple. In this temple the living God is at home; the whole being of the psalmist—soul (*nephesh* = throat), heart, flesh—longs to find a home there too. Just as the birds seek a secure place to raise their young, the psalmist seeks a shelter in the house of God.

The first stanza ends with a beatitude; the second stanza (6-8) begins with one: Happy are the pilgrims on the way. The psalmist turns from considering the goal of the journey to the journey itself. Even on the way to the sanctuary, God is the refuge of the pilgrim. Just as God provided water in the desert when Israel came out of Egypt, so God provides water now to sustain the pilgrim. The living God is the source of the psalmist's life. As the stanza closes, the pilgrims enter the city of God.

The third stanza (9-10) is a brief petition for the king, the Messiah (= anointed) who stands before God as representative of the people and who mediates God's protection and blessing to them.

The final stanza (11-13) returns to praise of God's sanctuary. Life in God's presence is the only genuine life. To be away from God is to be doomed to darkness and danger; God is sun and shield. To be away from God is the ultimate deprivation; God is the source of every good thing. A final beatitude closes the psalm: those who trust in God have found the end of their longing. How happy they are!

Holy Family C [opt] (2-3.5-6.9-10)

Blessed are they who dwell in your house, O Lord (5a).

The verses chosen from Psalm 84 for the Feast of the Holy Family C are taken from the first three stanzas of the psalm. They include the longing cry of the pilgrim, the double beatitude for those who stay in God's house and those who are on the way to it, and the prayer for the king-Messiah. The choice of Psalm 84 for this feast sets the agenda: family life must be considered in the light of the presence or absence of God. Home is where God is.

Two of the readings show us families on pilgrimage to the house of God; the third reading describes the goal of the pilgrimage, life in the abiding presence of God. Two of the readings also show us families in distress and the third suggests that conflict is part of Christian life. Psalm 84 reminds us that we are still pilgrims on the way; we have not yet arrived.

The first reading (1 Sam 1:20-22, 24-28) tells the story of the family of Elkanah from Ephraim. His two wives compete against each other. One longs for love, the other for children. One year when they came on pilgrimage to the shrine of the ark of the covenant, Hannah, the barren but beloved wife, went to pray before the ark. She begged the Lord for a son and promised him to the Lord. Eli, the priest of the sanctuary, blessed her and she left, satisfied that her prayer was answered. Indeed it was: the Lord remembered Hannah and she conceived a son, Samuel. In keeping with her vow, she brought him back to the sanctuary when he was weaned and consecrated him to the Lord.

Hannah came to the courts of the Lord, begging God to hear her prayer. She left, a witness to the truth of the psalm's beatitudes: happy are those who trust in God, who find refuge in God, who dwell in God's house (Ps 84:13, 6, 5). She came because of family troubles and received a family blessing. She found the presence of God, both in the sanctuary and in her son.

In the gospel (Luke 2:41-52) we find the family of Joseph on pilgrimage to the temple for the Feast of Passover. The parents begin the journey home, but the boy Jesus is not satisfied. His "soul yearns and pines for the courts of the LORD. [His] heart and flesh cry out for the living God" (Ps 84:3). He stays behind in the house of God. The distraught parents search for three days and finally find him in the temple. His response is simple and mysterious: "Why were you looking for me? Did you not know that I must be in my Father's house?" "Why were you looking for me?!" What parent of a twelve-year-old does not recognize that question! "Did you not know . . ." What parent has not been awed by the mystery of vocation glimpsed in a child! The scene closes with a simple statement: "He went down with them and came to Nazareth, and was obedient to them." Life has returned to normal—almost.

Each of these readings portrays a painful time in the life of a family. In each reading someone seeks the presence of God in the sanctuary (cf. Ps. 84). In each reading the presence of God is found also at home—in the child, in the parents, in the ordinary round of family life. This mystery is stated clearly in the reading from the First Letter of John (3:1-2, 21-24). The presence of the living God is within us. We are God's children already. If we believe in Jesus and love one another, we remain in God and God in us. Yet this is not a guarantee of an easy life. The world may not recognize us as God's children because we do not recognize each other! We long for the presence of the living God (Ps 84:2-3); we long to be at home with God (Ps 84:4-5). We proclaim those happy who dwell in God's house, yet the real beatitude is that God dwells in our houses! Lord of hosts, may we find you at home!

Dedication Lateran (3.4.5-6.8.11) [703]

How lovely is your dwelling place, Lord, mighty God! (2).

Psalm 84 is one of the choices for the Common of Dedication of a Church which is used for the Feast of the Dedication of St. John Lateran (see also Pss 95, 122). The emphasis in Psalm 84 is on the pilgrim's longing for God's presence in the holy place. Old Testament readings which fit particularly well with Psalm 84 are: Gen 28:11-18, in which the pilgrim Jacob finds God on the way; Isa 56:1, 6-7, which describes foreigners also coming to God's house; Ezekiel 43:1-2, 4-7, in which God returns to the temple after the Exile. A New Testament choice for the first reading might be Rev 21:1-5, which describes the goal of all our sojourning, the heavenly Jerusalem.

New Testament readings are: Eph 2:19-22, a home for everyone in God's house; Heb 12:18-19, 22-24, the city of the living God, the goal of our pilgrimage. Two gospel stories describe people who long for and find God's presence: Luke 19:1-10, the story of Zacchaeus; and John 4:19-24, the story of the Samaritan woman at the well.

Psalm 122

Psalm 122 is another of the Songs of Ascent (see Psalm 123). These psalms (120-134) are commonly understood to be pilgrimage songs sung on the way to the major feasts in Jerusalem (cf. Exod 23:14; Deut 16:1-17). The psalm is also one of the Songs of Zion (Pss 46, 48, 76, 84, 87).

The first stanza (1-5) expresses the joy on arriving in the holy city. Jerusalem is the city to which all God's people come. The double character of the city provides the reason. It is the city of David, the center of government. It is the city of the king to whom God promised a throne forever (2 Sam 7:16). It is also the city of God, the dwelling place of the divine name. Here David brought the ark and Solomon built the temple. Here God resides in a special way.

The second stanza (6-9) is a heartfelt exhortation to pray for the *shalom* of Jerusalem. *Shalom* is the situation when every person has what is needed for a full life. Jerusalem, the home of all God's people (cf. Ps 87:5-7), must be a place of *shalom*. Even the popular etymology of the name "Jerusalem" connects the city to peace, *shalom*. Jerusalem is the city loved and longed for. Jerusalem is the city in which we hope to be and to find all our loved ones when the kingdom of God comes in its fullness (cf. Rev 21:1-22:5). The living city of Jerusalem which we visit today is a place of strife and bitterness, poverty and despair. Yet that city remains the symbol of our hope. "For the peace of Jerusalem pray," *sha'alu shalom yerushalayim* (Ps 122:6).

1st Sun Adv A (1-2.3-4.4-5.6-7.8-9) [1]

I rejoiced when I heard them say: let us go to the house of the Lord (1).

The whole of Psalm 122 is used as the responsorial psalm for the First Sunday of Advent A. We begin the Church year singing the pilgrimage song which expresses our desire to be home at last.

The first Sundays of Advent direct our attention to the end of time when Christ will come in glory to call us home. Only in the last few centuries BCE did the idea develop that time would cease, the world would come to an end, and that God's victory over evil and vindication of the righteous would take place outside of history. Through most of the Old Testament period faithful people expected God's kingdom within history. They looked for the Day of the Lord when God would defeat their enemies and establish peace within their borders. Then the whole world would know that Yahweh is God of the whole earth and Jerusalem the center of divine blessing and power. This is the vision of Isaiah (2:1-5). All nations will come to Jerusalem to learn the way of God. *Torah*, instruction, will go forth from there. Justice and peace shall stream from Jerusalem and fill the world. God's kingdom will be established at last.

The psalm reminds us that this glorious vision is set in a real city, a city of pilgrims and markets, government offices and holy places. The real city is the symbol of our hope and the goal of our desires. We hear the lyrical words of Isaiah and we pray for their fulfillment. May the swords become plowshares. May peace reign in Jerusalem's walls. May God's kingdom come.

The New Testament readings shift the focus to the end of the world. Between the time of Isaiah and Jesus a new world view began to be expressed. In this world view, called apocalyptic, history is seen as too corrupt to be redeemed. God's victory over evil will come in a cataclysmic battle in which the world will be destroyed. But then faithful people will rise from the dead and live forever in God's kingdom, the new Jerusalem. Jesus is warning his disciples that the Day of the Lord will come suddenly, without any warning (Matt 24:37-44). His advice is not that we should worry, but rather that we should be prepared. The pilgrimage to the new Jerusalem will be announced, but we know not the day or the hour. If we are prepared we will be able to rejoice when we hear, "Let us go to the house of the Lord" (Ps 122:1).

Paul gives us specific instruction regarding preparation (Rom 13:11-14). We do know that it is time for us to stay awake in expectation. We do know that the day is coming nearer. We are called to live in the light, in peace and moderation, seeking no more than we need, respecting the rights of others. Living in this way is the foundation of *shalom*, where every person has what is needed. The way we prepare for the coming pilgrimage is by spreading *shalom*. Our care of the earth preserves it to supply others' needs; our attempt to simplify our possessions makes it possible for others to live also. Our openness to differences enriches the society in which we live. This is the peace of Jerusalem, the peace of all people, the peace of God's kingdom. This is the peace for which we pray; this is our preparation for the pilgrimage to that city where such peace will last forever.

Christ the King C (1-2.3-4.4-5) [163]

I rejoiced when I heard them say: let us go to the house of the Lord (1).

The first stanza of Psalm 122 is used for the responsorial psalm on the Solemnity of Christ the King C. The first stanza expresses the pilgrim's delight at arriving in the holy city. Jerusalem is the city of God's people, the city from which God's chosen king rules, the city in which God is present to the chosen people.

The imagery of king and kingdom controls this celebration. The perspectives range from David's reign in tenth-century Jerusalem to our hope for the kingdom of God at the end of time. Throughout the development of the theme of kingdom the capital city of God's king remains the same, Jerusalem, city of David and city of God. Jerusalem is David's city because he took possession of it with his own army and made it his capital city (2 Sam 5:6-12). David is the second king of Israel, anointed by Samuel after God rejected Saul (1 Sam 16:1-13). David was anointed king of the single tribe of Judah after Saul's death (2 Sam 2:1-4). He gained control of the whole kingdom, however, only seven years later when all the tribes of Israel came to him and proclaimed him king (2 Sam 5:1-5). His kingship was the golden age. He decisively defeated the archenemy, the Philistines; his other victories resulted in a substantial acquisition of yearly tribute. He brought the ark, sign of God's presence, to Jerusalem. God promised him that his dynasty would last forever (2 Sam 7:16). David becomes the representative and the symbol of God's rule in the midst of the people. Hope for the kingdom of God in the future coalesces around the figure of David.

Jerusalem is David's city and the city of God. There are found the thrones of the house of David (Ps 122:5). There God's people gather to live in peace, governed by God's chosen king. We rejoice at being invited to go there.

The gospels present Jesus as the son of David. Peter names him "Messiah" (Luke 9:20). "Messiah" means anointed, and implies accession to the throne of David. But Jesus' acceptance of the title "king" is limited. The magi come looking for the newborn King of the Jews (Matt 2:2). Nathanael refers to Jesus as the "king of Israel (John 1:49). All the other occurrences of the title are in the passion narrative. The people acclaim Jesus king as he enters Jerusalem (Luke 19:38; cf. Matt 21:5). He is condemned on the charge of blasphemy for having claimed to be the Messiah, which is interpreted for Pilate to mean king (Luke 23:2). Thus the charge against him which is nailed over his head at the crucifixion reads: "This is the King of the Jews." The story of the crucifixion is the gospel reading for this Solemnity of Christ the King (Luke 23:35-43). The bystanders taunt Jesus with the title: "Let him save himself if he is . . . the Messiah of God." One person at the scene, however, recognizes this dying man as a king. A thief crucified with him says, "Jesus, remember me when you come into your kingdom," and Jesus promises him a share in the kingdom. This is God's Messiah, son of David, heir to David's everlasting kingdom. This is the king who inaugurates the kingdom of God.

The author of the Letter to the Colossians (1:12-20) ponders the mystery. God "delivered us from the power of darkness and transferred us to the kingdom of his beloved Son." Our rescue has taken place "by the blood of his cross." Through his death and resurrection Jesus has established the kingdom and won the victory over evil. In him the promise to David has been fulfilled; in him the Day of the Lord has arrived. He is "the beginning, the first-born from the dead." Through him we are given peace, *shalom*, the fullness of everything we need. Through him we share in God's kingdom and become citizens of the new Jerusalem. It is he who issues the invitation to come. We rejoice when he says to us: "Let us go to the house of the LORD" (Ps 122:1).

Common End of Year (1-2.3-4.4-5.6-7.8-9) [*175*]

Let us go rejoicing to the house of the Lord (see 1).

Psalm 122 is the only suggestion for a common responsorial psalm for the last Sundays of the year (32-34). These Sundays turn our attention to the end of the world and the coming of God's kingdom. Psalm 122 is a good choice. One of the most easily grasped symbols of God's kingdom is the city of Jerusalem. The city of David, city of God, is the home of all God's people. There we will all live in peace.

Because of its connection to God's kingdom, Psalm 122 may be used with any of the final Sundays. The Sundays which may relate most easily to the content of the psalm are: the Thirty-Second and Thirty-Third Sundays of Year B in which the second reading from the Letter to the Hebrews (Heb 9:24-28; 10:11-14, 18; see Pss 146 and 17 for a fuller discussion) refers to the true sanctuary and sacrifice offered there; the Thirty-Third Sunday of Year C (see Ps 98) in which the gospel is Jesus' prediction of the destruction of the temple; and the Solemnity of Christ the King A and B (see Pss 23 and 93) in which the focus is on king and kingdom.

All Souls (1-2.3-4.4-5.6-7.8-9) [791]

I rejoiced when I heard them say: let us go to the house of the Lord (1).

Psalm 122 is one of several psalms suggested for the Common of the Dead. The whole psalm is used. Jerusalem is the city of God's kingdom which is the goal of our lives. In the resurrection we hope to be found citizens of the new Jerusalem. A few readings from the Common of the Dead use the same imagery of city and mountain: Isa 25:6, 7-9, God's banquet on the holy mountain; Phil 3:20-21, our citizenship in heaven; Rev 21:1-5, 6-7, the new Jerusalem; Luke 23:33, 39-43, Jesus the crucified king (see Christ the King C).

Dedication Lateran (1-2.3-4.4-5.8-9) [703]

I rejoiced when I heard them say: let us go to the house of the Lord (1).

Psalm 122 is one of three psalms suggested for the Common of the Dedication of a Church (see also Pss 84 and 95). All the verses are used except the beginning of the prayer for Jerusalem's peace (5-6). The omission is odd, especially for an occasion when the community of the Church is the focus. It might be well for us to add: "For the peace of Jerusalem pray."

Because the Church is the sign of the assembly of God's people and because Jerusalem functions in the same way, Psalm 122 is fitting with almost every reading in this common. Some readings, however, are especially apt. From the Old Testament: 1 Kgs 8:22-23, 27-30 and 2 Chr 5:6-10, 13–6:2, which describe Solomon's dedication of the temple; 1 Macc 4:52-59, the rededication of the temple by the Maccabees; Isa 56:1, 6-7, the welcome of foreigners into God's temple; Ezek 43:1-2, 4-7, God's return to the temple after the Exile.

From the New Testament: Acts 7:44-50, describing the building of the temple under David and Solomon; Rev 21:1-5 and Rev 21:9-14, the new Jerusalem; Heb 12:18-19, 22-24, the assembly of God's people at Mount Zion; and 1 Cor 3:9-13, 16-17; Eph 2:19-22; 1 Pet 2:4-9, which all describe the community of God's people as the temple itself.

From the gospels: John 2:13-22, Jesus' cleansing of the temple, Jesus himself as the new temple.

J. Canticles

Not all the "psalms" are contained in the psalter. Many poetic prayers can be found in the rest of the biblical text which fit the categories of the psalms. These prayers are called "canticles" to distinguish them from the prayers within the Book of Psalms. Traditionally canticles have been used as part of biblical prayer enjoying equal status with the psalms. The canticles represent various forms. The canticles which are found in the Sunday Lectionary include hymns (Dan 3:52-56 and Luke 1:46-55) and songs of thanksgiving (Exod 15:1-18 and Isa 12:1-6).

1. *Exodus 15:1-18*

The song in Exodus 15 represents the oldest version of Yahweh's victory at the Reed Sea.[1] It may date even to the twelfth or eleventh century BCE, placing it within a century or two of the exodus event itself. The song is attributed both to Moses (15:1) and to Miriam (15:21). The attribution to Miriam is probably older, since traditions tend to move from lesser known to more prominent figures. Miriam is here the leader of the liturgical celebration, praising the Divine Warrior who has won the victory (compare Jephthah's daughter [Judg 11:34], the women who meet Saul and David [1 Sam 18:6], and Judith [Jdt 15:14–16:2]).

Exodus 15:1-18 is a song of thanksgiving (see above for the description of the form). In Hebrew thanksgiving must become praise; the only possible

---

[1]For further information on Exodus 15:1-21 see the following: Rita Burns, *Exodus, Leviticus, Numbers* (OTM 3; Wilmington: Michael Glazier 1983) 112–115; Richard Clifford, "Exodus" (*The New Jerome Biblical Commentary* [Englewood Cliffs, N.J.: Abingdon, 1990]) 50; John Craghan, "Exodus (*The Collegeville Bible Commentary* [Collegeville: The Liturgical Press, 1989]) 96; Frank Moore Cross, *Canaanite Myth and Hebrew Epic* (Cambridge, Mass.: Harvard University Press, 1973) 121–144. Burns disagrees on the dating; she considers only 15:20-21 to represent the ancient tradition.

way to give thanks is to proclaim the goodness and power of the giver. The song may be divided into three stanzas: introduction, 1-3; Yahweh's victory at the sea, 4-12; Yahweh's gift of the land, 13-18.

The first stanza (1-3) announces the intent to give thanks and the theme of the thanksgiving: Yahweh has won a great victory. The power of the enemy (horse and chariot) has been crushed; the people have been saved. The second stanza (4-12) describes the battle more closely. It is a challenge to read these verses as a fresh and unique announcement without allowing other versions of the exodus event to influence our imaginations. There is nothing in this description about either splitting the sea or about Israel's passage on dry ground. Rather in this battle the sea is stirred up by a mighty storm; the Egyptians are hurled (from boats?) into the sea and drowned. The imagery reflects the Canaanite myth of Ba'al, the storm god, who defeats Yam, the sea god (cf. Pss 29, 89, 93). Yahweh has replaced Ba'al; the sea has lost its divine status and is just an instrument of Yahweh. The Egyptians who in their arrogance attack Yahweh are defeated by the two elements Yahweh uses for weapons: the wind and the sea. Yahweh is more powerful than any other god.

The third stanza (13-18) describes the procession of Yahweh's people into the promised land. The people have been "redeemed" (*ga'al*); Yahweh has acted as next-of-kin in ransoming them from slavery. They are surrounded and protected by the power of God. Therefore all the other peoples melt away in fear. Yahweh's people pass through their territory and pass over the Jordan (Josh 3–4) into the land given to them. Later generations would see the reference to "sanctuary" and "holy mountain" as the temple on Mount Zion. But in the ancient tradition the whole land of Canaan is Yahweh's inheritance and holy mountain. There the people are established; there Yahweh will be their king forever.

Easter Vigil 3 (1-2.3-4.5-6.17-18) [42]

Let us sing to the Lord who is gloriously triumphant (1).

In the Easter Vigil liturgy the thanksgiving song of Exodus 15 follows the prose version of the exodus event. The verses include the introduction (1-3), the first part of the story of the victory at the sea (4-6), and the final two verses of the entrance into the land (17-18). The verses omitted from the first stanza describe the great power of God in overthrowing the arrogant Egyptians; the listing of the terrified nations who witness the people's advance to the promised land is also omitted. Perhaps on this night there is a sensitivity to those once categorized as enemies.

There are actually three descriptions of the central event of the exodus in tonight's liturgy. Exodus 14:15-31 is a combination of two traditions:

the Yahwist story from the tenth century BCE and the Priestly version, written down in the sixth century BCE. In the earlier version Yahweh hides the Israelites by means of the cloud, sweeps the sea with a strong east wind, and leads the Israelites through. The Egyptians are prevented from pursuing because their chariot wheels are clogged by the mud and so Israel escapes. In the Priestly version the waters of the sea stand up like a wall so that the people may pass through. The Egyptians pursue them right into the sea and are drowned when the waters of the sea flow back on top of them. The third version, of course, is the song in which Yahweh tosses the Egyptians out of their boats and they drown in the deep water.

All these versions are preserved because they all contain the central truth: Yahweh saved a helpless people from the power of the Egyptians. This deliverance gave both parties their identity. God is Yahweh who delivered us from Egypt; the people are Yahweh's chosen, the next-of-kin redeemed from slavery.

The exodus is the central event for Israel. This is how they know who they are and who God is. We read this story as we keep vigil, making memorial of Jesus' resurrection, because that resurrection is our central event and the gift of our identity. Jesus is our next-of-kin through whom God has saved us from the slavery of death; we are the people baptized into his death so that we might rise with him into life. With Miriam we sing the victory song, celebrating God's triumph over death: "My strength and my courage is the LORD, . . . my savior!"

2. Isaiah 12:1-6

This short psalm at the end of the second collection of the oracles of Isaiah ben Amoz is a typical thanksgiving song. After the prophetic introduction it begins with a statement of intention: "I give you thanks, O LORD." The first verse continues with a description of distress and subsequent relief. God has been angry, but has now moved to consolation. This experience inspires the singer to proclaim God as the true salvation. The word "salvation" (*yeshuʿa*) occurs three times in the song, twice in verse 2 and once in verse 3. Every experience of salvation recalls the central experience of the exodus and so the singer echoes Miriam's Song at the Sea (Exodus 15:1-18): "My strength and my courage is the LORD [who] has been my savior."

The singer's own confidence leads to encouraging others that they too will experience God's salvation. On that day they too will sing a hymn of thanksgiving. Verses 4-6 present their hymn. It consists primarily of repeated calls to praise and thank the great God who has achieved the wonderful work of their salvation. The final call is to the city of Zion, home of the Holy One of Israel.

3rd Sun Adv C (2-3.4.5-6) [9]

Cry out with joy and gladness, for among you is the great and Holy One of Israel (6).

On the Third Sunday of Advent C all the verses of the song of thanksgiving in Isaiah 12 are used except the first verse. Thus the announcement of the song of thanksgiving and the description of distress and subsequent relief are missing. The responsorial psalm begins with the expression of confidence and the reference to the exodus deliverance. The singer's encouragement to others and their hymn of thanks conclude the psalm.

The readings for this Sunday present an exciting tension between joyful and fearful expectation. The Lord is indeed coming. Salvation and joy come with the divine presence. But we also know the dread of the winnowing fan which clears away the chaff.

The first reading (Zeph 3:14-18) is part of the joyful conclusion of the work of the prophet Zephaniah. This seventh-century prophet has already described the terrible destruction that will come on the Day of the Lord. A remnant, however, will be saved, "a people humble and lowly, who shall take refuge in the name of the Lord" (Zeph 3:12). It is this remnant that is encouraged to shout for joy in today's reading. They, the *'anawim* who know that their only help is in God, have heard the good news that the Lord is in their midst. God's response to their unconditional trust is delight, a delight that leads the Lord God to sing and dance for joy (Zeph 3:17-18).

Paul calls for the same unconditional trust in the Letter to the Philippians (Phil 4:4-7). There seem to have been some tensions in the Philippian community, but Paul tells them to abandon all anxiety and to be kind in all circumstances. With petition and thanksgiving they are to make their requests known to God. They are able to rejoice in peace because the Lord is indeed near and the Lord's peace is the guardian of their hearts and minds.

The gospel continues the introduction of Jesus by John the Baptist (Luke 3:10-18). John has warned the crowds not to rely on the fact that Abraham is their father, but rather to produce evidence of their repentance. Today's reading is the response of the crowd. They ask John how to live in the circumstances of their daily lives. John responds with simple principles of justice and charity. Those who depend on God for their needs have reason neither to hoard nor to take more than their just share. The wisdom of his response leads the people to wonder if John might be the Messiah. John then begins his announcement of the one who is to come. The coming one will baptize in the Holy Spirit and fire; he will separate the wheat from the chaff. Only if they are willing to live by God's justice can this announcement be good news. Only if they are willing to trust God unconditionally, only if the Lord is truly their strength and their courage, can they cry out with joy at the arrival of the Holy One of Israel (Isa 12:2, 6).

This is a sobering reflection for many of us in modern American society. How often, when we have two coats, do we give one away? How often do we insist that we be paid only what our work is worth? How often do we rejoice because our only hope is in God? It is worth pondering. Unconditional trust leads even the Lord God to sing and dance for delight. Unconditional trust draws the Lord into our midst.

Baptism of the Lord B [opt] (2-3.4.5-6)

You will draw water joyfully from the springs of salvation (3).

On the Feast of the Baptism of the Lord Year B the verses of Isa 12 used for the responsorial psalm are the same as those for the Third Sunday of Advent C (see above). The refrain is the singer's announcement to others of the availability of God's salvation.

The awesome gift of God's salvation overwhelms us on this feast. The first reading (Isa 55:1-11) is an invitation to celebrate a covenant meal with God.[2] The meal is a free gift as is the offer of covenant relationship. Acceptance of the covenant is not without demands, however. One must seek the Lord, turn to God for mercy. God's ways are mysterious to us and often counter to our human plans. The creative word of God, however, achieves its purpose of bringing life to the world. Water, the precious commodity without which we cannot live, is the prophet's image for God's gift of salvation. In the invitation to make covenant we are offered the water of hospitality. The word of God which creates and sustains life is compared to the water (rain and snow) which comes from God to make the earth fruitful. Water is a symbol of God's gift of life. God indeed is our savior; we shall draw water joyfully at the fountain of salvation (Isa 12:2, 3).

There are strong symbolic connections between the first reading and the gospel (Mark 1:7-11). Jesus, the Word of God, comes out of the water, and the Spirit, God's life, descends upon him. Jesus is the new covenant. Jesus is the Word which comes down from heaven and does not return there until he has accomplished God's purpose. Jesus, whose name, *Yeshu'a,* means "savior," is the fountain of salvation (Isa 12:3). Indeed he is our savior (Isa 12:2).

At his baptism Jesus hears the words, "You are my beloved Son; with you I am well pleased." In the second reading (1 John 5:1-9) we hear that

---

[2]For the insight that Isa 55 represents a covenant meal, I am indebted to Aloysius Fitzgerald, F.S.C., for a paper delivered at the Old Testament Colloquium, Conception, Mo., February 7-9, 1992.

"everyone who believes that Jesus is the Christ" is also a child of God. This is our salvation; this is the goal of the covenant, that we might share life with God in a bond as intimate as that between parent and child. This salvation, this covenant life, has been brought to us by "the one who came through water and blood." Jesus' life from baptism to death and resurrection has sealed the covenant bond between us and God. Jesus has become the fountain from which we drink of the Spirit, the water of salvation (cf. Isa 12:3). "Give thanks, . . . sing praise to the LORD for his glorious achievement!" (Isa 12:4, 5). God indeed is our savior! (Isa 12:2).

Easter Vigil 5 (2-3.4.5-6) [42]

You will draw water joyfully from the springs of salvation (3).

Isaiah 12 is used as a response to the fifth reading of the Easter Vigil. The verses are the same as those for the Third Sunday of Advent (see above). The refrain is the beginning of the prophet's encouragement to others who have heard his experience of God's salvation. The image being emphasized at tonight's celebration is water as the catechumens await their imminent baptism into the life of Christ.

Water is also a vivid image at the beginning and end of the reading from Isaiah (55:1-11). The prophet is encouraging the exiles to believe that God can and indeed will bring them home again. God has not forgotten the covenant with David. Its promises will be renewed now with the whole people. God has salvation ready for the people, free of charge. All they need do is come, listen, drink with joy. God's word, like the rain, gives life.

How great is the good news on the night when we celebrate the resurrection of Christ, who is God's word and God's salvation. This is the new exodus, when we are led through the water of death to new life. God indeed is our savior, in ways we could never have imagined. All we need to do is seek: Seek the Lord and we will be led to the springs of salvation! Shout with joy; "great in [our] midst is the Holy One of Israel" (Isa 12:6).

Sacred Heart B (2-3.4.5-6) [172]

You will draw water joyfully from the springs of salvation (3).

The refrain and verses from Isaiah 12 chosen for the Solemnity of the Sacred Heart B are the same as those for the Easter Vigil (see above).

This feast celebrates the mystery of God's great love for us which has become incarnate in Christ. It is a mystery we can scarcely believe. Hosea is the premier prophet of God's love. Hosea, who suffered through a troublesome marriage, knew how painful it could be to keep extending love to an unfaithful spouse. He understood God's grief over Israel. In today's reading he uses the image of parents with an ungrateful child (Hos 11:1, 3-4,

8-9). God loved Israel as a firstborn son, nurtured, protected, and caressed this favored child. Yet Israel turned from Yahweh to other gods. The strength of a mother's love is proverbial, yet even a mother may have to give up. God, however, does not give up. Even at the point where humans act out their anger, God continues to act out of mercy. God seems a too-indulgent parent.

Isaiah 12 lets us acknowledge God's overwhelming tenderness. "Though you have been angry with me . . . you have consoled me" (12:1). We confess what we have been accused of not knowing, that God is indeed our savior. We take as our own the victory hymn of the exodus, the paradigm of God's deliverance. It is in the exodus that God claims Israel as firstborn (cf. Exod 4:22; Hos 11:1). Through other people who sing with us, our thanksgiving expands to the whole world. Great in our midst is the God who loves us.

The gospel (John 19:31-37) shows us the extent of God's love. The scene set before us is of Christ dead on the Cross. We have been loved, even to death. But even death cannot conquer the power of this love.

Paul prays that indeed we might know the height and depth of God's love in Christ (Eph 3:8-12, 14-19), and that we might experience it to the point beyond knowledge. It is Paul's mission to proclaim this great mystery; it is ours to sing in thanksgiving. How can we ever believe the glorious achievement of God's love! "God indeed is [our] savior!" (Isa 12:5, 2).

3. Daniel 3:52-56

There are several additions to the Hebrew text of Daniel 3.[3] The additions comprise verses 24-90 in the Septuagint, the Greek translation of the Hebrew Scriptures. The additions are considered part of the inspired text by Roman Catholics, but are not used by Jews or Protestants. Such texts are sometimes referred to as "deutero-canonical," a second canon. The additional verses contain a prayer (24-45), a prose narrative (46-51), an ode (52-56), and a psalm (57-90).[4] They are expansions of the story of the three men who were thrown into the fiery furnace by Nebuchadnezzar because they refused to worship an idol. The men were saved by an angel. The ad-

---

[3]For further material on the additions to Daniel 3 see: Carey A. Moore, *Daniel, Esther, and Jeremiah: The Additions* (AB 44; Garden City, N.Y.: Doubleday, 1977) 39–53, 66–76; Louis Hartman and Alexander DiLella, "Daniel" (*The New Jerome Biblical Commentary* [Englewood Cliffs, N.J.: Abingdon, 1990]) 412; Toni Craven, "Ezekiel and Daniel" (*The Collegeville Bible Commentary* [Collegeville: The Liturgical Press, 1989]) 563.

[4]Moore, 40.

ditions represent their prayers and an added description of the angelic rescue.

The ode (52-56) is a hymn of praise. It is in the style of later Jewish blessings which begin "Blessed are you. . . ." The prayer is carefully crafted. Each pair of lines begins with the formulaic blessing and ends with a refrain. None of the six refrains are exactly alike; in each there is some small variation of vocabulary. The favorite prefix of the author is *hyper-*, which means "super" or "above." By using this prefix the author heightens the call for praise of God. God is to be "super-hymned" (52), "super-exalted" (52), "super-glorified" (53). Nothing is too much.

The blessings are standard praise. God is the faithful God of the ancestors. God's name, Yahweh, "the one who will be present," is worthy of all praise. God is to be blessed in the earthly temple and the heavenly temple; God alone is the everlasting king. God, enthroned upon the cherubim who guard the ark, looks from the heights to the depths. The implication is that God who is mighty cares for the lowly.

The whole ode is a call to praise God. "Blessed, blessed, blessed are you!"

Trinity Sunday A (52.53.54.55.56) [*165*]

Glory and praise forever! (52).

All of the little ode of praise from Daniel 3 is used for Trinity Sunday A. The readings for this Sunday emphasize the power of God's love for us. It is fitting for us to respond with the words of the men in the fiery furnace. We live surrounded by dangers; every day we walk through fire and are not burned. Every breath we take is a gift of the great God who loves us.

God's love saves us even from our own weakness and wickedness. At Sinai God made covenant with the chosen people. God and the people agreed to be bound to each other in a relationship as intimate as the relationship between husband and wife or between parent and child. The covenant demanded of both parties faithful love. But before they had even left Sinai the people broke the covenant. They made an image of God in an attempt to control the divine presence (Exod 32:1-6). The covenant could have ended right there. But moved by Moses' prayer, God relented and renewed the covenant (Exod 32:11-14). This covenant renewal is highly significant. The Sinai covenant is conditional; it can be broken. But in the foundational story God renews the broken covenant. Perhaps God will always renew it?

This Sunday's reading (Exod 34:4-6, 8-9) is part of the covenant renewal at Sinai. God again promises loving fidelity to the people. God proclaims that the divine name itself, Yahweh, means that God will be present to them forever. The name itself identifies God as merciful and gracious, slow to anger and rich in kindness (*hesed*) and fidelity. This is who God is: loving and faithful, present to forgive and deliver.

The gospel (John 3:16-18) proclaims the lengths to which God's faithful love will go: God loved the world enough to give the only Son, "so that everyone who believes in him might not perish but might have eternal life." God has kept the covenant; God lives the demand of loving fidelity. There are two demands made of God's people. The first is to believe in God's faithful love. The second is to live in the same loving fidelity. Paul exhorts the Corinthians to "live in peace" that "the God of love and peace" might be with them (2 Cor 13:11-13). Factions and disagreements have divided the Corinthian church. But the sign that God is present with the Christian community is the presence of God's love and peace. God loved us enough to send the Son to deliver us from death; we must have the same love for one another.

We hear the covenant demands; we stand in awe at the revelation of our God who is loving and faithful. We know the fiery furnace in which we live; we know how hard it is to be faithful in love and peace. But God has sent not an angel but Jesus to deliver us. We borrow the courage of the three men and focus not on our own weakness but the greatness of our God. "Blessed are you, O Lord!"

4. Luke 1:46-55 (Magnificat)

There are three canticles in the opening chapters of the Gospel of Luke: the canticle of Zechariah (1:68-79), the canticle of Simeon (2:29-32), and the canticle of Mary (1:46-55).[5] These canticles are generally considered to be pre-Lukan. They resemble Jewish literature from the period between 200 BCE and 100 CE. They depend heavily on the Greek translation of the Old Testament, the Septuagint, and are like chains of citations from other Old Testament psalms and hymns. Brown suggests that Luke got them from a group of Jewish-Christian *'anawim*, the lowly who are completely dependent on God.[6]

The Magnificat, as Mary's canticle is called from its opening word in Latin, is set in the story of Mary's visit to Elizabeth. This visit links the two birth announcement stories of Luke's first chapter and brings both pregnant women together. The canticle, which is only loosely connected to the story, forms Mary's response to Elizabeth's recognition of her as "the

---

[5]Sources for further study of Mary's canticle are: J. A. Fitzmyer, *The Gospel According to Luke I–IX* (AB 28; Garden City, N.Y.: Doubleday, 1981) 356–371; R. E. Brown, *The Birth of the Messiah* (Garden City, N.Y.: Doubleday, 1977) 330–366.

[6]Brown, 350–355.

mother of my Lord'' (Luke 1:43). Mary sings a song of praise to God who has done such great things.

The canticle is close to the form of the hymn (see above).[7] Rather than a call to praise, however, there is a statement of intent to give praise, somewhat like the first element in songs of thanksgiving (46-47). This introduction is followed by two stanzas (48-50, 51-53). The canticle concludes with a summary statement (54-55). The closest Old Testament model for Mary's canticle is the Song of Hannah (1 Sam 2:1-10).[8]

The introduction proclaims Mary's delight in the greatness of God. The following stanza (48-50) celebrates the mercy of the mighty God who cares for the lowly. Like the *'anawim*, Mary knows that God's power is used especially for the most needy. Verse 48 may be Luke's insertion into the text in order to relate the canticle to Mary's own situation. She is God's handmaid (cf. Luke 1:38); Elizabeth has already proclaimed her blessed (Luke 1:45). The stanza ends with a citation from Psalm 103:17 proclaiming the lasting fidelity of God whose "mercy is from age to age to those who fear him.''

The next stanza (51-53) is a declaration of reversals. God's power is used to help the lowly and to bring down the mighty. God's care is for the poor. Throughout the history of God with the people this special attention to the most helpless has been a characteristic of God. This characteristic is especially noteworthy in Jesus who humbled himself to take on our flesh, who did not think being equal to God something to be grasped at (cf. Phil 2:6-8). The psalm concludes with praise of the faithful God who continues to honor the unconditional covenant with Abraham, who continues to care for chosen Israel (54-55). Mary's child is the incarnation of God's fidelity to the covenant with the chosen people.

3rd Sun Adv B (46-48.49-50.53-54) [8]

My soul rejoices in my God (Isa 61:10; cf. Luke 1:46).

The responsorial psalm for the Third Sunday of Advent B is taken from Mary's canticle (Luke 1:46-55). Three verses have been omitted. The strong statement concerning God's reversal of the situation of the powerful and the lowly is left out (51-52) as is the reference to the covenant with Abraham (55). Both omissions are strange. God's exaltation of the lowly is suggested in the readings. The verse concerning God's faithfulness to Israel is included; why then is Abraham omitted?

[7]Fitzmyer (359) compares it to Psalms 33, 47, 48, 113, 117, 135, and 136.

[8]For a detailed review of the relationship of the canticle to its Old Testament background, see Brown, 358–360, and Fitzmyer, 366–368.

The Third Sunday of Advent has traditionally been a Sunday of joy. Mary's canticle captures the reason for such joy: God who is mighty has done great things for us. The prophet of the final section of the Book of Isaiah sings lyrically of the prophetic call and then proclaims the good news of Jerusalem's restoration (Isa 61:1-2, 10-11). The prophet has been anointed by God and thus filled with God's spirit. The prophet's commission is to proclaim the good news of a jubilee year, a year in which all debts are forgiven, all slaves are freed, and the land is returned to its original holders (Lev 25:8-22). This is a message of great good news for the dispossessed: the lowly, the brokenhearted, the prisoners. The year proclaimed by the prophet will be a new beginning for everyone.

The prophet is preaching to a disillusioned people. They have returned from the Babylonian Exile, but the labor of rebuilding has disheartened the people. The prophet describes the glorious restoration of Jerusalem which God will achieve through them. The covenant bond will be renewed; God's people will again rejoice in their status as bride. God will adorn Jerusalem with the bridal gown of justice and salvation. God's holy people will bring forth the good fruit of justice and praise. The intensity of the idealistic picture matches the despair of the people. The prophet proclaims to them that God is not only faithful but faithful beyond our imagining.

Mary's canticle proclaims the same truth. Who could have imagined what Mary knows about God's faithfulness and mercy? God's mercy is indeed from age to age. The hungry can hope not only for sustenance, but for every good thing.

The sixth-century prophet announces the good news of God's restoration of the people. Mary sings of God's faithfulness to Israel. John announces the good news that the moment of God's salvation has arrived (John 1:6-8, 19-28). John's preaching is so effective that some people think that God's salvation has arrived in him. John is perfectly honest: he is not the Messiah, not Elijah, not the prophet. He identifies himself with the words of a prophet of restoration (Isa 40:3): He is simply one who came to prepare the way. He proclaims his lowliness; his hope is in the God who regards the lowly and blesses them (Luke 1:48).

Paul presents a picture of the ideal life of the faithful person waiting for the fulfillment of God's promises (1 Thess 5:16-24). Joyful, thankful, prayerful, depending on God to make one holy—the description might well be applied to Mary. It is the ideal for us as well. We are God's people, waiting for our restoration. We know the good news of God's salvation which has come to us in Jesus. We also know that the fullness of the kingdom has not yet arrived. We are still waiting for "the coming of our Lord Jesus Christ." Only if our hope in God is firm will we be able to be truly joyful. God's great mercy is the source of our joy. In our God our soul rejoices!

III. Afterword

"If there is a theme [for the Sunday liturgy] it is in the antiphon of the Responsorial Psalm."[1] I have taken Ralph Kiefer at his word and used the Responsorial Psalm as the lens through which to look at the Sunday liturgies throughout the three-year cycle. Having followed this method for the whole Sunday Lectionary I would add this observation to Kiefer's comment. I find it true that the psalm is an excellent focus for the theme of the Sunday liturgy. For me the psalm is even more compelling, however, as the focus for prayer. The psalm is given us as a way to appropriate the message of the Word of God on each particular Sunday. Through the psalms the Word of God takes root in our very lives! May these reflections assist the people of God in continuing to sing the new song! "Let all the people say, Amen! Hallelujah!" (Ps 106:48).

[1] Ralph Kiefer, *To Hear & to Proclaim*, 81.

IV. Glossary

acrostic. A psalm in which each verse begins with the next letter of the Hebrew alphabet. See, for example, Psalm 34.

'adam. "Human being, humanity," Hebrew. The word applies equally to men and women.

'adamah. "Soil, ground," Hebrew. Cf. Gen 2:7.

'adonai. "Lord," Hebrew. After the Babylonian exile this word was substituted for the holy name, Yahweh, out of respect. See LORD.

'anawim. "Poor, lowly people," Hebrew. These people know their only hope is in God. Cf. Ps 34.

'ani. "Poor, lowly, afflicted person," Hebrew. Cf. Ps 34.

'apar. "Dry dust," Hebrew. Cf. Gen 2:7; 3:19.

apocalpytic. A world view which flourished in Judaism in the last two centuries BCE and in early Christianity. In this view, history is too corrupt to be redeemed. There will be a great cosmic battle between Good and Evil in which God will be victorious. Then God's faithful will be vindicated. The concepts of resurrection, angels, demons, and the cataclysmic end of the world derive from the apocalyptic world view.

ark of the covenant. A chest of acacia wood which symbolized the abiding presence of God with the chosen people. It supposedly contained the tablets of the law, a jar of manna, and Aaron's rod. It first appears in the desert period and was finally established in the Holy of Holies of Solomon's temple. It disappeared at the time of the Babylonian Exile (587 BCE) or earlier.

Assyrian captivity. The defeat and deportation of the ten tribes of the northern kingdom by Assyria in 722 BCE. The people of the northern kingdom were dispersed throughout the Assyrian empire and other peoples were settled in their territory, becoming the ancestors of the Samaritans. See "northern kingdom."

'awon. "Acting crookedly, perversion, sin," Hebrew. Cf. Ps 51.

BCE. "Before the Common Era," equivalent to BC, "before Christ." A term which can be used by Christians and non-Christians alike.

Babylonian exile. The exile to Babylon of the southern kingdom after Nebuchadnezzar's destruction of Jerusalem in 587 BCE. Through the suffering and struggle of the exiles to maintain their faith and their identity, Judaism was born. There was a return to Jerusalem in 539 BCE. See "southern kingdom."

bara'. "Create," Hebrew. This word is only used of God.

basar. "Flesh, meat," Hebrew. Cf. Ps 63.

Belial. "Worthless, evil," Hebrew. The word is sometimes used as a name for Satan, "the Evil One." Cf. Ps 41.

bicolon/bicola. The basic two-line form of Hebrew poetry. The lines are commonly parallel to each other. Each line is called a "colon."

books of psalter. There are five books in the psalter, divided in the following manner: Book I, Pss 1-41; Book II, Pss 42-72; Book III, Pss 73-89; Book IV, Pss 90-106; Book V, Pss 107-150. Each book ends with a doxology. The five-book structure may be an imitation of the Pentateuch, the first five books of the Bible.

CE. "Common Era," equivalent to A.D., "Anno Domini." A time designation which can be used by Christians and non-Christians alike.

cherubim. Mythical creatures, part human and part animal, who served as guardians of the throne in the Ancient Near East. Two cherubim guarded the ark of the covenant, the throne of God. Later piety defined cherubim as angels. Cf. Exod 37:7-9; Ezek 1:5-20; Pss 18; 80.

chiasm. A poetic device in which the elements of the first line are reversed in the second, forming an A:B::B:A pattern. The form is named for the Greek letter, chi, because of its X shape.

christ. "Anointed," derived from the Greek word *christos*. See "messiah."

confessions of Jeremiah. A group of laments found in the Book of Jeremiah (12:1-5; 15:10-21; 17:12-18; 18:18-23; 20:7-18) which portray Jeremiah's struggle with God over the terrible cost of his prophetic mission.

dakka'. "Crushed, humbled," Hebrew. From this meaning it comes to signify that which is crushed, i.e., dust. Cf. Ps 90.

deutero-canonical. The seven books which are not in the Hebrew Scriptures or Protestant Bible but which are found in the Roman Catholic and Orthodox Bibles. They include: Judith, Tobit, Wisdom, Sirach, Baruch, and 1-2 Maccabees, as well as additions to Daniel and Esther. These books circulated in the Septuagint (a Jewish Greek translation of the Hebrew Scriptures) and were already in use by Christians when the Jews decided not to include them in the Hebrew Canon.

'emeth. "Truth, trustworthiness, faithfulness," Hebrew. This word comes from the same root as the borrowed English word, "Amen."

'enosh. "Humankind," Hebrew. The word seems to be derived from a root meaning "weak, sickly."

Enthronement Psalms. A group of psalms (Pss 47, 93, 95-99) which celebrate the kingship of Yahweh over the whole world. Cf. Ps 47.

'eres. "Earth, land," Hebrew.

exodus. The departure from Egypt, ca. 1290 BCE. The central event in Israel's history with God and their beginning as a people.

fear of the Lord. The awe and wonder which comes from contemplation of the living God. It is considered to be the beginning of wisdom (Prov 1:7). Cf. Ps 130.

hanan. "To show favor, to be gracious," Hebrew.

Hanukkah. "Dedication," Hebrew. The feast which celebrates the rededication of the temple by Judas Maccabeus during the Maccabean revolt, 164 BCE. Cf. 1 Macc 4:36-59; 2 Macc 10:1-8.

hanûn. "Gracious, granting favor," Hebrew. Cf. Ps 51.

hasidim. "Loyal, faithful," Hebrew. The *hasid* is the person of *hesed*, faithful covenant love. See *hesed*.

hatta'. "Sin," Hebrew. This is the most common term for sin in the Hebrew Bible. It comes from a root meaning "to miss the mark, to be diverted from."

hesed. "Covenant love," Hebrew. This is the faithful love pledged between God and the people in the covenant. This love permeates the lives of God's people.

honneni. "Have mercy on me!" Hebrew. Cf. *hanûn*.

inclusion. A literary form in which the same word or phrase is repeated at the beginning and the end, forming an envelope around the intervening material.

ki tôb. "How good!" Hebrew. God's exclamation in the first account of creation, Gen 1:1–2:4a.

LORD. A form (note the small capital letters) which indicates that the Hebrew text contains the holy name, Yahweh. After the Babylonian exile the Jews ceased pronouncing the Name and substituted *'adonai* (see above), which means "lord." Out of sensitivity to Jewish piety, many English translations use the same substitution.

Maccabean Revolt. A revolt inspired by a terrible persecution under Antiochus IV Epiphanes, the Seleucid ruler of the territory of Israel (175–163 BCE). The revolt began ca. 165 BCE and resulted in almost a century of independence for the Jews.

messiah. "Anointed," from the Hebrew word *mashiach*. See "christ."

nadib. "Willing, generous," Hebrew. Thus it comes to mean "noble." Cf. Ps 51.

nephesh. "Throat," Hebrew. From this meaning it comes to signify that which gives a human being life. "My *nephesh*" is sometimes used as a substitute for "myself." Cf. Pss 42-43; 63.

niham. "Be sorry, repent," Hebrew. In various forms the word has a range of meaning from "console," to "avenge."

northern kingdom. The territory of the ten tribes of Israel after Solomon's kingdom divided in 922 BCE. The capital city was Samaria; the major religious shrines were at Bethel and Dan. See "southern kingdom."

'oz. "Power, might," Hebrew. Often used as a name for the ark of the covenant (see above). Cf. Ps 63:3; 78:61; 132:8.

passion predictions. Statements found in the synoptic gospels in which Jesus predicts his suffering and death (Mark 8:31-33; 9:30-32; 10:32-34 and parallels).

Passover. The memorial of the exodus (see above) in which God's people celebrate and make present God's saving act which delivered them from slavery and made them a people.

Penitential Psalms. Seven psalms (Pss 6, 32, 38, 51, 102, 130, 143) which have been traditionally recognized as particularly appropriate prayers of repentance for sin.

pesha'. "Rebellion, sin," Hebrew. Cf. Ps 51.

psalm titles. Phrases at the beginning of many psalms which give various aids to the person praying. Some titles indicate the collection in which the psalm was found, e.g., "of David" or "psalms of Korah." Some titles give musical indications like the tune, "to Lilies," or the manner of performance, "with strings." One title warns, "Do not destroy." Other titles help one pray the psalm by connecting it to an incident in David's life. Cf. Pss 54, 90.

rahamim. "Compassion, motherly feeing," Hebrew. This word comes from the root which means "womb." See *rehem*. Cf. Ps 51.

rahùm. "Compassionate," Hebrew. From *rehem*.

rehem. "Womb," Hebrew.

ruah. "Air in motion = breath, wind, spirit," Hebrew.

saddiqim. "The just, righteous," Hebrew. These are the people of *sedeq* (see below) who honor the demands of relationships.

Second Isaiah. Chapters 40-55 of the Book of Isaiah, attributed to a sixth-century prophet who preached during the Babylonian exile. The first section of the Book of Isaiah (chs. 1-35) is the work of the eighth-century prophet whose name the book bears. (Chs. 36-39 are a historical section.) The final section (chs. 56–66) represents the activity of one or more sixth-century prophets in Judah after the return from exile.

sedeq. "Just, righteous," Hebrew. Righteousness in biblical terms is always based on the demands of the relationship.

servant, suffering. A figure described in four songs of Second Isaiah (Isa 42:1-4; 49:1-7; 50:4-11; 52:13–53:12) who may represent Israel, Moses, a prophet, or one who is yet to come. Christian tradition has interpreted the passages as applying to Jesus.

shahar. "Pre-dawn light," Hebrew. Verb, "to look for." Cf. Ps 63.

shalom. "Completeness, peace, health, welfare, prosperity," Hebrew. From a root which means to be complete, to be in harmony, to give to another what is due. The peace signified by this word is a condition in which every person has what is needed for a full life. Cf. Pss 85, 137.

Sheol. The place to which every person goes at death; a place of no pain and no joy, no memory and no communication (cf. Job 3:13-19). The entrance to Sheol is through the grave. When the possibility of life after death began to be considered, belief in Sheol dwindled.

shùb. "Turn, return," Hebrew. In the prophets this term also connotes conversion and repentance.

Songs of Ascent. The fifteen psalms between Ps 120 and Ps 134 which have this title (see "psalm titles"). They are commonly understood to be songs of pilgrims "ascending" to Jerusalem. See Ps 123 for further description.

southern kingdom. The kingdom of Judah after Solomon's kingdom divided in 922 BCE. The capital city was Jerusalem and the temple was the chief religious shrine. The kings were from the Davidic dynasty throughout its history until the Babylonian exile. See "northern kingdom."

Sukkoth. The Feast of Tabernacles or Booths (*sukkoth*). A feast of the early fall at the time of the grape and olive harvest. The imagery of the feast includes the ideas of final defeat of Israel's enemies and the arrival of God's kingdom. Many of the descriptions are inspired by the violent storms at this time of year in Israel. Cf. Pss 65, 85.

tehom. "The deep, the primeval ocean, chaos," Hebrew. Possibly related to the Ancient Near Eastern goddess of the salt water, Tiamat, who is defeated in the battle of creation.

vengeance. A prayer often found in the psalms in which the psalmist asks God to destroy the enemies of God's people. Christians may understand this as a prayer that God will root out all evil—suffering, sin, and death.

vine. A common image for God's people, Israel. Cf. Ps 80.

water. An image for life and for God in the psalms; also an image of chaos and death. Cf. Ps 42-43.

yishre-leb. "The upright of heart," Hebrew. *yashar* means to be "straight, smooth."

Yom Kippur. Day of Atonement; the great day of fasting and repentance in the Jewish calendar.